AFRICAN AMERICANS AND THE COLOR LINE IN OHIO, 1915–1930

William W. Giffin

The Ohio State University Press
Columbus

Library of Congress Cataloging-in-Publication Data
Giffin, William Wayne, 1938–
African Americans and the color line in Ohio, 1915–1930 / William
W. Giffin.—1st ed.
    p. cm.
Includes bibliographical references and index.
ISBN 0–8142–1003–1 (cloth : alk. paper)—ISBN 0–8142–9081–7
(cd-rom)
    1. African Americans—Ohio—History—20th century. 2. Ohio—
Race relations—History—20th century. I. Title.
E185.93.02G55 2005
305.896'0730771'09041—dc22
                                2005015260

Cover design by Dan O'Dair
Type set in Goudy.

The paper used in this publication meets the minimum requirements
of the American National Standard for Information Sciences—
Permanence of Paper for Printed Library Materials. ANSI Z39.48–1992.

ISBN 978-0-8142-5420-2 (pb)
9 8 7 6 5 4 3 2 1

CONTENTS

List of Illustrations   v

Acknowledgments   vii

Introduction   1

PART ONE: BLACK MIGRANTS AND WARTIMES, 1915–1920

Chapter 1   The Great Migration and Its Impact   9

Chapter 2   The Color Line's Changing Dimensions   33

Chapter 3   New Organizations and Urban Issues   50

PART TWO: THE TWENTIES AND CULMINATING TRENDS

Chapter 4   Rising "Black Metropolises"   89

Chapter 5   Increasing White Intolerance   110

Chapter 6   New Leadership and Welfare Work   142

Chapter 7   New Leadership and Equal Rights Struggles   159

Chapter 8   Toward Black Political Independence   195

Conclusion   215

Appendix   232

Notes   235

Bibliography   279

Index   293

ILLUSTRATIONS

Maps

Map 1	Map of State of Ohio.	15
Map 2	Map of Columbus, Ohio, Showing Racial, National, and Industrial Localities, 1918.	36
Map 3	Distribution of the Cleveland Negro Population, 1930.	121
Map 4	Census Tracts of Cincinnati Basin, 1930.	122

Photographs

Photo 1	Wendell P. Dabney.	55
Photo 2	Jane E. Hunter.	58
Photo 3	Jennie D. Porter.	60
Photo 4	Harry C. Smith.	69

Tables

Table A1	Number and Percentage of Blacks and Whites in Ohio by State Population and Urban Population, 1910–1930.	232
Table A2	Black Population in Ohio Cities, 1910–1930.	232
Table A3	Number and Percentage Increase of Black Professionals, by Ohio City, Occupation, and Year.	233
Table A4	Court Suits Alleging Ohio Public Accommodations Law Violations, 1914–1919.	234

ACKNOWLEDGMENTS

Thanks are owed to those who gave me assistance or support in ways that facilitated the making of this book. My history mentors at The College of Wooster and The Ohio State University grounded me in the study of history. My history department colleagues at Indiana State University maintained a scholarly environment promoting research and writing. The University Research Committee at ISU partially funded research on some of the themes in this work. Librarians and archivists at many institutions were unfailingly helpful and kind to me. I wish to thank the staffs of Cincinnati Historical Society Library, Cincinnati; Carnegie Library, Wilberforce University, Wilberforce, OH; Cleveland Public Library; Cunningham Memorial Library, Indiana State University, Terre Haute, IN; Fisk University Library, Nashville, TN; Library of Congress, Washington D.C.; National Archives, Washington, D.C.; Ohio Historical Society Archives/Library, Columbus, OH; and Western Reserve Historical Society Archives/Library, Cleveland, OH. Thanks to Heather Lee Miller, The Ohio State University Press acquisitions editor who worked with great care and remarkable efficiency. Much gratitude, as well, goes to the Press's readers who gave much time to the manuscript and offered many insightful suggestions. I am most grateful to friends and family, some now gone, who gave me comfort and understanding as I advanced in this study.

WWG

Introduction

The examination of the Ohio color line presented in this book is a reflection of the renewed scholarly interest in the study of the African American past as seen from within statewide perimeters. Black historical themes in states are the foci of a spate of books and doctoral dissertations produced since the beginning of the 1990s. The states examined are mainly southern: Arkansas, Florida, Georgia, Indiana, Kentucky, Louisiana, Mississippi, Pennsylvania, and West Virginia.[1] Most center on the African American struggle for citizenship rights, while some give special attention to other issues, notably concerning color and class. Excepting one, each work covers several decades in the twentieth century or in a time frame spanning the nineteenth and twentieth centuries.

This Ohio book responds to a need for additional scholarship on black history in the World War I era and the 1920s, times that were fundamentally important in the shaping of twentieth century black experiences because they saw the culmination of trends that started in the nineteenth century and witnessed antecedents of the modern civil rights era.

Trends in the African American experience that were just getting well underway in the 1890s accelerated after 1915 and reached culmination in the 1920s. Among these trends were those that enlarged black urban populations through in-migration, broadened black urban community life, and magnified social welfare concerns in black urban neighborhoods. At the same time, mounting white hostility to blacks tended to further isolate African Americans in urban centers. Accompanying these trends was the development of a new black leadership that addressed welfare issues and equal rights grievances. Historian David A. Gerber (1976) carefully analyses these developments in their Ohio manifestations prior to World War I.[2]

This book asserts that the color line in Ohio grew more divisive in the period 1915–1930 when, as specialists in this field know, there was movement away from American principles of equality and justice. It is a reminder that the past does not always provide a comforting story of progress. Its analysis of racial discrimination and segregation in Ohio speaks to those historians who are still inclined to discuss Jim Crow as a wholly southern phenomenon.

Further, it provides a notable instance of the slavery era's legacy making its influence felt in the twentieth century. This book argues that the intensity of the Ohio color line varied from south to north in the period 1915–1930 and that these differences were rooted in the antebellum era prior to the Civil War when Ohio ties with the slave South were weakest in northern Ohio and strongest in southern Ohio.

A theme transcending this volume is that local people in Ohio took the initiative on color line issues. It was mainly black Ohioans working locally who acted on civil rights complaints and welfare concerns arising from the Ohio color line. Traditional studies, such as John Flint Kellogg's NAACP (1967), generally stress the roles of national figures and regional or national efforts to confront racial injustice. This book contributes to the more recent literature arguing that local initiatives were crucially important in twentieth century civil rights struggles, for instance, John Dittmer's Bancroft Prize winning Local People (1994), which clarifies the importance of local residents in campaigns for equal rights in Mississippi.[3]

The hardening of the Ohio color line in the period 1915–1930 occurred in a larger context of historical change in the nation. In the previous half-century, Ohio and much of the North experienced the compelling phenomena of urbanization, immigration, and industrialization and were transformed from largely rural and agricultural societies to modern ones. Ohio, like many northern states in 1915, encompassed numerous large cities with heavy industries and multi-ethnic populations. For over a century now, scholars have asked how African Americans figured in these changes, particularly those in the period 1890–1930. Research on black urban life done through the 1940s mainly was conducted by social scientists studying events in their own time, each focusing on themes such as race relations or black urban community formation in a single city.[4] Publishing in the 1960s and 1970s, historians associated with the so-called ghetto school discussed the social scientists' traditional black urban themes of the early twentieth century but placed them in a historical context that extended backward to related developments in the nineteenth century.[5] Later studies done by historians in the 1980s and after refocused scholarly attention away from black ghetto formation to issues of race, class, and gender with special reference to the African American Great Migration's contributions to the rise of the working class in black urban-industrial life.[6] Knowledge of African American urban history also has been enriched since 1990 by the appearance of numerous other scholarly studies. Each is set in one city, and most focus on citizenship rights struggles in a selected twentieth century period.[7]

This Ohio study comments on both traditional and current issues in the age-old scholarly discussion of black urban life. It deals with such older themes as black-white relations, black migration, and urban institution building as well as newer ones concerning color, class, and gender. The Ohio findings, for instance, support both the 1960s thesis that racial intolerance was an integral factor in early black urban community formation and assertions made in the eighties and nineties that black urban experiences also were affected by other factors that were inherent in urban growth, but different in each city.[8] African American urban studies often relate to a single city, while this Ohio book comments on several urban centers. It asserts that differences in black urban community formation in Ohio were shaped by color line variations from place to place and were related to localized demographic, spatial, and economic factors.

This book provides extended discussions of partisan politics, a relatively underresearched theme in early twentieth century African American history. Among the few such studies is one by Richard B. Sherman (1973), which mainly focuses on white Republicans in the period 1896–1933 making policies tending to abandon the cause of African Americans that the Republican Party had championed in the Reconstruction Era. The Ohio study shows African Americans as local activists who protested these policy changes, engaged in independent black Republican activities in the period 1915–1930, and helped prepare the way for the exodus of black voters from the Republican Party to the Democratic Party in 1936. Analyses explaining this black voter realignment mainly focus on 1930s events and black perceptions of President Franklin D. Roosevelt's New Deal policies.[9]

Ohio is a rich field for research and writing about African Americans, one yielding an extensive literature about the black history of the state, its region, and the nation. There is much fine published scholarship about Ohio's black history, especially in the nineteenth century field. Among these many works are David A. Gerber, *Black Ohio and the Color Line, 1860–1915* (Urbana, IL, 1976), Kenneth L. Kusmer, *A Ghetto Takes Shape: Black Cleveland, 1870–1930* (Urbana, IL, 1976), Kimberly L. Phillips, *Alabama North: African-American Migrants, Community, and Working Class Activism in Cleveland, 1915–1945* (Urbana, IL, 1999), and volumes in the *Greater Cincinnati Bicentennial Series*, edited by Zane L. Miller and Gene D. Louis, for example, *Race and the City: Work, Community, and Protest in Cincinnati, 1820–1970*, edited by Henry Louis Taylor, Jr. (Urbana, IL, 1993).

This Ohio book reflects a great deal of intense searching in original sources over quite a few years. It relies very heavily on these primary sources, for example, newspapers, particularly African American weeklies, census reports and other government documents, records of the NAACP and Urban League, and manuscript collections of individual African Americans. This research yielded an enormous amount of detailed information about individuals, organizations, and places across Ohio, from Cincinnati to Cleveland, and across all sorts of subject matter.

The book uses accumulation of detail to empower its underlying argument that the color line hardened and that resistance to it mainly came from local people. Instead of asserting the thesis with only some illustrative material, it gathers evidence from every corner of Ohio and almost every aspect of life from cradle to grave, at least from hospital to cemetery. Amassing detail upon detail, it leaves little room for doubt that the hardening of the color line, in its various shapes, was ubiquitous in Ohio and that it made life in these times more difficult for African Americans everywhere. The volume quotes generously from the primary sources, black and white ones; this allows the voices of that time to speak again, resurrects the rhetoric of the color line, and conveys variations in both the tenor of white intolerance and the spirit of black resistance.

This book treats the color line as a barrier dividing social groups, and it looks at both sides. It extensively documents the many ways that the Ohio color lines increasingly separated and divided. But much of this study is given to individuals and organizations in African American communities that acted to promote social justice. Importantly, the period 1915–1930 saw the early development of Ohio branches of national civil rights and race relations associations that were the organizational mainstays of the civil rights movement in the early 1950s. Also in this time, African Americans staged community boycotts and set a few Ohio precedents for the kinds of direct action mass protests common in the early 1960s.

Moving from city to city and from region to region as it does, this approach to the subject shows the ambiguities and complexities of the color line. It reveals the great variety within the state. It examines cities in each region and shows that black experiences were different in northern, central, and southern Ohio; for instance, Cleveland was typically the most progressive on equality issues and Cincinnati the least so.

There was variety within this larger pattern as well. Also, this approach shows that some whites crossed the line to work for justice. But it emphasizes the many and varied ways that African Americans acted in the face of the widening color chasm. The basic choices were accommodation or active resistance or wavering between the two, but there were variations of each. Sometimes a color line situation involved a personal decision, perhaps about whether to enter a restaurant or public park. Sometimes a decision concerned a larger community question, perhaps whether to advocate the desegregation of a public school that would bring integration at the expense of black teachers' jobs. Action was necessary to African Americans experiencing both the evolution of color lines and the formation of black communities in Ohio. All were in motion, executing complicated maneuvers of coping with always uncertain and changing circumstances in practically all aspects of life. Life along the color line was replete with challenges, some large, some small. There were failures and successes while color lines were inexorably extended. But, always, somewhere in Ohio local people resisted.

The book is intended for many kinds of readers. It makes a scholarly argument about the hardening of the color line in Ohio and the character of resistance there while providing a source of information and detail about dozens of themes of broad interest. It is meant to serve scholars interested in color issues. Naturally, it speaks to Ohioans especially. Further, it is intended to serve as a reliable and enduring reference for teachers, librarians, historical society staffs, museum curators, and others working on any number of programs and projects. Finally, it is hoped that the book speaks to general readers. It contains many stories of inherent interest revealing human conduct at its best and worst. One such instance involved a white sheriff who risked his life attempting to foil a white mob set on lynching the lawman's black prisoner. Another concerned an African American campaign to form a black regiment for service in World War I and the heroic conduct of Ohio's black combat soldiers in France. All of these stories help illuminate the reality of life along the color line for the Ohioans of this period.

PART ONE

Black Migrants and Wartimes, 1915–1920

CHAPTER ONE

The Great Migration and Its Impact

World War I and wartime black migration were the most powerful events affecting the African American experience in Ohio during 1915–1920. The war set the context for an unparalleled black in-migration to northern cities that changed black demographic character-istics in Ohio. Between 1910 and 1920, Ohio's African American popu-lation grew by 67 percent, rising to 186,187. Over 98.6 percent of this black population growth occurred in cities.[1] (See table A1. *Note:* All tables are presented in the appendix.) Black migrants were not counted systematically, but interested observers made estimates. In July 1917, a black social worker in Cincinnati, James H. Robinson, reported: "A con-servative estimate places the number of migrants who settled here during the past twelve months at 4,000 while easily 30,000 have passed through."[2] A long time African American resident of Cleveland, George A. Myers, believed that 25,000 black migrants entered Cleveland between January and October 1916.[3] A Cleveland daily newspaper esti-mated that 10,000 African Americans migrated to Cleveland during 1916–1917.[4]

Regardless of the specific numbers involved, the movement of so many people was dramatic and visible to the public through press reports. Major daily newspapers and African American weekly newspapers reported items about the numbers of black migrants arriving in Ohio. Also, the National Association for the Advancement of Colored People published migration reports in the NAACP journal, *The Crisis*, some-times stating numbers of black migrants entering Ohio. In 1916 and 1917 migration reports in the press were relatively common, especially in *The Gazette*, Cleveland's most enduring African American weekly. On June 10, 1916, *The Gazette* announced, "Another car-load of Afro-Americans arrived in the city, Tuesday morning, from the South, and others (individuals) from various parts of the state are coming daily to work."[5] Over 1,000 southern migrants arrived in Cincinnati on April 15, 1917, according to *The Crisis*.[6] The *Gazette* reported that train "carloads of Afro-Americans arrived in Cleveland and other cities in Ohio" on May 7, 1917, including fifteen hundred detraining in Cincinnati. While the black migration in summer and winter 1916 had been "confined almost wholly to men," this report stated: "A Sunday train from Cincinnati to Cleveland brought one car loaded with women and children, to join their men folks in Cleveland, Ashtabula and Buffalo. The party was from Biloxi, Miss."[7] Later in May 1917 the Toledo *Blade*, a major daily newspaper, reported the arrival in Toledo of 896 African Americans on sixteen rail cars.[8] Similarly, on August 31, 1918 *The Gazette* announced, "A large number of people from Alabama and Georgia arrived [in Cleveland] week before last."[9]

Although the wartime migration into Ohio continued through 1918, the "peak of the influx" was reached by April 1918, according to a *Gazette* report giving the observations of William R. Conners, executive secretary of Cleveland's Negro Welfare Association. Conners said that many migrants had "gone from Cleveland to other Ohio cities . . . and many returned South."[10] By March 1919, the migration into Ohio, at least into Cleveland, seemed to have stopped temporarily. The ticket agent at Cleveland's Union Station estimated that hundreds of African Americans had entrained for the South during January and February 1919.[11] Welfare Association officer Conners did not notice a significant exodus to the South in 1919, but he did see indications that the migration had slackened substantially. Conners reported: "Nearly all of our folks who came from the South during the war are Baptists and so far Baptist ministers haven't noticed any marked return to Dixie. At the same time hardly any new ones have come in."[12]

The great wartime black migration was based on a set of circumstances that prompted departure from the rural South and created incentives making relocation to the urban North attractive. Local statutes and state laws backed racial segregation and the disfranchisement of black voters in the South. African Americans were severely affected by the labor depression in the South in 1914–1915. The boll weevil plague of these years damaged cotton crops upon which many poor black farmers were dependent for their subsistence. Also, thousands of African Americans became homeless and destitute in the South because of floods in 1915.

Meantime, World War I indirectly created circumstances inducing African Americans in the South to move northward. War in Europe stimulated production in northern industries, increasing the demand for labor. The labor shortage in the North was potentially dangerous when United States entry into the armed conflict required vastly increased war production in northern industries. While labor needs grew the labor supply shrank as northern men, white and black, entered the military services. In the past, northern industry's increasing demand for labor was met by the employment of European foreign-born newcomers. But this time, European immigrants could not fill the gap in the labor supply. Dangers of wartime passenger travel on the Atlantic after 1914 caused immigration from Europe to decline sharply and then to virtually stop. Confronted by that labor market imperative, employers altered usual gender and racial hiring policies. Industries in the North employed black men, black women, and white women in some jobs previously done by white men only.[13]

Northern industrialists needed and actively recruited African American workers during 1916–1917. The need was greater in cities on or near the Great Lakes, such as Cleveland, where reliance on foreign-born white labor was greater than elsewhere in the region. Often industrialists sent labor agents into the South to recruit black workers. In Ohio, workers were most needed in factories, iron works, railroads, and coalmines. African American workers were needed in various kinds of factories including those producing tires and rubber, carbon, chemicals, valves, and munitions.

In Ohio, reports of urban industrialists seeking African American laborers in the South most often came from northern Ohio cities. The Goodyear Tire and Rubber Company in Akron issued calls for as many as three hundred African American workers at one time.[14] A firm in Sandusky promised to pay the railroad fare of those who would come to work in that northern Ohio city.[15] In Barberton the Pittsburgh Valve Company and the Columbia Chemical Company recruited southern black workers.[16] In Toledo the New York Central and the Pennsylvania railroads sought and hired black migrants from the South.[17] Agents from Cleveland looked for potential African Americans migrants in small southern towns on rail lines.[18] The Columbus Malleable Iron Works and the Ohio Malleable Iron Works were among the central Ohio companies that sent labor agents into the South.[19]

During 1916–1917 labor agents acting for northern industrial employers recruited African Americans in Alabama, Arkansas, Florida, Georgia, and Mississippi. Blacks, as well as whites, served as labor agents. Black Ohioans worked as labor recruiters for industries in several northern states, including Ohio. Joseph L. Jones and Melvin J. Chisum founded a Cincinnati employment agency that became a labor-recruiting center.

Their agency brought African Americans from the South and sent them to various parts of the North to work in manufacturing and munitions plants. According to one estimate, Chisum recruited thousands of African Americans during his forays in the South.[20] Meanwhile, some Cleveland industrialists paid labor agents one dollar for every African American worker recruited in the South. Agents representing Cleveland firms sometimes carried pictures of the homes of wealthy African Americans and showed them to southern sharecroppers as examples of "the sort of places you'd live in up in Cleveland."[21] After describing opportunities in Ohio, agents working out of Cleveland gave railroad tickets to African Americans taking their ease at railroad stations in small southern towns.[22]

As well as using labor agents in the South, Ohio manufacturers recruited Africans Americans already present in the state. Cleveland attorney Harry E. Davis noted that Cleveland employers were "appealing to our churches" and "literally combing the highways of the colored districts for workmen."[23] The National Carbon Company of Cleveland was one of the firms that sought the cooperation of African American ministers. The company's recruiting program included a plant inspection tour and dinner for black clergymen. By November 1917, the National Carbon Company had hired approximately one hundred African American employees and still needed about one hundred more.[24]

Regardless of their racial biases, whites in local and state government and in the newspaper business generally accepted the new racial hiring policies and the African American migration. They too understood that black workers were needed to fill vacant industrial jobs. For example, the Toledo *Blade,* using phrasing gratuitously insulting to African Americans, urged Toledo's whites to accept the permanency of the "Negro immigration" and noted that African Americans were entitled to freedom of movement.[25] Cleveland's director of public welfare, in response to an inquiry from the *Omaha Monitor,* an African American newspaper, said: ". . . our city offers opportunities for the industrious Negro from the South. . . . [T]here are a good many firms here that could use industrious Negro labor."[26]

During World War I the United States Department of Labor cooperated with northern industry's effort to increase production by recruiting and using black workers. The department's Director of Negro Economics, George E. Haynes, supervised a federal program meant to facilitate the employment of African Americans during the war. In various states, cooperative Negro Workers' Advisory Committees were organized at state, city, and county levels. A state level Ohio Negro Workers' Advisory Committee was established at a conference held in

Columbus in August 1916.[27] Subsequently, Negro Workers' Advisory Committees operated in thirty-one cities and counties in Ohio. A supervisor of Negro economics headed each Ohio committee. The Ohio supervisor for committees, in cooperation with the United States Employment Service, recruited and placed black workers in plants and industries that previously had not hired African Americans. According to Director Haynes, the Ohio Supervisors gave a large amount of advisory service, i.e., advised employers "about improvements and methods of dealing with Negro workers."[28]

Yet before the end of the decade, Ohio employers suspended their extraordinary efforts to recruit black workers in the South. Ohio labor market circumstances and racial bias eventually made the employment of black industrial workers less imperative. Ohio industry's labor shortage ended during the war as more and more African Americans were hired. Then the cancellation of war contracts and the return of war veterans during the postwar period caused a temporary labor supply surplus in Ohio. Active recruitment of black workers ended and the number of jobs available to African Americans declined. Meantime, the black migration to Ohio slowed in 1918, lessening even more after the war.[29] In comparison, the postwar boom's end eventually caused a short-lived black out-migration in western Pennsylvania where, according to historian Peter Gottlieb, many black southerners left Pittsburgh in 1920–1921.[30] Surely, the war's economic effects caused migration rates to fluctuate during 1914–1919. Emmett J. Scott's valuable essay on the World War I migration, published in 1920, stated that the movement "was fundamentally economic, though its roots were tangled in the entire social system of the South."[31] The Ohio record supported Scott's conclusion.

These economic and social forces did not simply control the lives of participants in the black wartime migration and carry them away. Migrants acted out of individual volition and initiative. Most African Americans in the South chose not to join the outward population movement. Those who did so made their own personal choices. Decisions were required, for example, about whether to migrate, where to move, and how best to reach a destination. Migrants employed a variety of tactics to survive the ordeal of their changing life circumstances in the South, in the North, during their travels, and at their destinations. Acting singly was sometimes the only recourse, but most often these strategies involved reliance on family, friends, and the cultural ways of the South. Departing African Americans saw migration as being in their own best interests in what seemed to be a time of hope raised by opportunities for urban industrial work. Convincing evidence supporting this characterization of black migrants is found in the work of historians who view the Great Migration as a historical process and examine its connection to the formation of the black urban working class.[32] These scholars emphasize that black migrants' coping capacities relied on human networks connecting their origins in the South and their settlement locations. Kimberly L. Phillips provides an important Ohio example calling attention to the links between African Americans in Cleveland and Alabama during and following World War I.

The black in-migration to Ohio cities after 1915 made the African American experience in Ohio largely an urban one. African Americans resided in small and large cities in every county in 1920, but more than ever before Ohio's black population was concentrated in large cities. Almost 80 percent of black urban residents lived in the nine Ohio cities whose total populations exceeded 50,000. (See map 1.) Black population growth rates were greatest in northern Ohio's large industrial cities. Black population increased eightfold in Akron, quadrupled in Canton and Cleveland, and tripled in Toledo and Youngstown. In prewar times black populations in these northern urban centers were smaller than those in Ohio cities to their south. The wartime labor shortage with its accompanying demand for black industrial workers was most intense in northern Ohio. Urban industries there were most affected by the virtual stoppage of immigration during the war. Ohio's northern region was more dependent on foreign-born labor than other less industrial parts of Ohio. In 1920 Cleveland's white foreign-born population was three times greater than Cincinnati's. Proportionately, there were many more immigrants in northern Ohio's large cities than in those of central and southern Ohio in 1920. African American population growth rates, while extraordinary, were not as sharp in the large cities of southern and central Ohio where there was less reliance on immigrant labor and where African Americans were relatively numerous before the war. Cincinnati's black population rose by half, while Columbus' and Dayton's grew by about three-quarters.[33]

These growth rates across Ohio brought the formation of population masses large enough to support urban black community life on a scale previously precluded by insufficient numbers. Cleveland's black population was only 8,448 in 1910, but it grew about 26,000 in the next decade. In numerical terms in-migration was advancing the growth of black cities within cities. In 1920, African Americans in each of three Ohio urban centers were as numerous as the population of a middle size city (a place of 10,000 to 25,000), as categorized in the United States census. The black population was 34,451 in Cleveland, 30,079 in Cincinnati, and 22,181 in Columbus. Black populations as large as small cities (places of 2,500 to 10,000) existed in Akron, Dayton, Springfield,

Map 1

Map of State of Ohio.

Source: David A. Gerber, *Black Ohio and the Color Line, 1860–1915* (Urbana: University of Illinois Press, 1976), p. 2. Map by James Bier. Reproduced with permission of the author.

Toledo, and Youngstown. (See table A2.) Black urban populations grew significantly, but in 1920 African Americans comprised only three percent of Ohio's total population. African Americans still were less than twelve percent of the whole population in all of Ohio's largest cities.[34] (See table A1.)

In consequence of both prewar and wartime migrations, many African Americans in Ohio were newcomers adjusting to city life during 1915–1920. Early twentieth-century migrants, regardless of their nationality, color, or gender, faced some of the same basic adjustment problems in urban centers. A newcomer needed to find shelter, make a living, and form comforting social relationships in unfamiliar and impersonal places. But racial prejudice sharply complicated relocation adjustments by African Americans. Employment and income were the migrant's greatest immediate concerns. Prior to 1916 potential jobs for African Americans in Ohio were scarce and largely found in domestic work and unskilled labor not associated with manufacturing. The paucity of jobs available to blacks meant that many migrants were jobless occasionally while some experienced sustained unemployment.[35]

Finding work, of course, was less difficult for migrants during 1916–1918 when the wartime labor shortage existed and Ohio's industries were seeking African Americans workers. Black men obtained jobs in foundries, factories, iron works, steel mills, and on railroads in unprecedented numbers. Meanwhile, black women were employed in a wider variety of jobs as racial hiring policies changed. Rachel S. Gallagher, director of the City Free Labor Exchange of Cleveland, described the results of these policy changes as they affected Cleveland in the spring of 1918. Director Gallagher reported that Cleveland's wage earning "colored girls" in 1916 had labored with few exceptions "in housework, as laundress and cleaning women, as maids," but in 1918 blacks were found in "nearly every field of women's work, and some work where women had not previously been employed." She gave examples of black women working in railroad yards, in packing houses, and in factories and plants making knit wear, sewn garments, buttons, paper boxes, cigars, and electrical supplies.[36] Similarly, in southwestern Ohio, African American women were employed as engine wipers at the Ivorydale Roundhouse of the Cincinnati, Hamilton and Dayton Railroad.[37]

Many African American newcomers, men and women, encountered difficulties while trying to obtain employment during 1914–1919, even in 1916–1918 when demand for black workers was comparatively high. An unassisted stranger in the city lacked information about the identities, locations, and job application procedures of employers hiring African Americans. Unemployment was inevitable, until the newcomer reached a source of necessary facts about job openings for African Americans. Presumably, the problem of acquiring such information was most quickly resolved by southern migrants who were guided by labor agents and by those who were knowledgeably informed by family or friends already located in Ohio destination cities. Eventually, some others obtained employment information from various local African American welfare associations or from the local offices of public agencies including the United States Employment Service and the Negro Workers' Advisory Committee of the United States Department of Labor. Black migrants were temporarily unemployed, for varying lengths of time. Organized job placement services did not reach all black migrants and some did not get jobs.[38] Often migrants who failed to obtain employment in one Ohio urban center moved on to another industrial city in search of work.[39]

Obtaining employment and adequate shelter were the most immediate problems of African American migrants settling in Ohio cities. Frequently in prewar times the migrants' employment and housing problems were equally difficult. But the difficulty of finding proper housing increased during wartime when getting a job was less difficult for African Americans. Wartime migrants arriving in industrial cities across Ohio found housing shortages causing overcrowding of dwelling units and homelessness. The housing situation in Cleveland was especially bad.[40] Cleveland's housing problems were observed and often reported by local black weekly editor Harry C. Smith. In May 1917, Editor Smith reported: ". . . the housing of the large number of our people who have come to Cleveland from the South in recent months and weeks is a serious problem. . . . It is distressing to meet daily numbers of these people almost begging places to stop and house their families, even temporarily."[41] Later in May, Smith noted: "Our local boarding and rooming houses are packed. Few additional places can be found."[42] In August 1917, the editor informed readers that hundreds of southern migrants were "living in old railroad cars, shanties, abandoned buildings, shacks and tents."[43] At about the same time the *Cleveland News* stated that thousands of black migrants were living in boxcars on railroad sidings in the city.[44] The federal labor department's Director of Negro Economics received information that migrants in Cincinnati and Columbus, as well as in Cleveland, were "crowded into basements, shanties, firetraps and other types of houses unfit for human habitation."[45] Homelessness and overcrowding occurred in smaller Ohio cities as well. In Toledo, some black employees of the New York Central Railroad were encamped in railroad cars with fifteen to twenty persons occupying a single boxcar.[46] There were exceptional instances in which employers, including the New York Central Railroad, provided company houses for southern migrants working for them.[47]

There was a nationwide housing shortage during World War I when increasing numbers of black migrants were looking for rooms to rent in Ohio. The building construction labor supply fell and the cost of building materials rose as men and commodities were absorbed in war mobilization.[48] New housing construction slowed and almost stopped. For example, in Cincinnati, the value of residential construction fell from about $7,000.00 to less than $700.00 from 1916 through 1918.[49] While African Americans migrants were worst hit, the effects of the housing shortage also touched middle class and working class whites. Thus, housing was an issue for white public officials and civic leaders and the major daily newspapers. The Cleveland Chamber of Commerce investigated local housing conditions in the summer of 1917 and concluded that housing needs were greater than ever. Chamber investigators said that workers were jammed together in almost every part of Cleveland. Overcrowding was worst in the vicinity of manufacturing plants. Black and white Cleveland residents needed an additional 10,000 low rent houses in 1917 according to a study announced by the Cleveland Real Estate Board's secretary. The *Cleveland Plain Dealer* and the *Cleveland News* covered the housing issue.[50] In Toledo, the *Daily Journal* ran stories exposing the effects of the local housing shortage.[51] The press and public officials understood that the effects of the housing problem were worst for black migrants. Ohio Governor James M. Cox ordered an investigation of African American housing conditions in the state in the summer of 1917.[52]

Black migrants had fewer options than whites in the search for shelter. The housing choices of African American migrants were limited by personal preferences, financial constraints, and color lines. Usually black migrants looked for shelter within or on the perimeters of black neighborhoods. Often migrants chose to locate in a specific black neighborhood because it was in proximity to family members or acquaintances or persons with similar geographical origins. Many times, black migrants preferred an African American neighborhood because it was seen as a haven in a city that was alien and even hostile to blacks. Irrespective of preferences, black migrants earning low wages in unskilled labor and domestic service jobs could not afford to pay high rents for housing, and existing African American residential areas generally were located in low rent districts. Preferences and incomes aside, racial practices of whites sharply restricted the residential choices of African Americans. For instance, poor black migrants often were excluded from low rent white neighborhoods where landlords did not rent rooms to African Americans. In these circumstances, black neighborhoods saw their boundaries expanding and their population densities increasing at the same time. In these areas, where over-crowded dwellings were commonplace, poor black migrants were especially vulnerable to exploitation by landlords.[53]

Nationwide rent profiteering was the bane of many urban tenants, white and black, during and after World War I. Landlords used the housing shortage as an opportunity to raise rents sharply. In some cities and states including Ohio, angry state legislators and municipal officials eventually formulated policies and introduced bills intended to counteract rent profiteering. For example, an anti–rent profiteering board was established in Cleveland.[54] Yet rents rises continued for the duration of the war. As early as June 1917 the Cleveland *Gazette* reported that landlords of rental properties in Cleveland's African American neighborhoods were raising rents substantially.[55] African Americans in Cleveland's Central Avenue district were still charged exorbitant rents in August 1918 according to reports in the same African American weekly and in the *Cleveland Plain Dealer*.[56] Some black Clevelanders reportedly saw rents rise by as much as 75 percent.[57] While rent gouging was a general phenomenon, rents were most disproportionate to the quality of properties occupied by black migrants or poor white immigrants. For example, profiteering landlords in Toledo raised rents on old dilapidated houses and dwellings unfit for human habitation.[58] Impoverished tenants inhabiting such places could not afford the higher rent unless they shared rental costs with others. More and more poor tenants had to live in the same rental unit and pool their funds to pay the rent. Thus rent profiteering contributed to overcrowding in black neighborhoods in Toledo and in other Ohio cities.

Housing and employment problems were only some of the hardships experienced by Ohio's black newcomers. Many African American migrants also were exposed to social difficulties historically associated with the nation's urban slum life since 1850. Relatively high rates of indigence, disease, and crime were endemic to urban slums wherever and whenever large numbers of impoverished migrants or immigrants were crowded in areas with substandard housing conditions. These social problems existed in Irish immigrant slums and other immigrant districts of cities across America on the eve of the Civil War. In 1859 in New York City 77 percent of all persons arrested for crime were foreign-born and 55 percent of them were Irish immigrants. At least 86 percent of all persons on public assistance in New York City in 1860 were foreign-born persons largely from Ireland and other lands of northwestern Europe. Meanwhile, mid-nineteenth century immigrants, including many of the Irish, contracted cholera, smallpox, and other epidemic diseases more frequently than persons in the native population.[59] Constrained only by their preferences and finances, most immigrants from northwest Europe ultimately moved away from the slums and their social problems. Eventually after 1900 few of the Irish, Germans, Swedes, and Norwegians appeared on lists of persons caught up in the social difficulties of slum life. Between the 1880s and World War I, their places in slums of the urban northeast were taken, sometimes literally, by immigrants from southern and eastern European countries. Until they too prospered and moved out of city slums, immigrants from Italy, Russia, Greece, Poland

and other southern and eastern European lands were exposed to the vice, crime and ill health associated with poverty in urban America.[60] In consequence of the wartime migration to northern cities, significantly more African Americans in Ohio were affected by the social ills of urban slums.

Deplorable housing conditions in city slums threatened personal and public health. Wartime black migrants to Toledo often inhabited vermin-infested houses, while some black newcomers to that city lived in small cellar rooms that were damp, dark, and insufficiently ventilated. Such conditions were ideal for the growth of disease-bearing microorganisms. In Toledo, adequate sanitation was virtually impossible to maintain in an overcrowded railway boxcar, a basement dwelling, a single room accommodating an entire family, or a house lacking running water. Contagious diseases spread more quickly in an overcrowded slum dwelling or district than in a less densely populated area. Yet, as Toledo health officials recognized, such housing conditions might cause a disease epidemic threatening to spread from the inhabitants of squalid dwellings into the citywide population.[61]

Ohio officials who investigated wartime housing conditions among black migrants were much concerned about general public health issues. Emmett J. Scott, who made a contemporary examination of the wartime migration, reported that the Council for Defense's Ohio branch and the Ohio Department of Health conducted a study of health conditions among black migrants in several Ohio cities. Scott summarized the Ohio health department's findings, stating: "The Negroes who were coming into the State [Ohio] were being crowded into the Negro sections of various cities in such a way that the health of these communities in many cases was being seriously threatened."[62] The health department was the first state agency to study the matter after Governor James M. Cox ordered an investigation of housing conditions among African American migrants.[63] Evidently, state and municipal officials were most interested in the public health dimension of housing problems experienced by wartime black migrants. The acting director of public welfare in Cleveland stated: "The large influx of laborers into Cleveland, especially Negro laborers . . . is causing a dangerous situation. There aren't sufficient houses . . . for families. As a result the health of hundreds is being undermined."[64] The Cincinnati Health Board held an extraordinary session, in June 1919, "to consider the Negro health problem" and concluded that a community health center was needed "for the sake of the Negro and the city," but funding was unavailable.[65] Meanwhile, death and illness rates were high among African Americans in Cincinnati, Cleveland, Columbus, and other Ohio cities. Statistical records of disease and mortality rates suggested that the health of persons inhabiting inadequate shelter was most at risk. For example, in 1920 in Cleveland, pneumonia- and tuberculosis-associated mortality rates of blacks were more than two times higher than those of whites.[66]

As the wartime migration to Ohio and other northern states ensued, greater numbers of African Americans encountered problems of urban vice and crime historically associated with the inner-city sectors where immigrants were most numerous. Streets known as "the tenderloin district" or "the red light district" existed in urban America for more than fifty years before World War I. Brothels, gambling houses, and saloons were concentrated in these few streets. Police authorities allowed illicit activities in "the tenderloin districts" because municipal administrations wished to isolate vice activities and their associated crimes in inner-city areas largely inhabited by low-income people, white immigrants and black migrants.[67]

During World War I, as in the past, newcomers in Ohio's inner-city wards faced the problems of vice and crime arising from drinking, gambling, and prostitution, as well as the greater possibility of arrests for vagrancy and loitering. Unlike in the past, most wartime newcomers were African American migrants from the South instead of white immigrants from southern and eastern Europe. When wartime migrants arrived in Ohio cities they found long established vice areas in or nearby African American neighborhoods. During the decade before the war, a "red light district" appeared at East 30th Street and Central Avenue in Cleveland. Although that vice area was in the middle of Cleveland's African American neighborhoods, it was visited by blacks and whites, foreign born and native born.[68] In 1916, the Cleveland *Gazette*, an African American newspaper edited by Harry C. Smith, reported and condemned the growth of the "speakeasies, gambling, and questionable houses" in that part of Cleveland.[69] Later, the *Gazette*'s editor criticized law enforcement in the Third Police Precinct, which encompassed the "red light district." He charged that policemen rarely patrolled "the roaring third" and usually appeared there only after a serious crime was committed.[70] Appearing before the Cleveland City Council in 1917, the newspaper editor gave testimony indicating that conditions in the Central Avenue "red light district" grew worse during the wartime migration. Harry C. Smith said, "Speakeasies, disorderly flats and a gambling den are in full operation" and added, "The hands of the police seem tied."[71] The *Gazette*'s editor and other anti-vice crusaders, white and black, did not persuade the city administration to eliminate the "red light district"; consequently, Cleveland's "tenderloin" enterprises flourished throughout the decade.

Evidently, while heads of vice-related businesses in the "roaring third" were unmolested by the police, increasing numbers of black residents of Cleveland's Central Avenue neighborhoods were arrested for relatively minor offenses after 1915. Apparently, these arrests made in Cleveland affected the racial composition of the inmates in the county workhouse at Warrensville, an institution for low-level offenders. According to a report made by a Cleveland city welfare department official in August 1917, the proportion of African Americans held at Warrensville increased rapidly in the previous year. Prior to the wartime migration the usual proportion of blacks in the county workhouse was about 10 percent. But in August 1917, 61 percent of the men and 66 percent of the women in the workhouse were African Americans.[72]

A "red light district" developed in a three-block corridor of Cincinnati's George Street well before World War I. Brothels existed on Longsworth and George streets by 1903. The bawdy houses, which were staffed by white and black women, catered to persons of every color and class.[73] Tolerated by the police, they openly advertised for business using "brightly lettered signs of 'Marie,' 'Lucy,' 'Kate,' 'Nellie,' 'May,' etc.," identifying their madams.[74] This "tenderloin" was located in an African American neighborhood on the western edge of Cincinnati's central business district. As the African American migration to Cincinnati increased in 1916–1917, many black newcomers to the city necessarily took living quarters near the "tenderloin" where vice and crime already abounded. In November 1917, under mounting pressure to oppose personal immorality and clean up vice in the city, Cincinnati municipal authorities ordered the closure of all brothels in the "red light district."[75] After evictions of madams and prostitutes, George Street buildings formerly housing brothels were used as tenement houses. "Negro tenants came and paid double-prices to rapacious landlords," according to Wendell P. Dabney, editor of an African American weekly in Cincinnati.[76] The former George Street inhabitants scattered, thereby diffusing vice activities. Dabney noted: "The Negro women . . . flocked into Carlisle Avenue, lower John and Smith Streets. They, still, a little more discreetly, however, followed 'Mrs. Warren's profession.'"[77] The closure of brothels in the George Street vicinity did not end the "tenderloin" phenomenon in Cincinnati. Eventually a different vice district developed. Some years later, Dabney reported that "crime runs riot as never before . . . in the downtown 'tenderloin district'" of Cincinnati.[78]

Likewise, in an essay about African Americans in Columbus, J. S. Himes, Jr., noted: "The mass migration of the World War brought an immediate harvest of new social ills. As the tight little community tried to expand with unaccustomed rapidity, a severe shortage of homes was experienced. . . . . Vice, crime, and delinquency reached a new high, the Bad Lands to the contrary notwithstanding."[79] Beginning in the 1890s a section of Columbus' East Long Street bordering black neighborhoods was known as the Bad Lands. It housed an array of "tenderloin" institutions of the usual types and, eventually, an opium den. Some Bad Lands brothels were shut down by a new city administration elected in 1909 with the backing of anti-vice crusaders. Yet saloons and some brothels in the East Long Street vicinity remained open. Meanwhile, the Columbus officials ignored the less visible "red light district" in a black neighborhood near Main Street and Seventh Street.[80] As the wartime migration accelerated, many more African Americans in Columbus were touched by the urban crime and vice problems.

Intensification of preexisting urban social-economic difficulties in black neighborhoods accompanied the rapid growth of Ohio's African American population after 1915. Yet in the broader context, the impact of the black wartime migration was certainly beneficial. The presence of black migrants was an economic asset in Ohio and elsewhere in the region as well.[81] A renewable labor supply and a growing consumer market were requisite to Ohio's continued economic development. When additional workers were needed, the black migration augmented the state's labor force enabling Ohio to reach high wartime production goals. Likewise, by increasing the state's African American population, the migration expanded the market for goods and services in Ohio, especially in cities. White as well as black entrepreneurs and professionals benefited when wage-earning black migrants acted as consumers. Some new black businesses were launched in response to the increased demand for goods and services during and after the war. Meanwhile, African American professional classes expanded to serve the needs of growing black urban populations. Further, the wartime migration broadened institutional life in black urban communities as African American churches made gains in membership and financial support in the latter half of the decade. The wartime migration's greatest economic effects were felt in Cleveland. The scale of the migration to Cleveland was greater than that to any other Ohio city, making Cleveland the location of the state's largest black urban population by 1920.

Undoubtedly, the aggregate income of African Americans in Ohio rose between 1910 and 1920 because the numbers of black men and women working in the state grew by tens of thousands. Surely, the wartime improvement of the occupational status of employed African Americans raised the group's total income as well. Proportionately more black males worked in industrial occupations during the wartime migration than in prewar years. Meanwhile, a smaller percentage of black men were employed in domestic service. By 1920 nearly two-thirds of Cleveland's employed black males worked in manufacturing and mechanical industries, while that proportion was little more than one-fifth in 1910. Meantime the percentage of Cleveland's black males working in domestic and personal service occupations fell to 15 percent in 1920 from 33 percent in 1910. More than half of the employed black males in Cincinnati and Columbus worked in manufacturing and mechanical industries by 1920. (In 1910, those proportions were one-quarter in Cincinnati and less than one-third in Columbus.) Also, in Cincinnati, Cleveland, and Columbus, greater proportions of African American industrial workers were in semiskilled and skilled occupations by the decade's end. Nevertheless, most African Americans still worked as unskilled laborers in Ohio industries. In 1920, 73 percent of black male industrial workers in Cincinnati were in the unskilled labor category, while the comparable figure was 64 percent in Cleveland and 59 percent in Columbus.[82]

Black entrepreneurs and professionals in Ohio cities soon felt the beneficial economic effects of the wartime migration. In January 1917, the Cleveland *Advocate*, an African American weekly, reported that ordinary black business and professional people in Cleveland were making more money than ever before.[83] Black business districts already existed in Ohio cities when African American newcomers arrived after 1915. They had developed in response to prewar black migrations. Cleveland's principal black commercial district was located on Central Avenue between East 25th Street and East 35th Street. In Cincinnati, many black businesses were concentrated in the vicinity of Fifth Street between Central and Smith. Columbus' black business districts were situated on East Long Street and on Mt. Vernon Avenue.[84]

The enlarged African American urban populations improved the financial viability of the black newspaper business in some Ohio cities. Consequently, after 1915 more black weekly newspapers remained in publication for longer time periods. Prior to 1900 Ohio's black urban populations were too small to generate subscriptions lists and advertising revenues that were large enough to sustain the continuous publication of black weeklies for more than a few years at most. Many such enterprises were started in Ohio and other Midwestern states during the period from the late nineteenth century to the end of the nineteen-twenties.[85] There was little difficulty in initiating a black newspaper in Ohio, but, since there were large obstacles to sustaining one, few of these newspapers were published successfully. Some printed only one or a few issues. Others continued publication for a few months or a few years. Only a handful maintained a continuous existence over a long period.

These were small weekly newspapers that carried news generally of special interest to the African American community. They were financed by income received from subscribers, commercial advertisers and, perhaps most importantly, from political advertisers. The owners and editors usually had sources of income other than that obtained from the newspaper enterprise. Four pages in length, the typical black weekly was headed by a publisher/editor assisted by a small and mainly female staff. Two women employed as business manager and stenographer comprised the Cincinnati *Union*'s office staff. A man and two women staffed Akron's *Black and White Chronicle*.[86] Although some black publishers maintained their own presses, ordinarily white-owned firms printed the black weeklies.

In Cincinnati, *The Colored Citizen*, *The Voice of the People*, *The Rostrum*, *The Brotherhood*, and *The Bee* were a few of the early black weeklies that were briefly published at different times. Wendell Phillips Dabney started publication of the Cincinnati *Union* in 1907. He was among the African Americans who were prominent in Cincinnati's Republican Party politics. Dabney served for many years as assistant paymaster in the Cincinnati treasurer's office. Cincinnati's African American community, which formed the state's largest black urban population before World War I, grew to almost 20,000 in 1910 and to 30,000 by 1920. Evidently the prewar and wartime black migrations to Cincinnati gave Dabney an economic basis sufficient for success. Still, Cincinnati could not support two African American newspapers simultaneously. Another weekly, *The Pilot*, owned by ten prominent black Cincinnatians, stopped publication after competing with *The Union* for about a year. Dabney published *The Union* continuously through 1920.[87]

The black community in Cleveland, whose population exceeded 30,000 by 1920, usually supported two African American weeklies at once after 1902. Harry C. Smith's *Gazette* was published continuously from 1883–1920. Smith was an especially enterprising and careful businessman, enabling the *Gazette* to succeed financially in the years before the Great Migration when Cleveland's black population was less than 10,000. For example, instead of depending wholly on a Cleveland readership, the *Gazette*'s editor sold subscriptions to the paper in smaller African American communities across Ohio. During 1903–1920, Smith's Cleveland competitors were the *Journal* (1903–1912), edited by Nahum D. Brascher, and the *Advocate* (1914–1920), edited by Ormonde O. Forte.[88]

Publishing a black weekly also was a challenge in Dayton, whose comparatively small African American population did not reach 9,000 before 1920. The *Informer*, the *Record*, and the *Citizen* were weeklies appearing

at different times in Dayton from 1900 to the World War. Early in the
century, John Rives founded the *Forum* in Dayton and published it
through the 1920s.[89] The *Ohio State Monitor* was published in Columbus
during the postwar period.[90] The Dayton *Forum*, the Cleveland *Gazette*,
and the Cincinnati *Union* were the only black weeklies that sustained
long lives prior to 1920.

As well as making existing businesses more profitable, the wartime
migration encouraged black entrepreneurs to start additional enterprises
relying on the patronage of African Americans. Between 1910 and 1920
the numbers of black retail dealers grew about fourfold in Cleveland,
increasing by 40 percent in Cincinnati and by 30 percent in Columbus.
The high wartime demand for housing in the vicinity of black neighborhoods created new business opportunities in the real estate field.
Although there were very few African Americans in the business,
between 1910 and 1920 the numbers of black real estate agents and officials doubled in Columbus and quadrupled in Cleveland.[91] The
Cleveland Realty, Housing, and Investment Company was organized by
a group of prominent African Americans, including Thomas Fleming,
Welcome Blue, and Nahum Brascher. After purchasing a great deal of
Central Avenue area property in 1917, the company sought black tenants by advertising in an African American weekly.[92] A company adver-
tisement in the *Cleveland Advocate* stated: "We have just secured the
group of seven apartment houses which are rapidly nearing completion
on East 40th Street between Central and Scovill Avenues. Three and
four room suites with bath, hot water, electric lights, gas ranges, heating
appliances, refrigerators, ... All for colored people."[93] This advertise-
ment, of course, shows that the black real estate company was not resisting the current patterns of racial segregation in residential housing.
Realtors of all colors profited during the wartime housing shortage, and
like their white counterparts black real estate dealers in Cleveland were
accused of rent profiteering.[94]

Many of the black migrants individually contributed to black business
growth by starting enterprises in Ohio cities, while the mass of wartime
newcomers stimulated black business expansion by enlarging the
African American markets in the state. The black migration to Ohio
was not wholly composed of working class folk from rural origins. A fraction of the black newcomers to Ohio came from urban settings to engage
in entrepreneurial pursuits. Black newcomers formed a variety of businesses in Cincinnati by the end of the decade. The migrant entrepreneurs came to Cincinnati from quite different backgrounds, but shared
similar commercial ambitions. For example, George Ryan Hicks moved
from Missouri to Cincinnati in 1916. His mother was a schoolteacher

and his father was a railway mail service employee. A native of Loveland in the Cincinnati area, Hicks was reared south of Columbus, Ohio, where he graduated from Chillicothe High School in 1904. After graduation from the Ohio State College of Pharmacy, 1910, he practiced pharmacy in Kansas City, Missouri, and in St. Louis. In 1916 Hicks and others organized the company that owned the Model Drug Store, at Fifth and Smith Streets in Cincinnati. Willie Harris migrated to Cincinnati in 1917 when he was twenty-three years old and in the same year opened a "first class tailoring establishment" on West Fifth Street. Harris was born at Birmingham, Alabama, where he apprenticed as a tailor after graduating from high school. G. W. Gamble, a native of South Carolina, came to Cincinnati in 1917, starting an ice, coal, and express business in 1920. Mrs. Flora Hector, born in Tennessee, relocated to Cincinnati in 1919, training as a beauty culturist and opening a beauty parlor in the city by the end of the year. William H. Hill left school at Warsaw, Kentucky, following his father's death and went to work at a youthful age to support his mother and siblings. Eventually Hill moved up the Ohio River to Cincinnati where he prospered and entered the undertaking business in 1919.[95]

The wartime business growth in Ohio's black urban residential districts represented the acceleration of a late nineteenth century trend toward increasing reliance on the growing African American market for services and goods. The phenomenon originated when Ohio's black urban communities were enlarged by migrations in the 1890s. Then most profitable black businesses, such as food catering, barbering, and tailoring, were still providing goods and services to an elite white clientele. The importance of white patronage of black businesses waned greatly before and during World War I.[96] Yet barbering and other businesses involving domestic and personal services continued to exist and thrived by serving African American patrons. The number of black male barbers increased during the decade and in 1920 reached 142 in Cincinnati, 167 in Cleveland, and 104 in Columbus.[97] Relatively small businesses were still typical enterprises in African American neighborhoods in the postwar period. For example, a 1919–1920 directory of black businesses in Columbus included automobile livery services, barbers, blacksmiths, caterers, confectionaries, dressmakers, drug stores, feed stores, furniture stores, house movers, hotels, painters, and plasters.[98]

Ohio's black professional classes also reaped the economic benefits of the large wartime black migration. Black professionals saw the economic opportunities that arose from the black migrations since 1890 and thereafter tended to establish practices based on black clients.[99] Nevertheless, some African American professionals, particularly lawyers, still followed the nineteenth century custom of retaining white clients. Ohio's black professional classes expanded greatly between 1910 and 1920. Teaching and clerical professions grew the most; for instance, the number of black clergymen in Cincinnati rose by 82 percent. There apparently was a fourfold increase of black clergymen in Cleveland. Although there were only 17 black churches in Cleveland shortly before the war, there were 73 black clergymen in the city by 1920. The number of black public school teachers often more than doubled in large Ohio cities, increasing tenfold in Toledo. Expansion in the legal and medical professions was significant but uneven statewide, and increases of black doctors and lawyers often did not keep pace with black population growth rates in Ohio's major cities.[100] (See table A3.)

The wartime migration also spurred African American institutional growth in Ohio cities. Religious institutions were most affected by black population increases. The majority of Ohio's black church members were Baptists before World War I. Likewise, in 1916, Ohio's 49,053 total black church memberships included 29,023 Baptist church members and 17,440 members of Methodist denominations, 11,149 of whom belonged to the African Methodist Episcopal church. The remainder of Ohio's black church members in 1916 were affiliated with the Seventh-day Adventist denomination, the Church of the Living God, Congregational churches, the Presbyterian church, the Protestant Episcopal church and the Roman Catholic church.[101]

The wartime migration quickened the numerical growth of Ohio's black church memberships, congregations, clergymen, and edifices. Recent scholarship suggests that this phenomenon was region-wide in the North.[102] Black churches in various denominations benefited from the incursion of migrants, but Ohio's black Baptist bodies gained the most because most church-affiliated black newcomers were Baptists. Only with some exaggeration, a Cleveland Negro Welfare Association official noted: "Nearly all of our folks [in Cleveland] who came from the South during the war are Baptists."[103] Consequently, Antioch Baptist Church, whose membership increased continuously, was the largest black congregation in Cleveland throughout the decade. In Cleveland the numbers of black churches of various kinds grew from 17 before the wartime migration to 44 in 1918.[104] In Columbus there were 14 black Baptist churches by 1920, up from 12 in 1916.[105] In Cincinnati 91 black clergymen were counted in 1920, while only 50 African American pastors were located in that city in 1910.[106]

Ordinary working people were mainly responsible for the growth of Ohio's black religious institutions during World War I, but black business and professional people also contributed to the expansion. Often new congregations were largely composed of poor migrants who were unable to finance the purchase of a church building. Excepting one, the black churches that were organized in Cleveland between 1916 and 1918 used rented buildings in that time.[107] Occasionally, a black urban church was founded through "chain migration" as virtually all of the members of a small congregation in the South moved north and reorganized in Ohio. For example, in Cincinnati, the Reverend Charles Williams "organized the Southern Baptist Church with eleven members who accompanied him from the South." The Reverend Williams was an active Baptist pastor, missionary, and church organizer in Mississippi before migrating to Cincinnati in 1917.[108] In contrast, members of Cleveland's old black business and professional families composed the congregations of Mt. Zion Congregational Church and St. Andrews Episcopal Church, both established long before World War I. The growth of Cleveland's new black business and professional classes in the war years brought membership growth at Mt. Zion Congregational Church and ultimately at the more exclusive St. Andrews Episcopal Church, while prompting the establishment of St. Mark's Presbyterian Church in 1918. Furthermore, thirteen other black congregations in Cleveland purchased church buildings in 1920.[109] Apparently, even the newer and poorer black congregations in Cleveland improved their financial affairs by the decade's end.

Prior to 1920, fraternal organizations as well as churches figured prominently in the social life of many Americans, white and black. Although some formed prior to 1800, most fraternal lodges in the United States were established in the nineteenth century. Autonomous fraternal orders were organized by African Americans and immigrants who were debarred from fraternal lodges whose members were of old British stock. By 1914 separate fraternal associations represented the wide spectrum of nationality and racial groups in Ohio and the nation. Historian David T. Beito calls attention to the important mutual aid dimension of black fraternal societies.[110] Whether composed of African Americans or others, the lodges offered their members benefits including insurance programs paying funeral expenses and opportunities to gain leadership experience through service in the orders' officialdoms. The lodges met a need for companionship, respect, and familiar surroundings, and that was most important to the foreign born and to African Americans who were coping in a larger society that was unwelcoming and sometimes hostile to them. Black social organizations exiting in Ohio before 1915 included the Masons, Knights of Pythias, Odd Fellows, United Brothers of Hope, Daughters of Hope, Good Samaritans, and True Reformers. Only churches surpassed such orders as centers of social activities in black communities. The black fraternal orders existed in Ohio cities, towns, and villages.

At times the Masons and Odd Fellows each sponsored scores of lodges in Ohio.[111]

Although past their nineteenth-century prime, black lodges were still significant in Ohio's African American social life during and after World War I. For example, in 1919 Columbus' black fraternal associations included Good Samaritans, Knights of Pythias, Court of Calanthe, and Biblus Kluklus. Columbus' three Knights of Pythias lodges claimed a combined membership of about 1,000. In Columbus, as elsewhere at the time, there were separate lodges for men and women. African American women conducted a large proportion of the black lodge activity in Columbus in 1919. There were three chapters and about 350 female members of the Court of Calanthe. Likewise, black women composed the officers and membership of two Good Samaritans lodges and one Biblus Kluklus lodge.[112]

During 1915–1920, an expanding black community life in Ohio also was conducted through voluntary associations other than fraternal orders. Generally, black social clubs and civic, business, and professional organizations were founded prior to World War I. Black women's clubs in Ohio, as elsewhere, were public-spirited. New studies are shedding light on the social service interests and political activities of black club-women in various states.[113] Black women's clubs in Ohio were organized along local, state, and national lines. Many of them were associated with the Ohio Federation of Women's Clubs (African American) established in 1901. Most black women's clubs in Ohio were designed to attain public goals and lend welfare assistance to the needy. In 1919, for instance, Columbus' black women's clubs included the George Steele Woman's Relief Corps, the Women's Independent Political League, and the Phillis Wheatley Club of St. Paul's A.M.E. Church. Service oriented black men were members of Columbus' Hi Y Club, an affiliate of the Young Men's Christian Association. Cleveland's Pleasant Company Club and Columbus' Fortnightly Club were examples of the many black social clubs that usually were intended to meet entirely recreational and social ends. Also, African Americans in Ohio participated in local black civic and business associations and national black professional organizations. These included the Cleveland Association of Colored Men, founded in 1908 as a civic organization dedicated to the advancement of African Americans. Cleveland's Caterers' Association, established in 1905, aimed to serve the interests of blacks at various levels of the food service business. Many black physicians in Ohio were members of the National Medical Association founded in 1895 by African Americans reacting to the exclusive racial policies of the American Medical Association.[114]

In conclusion, the black wartime migration significantly increased the African American populations of Ohio cities, especially Cleveland, Cincinnati, and Columbus. This provided African Americans in Ohio cities with the human resources needed to accelerate the building of large and heterogeneous black urban societies. The construction of such societies was not completed before the twenties, but much work on foundations and frameworks was done in the teens.

The complexities of black society were magnified as African American life in Ohio became increasingly urban and industrial in the period 1915–1920. The social-economic stratification of African American society assumed new dimensions. Unskilled workers in manufacturing became a major presence in black society's lower strata for the first time, although domestic service workers still composed a large cohort of that class.

Many in this sphere of black society were newcomers to the city who were exposed to the kinds of urban social pathologies—poverty, crime, and disease—that were common in white immigrant neighborhoods in earlier times. The city in history always was a locus of possibilities as well as problems. Accordingly, new jobs and wages in manufacturing improved the incomes of individual black workers and increased the aggregate income of local African Americans. These consequences of the black migration opened opportunities for the expanding upper strata of black society. Its members in business and the professions prospered as they increasingly served growing numbers of black patrons and clients, most of whom were working people in the under strata.

The enhancement of the financial, social, and cultural status of prominent blacks widened the income and life-style gaps between the poor and the prosperous in Ohio's black urban society. Affluent blacks in business and the professions usually possessed substantial dwellings outside of the most congested urban areas and near an edge of a city's evolving black district, for example, the Walnut Hills area of Cincinnati. The black upper strata's social and cultural activities were sedate and formal. Church congregations composed of prominent families conducted services in imposing traditional church buildings. Affluent blacks also comprised the memberships of an array of fraternal lodges, social clubs, and other voluntary organizations. In contrast, social and cultural life in the lower strata of black society was informal and necessarily less expensive. Kinship and friendship relationships were carried on, for example, by means of sidewalk and street corner talking or in church services, often held in storefronts. Sometimes such ties were enlivened by the kinds of nightlife existing in streets forming the "tenderloin."

People in Ohio's black society looked at urban-industrial life from many different perspectives. Each view was based on a set of life experiences common to a significant proportion of African Americans in the state. Clearly, persons on opposite sides of the economic spectrum had different economic interests and concerns. People in the same economic sphere differed from each other in the practice of social customs and cultural values. These differences reflected the existence of the various subgroups found throughout black society. Among them were the Ohio-born, natives of the South, women, and men. Individuals tended to associate with others whose values and life experiences were the most like their own. For instance, in Cleveland during the wartime migration, only families that were both old and prominent in the city's black upper echelon attended St. Andrews Episcopal Church. Meanwhile families that were newcomers in Cleveland's black business and professional classes worshipped at Mt. Zion Congregational Church and St. Mark's Presbyterian Church along with some of Cleveland's old and well established black families.[115]

Each social subgroup negotiated its own course through black society, none more distinctive than those formed on gender lines. Black women's occupations were clearly defined within each echelon of society— mainly limited to teaching and social work in the upper level and to domestic work at the lower, excepting during wartime when gender hiring patterns were temporarily altered. Organized social life among women existed in each realm of black society, with associations ranging from informal local groupings to clubs affiliated with statewide and national bodies.

The variety of subgroup experiences within African American society was overshadowed when black and white issues were placed at center stage. The color line encircled all African Americans as one group, and all African Americans experienced manifestations of color prejudice. Chapter 2 discusses the Ohio color line's variations and evolution in the wake of the wartime black migration.

CHAPTER TWO

The Color Line's
Changing Dimensions

The Great Migration of African Americans and the magnification of the Ohio color line occurred in parallel. Racial segregation and racial discrimination intensified in Ohio during and immediately after World War I. Residential segregation of African Americans in Ohio cities increased significantly. Racial separation was maintained in Ohio's business and professional activities, social life, and cultural institutions. Discrimination against Ohio's African Americans was noticeably greater in housing, schools, public accommodations, law enforcement, and press coverage. Ohio's white employers and private associations, such as fraternal organizations, generally drew color lines. Further, instances of violence against African Americans in Ohio were more frequent. In a narrow view, the growing intolerance in Ohio seemed to be a white reaction to the wartime black migration. Actually, the factors underlying this rising intolerance encompassed more than the migration, Ohio, and the war period.

During the period from 1882 to World War I, Anglo-Saxon Protestants across the nation became less tolerant of people who did not share their color, their land of origin, their cultural heritage, and their religious faith. The color bias against Native Americans, Chinese Americans, Japanese Americans, and African Africans was expressed in various ways. The federal policy of "civilizing Indians" (1877–1934) showed virtually no tolerance for Native American cultures.[1] The Chinese Exclusion Act (1882) and the Gentlemen's Agreement (1907–1908) respectively prohibited the immigration of laborers from China and Japan.[2] During 1890–1915, as horrendous lynching of African Americans proliferated in the South, southern states enacted laws that required racial segregation in virtually every aspect of life and that disfranchised African American voters.[3] Meanwhile, in the northern states extralegal racial discrimination and segregation rose. Race riots occurred in New York in 1900 and in Springfield, Illinois in 1908.[4] In the 30 years before World War I, nativists organized to oppose southern and eastern European immigrants, who were largely non-Protestants. For example, the Immigration Restriction League attempted to curtail immigration by advocating the passage of a federal literacy test bill that was repeatedly introduced in Congress (1898-1917). Meanwhile, some intolerant persons were emboldened by the development of a new pseudo-science that used grossly biased assumptions and concluded that humans were divided in a hierarchy of racial and nationality types headed by Anglo-Saxons and northwestern Europeans, who were superior to all others. William Z. Ripley's *The Races of Europe*, published in 1899, disseminated one such theory.[5] An anti-foreign thread ran through the Progressive Era's reform movements favoring prohibition, women suffrage, and municipal reform. Reformers inflamed intolerance by blaming immigrants for supporting conservative urban political machines that opposed reforms.[6]

The nationwide phenomenon of growing intolerance reached a new level of intensity and breadth during and shortly after World War I, when the increased black migration to Ohio was in progress.[7] Restrictions on immigration from Asia, ethnocentric federal policies on Indian reservations, and the legal racial caste system in the South carried over from earlier times. In addition, the Ku Klux Klan, revived in 1915, issued anti-Catholic, anti-Semitic, anti-foreign, and white supremacy propaganda through Klan organizations in the North as well as the South.[8] In 1916, Madison Grant published the *Passing of the Great Race* that was more influential than earlier pseudo-scientific works with racially biased conclusions. In 1917, the Congress passed and the President signed a literacy test bill meant to sharply curtail immigration from non-Protestant countries of southern and eastern Europe. Americans were further divided along ethnic lines by President Woodrow Wilson's rhetorical attempts to turn public opinion in favor of United States' entry into the war. According to Wilson "100 percent Americans" supported the war, unlike "hyphenated Americans." Official war propaganda sparked a hysterical reaction against German Americans and their culture in the United States. Some of the foreign born from southern and eastern Europe were the victims of a similar hysteria in the postwar Red Scare when nativists associated immigrants with Bolshevism.[9] Meanwhile, black men were lynched and whites initiated race riots in cities across the nation. Hollywood distributed racially insulting films like "The Birth of a Nation."[10] Also, in that time context, increasing racial segregation occurred in urban residential areas.

During and immediately after World War I, residential segregation of African Americans proceeded at a quicker pace in Ohio and elsewhere in the North. The wartime trend in Ohio lacked the duration and magnitude to cause the development of African American residential areas comparable to the very large all-black districts that appeared in New York City, Chicago, and Philadelphia before the war. In 1920, all-black districts of major proportions still did not exist in Ohio's urban centers or in many other northern cities where residential segregation increased in the previous decade.[11] Nevertheless, by the war decade's end, black urban concentrations in Ohio were significantly greater than before.

African American population densities increased in prewar black neighborhoods as well as in adjacent or nearby areas. Small predominantly black areas and streets existed in Ohio cities in 1914. These included parts of Central Avenue in Cleveland, East Long Street in Columbus, and the West End near the Ohio River in Cincinnati.[12] During the war, black population density in Cleveland grew in the area bounded by East 55th Street, Euclid Avenue to the north, and the Cuyahoga River to the west. In addition, a few smaller black residential areas gained population in other parts of Cleveland's East Side, while the West Side remained almost unoccupied by African Americans.[13] In Cincinnati the black population growth was largely concentrated just above the Ohio River in the city's lower West End, particularly within a north-south corridor composed of Cincinnati Wards 15–18.[14] Black population gains in Columbus were more widely distributed than in other Ohio cities. Prewar migrants to Columbus tended to locate in several African American neighborhoods in that city instead of congregating only in East Long Street's old black neighborhoods. By 1914 small black enclaves existed in each quadrant of an area encompassing downtown Columbus. Apparently, like earlier black newcomers, wartime migrants settled in black neighborhoods in various sectors of Columbus.[15]

Census figures reflected patterns of residential segregation existing in Ohio during the World War I and the postwar period. In 1920 Ohio's African American urban populations remained concentrated in a few census wards of each large city. In Cincinnati, seven wards encompassed 78 percent of all African Americans in the city. There were twenty-six wards each in Cincinnati and Cleveland. Sixty-three percent of Cleveland's black population was located in two wards. In Columbus, four of sixteen wards contained 53 percent of the city's black population.[16] (See map 2.)

Between 1910 and 1920, migration trends among whites as well as blacks raised the proportions of blacks in the inner city wards of Ohio's major urban centers. In-migration of blacks to old inner city districts

Map 2

Map of Columbus, Ohio, Showing Racial, National, and Industrial Localities, 1918.

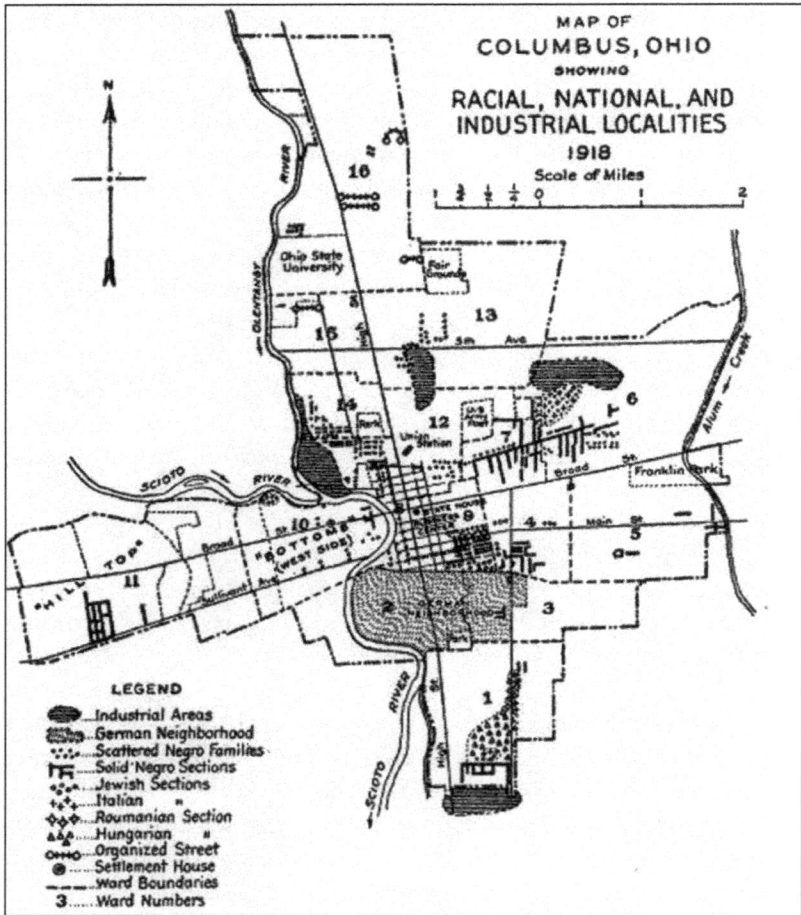

Source: Roderick D. McKenzie, "The Neighborhood: A Study of Local Life in the City of Columbus, Ohio," *American Journal of Sociology* 27(Sept. 1921), p. 148. Courtesy of The University of Chicago Press.

paralleled the out-migration of whites from those same areas. Undoubtedly, departing whites were engaged in flight from black new-comers, but at the same time they were participating in a larger phenomenon, nationwide suburban growth.[17]

The accelerating trend leading to the formation of large residential patterns composed of predominantly black census districts was shown in the 1910 and 1920 census figures for major Ohio cities. The trend was most advanced in Cincinnati and Cleveland. Black population growth after 1910 was significant in Ohio wards, but in 1920 only one predominantly black ward existed in the state. In 1910 African Americans in Ohio rarely comprised more than a quarter of a ward's population and never accounted for more than a third. However, in1920 the black proportion of the ward population was 52 percent in Cincinnati's Ward 18 and 40 percent in Cleveland's Ward 11. These percentages were much higher than those for wards elsewhere in Cincinnati, Cleveland, and other Ohio cities in 1920.[18] In Columbus, blacks were only a little more than a quarter of the population in Ward 7, which was the Columbus ward where African Americans were most populous. Blacks accounted for no more than 19 percent of the population in any Toledo ward. African Americans in Toledo resided in small neighborhoods, most notably in the areas of Toledo's Pinewood, Canton, Stickney, and Summit Streets.[19] Although the sizes of the state's black urban neighborhoods varied, residential segregation was the rule in Ohio's cities.

The residential segregation of African Americans in Ohio was largely the result of the fact that blacks were barred from certain houses, streets, and neighborhoods. Generally there was an informal, unstated understanding that dwellings in white neighborhoods would not be rented or sold to African Americans. Also, the residential exclusion of blacks sometimes was maintained by overt means, legal and illegal. Racially restrictive covenants in real estate agreements appeared in Ohio before the wartime migration. Historian Stephen Meyer demonstrates that such practices were widespread in the United States at the time.[20] For example, in 1914, there was in Cleveland "a noticeable tendency toward inserting clauses in real estate deeds restricting the transfer of the property to colored people, Jews, and foreigners generally," according to a National Association for the Advancement of Colored People branch report.[21] By 1915 many white residents of Greenlawn Avenue near East 105th Street in Cleveland northeast held property deeds with clauses designed to prevent sales to blacks. Nevertheless, an African American was able to purchase property on Greenlawn Avenue and maintain residence there even after white neighbors expressed objections. Greenlawn Avenue's white property owners met to discuss ways to remove the new black resident of the neighborhood. They claimed that the presence of African American or Jewish residents on the avenue depreciated property values.[22] Evidently the racially restrictive real estate agreement existed in Ohio even after 1917 when the United States Supreme Court ruled that such devices were unconstitutional. In 1919 a formal agreement meant to exclude blacks from houses in the vicinity of Vinal and Albert

Streets in East Toledo was signed by 146 white residents and filed in the Lucas County Recorder's office.[23]

Harassment and violence sometimes were used to prevent African Americans from occupying certain houses in all-white or racially mixed residential areas in Ohio. For example, in 1917, racial tensions rose in East Toledo as the wartime migration altered black residential patterns. An African American rented a house near a Bulgarian immigrant residential area in Toledo; the black renter subsequently received an anonymous note stating a racial epithet and threatening violence in imperfect English.[24] In 1917 and 1919, several houses occupied by blacks in Cleveland were vandalized by whites who broke windows and sometimes caused other more substantial damage.[25]

Meanwhile, whites in Ohio less often expressed their objections when African Americans occupied additional houses on already racially mixed streets adjacent to largely black neighborhoods. Indeed, some white property owners in such areas were financially interested in changing the occupancy of houses from white to black. Referring to Cleveland's racially changing areas in 1918, a Cleveland Negro Welfare Association official said, "landlords raise rents in houses occupied by white people to get rid of them, and then make a higher charge to colored tenants."[26] Some black tenants lacking rental alternatives were required to pay rents that were racially discriminatory. The Welfare Association officer noted that in some instances blacks in Cleveland's largely African American Central Avenue area paid more per room than whites living in the same district.[27] Similarly, in Cincinnati some whites exploited the housing crunch for African Americans. During and after World War I, land speculators in Cincinnati acquired West End tenement houses in racially changing areas. The new landlords raised rents and then sold the tenements, making inflated profits at the expense of new African American tenants.[28]

During 1915–1920, the separation of blacks and whites in Ohio's churches was more extensive than racial segregation in the state's residential areas. Church color lines in Ohio and across the country were shaped by a long a trend reaching back into the eighteenth century. Prior to 1800, blacks and whites in the South and North commonly attended the same church services. Increasingly from the 1790s onward African Americans worshipped in black churches affiliated with black Protestant denominations and, to a lesser extent, with white Protestant denominations. In Ohio and other states, few black churches were linked to any one white denomination by 1916; for example, only one of Ohio's black churches was associated with the Presbyterian Church in the United States of America, while two were connected with

Congregational churches. They included Cincinnati's Shiloh Cumberland Presbyterian Church and Cleveland's Mt. Zion Congregational Church, whose members were socially prominent African Americans. Eighty percent of Ohio's 392 African American churches belonged to black denominations. Most of them were affiliated with the African Methodist Episcopal church and the National Baptist Convention. Also, color lines existed in the joint activities of Ohio's clergymen. In large cities there were black ministers' associations, including the Baptist Ministers' Alliance in Cleveland and the Baptist Ministerial Association in Columbus. The distance between blacks and whites grew as white congregations relocated from church buildings in the vicinity of black neighborhoods to the suburbs. In Cleveland, over a dozen white churches sold their edifices to African American congregations in 1920. Racially integrated congregations were rare in Ohio during and after World War I. White Protestant churches did not encourage blacks to join. Perhaps excepting one family, African Americans did not attend white Protestant churches in Cleveland. Generally, the Roman Catholic church did not provide separate parishes for the comparatively few black Catholics in Ohio. In 1865 St. Ann's Church was established in Cincinnati, and in 1916 it still was the only black Catholic parish in Ohio. Sometimes, through 1920, attempts were made to involve blacks in Catholic church activities in Cleveland.[29]

This exclusive color line in churches mirrored the separation of blacks and whites that generally existed in Ohio's organized social life during 1915–1920, as noted in Chapter 1. In Ohio and throughout the country, Masons, Odd Fellows, and other fraternal societies and sororities were almost completely divided along the color line well before 1915. Likewise, racial separation also was perpetuated in various other kinds of voluntary associations including social clubs, civic organizations, and business and professional associations.[30]

During 1915–1920, there was less racial separation in Ohio public schools than in the state's churches and other private institutions and organizations. Generally, Ohio schools were racially integrated, but some segregated schools existed at each level of education. Segregation was more common in elementary schools than in high schools. Most segregated schools were in southern and central Ohio. In a few public school districts, schools were segregated because local authorities officially maintained dual school system policies. In other districts, schools were unofficially segregated because of the residential concentrations of blacks in those districts. Sometimes the gerrymandering of school district boundaries created racially separate schools.

This basic pattern of racial practices in Ohio's public schools existed from the late nineteenth century through 1920. Desegregation of public schools occurred after 1887, when the Ohio legislature prohibited racial segregation in the public schools. Dual schools systems were most common in southern and central Ohio in 1887. Desegregation proceeded rapidly in most school districts in those regions; however, it occurred slowly over several years in some places, largely in southern Ohio, where whites resisted school integration. Dual school systems contrary to state law were retained in a few southern and central Ohio school districts, particularly in Gallipolis, Baltimore, and Hillsboro. In the same regions, the gerrymandering of school district lines resulted in separate schools for blacks in Chillicothe and Xenia. Yet integrated schools were located across southern and central Ohio, notably in large cities. Black students attended various Cincinnati public schools. One black elementary school remained in Cincinnati after that city abolished its dual school system policy. Schools were integrated in Columbus, Springfield, and Dayton.[31]

Integration prevailed in northern Ohio's school districts, for example, in Cleveland and Youngstown. Blacks attended public schools in Cleveland in antebellum times.[32] Cleveland's schools were probably more integrated than those of any other city in the state. However, by the end of wartime black migration, some Cleveland schools had large African American enrollments resulting from the residential segregation of blacks in certain school districts. Fifty-six African American teachers were employed by the Cleveland school system in the school year 1918–1919. Most of them taught in predominately white schools. Only in a few cases was more than one African American teacher assigned to the same school. Few African American teachers were assigned to schools in predominately African American school districts.[33] In the school year 1919–1920, the number of African American teachers in Cleveland schools increased to sixty-eight.[34] In Youngstown and Columbus as well as in Cleveland, African American teachers regularly were assigned to teach in racially mixed classrooms during 1887–1915. But African American teachers elsewhere in the state generally were hired to teach only in black schools and in segregated classrooms in integrated schools systems.[35]

Forceful and enduring campaigns for the restoration of racially dual school systems were practically unknown in Ohio communities that abolished such dual school systems in accordance with state legislation requiring school integration. But interest in separate schools for African Americans mounted after 1900, and new all-black schools were established within the integrated school systems of Columbus and Cincinnati between 1910 and 1920.[36]

In Columbus there was no segregated public school between 1887 and 1911, and a few African American teachers were employed in several of the city's integrated public schools, mainly in ones with large black enrollments. The situation changed somewhat when the Columbus school board evidently attempted to appease whites advocating the introduction of a system-wide school segregation policy. In 1909, after preparing for a couple of years, the Columbus school board redrew the lines of some school districts using gerrymandered boundaries designed to form a district including a large body of black students. In 1911 African American students were admitted to Champion Avenue Junior High School, recently built in the new district that included black neighborhoods in an area of East Long Street. Some of the black students in the Champion Avenue school district lived across the street from an integrated school. White students in the district were sent to other junior high schools. All four African American teachers previously employed in various public schools were reassigned to the Champion Avenue Junior High School where they joined newly hired personnel, other black teachers, and a black principal.[37] Integration continued in schools at the elementary and high school levels within the district encompassing the Champion Avenue School; it was the only segregated school in any Columbus district then. Black students attended integrated schools in various parts of Columbus in subsequent years. For example, in 1919–1920, African American pupils were enrolled in Columbus East High School, Columbus North High School, and Columbus Commercial High School.[38]

In Cincinnati, a dual city school system including separate school boards was abolished a few years after 1887. But one all-black elementary school remained in an African American area of Walnut Hills. In 1901, at the request of many African American parents, the all-black institution's name was changed to the Frederick Douglass Elementary School in honor of the renowned black abolitionist. African American students in any Cincinnati school district were eligible to attend Douglass School on a voluntary basis. All the teachers and the principal of Douglass School were African Americans. In each of Cincinnati's other schools there were mixed classes, white teachers, and a white principal. In 1908 the parents, teachers, and principal of Douglass School urged the authorities to improve their educational facilities. In response, the school board approved the construction of a modern building for black students. The opening of the new Douglass School building in 1911 did not alter the integration status quo. There was still only one separate school in Cincinnati.[39]

In following years, however, support for the establishment of a second all-black public school developed among African American parents who were impressed by the quality of education in the new Douglass School and in private schools for blacks that appeared in Cincinnati between 1910 and 1914. An African American teacher previously employed at Douglass School, Jennie D. Porter, started a privately financed all-black kindergarten in 1911. Initially housed in a church, it moved to a larger building after winning local popularity and gaining enrollments. In 1914 the school superintendent and the school board, responding to voices in the black community, authorized the establishment of another separate elementary school, eventually named the Harriett Beecher Stowe School. Although approved on a temporary basis, the school endured and grew under the supervision of Principal Jennie D. Porter. In 1915 an African American teaching staff was employed and classes were held in the former Hughes School building. Enrollments increased regularly in the following years of the decade. Attendance was voluntary and all students retained the right to enroll in integrated schools in their own districts. In 1916 the school board approved the construction of a new building for the school, but the construction plan was not finalized before the end of the decade.[40] At the same time, the Cincinnati superintendent of schools refused to exclude black students from Walnut Hills High School. In 1916 many white students threatened to strike if the black students were not removed from the high school. In response to their threat to strike, the superintendent said, "to do so [to strike] would not only be a violation of the law, but also at variance with the spirit of our public schools."[41]

Meanwhile, a few separate schools for African Americans in Ohio received financial backing from white philanthropists ostensibly interested in "uplifting the Negro." The white philanthropists' control over black education in the United States is a subject of scholarly discussion.[42] Northern philanthropists since the Civil War had tended to fund separate black vocational training schools in states of the South and the North. White philanthropists contributing to black education in Ohio in this decade supported separate schools that emphasized industrial training. Sallie Peters McCall of Cincinnati was the white benefactor of the Colored Industrial School of Cincinnati established in 1914 with an endowment of $400,000.[43] Also, the philanthropy of a private company supported separate education for African Americans at Middletown in southwestern Ohio. In 1918 the American Rolling Mill Company constructed a building for the Booker T. Washington School, as it became known, and then donated the school structure to the city of Middletown. Three African American teachers staffed Middletown's separate school.[44]

Following the advent of the wartime migration, black migrant children were placed in special classes in the integrated public schools of some Ohio cities. Even in Cleveland, whose tradition of integrated education was extraordinarily long, some schools formed all-black classes in 1917. The segregated students were largely recent migrants from the South. Cleveland school officials justified their separation from other students on grounds that their scholastic achievement levels did not match their grade levels according to Cleveland public school standards. When African Americans in Cleveland questioned the practice, the school officials gave assurances that the segregation of black students from the South was temporary, indicating that it would continue only until the students were properly classified.[45]

African Americans were admitted to public universities and to several private colleges in Ohio during the second decade of the twentieth century. One private denominational institution in Ohio offered separate undergraduate education for African Americans. The Methodist Episcopal church founded Wilberforce University in 1856. Located at Xenia in southwestern Ohio, Wilberforce eventually was affiliated with the African Methodist Episcopal church. Wilberforce was distinguished as one of two enduring black colleges established in the United States before the Civil War.[46]

Ohio's racially integrated colleges and universities sometimes practiced racial discrimination. For example, administrators sometimes tactfully discouraged African Americans from entering specific programs at The Ohio State University. In reply to a prospective African American student's inquiry about an engineering program, the University president replied: "I should be very glad to aid you in any way possible in securing an education in Electrical Engineering."[47] Using discouraging words, the president concluded: "On one matter, however, I feel constrained to say just a word. The sentiment north of the Ohio River seems to be so persistent against the Negro in skilled labor that I doubt very much whether an educated Negro has a fair show or a show worthwhile in this part of the country."[48]

Many black students enrolled in The Ohio State University during this time and some participated in campus activities. A partial list of black students at the university in 1919–1920 included 47 names.[49] African Americans participated in some of the university's nonacademic activities. Daniel Ferguson was elected class orator for the Class of 1916.[50] William Mason of Cincinnati won first prize in an oratorical contest in March 1917.[51] George R. Dorsey was a member of the 1916–1917 debate team captained by John W. Bricker, who later served as United States senator representing Ohio.[52]

Several of Ohio's universities and colleges granted academic degrees to African Americans during 1914–1920. They included Antioch College, Case School of Applied Science, Denison University, Oberlin College, The Ohio State University, Ohio University, Ohio Wesleyan University, University of Cincinnati, Western Reserve University, and Wilberforce University. The numbers of African Americans graduating from each of these academic institutions ranged from zero to as many as eleven in a given academic year.[53]

Discrimination against African Americans in Ohio's public accommodations intensified as the state's black population grew during and after World War I. This increasing racial discrimination in the state's public places was rooted in a trend that was already in progress by the end of the nineteenth century. In the 1890s, while Ohio cities were receiving black migrations, some of Ohio's urban public accommodations departed from an earlier custom of admitting financially comfortable and socially prominent African Americans.[54] Commenting on the Cincinnati example of the phenomenon, Wendell P. Dabney, editor of the Cincinnati *Union*, recalled: "Colored people used to go to Parker's Grove, the site of our Coney Island. All of the picnic grounds were open to them, the beer gardens, theaters, Over-the-Rhine resorts, the Zoo café, dining room and most of the ordinary restaurants."[55] Subsequently fewer and fewer public places in Cincinnati welcomed blacks of any social economic status. Dabney explained: "Always a large increase in numbers of colored people has been followed by a large increase of prejudice."[56] By World War I, practices of racial exclusion and segregation were commonplace in Ohio's public places.

In southern and central Ohio, racial discrimination in public accommodations often was blatant during 1915–1920. Signs reading "For White People Only" or "Colored Trade Not Wanted" were posted in private businesses that were open to the public.[57] Hotels, theaters, restaurants and other public accommodations discriminated against blacks. For example, in 1915 one observer noted that in Columbus "there is not a moving picture house which does not openly declare seating our people in the last seats."[58] In 1919 all but one of Cincinnati's hotels excluded African Americans.[59] Restaurants in Springfield, Columbus, and other Ohio cities were accused of racial discrimination.[60]

In the meantime, racial bias also spread in the public places of northern Ohio where the commitment to equality traditionally was greater than in the state's other regions. After 1898 African Americans were increasingly turned away from hotels and other public places in Western Reserve towns and cities including Cleveland.[61] Discrimination against blacks was practiced less openly in northern Ohio than elsewhere in the state. Signs excluding African Americans were rarely seen in windows. A variety of subtler, but no less insulting, tactics were used to turn away black patrons.[62] In 1914 attorney Harry E. Davis of the Cleveland Branch of the National Association for the Advancement of Colored People reported: "Cleveland is, to a large degree, free from the baneful prejudice with which some of our brethren must contend. But there has been some trouble in the theatres, restaurants and other places of public accommodation, and some attempt at discrimination in institutions supported by public funds."[63]

By the eve of the wartime black migration, racial discrimination was widespread in Cleveland's downtown restaurants, hotels, and theaters, while racial bias existed in recreational facilities elsewhere in the city.[64] For example, the concessions at Cleveland's Luna Park were closed to African Americans except when the Cleveland Caterers' Association held its annual summer picnic there. On such days, however, the park swimming pool was always out of order and not open for use.[65] In a letter to the *Cleveland News* written in 1919, The Reverend O. W. Childers commented on the spread of prejudice in Cleveland's public places over the decade. Drawing on personal experiences in Cleveland, the pastor of the St. James African Methodist Episcopal Church wrote:

> Mr. Editor, how would you like to go about your daily duties always in fear you will disturb the quiet of the community and bring upon yourself woe simply because you are a colored man? We go into public places . . . always expecting insult and fearing for our safety. Only a few weeks ago four ladies of my congregation, some children and I were stoned on a streetcar of this city for no apparent reason than that we were colored.[66]

The level of white hostility rose in Ohio cities and in urban centers elsewhere in the country during and after World War I. The growth of racial intolerance was expressed in violence against urban African Americans as well as in increased racial discrimination in public accommodations. Periodic mob actions and race riots occurred in the United States prior to World War I. Major race riots broke out in East St. Louis, Chicago, the District of Columbia, and many other cities outside Ohio during the war and postwar periods. Typically, whites initiated the violence and blacks responded accordingly. Major riots involved large numbers and caused many physical injuries and fatalities.[67] The magnitude of racial violence in Ohio was comparatively small. Yet between 1915 and 1920, there was lynch mob activity in Lima, rioting in Cleveland and Youngstown, and racial incidents bordering on violence in Marion and

Toledo. Also, in a number of instances, white mobs harassed and some-times stoned blacks who were using a public facility or public area.

Perhaps an account of an attempted lynching in Lima during the summer of 1916 best illustrates the kinds of extreme conduct that arose from racial intolerance in Ohio at the time. On August 30, Allen County Sheriff Sherman Eley arrested Charles Daniels, an African American transient from Mississippi, for allegedly attacking Vivian Baber (white) in her home. Mr. and Mrs. Baber lived on a farm in Shawnee Township of Allen County, where Lima was the county seat. On the same day, a posse of two hundred men apprehended Daniels in the vicinity of the Baber farmhouse. Fearing trouble, Sheriff Eley took Daniels to Ottawa, some eighteen miles away. Ottawa authorities then transferred Daniels elsewhere. Meanwhile, a white mob formed at the Lima jail before dusk. The whites broke into the jail in search of Daniels. After failing to find him there, the mob broke into the Allen County courthouse and into the sheriff's home. Upon his return to Lima Sheriff Eley found the mob awaiting him. He escaped it temporarily, but was finally caught. The mob stripped off his clothes, beat him, and kicked him in an attempt to force him to disclose Daniels' whereabouts. The mob went so far as to string a rope from a telephone pole, place a noose around the sheriff's neck, and pull the rope taut before Eley revealed that he took Daniels to Ottawa. Traveling by car, many in the mob went to Ottawa, where they again failed to locate Daniels. In the meantime, Sheriff Eley escaped.[68]

Afterwards, Lima law enforcement officials got the situation in hand. Nevertheless, it was reported that "a strong undercurrent of feeling" against African Americans continued to exist. Upon the advice of Lima city officials, railroad and street paving contractors removed about 150 African American transient laborers from Lima. White men were hired to take their places. The police advised prominent African American residents of Lima to remain in their homes after dark.[69]

Charged with assault, Daniels was put on trial, found guilty, and sen-tenced to three to twenty years in prison. At the trial, "Mrs. Baber iden-tified Daniels as her assailant," according to a press account that said: "It was proven and admitted by the defendant that he had been near the Baber home shortly before the assault, but he steadfastly denied the charge."[70] Defense witnesses testified that Mrs. Baber had previously sin-gled out as the perpetrator a different black man, Charles Cole, when he, Daniels, and other county jail prisoners appeared before her.[71] Subsequently, several in the lynch mob were brought to trial, some were found guilty and some were given jail sentences.[72]

Minor riots occurred in Ohio as the wartime migration was reaching a peak in 1917. On June 11, Cleveland police were called out twice to quell rioting in the Central Avenue and East 14th Street area. The origin of the rioting was unclear. According to one account, the trouble grew out of a saloon incident. An African American representing himself as a beggar was chased from a saloon by a group of white men. Those seeing the African American being pursued by white men evidently assumed that he insulted a white woman. Rumors about the incident contributed to violence in that Cleveland neighborhood. Whites of foreign origin and blacks fought with fists, stones, and clubs. Scores of people were involved, but there were no serious injuries.[73] In the summer of 1917, white and black laborers participated in a Youngstown race riot. Evidently the violence in Youngstown ensued from a competition for jobs in the labor market there.[74] In 1919, vandalism and some violence occurred in Columbus when the Pennsylvania Railroad angered white employees by hiring black workers to break a strike.[75]

Rioting did not occur in other Ohio cities, but expressions of prejudice against African Americans occasionally raised concerns about the possibility of racial violence, for example, in Toledo and Marion. Racial tension was high in East Toledo during the summer of 1917. Several incidents suggesting possible hostilities between foreign-born whites and blacks in Toledo were reported in July.[76] In 1919 biased whites in Marion evidently vandalized property owned by African Americans and put out racist signs. Responding to this harassment, Marion police chief James W. Thompson took steps to protect Marion's black residents. The Marion police issued bulletins that declared: "Every protection will be given the colored citizens of Marion and those interfering with their rights will be punished to the full extent of the law."[77]

Also in 1919, white mobs physically attacked young African Americans who used Cleveland parks. On June 24 about thirty black children were attacked on a streetcar while returning from an afternoon excursion at Garfield Park. A mob of about fifty white men and boys stoned the streetcar and otherwise harassed members of the young excursion party that was under the supervision of three chaperones, including the Reverend O. W. Childers of St. James African Methodist Episcopal Church. Following complaints, the Cleveland Police investigated the violent incident. Also in the summer of 1919, whites threw stones at small black children who were swimming in one of Cleveland's park lakes. The lifeguards at the lake did not try to prevent this stoning. Afterwards, complaints were made and the lifeguards were dismissed.[78]

These racial incidents in Cleveland and elsewhere in Ohio were symptomatic of a hostile white reaction to the growing African American presence in the state that accompanied the wartime black migration to the North. The trend in every Ohio region was toward greater exclusion and segregation of African Americans in the period 1915–1920. The color line encircled all African Americans as one group, and all African Americans in Ohio experienced manifestations of color prejudice.

The nature of the Ohio color line, nevertheless, varied from region to region in 1920, being most rigid in southern Ohio. For example, racial segregation in hotels, restaurants, and other public accommodations was greater in Cincinnati than in Cleveland. Some all-black public schools existed in the state's southern and central regions, but there were no such separate schools in northern Ohio. The explanation of such differences in this time requires looking backward to Ohio's early history. Different color line customs were established in each Ohio region in the early nineteenth century, and these heritages were perpetuated in altered form through 1920. Starting early in the nineteenth century, white intolerance was most intense in southern Ohio, somewhat less so in central Ohio, and least intense in northern Ohio. Conversely, the color line was least restrictive in the northern region and successively more proscriptive in the central and southern regions respectively.

The factors influencing the initial character of black-white relations in Ohio were the geographical origins and settlement patterns of blacks and whites in pioneer Ohio and their proximity to the South, according to historians John D. Barnhardt, Robert E. Chaddock, and David C. Shilling. The racial perspectives of white settlers reflected their geographical backgrounds. In the early years of Ohio statehood, white natives of the South and their progeny constituted most of the population in many southern counties and a large part of the central region's population. Such migrants, often from Virginia and Kentucky, came with anti-slavery as well as anti-black views. Generally they were poor farmers who had owned no slaves. Previously disadvantaged in their economic, social, and political competition with slave-owning planters in the South, they did not wish to see slavery and a planter aristocracy established in Ohio. At the same time, their racial views were harsh and encompassed preferences for the kinds of black subservience found in the South.[79]

Other white settlers came from northeastern states and carried with them the values of that quarter of the United States, where a relative tolerance prevailed on issues of color. For instance, the first state constitutions of several New England states contained anti-slavery provisions. Some southern Ohio settlements, notably Marietta, were composed of New Englanders. But, especially after 1830, white migrants to central and northeastern Ohio counties frequently came from Pennsylvania and the eastern seaboard. Among them were anti-slavery English Quakers and immigrants from German provinces and Ireland.[80]

The white New Englanders' impact on settlement was greater in northern Ohio than in any other Ohio region. They were the earliest white settlers of that part of Ohio and, until midcentury, New Englanders comprised most people in the Connecticut Western Reserve, a large area encompassing present-day Cleveland. People of New England stock were a minority of the population in northwestern Ohio, but they were extraordinarily influential there.[81]

African American settlement patterns in the antebellum period also impacted the character of black-white relations in Ohio. White intolerance levels in Ohio regions were related to the distribution of African American population across the state. White intolerance was least pronounced in northern Ohio where African Americans were least numerous. Color bias was most evident in Ohio's southern and central regions where African Americans were most densely populated. Most African Americans in early Ohio came from southern states, and prior to 1860 the great majority of blacks in Ohio resided in the state's southern region, where Cincinnati housed Ohio's largest urban black population.[82]

An Ohio region's proximity to the slaveholding South also was a factor shaping the nature of its race relations early in the nineteenth century. The nearness of many southern Ohio counties to slave states reinforced and perpetuated southern Ohio's custom of strictly enforcing the color line. The state's Ohio River counties shared borders with either Virginia or Kentucky. Cross-river economic and social relations fostered a common culture in the Ohio Valley that was much influenced by the South's way of life, for example, regarding the roles of free blacks. The South's social-cultural impact on Ohio was minimal in regions located west of Ohio's boundary with Pennsylvania, and the color line was less vivid there than in Ohio's southern counties.[83]

The early nineteenth century regional model of white intolerance was perpetuated into the twentieth century as the color line heritage of each Ohio region was handed down from generation to generation. A tradition of protesting against color prejudice was a part of this legacy. Chapter 3 discusses social justice and social welfare issues and the activities of black leaders in Ohio. It asserts that the nature of protest activities in the period 1915–1920 varied from region to region under the influence of Ohio's nineteenth century black-white relations model.

CHAPTER THREE

New Organizations and Urban Issues

Social work institutions and civil rights organizations were established during and after World War I to deal with welfare concerns and civil rights issues that multiplied in Ohio cities during the wartime black migration. White hostility increased and acts of intolerance spread while the scale and complexity of the migrants' needs grew in those years. No other issues concerning African Americans in Ohio at the time received more public attention than those involving instances of white prejudice and social problems plaguing black migrants. Black civic leaders in cities across Ohio acted with renewed energy and participated in organized efforts to address these issues in the period 1915–1920. In earlier times, there were few urban organizations designed to assist black migrants in Ohio and to oppose racial discrimination there. The number of these organizations rose slowly between 1890 and 1910, but rapidly thereafter as Ohio's black urban population increased greatly.

Local people took the lead in struggles to overcome racial injustice and to resolve social problems in each major urban center in Ohio. Out-of-state reformers occasionally came to Ohio to assist these efforts, and statewide movements sometimes were launched; however, the orientation and leadership of these struggles were typically local, centered in a particular city, like Cleveland or Cincinnati. The character of these struggles, consequently, varied from city to city. These differences had antecedents in Ohio's early years of statehood, like the color line itself.

Ohio possessed a race-relations legacy that included a protest tradition whose intensity varied from region to region, being strongest in northern Ohio. What shaped the origins of this protest tradition? Prior to the Civil War, blacks and some whites in each part of Ohio criticized slavery and favored equality under the law for African Americans. But abolitionism and advocacy of equal rights were more prevalent in northern Ohio, especially in the Western Reserve, than in the other Ohio regions. This protest activity was an aspect of the regional pattern of black-white relations that developed early in the nineteenth century. The strength of white intolerance varied by region before the Civil War. Tolerance of dissent against the color line was greater in northern Ohio than in southern Ohio. As seen in Chapter 2, the dominant influence of relatively tolerant New Englanders in the settlement of northern Ohio shaped early black-white relations there. Also the northern region's distance from the South placed it well outside of the South's social-economic sphere of influence, which affected many Ohio counties located in the vicinity of the Ohio River Valley.

The antebellum form of black-white relations in Ohio, which embraced the protest tradition, was passed on as an inheritance to subsequent generations into the next century. Public support for treating blacks as equals in law fluctuated in Ohio during the period 1860–1915. Historian David A. Gerber's research shows that public backing for this principle increased across the state in the aftermath of the Civil War and then started decreasing in the 1890s as war memories faded.[1]

During the period 1860–1915, as in earlier times, the principle of equal rights for African Americans was asserted most insistently in northern Ohio. Regional differences in the effectiveness of protest were seen, for example, when there were issues about whether to establish separate public institutions for the welfare of African Americans. In northern Ohio, more than elsewhere in the state, such institutions were opposed as threats to equal rights for all. In Cleveland, prominent African Americans customarily insisted that publicly funded institutions be open to all regardless of color and objected to proposals for the establishment of separate institutions for blacks if their finances would depend on tax money or funds subscribed from the general public. Influential white civic leaders in Cleveland usually withheld their financial support and endorsements of such proposals when faced with this objection. When such propositions were made in southern and central Ohio cities, local African American spokespersons raised the same objection. The results were different there, for instance, in Cincinnati where certain prominent white philanthropists were inclined to disregard the objection and to financially back separate institutions for African Americans. Consequently, in 1915 separate institutions for blacks, such as homes for the elderly or children, were relatively common in Cincinnati but rare and poorly financed in Cleveland. At the same time blacks in Cincinnati were excluded from social institutions serving whites. Meanwhile blacks in Cleveland, at least on a token

basis, were admitted to such places, for instance, to one of the Young
Men's Christian Association facilities.[2]

The struggle against the Ohio color line after 1915 must be understood as an ongoing phenomenon that originated and took its basic form
in the previous century. This explains why the strength of protest varied
across Ohio's regions in the period 1915–1920. Equal rights advocacy
then, as in the past, was most effective in northern Ohio, while separate
welfare organizations for blacks were stronger in southern and central
Ohio than in the northern region. This struggle was related to major
themes in the nation's history, particularly movements for equal rights
and urban reform, as well as to Ohio's past.

Black Ohioans participated in the establishment of welfare
institutions and civil rights organizations during and after World War I.
These bodies were organized to deal with social problems and civil rights
issues that multiplied in Ohio cities during the wartime black migration.
While the scale and complexity of the migrants' needs grew in those
years, white hostility increased and acts of intolerance spread. Earlier on,
few urban organizations were in place to assist black migrants in Ohio
and to fight racial discrimination. These organizations were not to
increase rapidly in numbers and strength until after 1910, when Ohio's
black urban population began to increase greatly.[3]

The development of African American welfare organizations in Ohio
was related to national trends. Between 1865 and 1920, urbanization in
the United States was accompanied by the growth of urban social problems that caused concern among reformers. While the nation's cities
grew rapidly and prospered, many urban residents experienced poverty,
inadequate shelter, ill health, vice, and crime. Social reformers organized
to combat urban ills, for example, by establishing an array of associations
and private institutions to aid the needy and the troubled. These included settlement houses meant to facilitate the adjustment of immigrants to
urban life in America. Prior to 1890, only a small fraction of blacks in
the United States lived in cities, and urban welfare institutions were
rarely devoted to African Americans. But the gradual urbanization of
the nation's black population eventually made reformers conscious that
African Americans were increasingly affected by the problematical
aspects of the urban environment. Especially after 1910, urban welfare
organizations for blacks were founded in many states, including Ohio.[4]

Early concerns about the welfare of black migrants in cities inspired
the establishment of the National Urban League in 1911. Black and
white reformers supported it. The league's sponsors included Booker T.
Washington, president of Tuskegee Institute, while its financial backers
included Chicago philanthropist Julius Rosenwald. Branches, estab-

lished in large urban centers, were intended to ease the relocation difficulties facing largely rural migrants who were settling in cities and to improve employment opportunities for African Americans generally.[5]

Although there were exceptions, during this era of reform in the United States, African Americans in cities were debarred from existing private institutions intended to assist white newcomers or poor white people. Typically, shelters for single working women, homes for unwed mothers, orphanages, and similar refuges imposed color lines. Many social service institutions were sponsored by organizations involved in Christian activism. Among them were the Salvation Army, the Young Men's Christian Association (YMCA), and the Young Women's Christian Association (YWCA). The Salvation Army in the twentieth century was essentially an urban social service organization, although it had been founded in the nineteenth century as an evangelical movement in Great Britain and in the United States. The YWCA and YMCA maintained facilities in cities across the United States offering lodging, food, and recreation to female or male transients. These Christian social service organizations maintained a minimal presence in African American urban life before 1910, but this changed significantly in the war decade. Racial exclusion, nevertheless, remained a motive for the establishment of separate institutions providing for the welfare of African Americans.[6]

The trend of founding separate welfare institutions for African Americans in Ohio was strongest in large cities. Needs were the greatest where African Americans were most concentrated, in Cincinnati, Cleveland, and Columbus. This trend in Ohio began earliest in Cincinnati. During the century before World War I, African American welfare needs were relatively large in Cincinnati because that city attracted more black migrants and accommodated more black residents than any other Ohio municipality. In Cincinnati three African American welfare institutions were opened in the nineteenth century, and two more were formed shortly before World War I.[7] The New Orphan Asylum for Colored Children was incorporated in 1845.[8] The Crawford Old Men's Home (for African Americans, especially ex-slaves) was established in 1888, and the Home for Aged Colored Women was founded in 1891.[9] The Walnut Hills Day Nursery for Colored Children was incorporated in 1910, and the Home for Colored Girls was established in 1911.[10] All of these institutions for African Americans still existed in Cincinnati during and after World War I.

Welfare services for African Americans in Cincinnati expanded considerably from 1916 through 1919 as many more black migrants entered the city from the South. In 1916, the Young Men's Christian Association

(YMCA) dedicated a new building constructed to accommodate the Ninth Street Branch YMCA for black men.[11] In 1917, the Salvation Army opened the Evangeline Home for the care of unmarried black mothers.[12] In 1918 the Friendship Home for Colored Girls was founded as a shelter for working women over sixteen years of age.[13] In 1919 the Young Women's Christian Association (YWCA) founded the West End Branch for black women in Cincinnati.[14]

These separate welfare institutions for African Americans in Cincinnati were established through cooperative efforts of blacks and whites. Typically, a few African Americans took the initiative by proposing the creation of an institution for blacks, by promoting their plan within the black community, and by securing the support of influential whites. The Home for Colored Girls was established through the joint efforts of prominent Cincinnatians, black and white, who composed the membership of the Cincinnati Protective and Industrial Association for Colored Women and Children. Three white philanthropists each gave three thousand dollars toward the purchase of the building that was opened in 1914. Other funds for the Home for Colored Girls were raised by private subscription and, starting in 1915, the institution received funding assistance from the Cincinnati Council for Social Agencies.[15] Likewise, in 1912 a small group of African Americans formed a definite plan for a black YMCA branch building in Cincinnati. Once a survey of community opinion revealed that there was support for the idea, the plan's backers started a building campaign. Local African Americans contributed $15,000 of the total investment in the new Ninth Street YMCA building that opened in 1916. Chicago philanthropist Julius Rosenwald donated $25,000 toward the cost of the YMCA edifice, and an additional $50,000 came from Cincinnati whites.[16] Similarly, the Salvation Army of Cincinnati agreed to sponsor a home for unwed black mothers in response to a request from a small ad hoc committee composed of black and white female social workers and black weekly editor Wendell P. Dabney (see photo 1). A campaign to interest black churches and clubs in an unwed mothers' home was conducted by an African American Salvation Army ensign, Elizabeth Symmes; white philanthropist Mary Emery donated a building; other contributors provided funds to remodel and equip the structure; and the Cincinnati Council of Social Agencies agreed to provide partial funding.[17]

The character of Jacob G. Schmidlapp's interest in the welfare of the black community was unusual in Cincinnati, and he had no counterpart elsewhere in Ohio. Schmidlapp, a white Cincinnatian whose fortune was made in whiskey, led an effort to build relatively low rental apartment complexes for African Americans. Schmidlapp felt that it was his

Photo 1
Wendell P. Dabney.

With permission of Cincinnati Museum Center—Cincinnati Historical Society Library.

duty to try to improve the condition of housing available to African Americans, but his housing project efforts were not entirely philanthropic.[18] He and his white associates expected a 5 percent return on their investment in low-cost sanitary housing.[19] In 1915, Schmidlapp's Model Homes Company constructed the Washington Terrace apartments that eventually housed about 600 black tenants. Washington Terrace was founded on a community plan aiming to provide black tenants "social and civic opportunity and a stronger economic position."[20] Consequently, the apartment complex gave tenants access to a cooperative store, a large assembly room, a billiard room, and playgrounds for children. Schmidlapp took up the idea of building this African American community in the firm belief "that the Negro can best develop himself when surrounded by those of his own race."[21] Schmidlapp claimed success for this community plan, citing 1918 statistics indicating that the arrest rates and death rates of Washington Terrace residents were significantly lower than those for Cincinnati blacks generally.[22]

Prior to 1910 welfare institutions serving African Americans were almost nonexistent in Columbus, but several existed there by 1920. In earlier times, whites generally were unsupportive of the plans for social work among blacks that were occasionally proposed by some African Americans in Columbus. In 1902, however, a white woman's group opened a day nursery for black children. Subsequently, an African American women's club managed that nursery.[23] Interracial cooperation in social work improved as the wartime black migration to Columbus accelerated. The Young Men's Christian Association of Columbus formed a branch for African Americans in 1912. Lacking sufficient funding, the black YMCA initially was housed in two old adjoining buildings on Spring Street in Columbus. In 1916 the Spring Street Branch was included in the building fund drive of the Columbus YMCA's Central Association. A new building, costing approximately $131,000, was erected for this African American branch in 1917. Chicagoan Julius Rosenwald, president of the Sears & Roebuck Company, contributed $25,000 toward the construction costs. African Americans in Columbus pledged over $18,000 to the Spring Street YMCA building, while local white contributors covered the remainder.[24] Also in 1917, a group of Christian women opened the Columbus Home for Colored Girls on 17th Street.[25] In 1918 the Columbus Young Women's Christian Association established the East Long Street Branch for black women.[26] Institutions for African Americans' dependents, the Ohio Avenue Day Nursery and the Old Folks Home, also existed in Columbus at the end of the decade.[27]

Expansion of social welfare institutions for African Americans was slower in Cleveland than in Cincinnati and Columbus. Traditionally, there was less public approval of racially separate facilities in northern Ohio than in the state's other regions. Established in 1896, the Cleveland Home for Aged Colored People struggled financially, but endured through the World War I period. A day nursery, a children's home, and a settlement house for African Americans were opened in Cleveland before 1912, but all closed after short periods because of insufficient support from blacks and whites. A movement advocating a Cleveland YMCA branch for African Americans collapsed in 1911 for similar reasons. Prior to the wartime migration, Cleveland's black population was not large enough to finance more than one shelter like the Home for Aged Colored People. Furthermore, certain influential African Americans in Cleveland did not support secular institutions created solely for blacks. Those advocating racial integration of public facilities contended that the establishment of secular institutions for blacks promoted racial segregation in public life. They argued that African Americans should insist on using existing public welfare institutions instead of pressing for the creation of separate ones for blacks. Given this criticism, whites in Cleveland were relatively disinclined to financially support separate facilities for African Americans.[28]

In 1913 the Phillis Wheatley Home, a shelter for black working women, was opened in Cleveland and ultimately thrived there despite many objections. Upon entering the city as a young African American nurse, Jane Edna Hunter found that the only living quarters available to her in Cleveland were shabby and disreputable rooming houses. The Cleveland Young Women's Christian Association discouraged black women from membership. In these circumstances, Jane E. Hunter (see photo 2) concluded that Cleveland needed a home for African American working women. She founded the Phillis Wheatley Association with the assistance of Mrs. Levi T. Schofield, a wealthy white Clevelander who was president of the Cleveland YWCA. A local white philanthropist financed the rental of the house accommodating the association's activities. The Phillis Wheatley Association's white board of trustees, headed by Mrs. Schofield, hired Jane Hunter as a general secretary. Subsequently, the association offered employed black women room and board at a reasonable rate, while also providing employment assistance and vocational training.[29]

In June 1915 the Playhouse Settlement was formally opened in Cleveland's Central Avenue African American district. The Playhouse Settlement was established through the efforts of the Men's Club of the Second Presbyterian Church, a white congregation that was located near the Central Avenue African American area. Seeking advice about the settlement house plan, a committee of the Presbyterian men consulted Charles Chesnutt and several other outstanding Cleveland African Americans. Chesnutt fully supported the scheme, believing that blacks would be "the chief beneficiaries" of a settlement house in a black district. But he advised the group that the settlement house "not be conducted on race lines," saying: "A great many colored people object and properly so, to the policy of segregation which seems to regard them as

Photo 2
Jane E. Hunter.

With permission of The Western Reserve Historical Society, Cleveland, Ohio.

unfit to associate with other human beings, . . . and it would be difficult to reach many of them, even with a good thing, coupled with such a suggestion."[30] Russell and Rowena Jelliffe, white graduates of the University of Chicago's Graduate School of Social Service, were placed in charge of the Playhouse Settlement. The integrated settlement house became one of the Cleveland Community Fund's agencies in 1919.[31]

African Americans were involved in the administration of institutions for black dependents and working women in Ohio during 1915–1920. Governing bodies of these institutions often included whites, but black men and women generally were members of their governing boards. These institutional homes usually were entirely staffed and managed by African Americans. Most often they were supervised and staffed by black women. The Cincinnati Home for Colored Girls was typical; its first board of trustees was biracial. Among the board's African American members in 1914 were former state legislator George W. Hays, barbershop proprietor Fountain Lewis, newspaper editor Wendell P. Dabney, and social worker Mrs. J. P. Monroe, who was associated with the Cincinnati Better Housing League. The board's white members included the Procter and Gamble Company's James N. Gamble, businessman Jacob G. Schmidlapp, philanthropist Mary Emery, and other locally prominent women. Through the end of the decade, Mrs. Cora Oliver, a black social worker, was superintendent of this facility for "girls of school age from broken and improper homes."[32] In Cleveland, the Phillis Wheatley Association board of trustees, chaired by Mrs. Levi T. Schofield, was entirely white, but Jane Hunter, an African American, was supervisor and general secretary of the Phillis Wheatley Home for employed women.[33] An African American, Mrs. Isabella Ridgeway, was superintendent of the Old Folks Home in Columbus. All of the trustees of that home for elderly African Americans were black men, mostly clergymen.[34] Meanwhile in Ohio, African Americans participated in the administration and work of racially separate institutions affiliated with the Salvation Army, the YWCA, and the YMCA. Prominent white and black citizens of Cincinnati served on an advisory committee of the Salvation Army's Evangeline Home for unwed African American mothers. The committee's black members included Jennie D. Porter (see photo 3), a highly respected teacher, and Edmund H. Oxley, Rector of St. Andrew's Episcopal Church. The Evangeline Home's medical staff was composed of seven black physicians who served gratuitously. Typically, African Americans filled the executive secretary positions and management committee memberships of black YMCA and YWCA branches in Ohio. Anna Hope was the original executive secretary of Cincinnati's West End Branch YWCA.[35] Nimrod B. Allen was the first executive secretary of Columbus' Spring Street Branch YMCA. The "leading colored men of the city" composed the Committee of Management that administered the black YMCA branch in Columbus. Likewise, in Cincinnati only African Americans were members of the Ninth Street Branch YMCA's Committee of Management in 1916.[36] As these examples indicate, the black leadership of social work institutions in Ohio came from the business and professional classes. White backers of these institutions similarly came from backgrounds in business or industry. Scholars find this class dimension in other states where, as in Ohio, middle class values shaped social work goals and efforts in black neighborhoods.[37]

During and after World War I, recently established African American institutions and associations addressed problems confronting black migrants in Ohio cities. In Cincinnati, Columbus, and Cleveland, African American institutions providing temporary shelter brought some relief to people facing the severe housing shortage of the period. Most of these facilities provided rooms for females. Homes for employed single black women offered their residents temporary shelter, board, and recre-

Photo 3
Jennie D. Porter.

With permission of Cincinnati Museum Center—Cincinnati Historical Society Library.

ation. Also, young female residents, including many vulnerable new-comers, were shielded from the dangers of involvement in vice and crime that flourished in some overcrowded urban areas. This shielding is an Ohio instance involving what Hazel Carby's insightful essay charac-terizes as "Policing the Black Woman's Body" by enforcers of middle class standards.[38] Cleveland's Phillis Wheatley Home, which was accom-modating 170 young women annually by 1916, enlarged its capacity by acquiring buildings during the war.[39] Attempting to further aid black women seeking rented rooms, the Phillis Wheatley Association cooperated with the United States Homes Registration Bureau, which canvassed and registered available living quarters in Cleveland and in other cities of the country. In 1919 the Cleveland agency of the bureau maintained a special office in the Phillis Wheatley building.[40] Certainly, the Phillis Wheatley Home was the most outstanding shelter for black working women in Ohio during the wartime migration. Columbus' Home for Colored Girls was a comparatively small facility. Located in a two-story frame house, it was supported by a group of Christian women, undoubtedly with relatively limited funds. Nevertheless, this Columbus Home offered shelter and policed conduct, as it tried "to promote the social, moral, intellectual, industrial, and religious advancement of women and girls."[41] Also, rooms at affordable rents were available to adult women at Cincinnati's Friendship Home for Colored Girls. The African American YWCAs in Columbus and Cincinnati, established respectively in 1918 and 1919, were opened too late to accommodate newcomers at the peak of the wartime migration.[42]

While providing inexpensive lodgings in dormitory rooms, black YWCAs and black YMCAs in Cincinnati and Columbus also served as social and recreational centers late in the decade. The Ys were intended to give black newcomers and young people alternatives to social life in saloons and on street corners. The facilities of Columbus' Spring Street Branch YMCA and Cincinnati's Ninth Street Branch YMCA included swimming pools, gymnasiums, billiard tables, bowling alleys, and cafeterias as well as banquet, meeting, and reading rooms. In Cincinnati, the West End Branch YWCA offered patrons use of its swimming pool, gymnasium, and tennis and basketball courts. The West End Branch YWCA's Tea Room served inexpensive wholesome meals to nonresidents as well as residents, and its public meeting rooms often were used by other organizations in the black community.[43]

New African American welfare associations appeared in Cincinnati, Columbus, and Cleveland in 1917 when the gathering momentum of the black wartime migration focused public attention on problems affecting African Americans in urban Ohio. Ultimately, these Ohio associations were affiliated with the National Urban League, but their origins were rooted in local initiatives. After local black and white investigators studied conditions of migrants, major civic organizations in each city proposed and financially backed the formation of a new African American welfare association. The association in each initially was seen as an agency mainly for the reorganization of welfare services already available to African Americans in the city.

As the presence of black migrants in Cincinnati became increasingly evident during May 1917, the Cincinnati Council of Social Agencies reported its intention to survey the "Negro Problem" in the city.[44] Later in the year, the Negro Civic Welfare Association was established as a department of the Council of Social Agencies and the Cincinnati Community Chest, a leading public charity organization. In 1918 the Negro Civic Welfare Association formulated a citywide social service program based upon a broad survey of social conditions among all blacks in Cincinnati. The program was designed to coordinate the city's existing African American welfare activities and promote further social work among blacks generally. The intention was to serve a broad African American clientele including migrants. The Welfare Association usually worked through other agencies, for example, by encouraging Cincinnati's Better Housing League to help black migrants who were searching for better shelter and to otherwise assist African Americans. Starting in 1918, the Better Housing League provided landlords with a visiting housekeeper service through which black tenants received information about good housekeeping practices.[45] Similar domestic agendas existed in other states.[46] The Welfare Association's program aimed to create linkages among social work agencies and to enhance the efficiency and financial resources of the city's black welfare institutions.[47] Accordingly, in 1919 the New Orphan Asylum for Colored Children, the Crawford Old Men's Home, and the Home for Aged Colored Women became affiliated with the Cincinnati Community Chest. Meantime, the Orphan Asylum for Colored Children was remodeled.[48] During 1917–1919 the Negro Civic Welfare Association's efforts were devoted mainly to social services planning and harmonizing the efforts of Cincinnati's comparatively large number of black social work institutions. Employment assistance for black men and women seeking jobs in Cincinnati manufacturing plants began after the wartime migration. The Welfare Association initiated a program of industrial welfare work in 1920. At the same time recreational programs were started in the West End, Walnut Hills, and other black communities in the Cincinnati area.[49]

The Columbus Urban League evolved from the Federated Social and Industrial Welfare Movement for the Negro, or the Negro Welfare League, as it was known informally. The Negro Welfare League grew out of an interracial meeting held in early 1917 to consider problems experienced by the large number of black migrants from the South who were just then entering Columbus. Those attending the meeting represented the National Association for the Advancement of Colored People, the YMCA, church groups, and schools. Several municipal government officials attended. Subsequently, black migrants arriving by train at Columbus' Union Station were met by a "travelers' aid" worker of the Negro Welfare League who assisted them in seeking contacts with social agencies, relatives, or friends. In 1918 the Negro Welfare League was reorganized as the Columbus Urban League, affiliated with the National Urban League. At the end of the decade, the featured work of the Columbus Urban League included placing unemployed persons in jobs, improving the efficiency of employed workers, and making adult education classes available to unschooled persons. Still at a formative stage, the Columbus Urban League sought contributions in 1920 to pay the salaries of the executive secretary, traveler's aid, and home visitor. Also, contributions were needed to purchase office equipment and to acquire a building to serve as a community center.[50] The Columbus Urban League evidently was not as well funded as its counterparts in Cincinnati and Cleveland.

In December 1917 the Negro Welfare Association was founded in Cleveland in response to mounting social problems experienced by thousands of recently arrived black migrants from the South.[51] The Cleveland Negro Welfare Association shortly became affiliated with the National Urban League, but its antecedents and funding were much tied to Cleveland.[52] In the summer of 1917 one of the city's major civic organizations, the Cleveland Welfare Federation, appointed a biracial committee to study welfare problems arising from the wartime migration.[53] The original idea of the Negro Welfare Association and most of its funds came from the Cleveland Welfare Federation.[54] The Negro Welfare Association was meant to assist the adjustment of migrants to new living and working conditions in Cleveland, while improving their housing conditions and providing employment services. The association was designed to develop cooperation among existing welfare agencies serving black clients and to create new ones when necessary. After opening offices in the Phillis Wheatley Association Building at East 40th Street and Central Avenue, the association began operations on a first year budget estimated at $5,000.[55]

According to Emmett J. Scott's contemporary study of the black wartime migration to the urban North, Cleveland led other cities in Ohio in dealing with welfare problems of the migrants.[56] Black and white civic organizations took an active interest in their difficult situation. In 1917 both the Cleveland Chamber of Commerce and the Cleveland Welfare Federation sponsored investigations into the welfare needs of black migrants.[57] Nevertheless, many black migrants received no assistance in finding satisfactory housing before the winter of 1917–1918, when the Cleveland's Negro Welfare Association began to coordinate the migrant aid efforts of local African American churches and other organizations.[58] The Negro Welfare Association's annual report for 1918 recorded a variety of services aiding migrants. The association was most active in providing employment assistance, placing almost all of its 1,500 job applicants during the year. The association also urged greater efficiency among black industrial workers, gave clients advice concerning housing conditions, organized several "Home Economics Clubs," and conducted surveys and investigations revealing conditions, needs, and wishes of African Americans in Cleveland.[59] In 1919 the Negro Welfare Association helped establish a Community House to serve unemployed war veterans in the East 40th Street and Central Avenue area.[60]

African Americans with strong academic credentials and backgrounds in social work served as executive secretaries of black welfare associations in Ohio during and after World War I. James Hathaway Robinson, who was born at Sharpsburg, Kentucky, in 1888, became executive secretary of Cincinnati's Negro Civic Welfare Association in 1917. Robinson graduated with a B.A. degree from Fisk University in Nashville, Tennessee. At Yale University he earned the M.A. degree and completed the residence requirements for the Ph.D. degree with a major in sociology. Then with the benefit of an Urban League fellowship, Robinson studied sociology and social work in the Graduate School of Columbia University during 1914–1915. Robinson was a member of Cincinnati's Douglass School faculty when he was appointed executive secretary of the local Welfare Association. Using his formal training in social services, Robinson constructed an elaborate and sophisticated survey of the social-economic conditions in Cincinnati's black community. Robinson's Cincinnati survey and the planned welfare program based on it received national recognition in the field of social work.[61] William R. Conners was hired as executive secretary of Cleveland's Negro Welfare Association, starting in January 1918. Conners received his undergraduate degree from Biddle College (later Johnson C. Smith University), Charlotte, North Carolina. He was a teacher at Livingstone College in Salisbury, North Carolina and then became a school principal in the Philadelphia area. Meanwhile, Conners studied at the University of Pennsylvania where he earned a master's and a doctorate. In 1917, Conners was secretary of the Housing and Industrial Bureau in the National Urban League's New York Office. He was sent to Ohio to assist local organizers who were forming Cleveland's Negro Welfare Association as an Urban League affiliate.[62]

The black welfare associations in Ohio operated with biracial executive boards. In Cleveland, blacks and whites were members of the Negro Welfare Association's Board of Trustees. James H. Robinson's plan for a black welfare association in Cincinnati called for an advisory group including black professionals and others who were well informed about Cincinnati's black community. Most members of the Cincinnati Negro Civic Welfare Association's biracial board of directors were whites.[63] Through 1920, a biracial executive board provided the sole governance of the Urban League's affiliate in Columbus, evidently because it lacked the funds for an executive secretary's salary. The board president was the Reverend Irving Maurer, the white pastor of the elite First Congregational Church in Columbus. Dr. William J. Woodlin, a black physician, was first vice president. Its secretary was an African American, Ann Hughes, who was superintendent of the Ohio Avenue Day Nursery for black children. The regular members of the board included several African American physicians, clergymen, and social workers. One of the African American board members, Nimrod B. Allen, was a likely candidate for the vacant executive secretary post. Allen, born at Gerard, Alabama, in 1886, was the son of a minister and educator. As a youngster, Allen worked on the *Southern Christian Recorder*, edited by his father. He attended Wilberforce University in Xenia, Ohio, receiving the B.A. from that traditionally black institution in 1910. Allen acquired some training in social work while studying at Yale University, where he was awarded the S.T.B. in 1915. Returning to Ohio in the same year, Allen became executive secretary of Columbus' Spring Street YMCA, a position that he held through 1920. Meanwhile he helped organize the local Negro Welfare League and the Urban League's Columbus affiliate. Allen was appointed as the executive secretary of the Columbus Urban League in 1921.[64]

Generally, social services for African Americans in Ohio cities were not coordinated at the state level. But early in the war period a statewide organization formed in response to widespread publicity and concern about the welfare implications of the black migration into Ohio. The Ohio Federation for Uplift Among Colored People arose from a statewide conference on migrant problems held in Columbus in 1917. Among the leading black citizens of the state who had called for this large interracial meeting were J. Walter Wills, president of the Cleveland Association of Colored Men, and Charles S. Johnson, superintendent of the Champion Chemical Company of Springfield. The Ohio Federation cooperated with or established welfare organizations in Ohio cities, including Cincinnati, Cleveland, Dayton, Sandusky, Akron, Springfield, Xenia, Urbana, Piqua, Troy, and Chillicothe. It also maintained a lecture bureau and supported the war effort, for instance, by promoting the sale of United States Thrift Stamps.[65] The Ohio Federation for Uplift Among Colored People evidently disintegrated after 1918 as the African American migration into Ohio temporarily subsided.

During and after World War I, African Americans in Ohio organized to protest racial discrimination as well as to aid African Americans needing employment, housing, and medical assistance. Branches of the National Association for the Advancement of Colored People (NAACP) were established throughout Ohio during the second decade of the twentieth century. The Ohio branches were affiliated with the parent organization's national offices in New York City. The original plan to form the NAACP was made in 1909 at an interracial conference attended by W. E. B. Du Bois and other young African American members of the Niagara Movement who adamantly demanded an end to all racial discrimination and segregation. Also present were Jane Addams, John Dewey, and other white notables who were troubled by the recent Springfield riots and the prospect of escalating racial violence. Formally organized in 1910, the NAACP set out to combat racial inequality and brutality, especially in the forms of lynching and southern state laws that caused racial segregation and the disfranchisement of black men.[66]

NAACP affiliates were started in many of the nation's cities. The first Ohio NAACP branch was organized at Cleveland in 1912. NAACP branches were formed at Cincinnati, Columbus, Dayton, Springfield, and Toledo in 1915. During the period 1916–1919, NAACP branches were established at Akron, Lorain, Oberlin, Wellsville, and Youngstown in northern Ohio. Meanwhile, NAACP branches were started in central Ohio at Urbana and in southern Ohio at Middletown and in Greene County.[67] Like their parent organization, Ohio's NAACP branches were racially integrated, but most NAACP members and leaders in Ohio were African Americans.[68] Usually, African Americans held the local offices; for example, in 1917 the president of the Cleveland NAACP branch was the Reverend Horace C. Bailey, pastor of Antioch Baptist Church.[69] Likewise, in 1919 the Columbus branch's president was the Reverend Edward L. Gilliam, an African Methodist Episcopal church pastor, and its secretary was attorney S. T. Kelly.[70] More NAACP affiliates were formed in Ohio during the decade than in most states.[71] However, interest in Ohio's NAACP branches tended to decline after the original efforts to organize them. For example, the Cincinnati NAACP branch "in its early days had a large and loyal membership," according to Wendell P. Dabney, but "interest in it gradually died."[72]

The Cleveland affiliate was the most vital NAACP branch in the state, and its public meetings were generally well attended. Even so, the NAACP's Cleveland membership was small, and its branch there lacked sufficient funding.[73] In Cleveland the NAACP interested itself in employment and housing problems, occasionally asserted itself in cases of racial discrimination, and hosted lectures by national civil rights leaders, including Joel Spingarn.[74] The first district conference of the NAACP was held in Cleveland in May 1916. Delegates attending the conference came from branches in Ohio, Michigan, and Pennsylvania, which were the states comprising the Great Lakes District.[75] In June 1919 Cleveland was the site of the Tenth Anniversary Annual Conference of the national organization.[76] While active in these ways, the Cleveland branch was criticized for ineffectiveness, as were others in the state. Silas D. McElroy, a Cleveland member, held, " . . . the local branch ought to do something far more practical for the race than merely hold meetings, with white speakers as a rule, and take in new members at one dollar each a greater part of which is sent to the National Association headquarters in New York City."[77]

The existence of NAACP branches in many Ohio cities created the potential for formally organized campaigns against racial bias in the state. But that potential was little realized before 1920. The NAACP occasionally opposed racial discrimination and sometimes succeeded. The NAACP was one voice among others advocating civil rights in Ohio. As in the past, opposition to racial bias in most instances was led not by civil rights organizations, but by individual African Americans acting on their own initiative or as spokespersons of traditional black institutions and associations including churches and newspapers. Some black persons who took these initiatives were acquainted with or were known to influential whites. Their acquaintances and reputations among white notables often arose from their active participation in partisan politics, almost always as Republicans. Commonly, white civic leaders and public officials involved in a particular issue were contacted on a personal basis. Black leaders individually or in committees addressed white leaders through personal conferences or through correspondence. The African American spokespersons described the nature of the grievance and requested action remedying the problem. When matters were not resolved in this way the issues were sometimes taken to the courts. In other circumstances, black persons whose civil rights were infringed upon acted directly and without group support, starting private legal proceedings under Ohio equal rights legislation. In still other cases of racial discrimination, black individuals brought attention to injustices by writing letters to the editors of local African American weekly newspapers or major dailies. In extraordinary instances, ad hoc groups of local black citizens formed to petition for redress of grievances, for example, concerning racial segregation in a public school. African American state legislators were expected to take leading parts when the Ohio legislature was capable of affecting the outcome of equal rights issues.

During its first decade of existence in Ohio, the NAACP did not lead the opposition to color line practices in public accommodations. Typically, African American individuals opposed racial bias in Ohio's public places during the decade when restaurants, theaters, parks, and other commercial venues increasingly excluded blacks or required racial segregation. An interested observer made a comparison of differing reactions to racial discrimination in Cleveland and Columbus that could have been made in regard to Cleveland and other Ohio cities. He wrote, "In Cleveland, although discrimination is clandestinely practiced, there is a conviction on the part of prejudiced whites that our people will fight in the courts thereby keeping prejudice and discrimination to a minimum; while here in Columbus there has been but one civil rights case tried in ten years, the prejudiced whites have no awakened public conscience."[78] African Americans in Cleveland were more inclined to act against racial discrimination in public places than black citizens of other Ohio cities. In May 1917 the black ushers of Cleveland's Miles Theatre, evidently acting on their own initiative, quit in a body when a patron was refused a ticket on the main floor because of her race.[79] Editor Harry C. Smith (see photo 4) regularly used the Cleveland *Gazette* to vehemently criticize racial exclusion and segregation. Over a period of many years, *The Gazette* excoriated Cleveland's Luna Park and the African Americans who patronized it. Luna Park's concessions were closed to African Americans except when the Cleveland Caterers' Association held its annual summer picnic there. In 1919 the Cleveland Association of Colored Men used its influence to discourage the Caterers and other African American organizations from using Luna Park. The Caterers Association subsequently held its outing at another park.[80]

In several Ohio cities, African American individuals started legal proceedings against public accommodations, alleging racial discrimination in violation of Ohio's late nineteenth century civil rights statutes. More civil rights suits were filed in Cleveland than elsewhere in the state. The civil rights cases involved alleged racial discrimination in restaurants and theatres. African American plaintiffs won most of the suits involving restaurants but lost most of those against theatres. (See table A4.) Ohio statutes permitted courts to award at most $100 to victims of racial discrimination. Usually the black litigants were businessmen, lawyers, and other professionals. Few civil rights suits were filed because members of the African American community generally were unaware of the existence of laws prohibiting racial discrimination in public accommodations, lacked money to initiate litigation, desired to avoid the notoriety of a court case, or wished to avoid the degrading experience of being refused service.

African American resistance to racial discrimination most often

Photo 4
Harry C. Smith.

With permission of The Western Reserve Historical Society, Cleveland, Ohio.

occurred in the state's large urban centers but sometimes was mounted in small Ohio cities. During 1916 through 1918, Gallipolis was the scene of a campaign to end racial segregation in a public high school. In the war decade Gallipolis' total population did not exceed 6,070, and its black population declined from 684 to 482.[81] Located on the Ohio River border with West Virginia, the city's racial practices reflected those of the South. Gallipolis was one of the few Ohio cities maintaining separate schools for African Americans in the twentieth century. Lincoln Elementary School for African Americans was opened in Gallipolis in the late nineteenth century. During the 1880s, black students were refused admission to Gallipolis' Union High School and were discouraged from attempting to register at Gallia Academy, another secondary school in the Gallia County seat. African American parents persistently tried to enroll their children in the high school, and the board of education responded by adding two rooms to the Lincoln Elementary School. Thereafter, a "high school education" was purportedly available to African Americans in those rooms. The "high school" for African Americans employed one teacher until 1900, when a second one was hired. Commenting on the unsatisfactory character of the "high school" in the Lincoln Elementary facility, a black Gallipolis citizen wrote: "An obsolete, dilapidated building, inadequate in every respect for the needs of the scholars, has been given us for years, also, teachers, who are not always appointed without political consideration. Thus was lowered the intellectual and moral standard of the institution. . . ."[82]

The issue of new school construction in Gallipolis was raised in 1916 when the Gallia Academy trustees offered to transfer that institution to the local school board if it would authorize the construction of a modern high school building. Accordingly, the property was transferred and Gallipolis High School was erected. African Americans were not permitted to attend the new high school. Responding to complaints about this, the Gallipolis school board repaired the dilapidated Lincoln School. Two years later, in May 1918, black residents petitioned the board of education to substantially improve Lincoln School or to admit African American students to the new high school. The board ignored the petition. The following September some eligible students from Lincoln School sought admission to Gallipolis High but were refused.[83]

Several factors made it difficult for the advocates of high school integration to gain the active support of the whole African American community in Gallipolis. Some were affected by apathy resulting from the failure of previous attempts to influence the board of education. Some in the black community opposed "mixing the schools." In this regard, a black resident of Gallipolis commented: "These conditions [at Lincoln School] were tolerated for years, the personal interest of the few being of more value than the future possibilities of the many!"[84] Undoubtedly, his reference was to the few African American teachers and their students. Outside of Cleveland, Ohio school boards only employed black teachers to instruct black students. Unemployment of black teachers would likely follow high school integration. Nevertheless, local activists obtained the services of a Columbus attorney. An injunction suit against the school board was filed in common pleas court. On November 18, 1918, the court found that the Gallipolis Board of Education had "willfully, arbitrarily and illegally" maintained a separate high school for African Americans and enjoined the board from maintaining such a high school. In a session at Ironton, a circuit court of appeals upheld the decision.[85]

During and after World War I, African Americans in Ohio criticized racial discrimination in employment, housing, and law enforcement; opposed color lines in public schools and in public accommodations; and addressed issues of racial violence.

Exhibition of racist motion picture films in the state was at the center of the most extensive and sustained opposition to color bias by black Ohioans at the time. African Americans everywhere were offended by the racial contents of "The Birth of a Nation" and other films exhibited nationwide during World War I. There were intense controversies in many states as NAACP representatives and other voices of black protest objected when these films were exhibited. Racially biased films were shown in Ohio cities during March 1915 through October 1918. Throughout that period and in every section of Ohio, African Americans urged theater owners and public authorities to edit the films or stop their exhibitions. While by no means alone in these campaigns, the NAACP actively opposed these motion pictures in several Ohio cities. Other expressions of protest came from individual African Americans, especially newspaper editors and clergymen. African American women's associations and ministerial alliances joined the controversies. Eventually, an African American state representative sought a legislative remedy. African Americans approached and pressured whites in authority, including Ohio mayors, police chiefs, governors, and state film censorship board members.

In March 1915 a motion picture released in Cleveland by the Fox Film Corporation carried a title bound to offend African Americans. The black Ministers' Alliance in Cleveland held a meeting to discuss the showing of "The Nigger" at the Standard Theatre and adopted a strong set of protest resolutions. The ministers visited Cleveland Mayor Newton D. Baker to protest the exhibition of the film. Also, Harry C. Smith, editor of a local African American weekly, called upon the mayor and the chief of police in connection with the film. Smith reported the mayor's statement that the film "would be banished from the city if it was as represented by us."[86] The chief of police ordered an investigation, sending officers to see the film. The officers claimed that it did not warrant an order of suppression and reported that the state board of film censors had approved the film for showing.[87] In reply to a letter from Editor Smith, Governor Frank Willis wrote, "I shall take immediate steps to bring this [the film] to the attention of the State Moving Picture Censor Board in order that this film may not be exhibited at any point within the limits of this state."[88] The governor was given a copy of a review of the film taken from a motion picture industry journal. The *Moving Picture World* stated:

> Repulsive, harmful and void of any moral lesson worth pointing out in a picture purporting to be founded on Edward Sheldon's play, "The Nigger." . . . . A drunken Negro, frothing at the mouth, is shown in a close up as he hides behind a tree, waiting to assault a little (white) girl wandering through the woods. The child dies from the effects of what a sub-title describes as "the usual crime," and after that we have a manhunt with bloodhounds, a lynching and the spectacle of a Negro being burned at the stake. Nothing so nauseating as "The Nigger" has been shown on the screen as seen by a representative of the *Moving Picture World*, it is a brutal appeal to most dangerous human passions and prejudices.[89]

Mayor Newton D. Baker, also replying to an inquiry by Editor Smith, said that he had contacted the state censor board. The board had informed him "that the film in question . . . contained none of the disgusting and inflammatory details in . . . the *Motion Picture World*." Baker assumed "these objectionable things had been eliminated before the film was exhibited to our Censor Board."[90] Editor Smith replied that the chief of police had informed him that ten feet of film had been eliminated. Smith stated positively, however, that objectionable features remained. These features included scenes showing the Negro hiding "behind a tree waiting to assault the little white girl," the dead child, the manhunt, "the flames indicating the lynching and burning at the stake," and a "'race war'" during which whites were killed by Negroes.[91]

The controversy about the showing of "The Nigger" in Cleveland was resolved when the Censor Board withdrew its approval of the film. Governor Willis informed Editor Smith, "As soon as I heard from you I got in touch with the President of the [Censor] Board. Upon further consideration the Board adopted a resolution rescinding the certification that had been issued for the very objectionable film, 'The Nigger.' Notification was sent to the Fox Film Corporation at Cleveland, Cincinnati and New York. Also authorities at Cleveland were notified."[92] The showing of the film was then discontinued by action of the Cleveland police.[93]

A new version of "The Nigger" with a different name did pass the state's board of film censors. Chairman of the Board Charles G. Williams explained that "a new picture" had been "submitted to the Board under the name of 'The Mystery of Morrow's Rest' without the objectionable parts." According to Williams, however, some film exhibitors advertised the revived film as "The Nigger" or showed the original version under the new title.[94] The local NAACP branch discovered that the Majestic Theatre in Springfield was attempting to show the original film under the title "The Mystery of Morrow's Rest." The local NAACP branch then complained to the Springfield city manager, who informed the state censor board. Subsequently the board stopped the showing of the film.[95]

Municipal officials in several Ohio cities took action against "The Mystery of Morrow's Rest" once African Americans made objections to it. In June 1915, Mayor Hartenstein of Youngstown reported:

> . . . I advised the management of the theater not to produce it because of its tendency to arouse race prejudice. The manager faithfully promised me he would obey my request. When several prominent Colored residents called and objected to the picture, I informed them it would not be produced. [Later] I found out that the picture called "The Mystery of Morrow's Rest," advertised to appear at the Dome . . . was really "The Nigger" under another name. I immediately instructed [Police] Captain Jenkins to stop the show, and he obeyed my orders.[96]

The exhibition of the film also was stopped in Steubenville and Toledo under similar circumstances.[97] "The Mystery of Morrow's Rest" was shown in Lorain despite protest. Ruth Anna Fisher of Lorain's Colored Women's Association stated: ". . . the unpleasant . . . feature of this case was the apparent indifference of our city officials in the matter. The chief of police passed the case on to the mayor; and he in turn gave it over to the city solicitor who was glad to do nothing about it."[98]

"The Birth of a Nation," epic film maker D. W. Griffith's version of Thomas Dixon's overtly anti-black fiction, was released nationwide in 1915 and shown through the war years. Griffith's professional reputation and the extraordinary technical quality of his film in combination with its emotional content quickly made "The Birth of a Nation" a major commercial film. The motion picture seemed to inflame racial passions as the lynching of black men increased and race rioting spread in the United States. Meanwhile, the NAACP's New York headquarters orchestrated a campaign designed to stop the screening of "The Birth of a Nation," and African Americans throughout the land opposed it.[99] Beginning in the summer of 1915 African American leaders from Cleveland and around Ohio urged state officials to prevent the showing of "The Birth of a Nation." At the end of September the promoters of the film applied to the State Board of Motion Picture Censors for permission to exhibit it in Ohio. In response, a biracial protest against "The Birth of a Nation" was filed with the state censors' board by Columbus civic leaders including representatives of the National Association for the Advancement of Colored People, Mayor George J. Karb, Dr. Washington Gladden, pastor of the First Congregational Church, Rabbi Kornfield, and Editor James Carroll of the *Catholic Columbian*. The censors' board subsequently denied the application of the film's promoters.[100]

Chairman of the Ohio Board of Motion Picture Censors Charles G. Williams, in giving his official opinion on "The Birth of a Nation," commented upon the protests against the film. He said that the Ohio Board of Motion Picture Censors received information indicating that "the entire Colored race" seriously objected to the film. The Governor's office received many protests against "The Birth of a Nation." Governor Frank B. Willis repeatedly asked the board to carefully consider the motion picture and "urgently recommended" rejection of the film if the board found that it was "of such a character as to reflect upon the Colored race" and tended "to arouse racial hatred and prejudice." According to Williams, the owners of the film submitted many statements praising "The Birth of a Nation." These included recommendations by "reputable individual citizens" that the film be shown. Supporters asserted that it was of "dramatic and historical value" and that it was the "most gigantic production from the standpoint of cast and spectacular achievement" ever made by the film industry.[101]

After viewing "The Birth of a Nation," the Board of Motion Picture Censors admitted that it had "a great dramatic value" and that it was "stupendous from the standpoint of camera achievements." But the board concluded that the film reflected "unfavorably on the colored race" and that it misrepresented history. Williams wrote:

> The entire latter half of said film is devoted to scenes and subtitles portraying Colored men engaged in all sorts of vicious conduct toward whites of the South during the Civil War and Reconstruction Period following. There are many mob scenes where Negroes are in the most repelling way attacking white citizens, and scenes where Negro men are forcing their attention upon white women and are engaged in all sorts of ridiculous and knavish conduct, not only as individuals, but as a race. True, they were led in many instances by what the film terms "scalawag carpetbaggers"; but this only further reflects upon the government of that period. ... [The] child unfamiliar with the real facts of history, would upon

viewing the film immediately conclude that the result of the Civil War was the greatest crime in the annals of history, rather than, the prevention of human beings being driven by the lash and being sold upon the auction block.[102]

Defenders of "The Birth of a Nation" held that the film was not objectionable because it concerned events of a time long ago. While the film was set in the past, the Ohio Board of Motion Picture Censors concluded that it affected current life. Chairman Williams said: "[I]t strongly tends to arouse hatred and prejudice among the coming generation against a race that is living in our midst." Noting that "The Birth of a Nation" seemed to condone lawlessness by the Ku Klux Klan and racial violence against African Americans in the past, Williams stated:

> The play also represents the Ku Klux Klan in such a manner that their conduct would be applauded. It tends to justify that organization in capturing the Negroes and, as masked vigilance committees, trying them at night, convicting them of supposed outrages, executing them and placing their bodies at the doors of state officials who sympathized with their cause. . . . [T]he same spirit that urged their activities at that time is the same that prompts such appalling conduct in recent times as to cause Negroes to be lynched, making lynching day a day of celebration. . . . . Films which present scenes of this character in a manner which to the on looker seems to be justified cannot fail to be harmful.[103]

The Ohio Board of Motion Picture Censors rejected "The Birth of a Nation" in its entirety instead of approving an edited version of it.[104]

In January 1916 the owners of "The Birth of a Nation," through Attorney Joseph W. Heintzman of Cincinnati, threatened to file an injunction suit in the Supreme Court of Ohio or in a federal district court if the Ohio Board of Motion Picture Censors did not revise its ruling on their film.[105] In response Ohio Attorney General Edward C. Turner personally reviewed the motion picture and subsequently supported the board of film censors' decision. Turner gave the opinion that the picture should have been entitled "An Insult to the Nation."[106] On January 18 the Epoch Producing Company, the owners of the film, filed a suit to restrain the censors' board from prohibiting the showing of "The Birth of a Nation" in Ohio.[107] A federal district court dismissed the case on the grounds "that an adequate legal remedy is afforded by Ohio statute in provision for appeal from the ruling of the state board of motion picture censors to the Ohio Supreme Court."[108] The state supreme court subsequently upheld the board's ruling on "The Birth of a Nation."[109]

The decision of the Ohio Supreme Court regarding "The Birth of a Nation" did not end the controversy over the film. Attempts to have it shown in Ohio were renewed in 1917 after a change in the administration of state government. Democratic Governor James M. Cox succeeded former Republican Governor Frank B. Willis. A revised version of the film passed the state censors' board on February 1, 1917.[110] Two days later George A. Myers, who was perhaps the most widely known black man in Cleveland, asked the chairman of the Democratic party organization in Cuyahoga County to use his influence with Governor Cox to have the film prohibited.[111] The county Democratic leader informed the governor that he had seen "The Birth of a Nation" while in New York City and advised, "I doubt very much the wisdom of allowing it to be shown in Ohio."[112] Nevertheless, the film was exhibited in theaters around the state, beginning in March, but not without the continued opposition of African American activists and interested white citizens.

In March a committee of Dayton African American leaders actively campaigned against the showing of "The Birth of a Nation" in that city. The committee obtained the cooperation and aid of the Greater Dayton Association (a business organization), the Dayton Federation of Churches, and the Young Women's Christian Association of Dayton. The film's opponents appealed to local authorities in Dayton, which employed the city commission form of municipal government. The Dayton City Commission passed a resolution condemning the exhibition of "The Birth of a Nation." The commission then considered the passage of a city ordinance that would have prevented the screening of the motion picture.[113] Among the interested parties who gave pertinent testimony before the commission were conservative African American newspapermen George L. Knox and A. E. Manning, publishers of the Indianapolis *Freemen* and the Indianapolis *World* respectively. Knox and Manning spoke in favor of "The Birth of a Nation," and their testimony evidently dissuaded the Dayton city commissioners from enacting an ordinance prohibiting the film's appearance in Dayton, according to the Dayton *Forum*, an African American weekly.[114]

Early in April 1917, when the opening of "The Birth of a Nation" at Cleveland theaters was advertised, local civic leaders began to protest against it. For example, the Cleveland Minister's Union (white) sent letters opposing the film to Mayor Davis and Governor Cox.[115] Mayor Davis repeatedly stated that he would do all in his power to prevent the showing of the picture in Cleveland. On March 29 the mayor issued an order to stop the exhibition of "The Birth of a Nation" on the grounds that "it might tend to incite riots."[116] The Epoch Producing Company subsequently filed an injunction suit in the local federal district court to restrain the city officials from interfering with the presentation of the film.[117] Meanwhile, the Cleveland City Council passed a resolution disapproving of "The Birth of a Nation" and then passed an ordinance prohibiting its exhibition and the use of advertising that tended to cause riots.[118] The film company's injunction suit was dismissed from the federal district court, whereupon it was carried to the local common pleas court. The common pleas court ruled that city officials had no right to interfere with the presentation of "The Birth of a Nation" because the state censors' board had approved it. Meanwhile, the Cleveland Branch of the National Association for the Advancement of Colored People, the Cleveland Association of Colored Men, and the Cleveland Federation of Colored Women's Clubs had joined in a united fund-raising campaign to hire lawyers to assist the city attorneys in the case.[119]

In Cincinnati the local branch of the National Association for the Advancement of Colored People appealed to the mayor to prohibit the showing of "The Birth of a Nation." The request proved to be fruitless. Furthermore, NAACP Branch President William Stevenson's effort to obtain a court injunction against the film was thwarted by a lack of funds.[120]

Opposition to "The Birth of a Nation" was taken to the Ohio General Assembly in 1917. Hamilton County State Representative A. Lee Beaty was the only African American in the state legislature at the time. On January 30 Beaty introduced House Bill No. 227 that provided a fine of up to one thousand dollars against any person "who shall advertise, publish, present or exhibit in any public place in this state, any lithograph, drawing, picture, play, drama or sketch that tends to incite race riot or race hatred, or shall represent any hanging, lynching or burning of any human being. . . ."[121] It was hoped that such a measure would have the effect of preventing the exhibition of "The Birth of a Nation" and similar films. Several African American leaders spoke in favor of House Bill No. 227 before a hearing of the House Judiciary Committee, to which the bill had been referred.[122] On February 19, Beaty presented the House with a petition of two hundred forty-one Franklin County citizens favoring the bill.[123] House Bill No. 227 received support from other parts of the state. The Baptist Ministers' Alliance and several other African American church groups in Cincinnati passed resolutions in favor of the measure. William Stevenson, who was president of the Cincinnati NAACP branch, gave several speeches in support of the bill and circulated a petition that was sent to the state legislature.[124]

Both Democratic and Republican members of the Ohio House of

Representatives offered Beaty support for House Bill No. 227. But an editorial in *Dayton News* made some of them anxious about siding with Beaty. Governor James M. Cox was the publisher of the Dayton *News*, and many assumed that its editorials reflected the governor's opinions. The *News* editorial was favorable to "The Birth of a Nation." The editor asserted, "[I]t is only the Negro politicians who are trying to stir up a tempest in a teapot" about the picture and "it is hoped that they will not succeed."[125] Beaty and the other proponents of House Bill No. 227 were fearful that it would die in committee unless it was forwarded to the whole house well before the end of the legislative session in March. Consequently, they took steps to bring it up for a vote. On March 2, Beaty succeeded in having the bill taken from the judiciary committee and placed upon the calendar. A few days later he failed in an effort to have it moved up on the calendar. Nevertheless, House Bill No. 227 passed the house with a unanimous vote on March 9.[126] The next day it was received by the senate, given a second reading, and sent to the senate judiciary committee. On the last day of the legislature, March 21, Senator White of Columbiana County tried to bring the bill to a vote by moving to have it taken from the judiciary committee. The motion failed and House Bill No. 227 was thus killed.[127]

State Representative Beaty concluded that former Republican Governor Frank Willis precluded the possibility of bipartisan support for the bill in the senate and thereby caused its death. Beaty stated: "I had hopes of bringing it [House Bill No. 227] to a vote until Willis wrote a letter to the Republican Senators urging that all vote for it. The letter became public, party lines were drawn and I now realize that Democrats in control of the senate will not let it came to a vote."[128] State Senator George D. Jones, who was a Democrat and Columbus NAACP branch president, had offered to promote the passage of the bill in the senate. But after Willis' appeal, Jones had withdrawn his support and had abstained when the crucial senate vote on the bill was taken.[129] However, Editor Harry C. Smith of the Cleveland *Gazette*, a black weekly, believed that the Ohio General Assembly's Democratic majority was responsible for the death of House Bill No. 227.[130]

"The Birth of a Nation" was free to run in Ohio from early 1917 until October 1918. During that period it was shown in many Ohio cities including Cleveland, Dayton, Columbus, Cincinnati, Toledo, and Lorain. African American leaders continued to express opposition to the showing of the film.[131] After the motion picture was shown in Ohio for over a year Governor Cox took steps to prevent further release of it in the state. Harry C. Smith, editor of the Cleveland *Gazette*, was informed that the producers of "The Birth of a Nation" agreed voluntarily to stop showing it in Ohio after October 1, 1918, "at the request of Governor Cox."[132]

Surely, "The Birth of a Nation" and other contemporary films depicting racial violence contributed to the trend of rising white hostility toward blacks that included the spread of race riots in urban America or at least reflected that social phenomenon of the time. Deadly violence occurred in many cities including East St. Louis, Chicago, Omaha, and the District of Columbia. The African American community of Ohio was concerned about the nationwide epidemic of race riots and racial incidents. In Ohio, meetings were held and resolutions protesting violence against African Americans were adopted. In Cleveland, for example, the Ministers' Alliance, the National Association for the Advancement of Colored People, and the Cleveland Association of Colored Men passed a resolution strongly condemning "the appalling outrages committed upon citizens of the United States and residents of East St. Louis, Illinois" and sent it to Representative H. I. Emerson, of the 21st Ohio Congressional District.[133] Similarly, a meeting to protest against the Omaha riot was held at Cleveland's Metropolitan Church.[134]

African American activists in some Ohio cities organized to prevent local riots. In August 1918 about fifteen representative citizens of Cleveland's East End joined an *ad hoc* committee that was formed to report racial incidents and seek protection for members of the African American community. The committee was created in response to a series of incidents involving whites molesting blacks on East End avenues and streetcars in the summer of 1918. The committee, in cooperation with the local NAACP branch, sought and secured promises of protection from Cleveland's director of public safety.[135] In 1919 some one hundred African Americans in Franklin County organized the Columbus Citizens' Law and Order League. The purpose of the league was to prevent African Americans from taking any action that might lead to rioting. The means of achieving the objective was to be "instruction on the advantages of being law abiding citizens."[136]

Prominent African Americans in Ohio publicly stated their views concerning the racial violence of the period. While some of these statements were directed toward whites, others were addressed to blacks. Harry C. Smith, using the editorial voice of the Cleveland *Gazette*, repeatedly warned his readers that they might be subjected to mob violence. Often in the race riots at that time, armed white mobs invaded black residential areas. Smith's repeated advice was that the *Gazette*'s readers should arm themselves in order to protect their homes against such violence. In 1919, following the riots in Chicago and in the District of Columbia, Smith wrote an editorial entitled, "The Mob: A Warning."

He warned, "Cleveland may be the next riot storm-center" and advised, "have a U.S. Amy Riot Gun in your homes."[137] Subsequently, a Cleveland daily newspaper quoted the editorial and implied that Smith was inciting a riot.[138] In response, Smith stated: "*The Gazette* is unalterably opposed to the mob and our readers well know this." Advising citizens to have protection in their homes, Smith asserted, "whether it be against a thief, a would be murderer or a mobocrat is no crime, is not contributory to the same, is not without the law but clearly within the law and good sound advice." In further rebuttal, Smith wrote:

> *The Gazette* stands for law and order! No agency among our people of this community has more constantly and incessantly for years urged our people to be law abiding to the last degree but at the same time to be MEN and WOMEN who know their rights and privileges as citizens, and to insist upon them . . . in a proper way.[139]

The race rioting in contemporary America also was the subject of public comments made in the postwar period by William S. Scarborough, president of traditionally black Wilberforce University near Xenia, Ohio. His audience was the largely white readership of a national magazine, *The Independent*. He offered a means to solve the problems of racial violence. After describing the injustices suffered by African Americans, especially black soldiers, Scarborough said: "There is but one remedy for the riots, and that is justice—a willingness to accord every man his rights—civil and political. . . ." On the one hand he appealed to the whites' sense of fair play. On the other, he noted in very mild language that African Americans would defend themselves physically if necessary. Scarborough wrote:

> The Negro is law-abiding and only occasionally shows a retaliatory spirit. Will not the American white people come halfway—put aside their prejudices and play fair with this people that has done so much to help win the war? Negroes are not rioters, but they can be made so.[140]

Race riots in Chicago and other cities during1919 occurred while the United States was experiencing the postwar Red Scare. Ohioans felt the anti-Bolshevik hysteria that exaggerated the potential for violence by political radicals. In Cleveland parading Socialists were attacked and Socialist headquarters were ransacked on May Day, 1919.[141] One aspect of the Red Scare in Ohio and the nation was an anxiety that the Bolsheviks would successfully recruit African Americans, with violent results. James W. Faulkner, a *Cincinnati Enquirer* columnist, reported that African American political leaders of Cleveland were discussing "overtures of the Socialist party for a union of forces."[142] Faulkner's report named Harry C. Smith, who was a businessman, ardent capitalist, and lifelong Republican. Speaking as the proprietor of the Cleveland *Gazette*, Smith scoffed at Faulkner's assertions and added: "Negro leaders of [Cleveland] . . . are impatiently waiting for the opportunity to vote a straight Republican ticket at the next national election. They want no union with other parties. . . ."[143] Subsequently, reports were circulated that International Workers of the World agents were attempting to incite blacks to mob violence in Akron, Cleveland, and other Ohio cities.[144] Early in October 1919, Akron police raided International Workers of the World headquarters in that city, arrested its organizers and confiscated pamphlets. The pamphlets were reportedly "violent in tone"; that is, they urged blacks to retaliate against whites for injustices they had suffered.[145] Yet there were no reports of black Ohioans initiating retaliatory violence against whites. These fears about the loyalty of African Americans, Bolshevism, and violence are illuminated by current studies examining the federal government's surveillance of alleged African American radicals during the war.[146]

New research comments on issues of wartime patriotism among African Americans.[147] In Ohio, the fulfillment of wartime citizenship responsibilities was used to buttress claims to citizenship rights. Many blacks backed the war, professed loyalty to the war's democratic ideals, and then called for the realization of these war aims. Black men joined the armed services as volunteers and draftees. Some black Ohioans were inducted directly into the United States Army. Others entered the national service as volunteer members of Ohio's state militia units. African Americans from Ohio served in combat and noncombat roles. Black Ohioans enrolled in the Officer Training School at Fort Des Moines, Iowa, and in Students' Army Training Corps programs on college campuses. African Americans from Ohio were among the military officers, physicians, female nurses, and war correspondents of World War I. Some of the black combat units representing Ohio won war honors. Meanwhile, African Americans on the home front in Ohio did their bit for the war effort, for example, by backing the government's war loan campaigns. The African American contributions to the defense of democracy during the war made black Ohioans feel even more entitled to racial equality under the law.[148]

During the conflict, the United States War Department created two black combat organizations: the 92nd Division, draftees, and the 93rd Division (Provisional), largely National Guardsmen. These black divisions were trained at a variety of camps in the United States, sent overseas at different times, and assigned to various divisions of the French army. A large proportion of the black Ohioans who served in World War I were draftees in the National Army. Under the Selective Service Act of May 1917, 7,861 blacks and 139,695 whites from Ohio were drafted for duty in the war.[149] Many Ohio draftees, both black and white, were trained in Ohio at Camp Sherman near Chillicothe.[150] Ohio's black draftees served in 92nd Division units including the 317th Engineers Regiment, the 317th Engineers Train, the 325th Field Signal Battalion, and the 365th Infantry Regiment.[151]

Many black Ohioans were schooled as officers in various officers training camps. Some entered the Officers Training School at Fort Des Moines, Iowa. Eighteen Ohio men were among those who received commissions at Fort Des Moines in October 1917. Two were commissioned as captains, nine as first lieutenants, and seven as second lieutenants.[152] Later, many other black Ohioans received commissions.[153] Wilberforce University, a traditionally black college in southwest Ohio, alone sent two hundred African American students to the regular army's officers training camps.[154] Wilberforce University also participated in the Students' Army Training Corps Program involving about five hundred fifty educational institutions nationwide, including approximately twenty African American institutions. The program's purpose was to use educational facilities to complement the training programs of the regular army camps.[155]

The Surgeon General's Office, United States Army, accepted few of the African American physicians and nurses who wanted to serve in the war.[156] Charles Garvin, a Cleveland physician, was an exception. Garvin, a lieutenant, was a member of an otherwise white hospital contingent created in Cleveland in the summer of 1917 for immediate service in France. Eventually he was transferred to the medical section at Fort Des Moines because he was an African American.[157] Garvin subsequently attained the rank of captain and commanded the African American 366th Ambulance Corps, which served in France.[158] Until the war was nearly over, the Surgeon General's Office and the Red Cross refused black women who volunteered for the nursing service; then in July 1918, the authorities accepted about a half dozen African American nurses, four of whom were assigned to Camp Sherman in Ohio.[159]

Many black Ohioans volunteered for military service in the Ohio National Guard's Ninth Separate Battalion, a black unit that was organized in 1881. The battalion was composed of Companies A–D, stationed in Springfield, Columbus, Dayton, and Cleveland respectively. As war loomed during 1916–1917 certain socially and politically prominent

African Americans across Ohio made an elaborate and persistent effort to obtain governmental approval of their proposal to enlarge the black battalion to a regiment. The proposed regiment's advocates used their direct acquaintances with whites in authority positions, including the Ohio governor, the Ohio adjutant general, and most notably the Wilson administration's secretary of war, who was Clevelander Newton D. Baker. Ultimately, their proposition was rejected but not before it reached the desk of President Woodrow Wilson.[160] At first the black battalion was sent with the Ohio Guard to Alabama for training at Camp Sheridan.[161] Later, it was transferred to Camp Stuart in Virginia, where it was designated as the Second Battalion of the 372nd Regiment in the 93rd Division that was composed of black national guard units of many states. At Camp Stuart, two black Clevelanders, Major John C. Fulton and Captain William R. Green, were reportedly retired by reason of physical disability. The black press suspected that the alleged ill health was being used as an excuse to remove black officers above the rank of captain.[162] The Ohio battalion embarked for France with the 372nd Regiment on March 30, 1918.[163]

The 372nd Regiment, with its contingent of Ohio National Guardsmen, was one of the two combat regiments in the African American 93rd Division that were brigaded with the famous 157th or "Red Hand" Division of the French Army. The 372nd Regiment's most notable combat duty was done under heavy shelling in defense of "Hill 304" in the Verdun Sector during the summer 1918. A press report about black men defending "Hill 304" stated:

> [A] company of the Old Ninth Ohio Battalion . . . laid in an open field all night, awaiting orders to go into action, while all the time the Germans were dumping 210 shells and 88 machine gun fire at them. But even in the face of such a murderous fire, the line stood firm. Anderson Lee and William Chenault, of Dayton, were killed.[164]

The 372nd Regiment also participated in the Champaigne offensive in September 1918. General Goybet, Commander of the 157th Division, praised the "dash" and heroism of the men of the black regiments under his command. Prior to disembarkation from France, Vice Admiral Moreau decorated the colors of the 372nd Regiment with the Croix de Guerre.[165]

African Americans aided the war effort on the home front in the United States as well as in Europe. President William S. Scarborough of Wilberforce University was a member of Governor James M. Cox's War

Cabinet in the Ohio Branch of the Council of National Defense.[166] Blacks generously supported the five war loan campaigns.[167] The Fourth Liberty loan, for instance, received contributions of fifteen thousand dollars from pupils at Stowe School in Cincinnati, five thousand dollars from Big Four Roundhouse employees in Columbus, and over four thousand dollars from coal miners at St. Clairsville.[168] The African American press in the state played an active role in promoting the loan campaigns.[169] Journalists Harry C. Smith of the Cleveland *Gazette* and Ralph W. Tyler of Columbus attended an extraordinary national conference of black newsmen in June 1918 that was held to discuss press coverage of African Americans in the war. In September 1918, the Wilson Administration's Committee on Public Information designated Tyler "as a regularly commissioned war correspondent to specialize on the conditions surrounding the colored troops in France. . . ."[170] Tyler had served in various departments of the *Columbus Evening Dispatch* and the *Ohio State Journal*. He had been a contributing editor for the African American *Cleveland Advocate* and secretary of the National Colored Soldiers Comfort Committee. Tyler reached France just prior to the Armistice and observed some of the final combat of the war. His dispatches included glowing accounts of the African Americans' role in the war.[171]

African Americans assisted private organizations, including the Red Cross and the YMCA, which sponsored separate social centers for black and white trainees. These facilities were intended to maintain the soldiers' morale while they were in training in the United States. African Americans, for instance, staffed "Community Houses" for black soldiers that the War Camp Community Service sponsored in many Ohio cities. The establishment of "Community Houses" for soldiers foreshadowed the establishment of similar projects for the greater African American community during the war in many cities in Ohio and across the country.[172]

What was the war's significance in the history of Ohio's black-white relations? African American participation in World War I raised a new spirit of resistance to the color line in Ohio. This spirit, which arose in Ohio and elsewhere, underlay what historians of black history in the United States have long since called "the New Negro" movement of the 1920s.[173] African Americans who performed military service to defend democracy in Europe experienced a white society in France that was relatively free of racial discrimination. The wartime crusade for democracy abroad and at home inspired African Americans to greater insistence on equal rights promised in the democratic ideal. Like many African Americans who were in France during the war, Ohioan Ralph W. Tyler appreciated the French people's comparative lack of racial prejudice. He wrote: "I am stuck on France. I feel free over here—absolutely . . . free. Were I a young man I would never return, and as it is, were it not for the fight I ABSOLUTELY KNOW we face on returning I would prefer to stay here where you have real democracy. But to stay, and fail to get into the fight back home would stamp me as a coward, which I am not."[174] The war effort in Europe and on the home front inspired other black Ohioans to contest the color line. Blacks objected to the color line in military and civilian life during the war. The black press in Ohio, for instance, called attention to the inequitable shelter and treatment accorded blacks in military encampments and to the exclusion of blacks from the officers' corps above certain ranks and from the nursing corps.[175] In 1918, black parents in the southern Ohio town of Gallipolis challenged the existence of an inferior segregated high school that they had tolerated for years. Explaining why the parents acted when they did, a local observer wrote: "But with hundreds of thousands of our boys fighting to make 'the world safe for democracy,' and the race at home being loyal to its government in every particular, it became our duty in this city, to see that this 'democracy' here did not degenerate into a mere catchphrase."[176] The struggle to promote the nation's democratic principles at home increasingly required the use of organization.

In summary, persistence and change shaped the struggle to affirm equal rights and to sustain the needs of African Americans in Ohio during the period 1915–1920. Early nineteenth century regional differences in the nature of protest persisted through 1920; however, the style of African American leadership changed with the times. The enormous proliferation of sundry kinds of voluntary associations was a characteristic of modernization in the United States following the Civil War, especially in the Progressive Era after the turn of the century. Americans of practically every color, class, and gender became increasingly organized.[177] Blacks in Ohio, for instance, joined affiliates of the NAACP and the National Urban League, founded in the decade after 1910. In Ohio, this was a decade of transition from African American leadership exercised through informal networks of prominent individuals to leadership conducted through organizations. The leadership changeover was incomplete in 1920. Ohio's NAACP branches and Urban League affiliates were still approaching maturity at decade's end. These new organizations had created bureaucratic forms, defined issues of concern, and set some precedents for action, establishing the basis for more effective work in the future. Meantime, old networks of influential individuals were intact and functioning, although weakened a bit by advancing age, competition from new organizations, and decreasing Republican party support of African American interests in the partisan arena. The new-style organized leadership coexisted with the old-style individual networks in the period 1915–1920. Sometimes the two leadership sets addressed the same particular cause, each working independently of the other and each using its own methods and techniques. The rivalry's future in the 1920s was predictable in the teens. The new organized leadership was young and gathering strength while the old one was showing some signs of decline.

PART TWO

The Twenties and Culminating Trends

CHAPTER FOUR

Rising "Black Metropolises"

The urbanization of Ohio's black population reached a new level in the 1920s. This was the consequence of the black migration to Ohio cities that began slowly in the nineteenth century, gained momentum after 1890, accelerated sharply during World War I, and persisted at a high rate in the 1920s. What may be called "black metropolises" existed for the first time in Cleveland, Cincinnati, and Columbus. Various words are used to identify these great black urban enclaves that matured in the United States during the twenties, but a wholly proper name is elusive because no one term is entirely and literally descriptive of them. In the 1960s "ghetto" was the term that urban historians preferred.[1] Each large black area in urban Ohio was a ghetto, which is defined as a district where an ethnic group is required to dwell. A ghetto perspective that employs residential proscription as a lens tends to narrowly focus attention on problems in black urban life while marginalizing its benefits. In the 1940s, sociologists St. Clair Drake and Horace R. Cayton used the phrase "black metropolis" in a figurative reference to black urban districts.[2] Their study featured urban pathologies; however, the "black metropolis" is a metaphor broad enough to cover discussion focusing on positive as well as negative aspects of the black urban experience. The "metropolis" concept in the history of the modernization in the United States views the urban center as being at once an incubus of social ills and an engine driving opportunity, expansion, prosperity, and special accomplishment.[3]

In many respects this metropolis model was reflected in black Cleveland, black Cincinnati, and black Columbus. The size of the black population concentration in each of these urban centers was comparable to that of a large city. In a sense, these were black cities within cities. Actually, they were very large districts with nearly all-black neighborhoods. Growth was the norm in many categories of life in Ohio's black metropolises. For instance, as black populations increased, black residential areas, businesses, professions, hospitals, and churches expanded accordingly and in proportions unprecedented in the state. Ohio's black urban society experienced a measure of the decade's prosperity, which was spread unevenly, in the form of relative affluence for the business and professional classes and some occupational gains for working people. Meanwhile, African Americans in Ohio industriously constructed urban structures of many kinds, economic, social, cultural, and political. Consequently, Ohio's black metropolises generally possessed the spectrum of urban institutions found in cities across the state and the nation. This indicates that local people in Ohio's black neighborhoods saw opportunities and realized them. The most notable achievements were in the building of essentially black cities, each with its wide-ranging institutional structures. Characteristic urban problems, as well as possibilities, existed in Ohio's black metropolises. These troubles, such as poverty and crime, were complicated by color lines that circumscribed the black neighborhoods. This study shows that African Americans in Ohio cities were not passive in the face of life's challenges in the twenties, but active and assertive in seizing urban opportunities and in combating urban problems.

Impacted by the black migration of the 1920s, Ohio's African American urban population grew, reaching unprecedented raw numbers. Black population growth in Ohio occurred largely in major urban centers. In 1930, 72 percent of all black Ohioans lived in cities whose populations were 50,000 or more. Cincinnati, Cleveland, and Columbus each possessed black populations over 30,000 in 1930, and black totals in other Ohio cities exceeded 10,000. (See table A2.) Growth during the 1920s was greatest in northern Ohio's major urban centers, where black population more than doubled in Cleveland, Toledo, and Youngstown. In the southern area, Dayton's black population nearly doubled and Cincinnati's grew by almost three-fifths. In central Ohio, Columbus' black population grew by almost half, but Springfield's rose less than two-tenths. African Americans in 1930 were 12 percent or less of the whole population in each large Ohio city.[4] African Americans statewide rose to 309,304, which was 4.7 percent of Ohio's total population in 1930.[5] (See table A1.)

In the 1920s, as in the past, African American migrants were attracted to Ohio because its social-economic conditions were more favorable than those of the South. An impoverished potential migrant from Houston, Texas, expressed a typical motive of black migrants when he inquired about opportunities in Columbus, Ohio. The Texan asked "whether there be any chance for the man Seeking work and a place for himself and family to sleep at night with both eyes shut?"[6] He added: "I am a married man, wife and 2 children and wants to locate where my children will have a chance in life to make good and wages is beyond starvation prices of course. No need to tell you of Texas. You are reading."[7] Historian Peter Gottlieb points out that a spirit of hope was characteristic of black southerners migrating to cities in the East and Midwest during World War I and the 1920s. Economic circumstances in much of this period supported a belief that personal advancement was possible for African Americans who seized the initiative and removed from the South.[8]

The rate of black migration to Ohio evidently rose and fell with the degree of economic opportunity in the state. African American workers in Ohio cities experienced general unemployment as postwar economic readjustments caused a depression in 1921–1922.[9] In times of economic difficulty African Americans were usually the first to lose their jobs. In 1921 a local researcher wrote, "Several factories [in Columbus] have indicated that they expect to reduce the number of negro [sic] workers and employ white workers in their stead."[10] However, employment of black workers was relatively high in Ohio between 1922 and 1927. The economy of the state and the nation expanded during this era of business and industrial prosperity. Moreover, the Congressional immigration restriction legislation of 1924 sharply cut the flow of immigration and further reduced the supply of foreign-born white workers. These two factors caused a relatively high demand for African American labor. By the summer of 1922 Ohio employers experienced a labor shortage that was filled in part by black workers. During the summer of 1922, approximately fifteen hundred African Americans from the South migrated to Youngstown and found employment in the steel mills there.[11] Similarly, in June 1923 an African American journalist observed, "Owing to the shortage of labor a number of our people are still migrating from the South to Cleveland."[12] Almost two-fifths of the job applicants placed in work by the Negro Welfare Association of Cleveland in 1923 had been in the city only two months.[13]

Business prosperity in Ohio, as in the country as a whole, continued until near the end of the twenties. Marginal labor was adversely affected as the economic expansion began to level off in the second half of the decade and the introduction of improved industrial technology reduced the need for manual labor. In Columbus, according to one observer, "The depression for marginal labor, especially colored labor, set in as early as 1927."[14] In 1926 Clevelander George A. Myers noted that black migration to Cleveland was "on the wane, the demand for labor not being so great as it was for the past few years."[15] In October 1927 thousands of

African Americans in Cleveland were reportedly unemployed.[16] Thus, black workers began to experience economic difficulty even before the financial disaster of 1929 and the Great Depression that followed it.

During the 1920s black newcomers in Ohio cities, like migrants in earlier times, were required to make a difficult adjustment to urban life in hard circumstances. Obtaining employment and income, at least in the decade's flush years, was often less problematical than finding adequate lodgings. Many African American migrants to Ohio cities were crowded in dwellings that were inadequate for human habitation. The causes of the phenomenon were familiar. Racially exclusive policies of many white property owners still limited the number of dwellings available for occupancy by African Americans. The wartime shortage of new housing continued to exist nationwide into the 1920s. Migrant families and individuals with meager incomes shared rooms with others because separately they could not pay the relatively high rent for scarce housing space in African American areas. During the 1920s shortages of housing were noted across Ohio from Cincinnati to Toledo.[17] Cincinnati Better Housing League information, published in 1926, said: "So as far as new housing goes nothing has been done for the colored population except the [few] houses built by the Model Homes Company [prior to 1920]."[18] In Cincinnati, housing options were further limited when private urban redevelopment enterprises in the Basin area cleared old dwellings available to blacks for the construction of business and club edifices.[19] The Cincinnati Better Housing League reported at mid-decade that Cincinnati's West End was "a highly congested area built up with tenement and business houses, factories and railroads."[20]

Generally the housing open to black migrants in Ohio was old, dilapidated, and comparatively expensive as well as overcrowded. Systematic surveys of African American dwelling units in Columbus indicated that housing conditions of blacks there were far below the average for that city.[21] Despite the inadequate character of rental housing accessible to African Americans in Ohio, blacks were required to pay exceptionally high rental rates. The editor of the Cleveland *Gazette* noted: ". . . our people of this section [of Cleveland] pay higher rent proportionately, for the worst living quarters in the city, than is paid by members of other groups in other sections of the city."[22] Comparing housing costs of black and white tenants in Cincinnati, the city's Better Housing League indicated: "Negro tenants pay higher rent for similar accommodations."[23] The wartime rent profiteering phenomenon continued into the 1920s. In Cincinnati the average rental of tenement flats occupied by black families increased from approximately four dollars per room per month in 1918 to over seven dollars per room per month in 1925."[24]

Contemporaries recognized the connection between high housing costs and residential congestion. In 1922 housing problems created "almost desperate" circumstances for black families in Cincinnati, according to the local Better Housing League. In 1923 a league worker reported that 94 people were occupying 12 rooms in a George Street tenement in Cincinnati's African American West End.[25] In 1925 Clark L. Mack, Labor Commissioner, Cleveland Chamber of Commerce, reported: "High and exorbitant rents are frequently being charged colored people in certain sections of the city [Cleveland] resulting in overcrowding and the spread of disease."[26] Commenting on serious overcrowding in African American areas of Cleveland in 1926, City Health Commissioner Harvey L. Rockwood noted that there were single dwelling units in Cleveland that were occupied by fifteen to twenty people.[27]

Many African Americans residing in Ohio cities during the 1920s were exposed to various social problems that were historically endemic in urban areas where low-income people occupied residential housing that was old, deteriorating, and overcrowded. Among them were serious public health hazards. Ohio public health officials reported that poor housing conditions disproportionately threatened the physical well being of African Americans. The Cincinnati Health Commissioner, Dr. W. H. Peters, asserted that "bad housing" was "the chief predisposing factor" contributing to extraordinary ill health among blacks in Cincinnati during the early 1920s. His statement, published in a 1925 issue of *Cincinnati Sanitary Bulletin*, noted that African Americans contributed more than their "quota to the death toll of Cincinnati from practically every important cause of death."[28] Infant mortality per 1,000 births was greater for blacks in Cincinnati. Almost three times as many black children as white infants died within their birth year. Peters also reported: "As compared to the white race, over four times as many colored people die of tuberculosis per 1,000 of population."[29] Regarding Cincinnati deaths from all causes, the black morality rate was almost double the white death rate per 1,000 persons in 1924.[30] Cleveland Health Commissioner Rockwood made similar points about the effects of overcrowded housing in a paper, "Effect of Negro Migration on Community Health in Cleveland," presented to the National Conference on Social Work in 1926. Rockwood stated that the death rate among blacks in Cleveland increased 80 percent from 1920 to 1926 while the death rate among other Clevelanders remained nearly stable for the same period.[31] According to statewide vital statistics Ohio mortality rates were still about 70 percent higher for blacks than whites in 1930, respectively 18.8 and 11.1 deaths per 1,000 persons. Death rates and presumably health status improved marginally for both blacks and whites by the end of the decade.[32]

Likewise, crime threatened African American residential areas that became increasingly congested as black migration to Ohio cities continued during the 1920s. Crime reached new levels in some African American sections of Cincinnati, Cleveland, and Columbus by mid-decade. Writing in 1926, Cincinnati black weekly editor Wendell P. Dabney said: "Queen City crime runs riot as never before, and in the 'Black Belt,' that is, the 'downtown tenderloin' district, vice . . . rears its hideous head. . . ." He observed, for instance, that prostitution still was being practiced openly in many downtown public places in this district. Further, Dabney lamented, "The proportion of colored criminals [in Cincinnati] is appalling."[33] The causes were evident to him. In previous years thousands of black migrants from the "most benighted southern counties" had settled in Cincinnati. He explained: "They crowded into the tenements, already over full, . . . in the West End. Walnut Hills and the suburbs, the habitat of very reputable [black] families had no room for these refugees. The terrible congestion brought both sexes of all ages together. . . . The glaring poverty . . . , permeated all phases of daily existence, intensifying its horrors, furnishing ever-insistent incentive to theft or harlotry."[34] In addition to difficult living conditions, Dabney said that the sources of crime in impoverished black residential areas were the liquor trade and lax law enforcement caused by political influences.

Crime increased in Cleveland neighborhoods where black migrants were crowded together. For example, one issue of an African American weekly reported several murders committed in the area of Central and Scovill Avenues during the previous weekend. Putting the incidents in context, the Cleveland *Gazette's* report noted: "'Speakeasies,' 'Boot-leggers,' 'dope sellers,' prostitutes, gamblers, loafers, etc., are so numerous and work so openly and brazenly that it is not at all strange that here of late practically every Saturday and Sunday are almost as bloody days, with many crimes, as there were last Saturday and Sunday. They yell, curse and swear, using the vilest of language with the greatest impunity in the public highways at anytime of the day or night, and in the hearing of women and children, too and little or no effort is made to stop them. It seems as if the police fear to say much if anything to them."[35] Others, including Cleveland Councilman Peter Witt, believed that inadequate policing contributed to the growth of crime in some black districts. Witt, who several years earlier had been special assistant to Progressive Mayor Tom L. Johnson, excoriated Cleveland city officials for the lawlessness in the largely black third police precinct. This white councilman stated: "The vicious and criminal element operates in the 'Roaring Third' precinct through the connivance of city authorities. The

'Roaring Third' does not mean that the great majority of people in the district are vicious, but that the criminals are suffered to operate there."[36]

Statistics drawn from police and court records in the 1920s showed relatively high crime rates in Ohio's black urban communities while migration from the South was ongoing. Although the police rarely interfered with the various illicit vice enterprises in black urban areas, a disproportionate number of African Americans in Ohio were arrested, convicted, and sentenced. Undoubtedly, worsening housing conditions in some black neighborhoods contributed to social disorganization and crime; however, the crime statistics among African Americans also reflected evident racial bias in the Ohio criminal justice system. A disproportionate number of blacks were arrested and sentenced. In both Cincinnati and Cleveland, the percentage of black youngsters committed to juvenile detention homes was significantly greater than the black proportion of the city's population.[37] In Columbus, the juvenile delinquency rate among African American youngsters was the highest of any ethnic group there.[38] Among those arrested in Cincinnati, blacks were more likely to receive jail sentences than whites. The disparity was evidenced in statistics on the "Number of Arrests, 1920 to October 1, 1925," provided by the Cincinnati Police Department. In an average year during that time blacks composed about 17 percent of the arrests in Cincinnati, but blacks comprised approximately 47 percent of those sentenced to jail from June 1924 to June 1925.[39] Meanwhile, African Americans were about 11 percent of Cincinnati's population. In criminal courts across the state, proportionately more blacks than whites faced incarceration. In 1930, when African Americans were 4.7 percent of state's population, blacks were 23.8 percent of all prisoners received from Ohio courts.[40]

The social-economic problems accompanying the black migration to Ohio in the 1920s received more public attention than the movement's positive effects. The enlargement of black populations was fundamental to economic, social, cultural, and political advances in Ohio's African American urban communities during the decade. A black community capable of supporting a broad institutional life existed in each of several Ohio urban centers by 1930. Increasing numbers of employed persons further raised aggregate income in black communities. Although severely restricted by racial bias, upward occupational mobility boosted incomes of some African Americans. The resulting growth of the African American consumer markets in Ohio cities fostered the continued expansion of black business and professional classes. Also during the 1920s, unprecedented numbers of black institutions, especially churches, were founded with the financial support of black working people.

In Ohio during the 1920s African Americans' group purchasing power rose with the increasing number of black Ohioans earning wages and salaries. Gainfully employed black men and women increased from 99,193 to 145,379 between 1920 and 1930.[41] The improved occupational status of black Ohioans also increased the group's combined income. The percentage of employed black males working in industrial occupations in the 1920s was well above the prewar figure. In Cleveland, almost half of the employed black males were in manufacturing and mechanical industries in 1930, while only about a fifth of the men were in domestic and personal service jobs.[42] Meanwhile, in Columbus and Cincinnati about 40 to 45 percent of employed black men worked in those industries.[43] In Ohio industries, a larger proportion of blacks worked in semiskilled and skilled positions than before the war. In exceptional instances, Ohio industry employed African American workers in white-collar and supervisory positions as well as in skilled and semiskilled jobs. Cleveland's Negro Welfare Association placed six personnel workers and eight foremen in local industries in 1920.[44] In Cleveland, scores of black women operated power machines in the plants of the Liberty Garment Company and the Manual Products Company.[45] In 1921 the Jeffrey Manufacturing Company of Columbus employed an African American, Harry Alexander, in its bookkeeping department.[46] Even so, most black industrial workers in the state were employed in unskilled labor occupations. In 1930, 80 percent of black male industrial workers in Cincinnati were in the unskilled labor category, while the like figure was 65 percent in Columbus and 61 percent in Cleveland.[47]

African American occupational gains made in Ohio during World War I were maintained during the 1920s, but they were somewhat eroded. The proportions of employed black males in skilled occupations, in semiskilled work, and in unskilled labor in Ohio industry were less favorable to African Americans in 1930 than in 1920. The occupational standing of black Ohioans, however, was considerably higher in 1930 than in 1910. In Cleveland, for example, the proportion of employed black men occupied in manufacturing and mechanical industries grew from 22 percent in 1910 to 48 percent in 1930, and the actual number of black male industrial workers rose from 755 to 12,121.[48]

While African Americans experienced some upward occupational mobility in the 1920s, domestic and personal service work was still a significant source of income for black Ohioans, especially females. The proportion of employed black males working in domestic and personal service increased marginally in major Ohio cities. About a fifth of the employed black men in Cleveland held domestic and personal service jobs in 1930. Traditionally, African American women in Ohio were largely restricted to domestic and personal service occupations. A relatively high percentage of employed black women worked in industry during World War I, but those gains were lost in the next decade. The proportion of employed black females working in industry was smaller in 1930 than in 1910. Conversely, the percentage of black working females with domestic and personal service jobs was larger in 1930 than in 1910. In Cincinnati 90 percent of employed black women were domestic and personal service workers in 1930. At the same time, over 121,000 black women were working and earning incomes in Ohio.[49]

Black occupational gains in the state after 1910 were marginal because the Ohio color line in employment was still much in effect. White owners and managers of commercial enterprises remained least inclined to employ African Americans. Influential black Clevelander George A. Myers reported an example of that form of racial discrimination in 1926. He wrote: "We have many . . . graduates of High Schools and Colleges, capable of office, banking and other commercial opportunities, but like every avenue which leads to the good, are closed in the face of negro [sic] youth. . . . . There is not a bank in Cleveland that employs any of our group as a clerk, teller or bookkeeper, scarcely an office that uses any as clerks or stenographers and no stores, though our business runs up in the millions; [sic] that employ any as sales-women, salesmen or clerks."[50] African Americans largely obtained occupations in commerce through self-employment or employment in black businesses.

Black migration during the 1920s boosted business in black commercial districts founded before the war, for example, Central Avenue in Cleveland, Fifth Street in Cincinnati, and East Long Street in Columbus. Black-owned business also developed in newer black neighborhoods of Ohio cities. In contrast to prewar times when the black population was much smaller, there were enough black consumers to support relatively large numbers of African American enterprises by 1930. Commenting on local black business activity in 1922, Columbus Urban League executive secretary Nimrod B. Allen said: "There are nearly one hundred business enterprises on East Long Street and vicinity, embracing haberdasheries, photographers, optometrists, music shops, music studios, beauty parlors, printing establishments, corporations, tailors, etc."[51] Writing in Cincinnati at mid-decade, black weekly editor Wendell P. Dabney observed: ". . . [W]e have hundreds of business houses. A multiplicity of certain kinds, a scarcity of others. Naturally those necessitating small capital . . . are the most numerous." He indicated that the more successful black enterprises in Cincinnati were barbershops, beauty parlors, restaurants, lodging houses, undertaking establishments and a chain of drug stores.[52] In 1926 local African American civic leader George A. Myers listed and discussed types of black businesses in Cleveland. Building construction, insurance, and finance companies were noted. Myers also referred to "A few small stores and several very prosperous Undertakers and Real Estate Dealers."[53] Actually Myers understated the magnitude of Cleveland retail stores owned by African Americans. According to the census bureau there were 215 Cleveland stores "operated by Negro proprietors" in 1929. The total payroll of these stores was $108,666 and their total net sales were over a million dollars.[54]

The 1920s black migration expanded potential subscriber pools of black weekly newspapers in Ohio cities. This enabled proprietors of well-established black newspapers to continue in business through the decade and motivated other African Americans to start new weeklies. Although readership grew in the twenties, black weeklies were still financially challenged and only the fittest survived. Among the prewar black weeklies that continued publication through the twenties were editor Wendell P. Dabney's Cincinnati *Union* and editor John Rives's Dayton *Forum*. William B. Johnson published and edited the *Black and White Chronicle* in Akron from 1924 into 1930. Black newspapers published for two years or less in the twenties included the Cincinnati *Optimist*, the Springfield *Informer*, and the Akron *Informer*. Short-lived black weeklies published in Columbus late in the decade were the *Columbus Weekly News*, the *Ohio Recorder*, the *Columbus Voice*, and the *Ohio Torch*.[55]

Cleveland produced more sustained black newspaper enterprises than any other Ohio city in the 1920s. Harry C. Smith maintained continuous publication of the Cleveland *Gazette* during the decade. The *Gazette* sometimes competed with as many as three local black weeklies in the 1920s. The *Cleveland Advocate* was published from World War I to 1922. The *Cleveland Call* was founded in 1920 by Garrett A. Morgan as an advertising medium for his business involving the manufacturing and sales of hair and beauty products. Also in 1920, the Cleveland *Post* started publication as the voice of a black fraternal organization. Published intermittently, these new weeklies were financially disappointing. Ormande O. Forte, former editor of the defunct *Cleveland Advocate*, reentered the competition by founding the *Cleveland Herald* in 1924. The *Herald* was published irregularly during the rest of the decade. Attempting to survive this competition, the owners of the *Post* and the *Cleveland Call* pooled their resources by merging their weeklies in 1926. The new *Cleveland Call and Post* was not financially successful until the 1930s. Remarkably, the *Gazette*, the *Herald*, and the *Call and Post* existed in Cleveland at decade's end.[56]

In line with a prewar and wartime trend, Ohio's new African American enterprises catered to blacks rather than whites in the 1920s. The postwar decade saw further decline of the old style black businesses providing personal services to white patrons. In the previous century, successful black businesses usually relied on white patronage. In time more whites entered the personal service business and acquired a larger share of its white clientele. In 1930 black tailors, barbers, and food caterers with white clienteles were exceptional in Ohio. In Cincinnati, white hotels provided food-catering services for large social events of the kind previously handled by financially successful black caterers. Some African Americans, who were former hotel cooks and waiters, made minimal profits by catering smaller affairs like house parties. A few of Cincinnati's older black food caterers, including Edith Fossett Miller, maintained profitable businesses into the 1920s. Many of Cincinnati's old and wealthy white families employed the Fossett catering services for generations. This Cincinnati family was descended from the Fossetts who were in charge of Thomas Jefferson's Monticello kitchens and dining room.[57]

Hundreds of African American barbers served black patrons in Ohio during the 1920s.[58] Unlike prewar times in Ohio, there were very few black barbershops frequented by whites in 1930. Still patronized by whites in 1926, Skillman's barbershop in Cincinnati was exceptional. It was one of the few remaining black barbershops occupying high rent buildings in downtown Cincinnati. Skillman's location on lower Vine Street previously accommodated the large shop of Fountain Lewis, Jr., who learned the barbering trade from his father. In earlier times, Fountain Lewis, Sr.'s shop in Cincinnati was "the great resort of bankers and aristocrats," according to Wendell P. Dabney, who noted, "Grant, Lincoln and other famous dignitaries were soothed into slumber by the rhythmic music of his scissors."[59] Black barbers received little competition from whites in the elder Fountain Lewis's time. Eventually, in Cincinnati and elsewhere, more whites entered the business, and younger whites were more inclined to patronize white barbers. After years of successful business Fountain Lewis, Jr. closed his large barbershop and joined his son in an undertaking enterprise.[60]

In Cleveland, George A. Myers's experience reflected changing white attitudes toward African American barbers. Myers was employed in a Cleveland hotel barbershop in 1879 when he was a young man. Backed by prominent white men in 1888, Myers became the owner of the new Hollenden Hotel's barbershop. Offering the most modern facilities and outstanding service, Myers's shop was reputed as a fashionable place in one of the city's major hotels. Local and visiting dignitaries including some famous persons, such as Marcus Hanna, patronized the Hollenden barbershop. In 1920 Myers employed 35 barbers, hairstylists for women, manicurists, podiatrists, porters, and cashiers. When Myers announced his retirement plans in 1930, the hotel management informed him that the barbershop's African American staff would be replaced with whites after his departure.[61] Also in 1930, the prominent black Clevelander Charles W. Chesnutt wrote: "The increase in white barbershops [in Cleveland] has almost put the Negro barber out of business, so far as white patronage is concerned, and the Barber's Union, in which no Negro is admitted to membership, has been trying to complete their ruin by proposing a state barbers' licensing law, requiring examination and acceptance by a committee dominated by the union."[62]

Black undertaking businesses grew in Ohio during the 1920s when African American families ordinarily used the services of black undertakers. In 1926 local weekly editor Wendell P. Dabney wrote: "Over a half century ago, when Negroes died [in Cincinnati], white undertakers buried them. Now very rarely does any white undertaker bury a colored person."[63] Greater black mortality naturally followed the extraordinary black in-migration and the African American population growth in Ohio after 1915. More black families needed funeral services, and new black undertaking firms met that demand in Ohio cities. African American funeral businesses expanded most in urban centers with the largest black populations. In Cleveland, J. Walter Wills' "House of Wills" and nine other black funeral homes employed 32 African American undertakers in 1930. Wills undoubtedly was the most enterprising and financially successful black funeral home proprietor in Cleveland and perhaps in the state during the decade. There were considerably more African American funeral homes in Cleveland, Cincinnati, and Columbus than in other Ohio cities. In 1930, five black undertakers were employed in Dayton.[64]

In Cincinnati, many blacks entered the funeral business early in the decade once African American deaths in the city increased sharply, rising from 674 to 921 during 1920–1923. Seventeen black undertakers served there in 1926. Relative newcomers to Cincinnati were among those who formed new black undertaking businesses in the city. Former school principal Inez Renfro and United States postal employee St. Julian Renfro came to Cincinnati from the South in 1913. This married couple entered business together as funeral directors in 1922 when he finished training at the Cincinnati College of Embalming. Another wedded pair, Ruth H. Walker and Leroy J. Walker, also opened a funeral home in 1922. Born in North Carolina, the Walkers moved to Cincinnati in 1914 and eventually enrolled in the Cincinnati College of Embalming. After passing the state board's examination, they were certified as Class A embalmers in 1920. Some new black undertakers were older veterans of successful businesses in Cincinnati. Fountain Lewis, Jr., the former proprietor of a large down-town barbershop, invested in his son Fred's undertaking venture. Walter S. Houston, an experienced grocer who owned Cincinnati property valued at $50,000, also launched a new black funeral estab-lishment early in the decade.[65]

In 1930 Ohio's new black retail businesses were in black neighbor-hoods, and with few exceptions their customers were African Americans. The wartime expansion of African American retail stores continued dur-ing the 1920s, but at a somewhat slower rate. Between 1920 and 1930 the number of black retail dealers more than doubled in Cleveland, growing 35 percent in Cincinnati and 13 percent in Columbus. The dramatic transformation of black retail business in Cleveland was most graphical-ly indicated by the growth of the actual number of black retail dealers from 28 in 1910 to 286 in 1930.[66] In Ohio statewide, black proprietors operated 790 stores with about $400,000.00 in total payroll and over $4,400,000.00 in total net sales in 1929.[67]

During the 1920s African Americans in Ohio entered the real estate business in greater numbers than ever before. Continuing black migra-tion to Ohio cities maintained a high demand for housing in traditional-ly African American neighborhoods and their vicinities. Between 1920 and 1930 the numbers of black real estate agents and officials quadrupled in Cincinnati, tripled in Columbus, and doubled in Cleveland. In 1930 there were 39 black realtors in Cleveland, 18 in Columbus, and 14 in Cincinnati.[68] Since real estate clients needed financial assistance in the purchase of homes, some black entrepreneurs were associated with both mortgage granting companies and realty firms. The most enterprising African American then in Cleveland undoubtedly was Herbert Chauncey, a Georgia native, who acquired a license to practice law in Ohio. Supported by local African American investors, Herbert Chauncey organized a savings bank and a real estate company in Cleveland. Likewise Chauncey established an insurance company and a weekly newspaper, the Cleveland *Post*.[69] Born in Covington, Kentucky, Horace Sudduth was a prominent African American civic leader in Cincinnati and a successful entrepreneur. He was the owner of the Sudduth Real Estate Agency and president of a savings association owned by African Americans in Cincinnati.[70]

New black-owned savings banks in Ohio were a welcome alternative to white-owned banks that practiced racial discrimination in making home mortgage loans. It was, however, the growing numbers of potential African American savers and credit consumers that most impelled the proliferation of black savings and loan associations in Ohio during the 1920s. In the decades before World War I, when the black population was relatively small, African American banking enterprises in Ohio usually were short lived.[71] The Star Building and Loan Association of Toledo was Ohio's only African American banking institution when it was incorporated in 1913.[72] Several black financial enterprises appeared in Ohio after the war. Organized by Herbert S. Chauncey and other black investors in 1919, Cleveland's Empire Building and Loan Association prospered during the 1920s as the value of its deposits, capital stock, and assets grew. Meanwhile the Cleveland Finance Company existed under black ownership. In 1922 African Americans in Columbus owned the Credential Mortgage Company, the Adelphi Loan and Savings Company, and the Columbus Industrial Mortgage and Security Company.[73] African Americans in Cincinnati, including Horace Sudduth, established the Industrial Savings and Loan Company. Black investors also started the East End Investment and Loan Company in Cincinnati. Each maintained a branch office in Cincinnati's Walnut Hills area as well as a main office in 1926. Late in the decade, African Americans in Akron formed the People's System Finance Company.[74]

New African American insurance businesses also appeared in Ohio during the 1920s. Formed in 1919, Columbus' Supreme Life and Casualty Insurance Company was the most ambitious black insurance firm in the state during the decade. In 1922 Supreme Life extended its operations in Ohio and entered insurance markets in West Virginia, Arkansas, and the District of Columbia.[75] In 1928 the Columbus-based insurance company purchased a building in Cincinnati and opened a branch office there.[76] The Anchor Life Insurance Company, another black enterprise, existed in Cleveland by 1926.[77] Some insurance agents in Ohio represented out-of-state African American enterprises, including the Columbian Fraternal Association.[78] These black ventures hired African Americans to sell insurance; consequently the number of black insurance agents in Ohio increased sharply between 1920 and 1930, from 8 to 95 in Cleveland, 2 to 29 in Cincinnati, and 8 to 26 in Columbus.[79] Major black insurance companies in Chicago and Atlanta during this period are subjects of recent book length studies.[80]

The widening scope of black commerce was accompanied by the rising importance of African American business associations in Ohio during the 1920s. Relative newcomers as well as long-time Ohio residents contributed to these African American business activities. Writing in 1922, Columbus Urban League executive secretary Nimrod B. Allen stated: "Columbus' Negro citizens have made very noticeable and rapid progress within the last few years. The citizens credit this progress to the influx of Southern Negroes . . . who were used to being in business for themselves."[81] Recent scholarship calls attention to the success of black business enterprises in the South prior to World War I.[82] Newcomers contributed much to the Business and Professional Men's Club that was affiliated with Columbus' black YMCA Spring Street branch. According to Allen, the club was meant to offer black businessmen what the Kiwanis and Rotary gave to whites. It met weekly and, according to Allen, was "addressed by men of affairs in and out of Columbus" who inspired members to take actions that were responsible for much black business progress in Columbus. An insurance company, finance companies, and other enterprises grew out of the club's network of black businessmen.[83] Elsewhere, energetic entrepreneur Herbert S. Chauncey successfully led an effort to organize the Cleveland Business Men's Association in 1925. The Cincinnati Business Men's Association already existed in 1926 when the Akron Negro Business League was organized.[84]

Black professional groups in Ohio were greatly enlarged under the impetus of the black in-migration during the 1920s and the consequent African American population growth in the state. Ohio's black clergymen, teachers, physicians, and lawyers devoted their services almost entirely to the needs of African Americans and saw white clients even less often than in the recent past. Black professional classes expanded at high rates between 1920 and 1930; however, while there were some exceptions, the growth of black professional groups did not keep up with the increase of black population in Ohio cities. Most black professionals in Ohio were clergymen or teachers, largely women. Increases in the number of black teachers were greater in the downstate cities that maintained schools whose students and staff were all African Americans. Most black ministers served in Ohio's three largest cities. Black physicians and attorneys also increased at high rates in some Ohio cities, but there were relatively few African American doctors and lawyers anywhere in the state.[85] (See table A3.)

Although the black business class experienced unparalleled prosperity in Ohio during the 1920s, its gains were relative and limited. Expressing the optimism of the decade, local Urban League officer Nimrod B. Allen asserted: "it is no wild fancy to predict that the next generation will find a score or more of Negroes of real wealth from business accumulations on [Columbus'] East Long Street; even now [1922] we have those who count their monthly incomes in the thousands."[86] Yet, only in comparison with the precarious existence of the black business and professional communities in prewar years could the situation in the 1920s be regarded as progress. Two prominent African American elders in Cleveland, George A. Myers and Charles W. Chesnutt, were well aware of the extraordinary proliferation of black enterprises, but they saw these gains in the context of citywide business. In Cleveland, the role of "the Negro in business" was "limited" in 1926, according to Myers. For example, Cleveland's African American insurance and finance companies were, Myers noted, "all conducted by earnest and honest men, but handicapped by lack of capital and the confidence of the masses."[87] In 1930 Chesnutt wrote: "The development of business among Negroes in Cleveland has been backward, for obvious reasons— the lack of capital, experience and inherited business attitude."[88] Similarly, most African American businesses in Cincinnati were based on small capital investments in 1926, according to local black weekly editor Wendell P. Dabney. He stated: "There are no big colored groceries or general stores."[89] Explaining the phenomenon, Dabney indicated that lower prices and advertising attracted many black patrons to larger groceries and retail stores owned by whites, who achieved economies of scale and advertised effectively.[90]

Likewise, African Americans in professional life made relative gains in Ohio during the 1920s. In Cincinnati black teachers earned salaries remarkably higher than those of their counterparts in the past, while black physicians and dentists also experienced comparative opulence. "Our professional men and women are doing well, more doctors, lawyers and teachers than ever before in the history of the city [Cincinnati]," said Wendell P. Dabney, who also noted, "The colored professions do not enjoy so much white patronage as in earlier days."[91]

In this decade, black professionals in Ohio were dependent more than ever on black clients whose incomes were curtailed by color lines in the job market and other factors. Potential black clients were mostly persons employed in manufacturing or domestic jobs. This growing financial reliance of black professionals on black workers was occurring outside Ohio as well. Historian Joe William Trotter, Jr. finds this linkage between a black professional class and a new black working class in southern West Virginia in the period 1915–1930.[92]

The increasing number of black professionals in Ohio intensified competition for black clients, and this further restricted the incomes of some African American professionals, especially in Cleveland. The enlargement of black professional classes in Ohio was greatest there. Commenting on black professionals in 1926, George A. Myers said that there was in Cleveland a "superabundance of doctors, dentists and lawyers, which of necessity makes a survival of the fittest, and a meager living for the many."[93]

African American churches were the greatest institutional beneficiaries of Ohio's black in-migration during the 1920s. Black church membership, congregations, clergymen, and buildings increased apace with Ohio's black population growth. In 1926, there were 119,529 black church members in Ohio, more than double the number in 1916. Often membership rose rapidly in new black churches. In Cincinnati the New Hope Baptist Church was organized with 16 members in 1922, and its membership grew to 580 within three years. Like most black church members in Ohio before 1916, the majority of African American new-comers were Baptists. In 1926 African American church membership in Ohio included 74,048 Baptists and 36,591 Methodists, while another 8,890 black church members were Adventists, Presbyterians, Episcopalians, Roman Catholics, and affiliates of several other church bodies. Between 1916 and 1926, the number of black church congregations in Ohio rose from 392 to 622.[94]

During the 1920s expanding black congregations in Ohio were housed in buildings ranging from large and costly traditional church edifices to low-rent rooms in various kinds of structures. In Ohio's great urban centers, small black congregations composed of recent migrants worshiped in stores and other rented buildings that were not constructed as churches. In his brief history of African Americans in Columbus, J. S. Himes, Jr. commented: "In some instances entire congregations, pastor, members and ritual, migrated to Columbus and set up church in . . . an empty store building, a vacant dwelling, or an abandoned church edifice."[95] Feeling unwelcome, some other migrants left formal black churches in Columbus to join an existing storefront congregation or to form another newcomers' church.[96] In Cleveland, the members of Zion Hill Baptist Church were black migrants who came from Alabama as a group headed by the Reverend Charles C. Ailer. Many black migrant congregations using untraditional structures in Cleveland were found on Scovill Avenue and Central Avenue.[97] In Cincinnati the Holiness Assembly Church, the Spiritualist Church of God, and similar black churches conducted services that undoubtedly were attractive to some nostalgic newcomers. In ways familiar to natives of the rural South their religious services touched emotions while providing the supports of friendships and kinships.[98] Black migrant churches surely comforted many lonely rural newcomers while they became accustomed to living in Ohio cities.

The storefront church phenomenon in the 1920s was overshadowed by the great increase of church buildings owned by African American congregations in Ohio. In the wake of in-migration to Ohio and the prosperity of the decade, black congregations usually included more members and many with higher incomes than in the past. Those new circumstances enabled African Americans to finance the purchase of existing church buildings or the construction of new ones. African Americans rarely built new churches because church buildings often stood vacant in Ohio's expanding black urban districts. Numerous white congregations that vacated churches in Ohio's racially changing neighborhoods were agreeable to selling their old church properties to African Americans. In Cleveland most black congregations that were in the market for church property were able to acquire church edifices previously used by whites; consequently, few new African American churches were built there.[99] Similar circumstances existed in Columbus, where the number of church edifices owned by African Americans increased from less than twenty before 1915 to about 100 in 1931. In his account of African American life in Columbus, J. S. Himes, Jr. said that only about a half dozen of those 80 additional black church buildings were new constructions. Himes explained: ". . . colored congregations bought, often at fabulous prices, church buildings abandoned by white congregations who moved out in the face of the swelling tide of color."[100]

Although exceptional, new churches financed by black congregations were built in Ohio in the 1920s. Generally, the members of those congregations were either unusually numerous or relatively affluent. Often the black pastors who led church building campaigns were themselves migrants with impressive ministerial credentials. In Cincinnati the Antioch Baptist Church was the largest black congregation, and its membership grew as black in-migration proceeded. In 1923 The Reverend W. Henry Williams, D.D. was called to Antioch Baptist Church with a mandate to build a new edifice. An alumnus of Kentucky's Simmons University, he had received an honorary doctorate from Selma University in recognition of his long and successful Baptist pastorates in Somerset and Owensboro, Kentucky. Starting in 1925, Antioch Baptist erected a Gothic style brick and stone church with an auditorium seating two thousand people. Costing over $200,000, the new building included offices, library, kitchen, dining room, social hall, and gymnasium. At the same time, the congregation of Cincinnati's Mt. Zion Methodist Episcopal Church constructed a house of worship with an attached community house costing $110,000 in all. The pastor in charge of this building campaign was a thirty-five year old native of New York City, The Reverend Stanley E. Grannum, who was a Wesleyan University (Connecticut) A. B., Boston University Graduate School, S. T. B., and former pastor of black churches in Boston and New York City. The new Mt. Zion M. E. Church was located in Walnut Hills, which was the residence of many of Cincinnati's financially successful African Americans.[101]

The rising number and value of church buildings owned by Ohio's black congregations were measures of the demographic and economic growth of African Americans in Ohio after the start of the great wartime black migration. Between 1916 and 1926 the value of church edifices owned by African Americans in Ohio rose from $2,237,987 to $9,113,989, while the number of those properties increased from 367 to 523.[102] Expansion during these years allowed many black congregations to finance the purchase or the construction of church edifices, but the resulting increase of church indebtedness made the same congregations more vulnerable to financial pressures and possible hard times in future. This phenomenon was most pronounced in Cleveland, Cincinnati, and Columbus but also occurred in other major Ohio cities including Akron. J. S. Himes, Jr., pointed out that the "financial difficulties of Negro churches" in Columbus and in other cities constituted a noteworthy dimension of the black experience in this growth period.[103]

The effects of the continuing black migration to Ohio in this decade invigorated organized African American social life outside of churches. During the 1920s, as in the past, blacks and whites with business and professional backgrounds still participated in separate fraternal associations. These orders were in the early stages of a long-term decline. They were being undermined by competition from motion pictures, radio, and other newer social life alternatives. Nevertheless, Ohio's separate black and white fraternal associations remained robust throughout the decade. Most of the black orders then existing in Ohio were established much earlier, some in the nineteenth century. They included the Masons, Odd Fellows, Knights of Pythias, Elks, and United Brothers of Friendship.

The Prince Hall Grand Lodge of Free and Accepted Masons of the State of Ohio was founded in 1848. Eventually, its lodges existed throughout the state, and in some places there were proportionately as many black Masons as white ones.[104] Although they were relatively less numerous than that, black Masons were active in Ohio during the 1920s. They were present in the state's small cities as well as in its large urban centers. For example, black Masons in Cleveland, Canton, and Newark, respectively, hosted the 75th through the 77th annual meetings of the Grand Lodge of Ohio.[105] Sometimes new black lodges were opened in the state during the decade. In 1920 black Masons chartered Cleveland's William T. Boyd Lodge. In 1922 black Masons planned to build a temple in Columbus at 19th and Long Streets, where they had recently purchased land. In 1926 eleven lodges, chapters, and other black Masonic bodies existed in Cincinnati. Often vocationally successful African Americans in Cincinnati were members of Masonic orders. A large proportion of Cincinnati's black physicians belonged to a Masonic order and to one or more other black fraternal associations in the 1920s.[106]

African Americans in Ohio conducted separate social activities in other fraternal associations and in a variety of social clubs, civic organizations, and women's clubs in the 1920s. In Cincinnati there were ten Knights of Pythias bodies among well over a hundred lodges, chapters, temples, and other such affiliates of black fraternal organizations in 1926. Some African American social organizations were prosperous as well as active. Black Odd Fellows owned property including an impressive lodge hall on West Ninth Street in Cincinnati and a three-story building at Garfield Avenue and Long Street in Columbus. In 1925 the Cincinnati Federation of Women's Clubs purchased a fine Victorian Era brick mansion on Chapel Street and fitted it out as a clubhouse. Meantime, Cincinnati's many black men's clubs, such as the Argus Club, possessed no property. These men's clubs held their monthly or annual gatherings in private homes. However, members of the Crescent Club, whose members included black weekly editor Wendell P. Dabney, leased clubrooms in Cincinnati's Sterling Hotel.[107]

Altruism was commonly practiced by the separate organizations involved in African American social life in Ohio during the 1920s. Black weekly editor Dabney observed that scores of black fraternal lodges in Cincinnati were "doing well in the field of charity."[108] Black women's groups were characteristically identified with altruistic causes. Often black women's clubs attracted middle class persons interested in social work. Mrs. Mamie Trotter, for example, was Lady Manager of the Colored Orphan Asylum and Parliamentarian of the Cincinnati Federation of Women's Clubs. Mrs. Estelle Rickman Davis served as President of the Ohio Federation of Women's Clubs in the early 1920s and as an officer of Cincinnati's YWCA West End Branch, Home for Aged Colored Women, and Union Baptist Church Missionary Society.[109]

In summary, black Columbus, black Cincinnati, and black Cleveland became African American metropolises in the 1920s. These great black populations were comparable in size to that of a large city, ranging from 30,000 to 70,000.[110] Each black metropolis possessed urban establishments similar to those found in actual cities with tens of thousands in population. Black commercial districts housed many kinds of businesses, such as food catering, barbering, tailoring, saloon keeping, news publishing, undertaking, retailing, insurance, banking, and real estate. African Americans owned and/or managed, staffed, and patronized these institutions. African Americans in each black metropolis offered a gamut of professional services, for example, medical, dental, legal, pedagogical, and pastoral or ministerial services. Various black business and professional associations existed to represent these economic interests. Churches, schools, hospitals, YWCAs, YMCAs, fraternal orders, women's clubs, welfare organizations, and equal rights associations exemplify other kinds of urban structures found in Ohio's black metrop-olises. Local people in black Cleveland, black Cincinnati, and black Columbus built these African American cities within cities. While foun-dations were laid earlier, most of the construction was in the period 1915–1930. The black districts reached metropolis dimensions in the twenties when the growth of black community infrastructure was greater than in any previous decade. This was a decade that saw opportunity, prosperity, and achievement in black metropolises. In contrast to the past, as Charles Dickens said of another age, "It was the best of times, it was the worst of times." In the twenties black districts in Ohio cities also experienced the intensification of residential congestion, disease, crime, and other characteristically urban problems. At the same time, white intolerance rose to a shrill pitch. As the following chapter shows, the Ohio color line, more divisive than ever, circumscribed and delimited both the positive and negative developments in the black urban experi-ence in this state.

CHAPTER FIVE

Increasing White Intolerance

White intolerance in the United States reached a post–Civil War peak and the Ohio color line became more unyielding and restrictive in the 1920s. After increasing for decades, intolerance reached a benchmark high across the nation at mid-decade. Anglo-Saxon Protestant hostility toward the foreign born, Catholics, Jews, African Americans, and other nonwhites contributed to the rise of the Ku Klux Klan in the period 1915–1925. The Klan was highly organized in Ohio, Indiana, and many other northern states, as well as in the South. It successfully recruited Anglo-Saxon Protestants while preaching white supremacy and family values. The 1924 election victories of Klan-endorsed Republican candidates for statewide offices in Indiana were evidence that the Klan viewpoint was popular in the Midwest. Also signaling the high level of intolerance in 1924, the United States Congress passed the Johnson-Reed Act containing the most racially restrictive immigration regulations in the nation's history. It prohibited immigration from Asia, whose populations were nonwhite, and established quotas permitting relatively little immigration from southern and eastern European countries whose people were largely non-Protestants. Meanwhile, African Americans were lynched and anti-lynching bills failed in the United States Congress when they were filibustered by southern Democrats and rejected by the Republican party. A legal racial caste system was completed in former slave states, and informal racial segregation was a fact in every region of the country during the decade.

Black and white Ohioans were separated more than ever in the 1920s as the color line was further solidified across practically every area of life. Ohio's long established patterns of racial segregation and discrimination were enlarged to encompass unprecedented numbers of people, locations, institutions, and other aspects of life. The residential segregation of African Americans reached ghetto proportions for the first time in some Ohio cities by 1930. Racial discrimination and segregation were increasingly common in residential housing, schools, and public accommodations, while color bias was still seen in law enforcement and the print media. White employers and various private organizations continued to bar or discriminate against African Americans. Racial incidents sometimes turned violent as instances of racial harassment multiplied. This mirrored the growth of white intolerance, which accelerated during World War I and continued in the postwar decade.

Intolerant whites in Ohio assumed the credibility of a white supremacy concept, which contrasted a stereotype of whites with superior characteristics and a false image of blacks possessing undesirable traits. Manifestations of the white supremacy thinking ranged from less to more hostile reactions to African Americans. Avoidance of racially mixed company was an example of a passive reaction. Towards the middle of the continuum were innumerable acts of overt racial discrimination or segregation, which were more aggressive, but nonviolent. The most hostile reactions were violent in nature. White supremacy views ran across class lines; consequently, the Ku Klux Klan drew membership from all social-economic classes. This ideology was widespread in Ohio before and after World War I, but this racial and ethnic thinking was lacking in organization until the Klan adopted it. The Klan's organized conduct affecting blacks ranged from mild to aggressive actions, mirroring that of individual white supremacy adherents in the general public. The most militant white supremacists in and out of the Klan employed violent tactics, rioting, vandalism, threats of violence, and physical harassment. Racial violence was uncommon in Ohio, but belief in white supremacy undoubtedly was the norm in white society. The popular press in Ohio reflected the fact that this was a standard white view. Black stereotypes commonly were used in daily newspaper reporting about African Americans.

During the 1920s white Ohioans still candidly expressed their assumption of white supremacy. For example, the editor of a reputable Cincinnati daily newspaper, writing in reference to immigration restriction legislation, favored the exclusion of Japanese immigrants but was willing to welcome "people from all white lands."[1] Yet, white Ohioans generally failed to recognize their own prejudice; most of them probably sincerely believed that they were not anti-black. Undoubtedly many white people in the state felt a paternalistic sympathy for blacks that moderated their white supremacy views. An articulate and extraordinarily revealing expression of this attitude of white superiority mixed with paternalism was revealed in a letter of inquiry about the activities of the Columbus Urban League. The author was a middle class white woman residing in Columbus. Her letter was addressed to the local Urban League president, a white man, who was also the pastor of the Columbus First Congregational Church. She wrote:

The Negro problem is one which we should all get together upon as it seems as if it may be a very ugly one to bequeath to our children. I said the other day (thoughtlessly) "The Columbus Urban League is one Philanthropy to which I would not subscribe as the Negroes are spoiled already" but I am open to conviction.

The deepest sympathy is of course due them and I have read many an article by DuBois which wrung my heart, but when I see how his teachings of race equality (that they must stand upon their rights to get anywhere) is putting them on the defensive and wiping the care-free smile from their faces. I cannot help siding with Booker Washington's theories as being best for their "pursuit of happiness."

It seems to me there has been a definite propaganda at work along the former lines; whether emanating from their churches or from your League I do not know but I do know the kind-hearted, willing, happy worker has gone and instead we have an imitation of the white race at its worst and a suspicious unkind spirit of rivalry.

Like the letter writer, many whites in Ohio and other states felt genuine concern about the hardships of impoverished African Americans living in the urban North or in the rural South. Surely they were touched by the human difficulties of African Americans caught in urban slums with their deteriorating housing, health threats, and attendant social problems. Undoubtedly these whites recognized that such inequity was a race-relations problem that carried the potential for greater racial friction in future. Paternalistic whites were interested in improving the general welfare of African Americans but objected to efforts meant to bring racial equality because they did not see black people as their equals. The altruistically inclined whites often saw distorted images of African Americans. Certain ethnic stereotypes had evolved over the country's colonial and national history. For example, African Americans were pictured as big, strong, carefree, happy, willing workers who were especially suited to manual labor. In this stereotypical perception, an affectionate bond between white mistress and black servant was the norm. Also according to this biased view African Americans lacked intelligent views and were easily misguided. In accord with such views whites, including many of those who were relatively sympathetic to blacks, approved a color line etiquette with a wide array of taboos. These ranged from proscriptions against racial intermarriage to rules against entering a white dwelling by the front door.

In writing to the local Urban League president, the white Columbus woman discussed her relationship to two young black women whom she employed. In that part of the letter she again made remarks rooted in racial imagery that was in common usage among whites of her background. She continued:

> I have two colored girls working for me doing the housework and because they are of the best type of their race they have seemed illuminating. They have been up from Louisville two years and when they first came they were so kindly and so cheerful, but I have seen a distinct change in their attitude—towards service—not at all towards me, for I am fond of them and they are fond of me. I have the utmost confidence in their honesty and decency. They are good—I was about to say "Christian girls," but is it Christian to begrudge service and consider certain tasks beneath one? Christ's washing of the feet proves not. Of course, their lack of an intelligent view of the matter I make allowance for, but is it right to make them unfit for and discontented with manual labor?
>
> It is really amusing. These girls of mine are big strong healthy girls but they think because I occasionally lie down in the after noon it is the thing to do so up they go leaving me to the mercy of the telephone and door bell. I have never had white girls refuse to help in housecleaning time and these girls had they followed their natural kindly instincts, would not have done so, but they felt they must "stand on their rights," so let me work all day alone while they did their regular tasks only and went to their rooms for two hours every afternoon. They used my front door for themselves and their callers until I forbade it and then resented it. To be sure I could give no real reason for not [permitting] it, but if your Christianity carries you that far does it stop this side of intermarriage?

Moderately biased whites had certain racial expectations. They expected African Americans to be kind, courteous, and service oriented in dealings with whites. Blacks were supposed to be deferential to whites in employers' homes, on streetcars, and in other public places. Lack of deference was seen as aggressiveness or gratuitous assertion of rights. These whites assumed that blacks naturally would obtain and accept less than whites, for example, smaller incomes and less expensive clothes. Efforts in aid of economic, cultural, and social betterment were perceived as unnatural and objectionable attempts to emulate whites. Generally whites were offended whenever African Americans showed dissatisfaction with the color line. Accordingly, white moderates concluded that the pursuit of equal rights was not in the interest of good race relations. The foregoing letter to the Columbus Urban League president revealed its author's disagreement with W. E. B. Du Bois' "teachings on race equality" that emphasized protest against discrimination. The letter concluded:

> At any rate the comfort of Negro servants is gone with this "chip on the shoulder" attitude. Demanding as they do, equal wages with whites, I feel as if I would never have them again. Is it doing them a kindness to make so many employers feel the same way?
>
> It is not only in household labor that this attitude manifests itself. I only speak of that which I know most intimately. Hearsay evidence is abundant everywhere. Any one who uses the Long Street [trolley] cars can testify that the aggressiveness of the Negroes demonstrates the need of a school of manners and Christian kindliness rather than equal rights.
>
> Have not most of them more money than it is good for them now? My girls spend nearly as much for their clothes as I do and certainly think of little else. They have a superficial smattering of learning which they like to air but their end and aim of existence is to get through "work" and to be "out."
>
> To be sure discontent and unrest are the faults of the age, but is your organization fostering or lessening them? What are you giving the Negroes to take the place of their happiness if you are not giving them the ideal of service? I feel confident you must at least be trying to give them that but what then is the strong influence opposing it?[2]

The racial comments in this letter were stated in language that was at once forthright and muted. The letter's author was probably more knowledgeable about the views of black ideologues W. E. B. Du Bois and Booker T. Washington than most whites in the state. Like many other white Ohioans, the letter writer clearly opposed race relations based upon equal rights but otherwise wished African Americans no harm. Also, like so many whites in Ohio, the writer became defensive as race relations changed and racial tensions rose in the state during and after World War I.

White intolerance of African Americans in Ohio remained relatively high in the 1920s after rising significantly during the wartime migration. The growth of the Ku Klux Klan in Ohio paralleled the increased white hostility to blacks. Klan activities were the most organized expressions of white supremacy radicals in Ohio during the decade. In contrast to white moderates, Klansmen advocated further racial proscription and sometimes perpetrated violence against African Americans. The nineteenth century Klan was basically confined to the South, but the reincarnated twentieth century Klan also was organized in many northern and western states. The Ku Klux Klan gained membership in Ohio and in other Great Lakes states early in the 1920s. The Klan first began to recruit in Ohio from a base of operations in southwestern Indiana. Klan units were formed in Cincinnati and Springfield late in 1920. A Columbus dentist, Dr. Charles L. Harrod, was the organizer of the Franklin County Klan and was the first "King Kleagle" in Ohio. Harrod's Columbus office was the Ohio Klan's principal recruiting headquarters. Busily recruiting in urban and rural areas, Klan organizers obtained members in every region of Ohio. As in other states, Ohio Klan membership was high in large cities including Akron, Dayton, and Youngstown. The Klan was also well entrenched in Ohio's rural areas, such as Pickaway and Washington Counties on the Ohio River and Butler County on the southwestern boundary with Indiana. The Klan's large membership made it a significant presence in Ohio. In 1927 the Klan claimed an Ohio membership of three hundred thousand. According to Kenneth T. Jackson's estimates, Klan membership was higher in Ohio than in any other state excepting Indiana.[3] The number of Ohio Klan members by any estimation, nevertheless, composed a small fraction of state's white population that totaled 6,331,136 in 1930.[4]

In the nineteenth century, the Ku Klux Klan was essentially a race organization antithetical to African Americans. The twentieth century Klan represented ethnic biases and racial ones. Klan members reacted to the mass immigration of European non-Protestants and to changing race relations in the decades prior to 1920. Consequently, in Ohio and other states, Ku Klux Klan propaganda and activities were anti-foreign, anti-Catholic, and anti-Semitic as well as anti-black. While appealing to prejudices, the Klan attempted to convince potential members that it was engaged in a moral crusade. The Klan pictured itself as the champion of white Protestant family values including support of law and order.[5] There is an extensive literature on the Ku Klux Klan in Midwestern states during the 1920s. Older studies point to the Klan's nativism, racism, and religious bigotry in explanation of its rise to prominence in the twenties. Newer and often more sophisticated analyses draw attention away from intolerance aspects. They argue that the Klan's attractiveness came mainly from its identification with traditional values. William D. Jenkins and Leonard J. Moore, respectively, find that Klan members in Ohio and Indiana mirrored the whole spectrum of the white Protestant population. They argue that middle class members of mainstream denominations joined the Klan because they perceived it as a political agent for moral reform on such issues as vice and political corruption.[6] But regardless of the primary motivation of its members, the Klan used a threatening public rhetoric of religious bigotry, xenophobia, and white superiority. The foreign born, non-Protestants, and African Americans consequently were concerned about the Klan's growing presence and power in the public sphere.

The Klan's heritage of violence against blacks made its self-proclaimed law-abiding image seem implausible. The public knew well the Klan's identification with arson, beatings, and lynching going back to the Reconstruction Era in the South. Evidently to alter perceptions of the Klan as a lawless organization, Klansmen often denied hostility toward African Americans. Although avowedly white supremacist and segregationist, the Ohio Klan protested that it was not unsympathetic to blacks. In order to demonstrate their "love of the Negro," Klansmen occasionally made dramatic financial contributions to black churches. For example, in December 1923, about forty Klansmen marched into a black Baptist Church at Wadsworth in northern Ohio and gave its pastor a one hundred dollar contribution.[7] Klansmen made a similar demonstration at a black Baptist Church in Cincinnati in April 1926.[8] Such events surely were intended to attract press attention, and they were often reported widely. The *New York Times* carried the story of the Klan contribution to the black church in Cincinnati.

Ohio Klansmen even presumed to create a separate black branch of the Klan in 1924. Youngstown Klan officials, through a black agent, Paul Russell, organized the Loyal Legion of Lincoln, which was intended to be a national organization headquartered in Youngstown. The Loyal Legion shortly became defunct when Grand Scorpion Russell apparently absconded with funds collected from white Klansmen to finance the organization.[9]

The Ku Klux Klan entered the political arena to gain power and promote its ethnic and racial agenda in Ohio. The Ohio Klan initiated its first intensive political program in 1923. Five Mahoning Valley cities elected Klan mayors that year, and Klan candidates were elected in various other parts of the state.[10] Shortly after the general election in November 1924, Ohio Grand Dragon Clyde W. Osborne claimed that enough Klan candidates won seats in the state House of Representatives and Senate to give the Klan control of the Ohio General Assembly in 1925.[11] Later Osborne more modestly claimed that forty-five members of the House were Klansmen.[12] It appears, however, that there were never more than twenty Klansmen in the General Assembly.[13] Nevertheless, in 1925 Klan state representatives introduced legislation reflecting their organization's anti-Catholicism, anti-Semitism, and white supremacy attitudes. One of these bills prohibited marriage between whites and nonwhites.[14] Other such proposed legislation included bills that required all students to attend public schools, thereby disallowing enrollment in Catholic parochial schools, excluded Catholics from teaching in public schools, and required Bible reading in the public schools. These Klan backed bills did not pass the Ohio legislature, excepting the latter, which was vetoed by Governor Vic Donahey.[15]

Occasionally Ohio Klansmen demonstrated their white supremacist views with violence or threats against African Americans. For example, in February 1923 Klansmen in white sheets harassed four black families in Cleves, a very small Ohio River town just below Cincinnati. They fired several gunshots and attached a note to the door of each African American home. The notes warned the families to leave town "by nightfall" and were signed "KKK."[16] Also in 1923, Klansmen burned "fiery crosses" in the African American section of Urbana.[17] In 1920 blacks were 11 percent of that Central Ohio town's 7,621 people.[18] The Ku Klux Klan exacerbated racial problems in Ohio, sometimes inspiring violence against blacks and generally exploiting color prejudice; however, it was not responsible for all racial violence or color lines in Ohio during the 1920s. White hostility and racial discrimination existed in Ohio prior to the Klan's rise and after its fall from prominence. In Ohio and elsewhere the Ku Klux Klan went into decline after a nationally prominent Klan leader was convicted of second-degree murder on the deathbed testimony given by young woman that he savaged and raped. Ohio Klan membership fell rapidly in 1926, and by the end of the decade the Klan was insignificant in the state.[19]

The potential for racial violence in Ohio was substantial through the 1920s as race relations remained tense. Actually racial outbreaks in the state were infrequent during the decade, but they included a classic race riot in the central Ohio city of Springfield. These incidents involved white mobs, lynching threats, criminal allegations against black men, and rumors of anticipated violence. In March 1921 a race riot broke out in Springfield for the third time in the twentieth century. Earlier, in 1904, a Springfield mob lynched a black man, who allegedly killed a white policeman, and destroyed dwellings in a local black area known as the "Levee." In 1906, another mob in that city burned another African American section following the murder of a white railroad worker. In both riots the state militia was called upon to put down disorder.[20] The 1921 Springfield riot was evidently precipitated when an eleven-year-old white girl was assaulted on March 7. An African American allegedly was seen in the vicinity of the assault shortly before the girl was attacked. The local press ran daily stories about the alleged presence of a black man and about the physical condition of the hospitalized girl. Two days later, a white mob formed at the jail in response to false rumors that the assailant had been captured. The sheriff told the assembled whites that the capture rumors were erroneous and proved it by allowing some of them to inspect the jail. On the evening of March 10 a second and larger white mob formed in Springfield's black business district and harassed departing basketball fans who had watched a game played at the African American Center Street YMCA building.[21]

The next morning, March 11, it was rumored in Springfield's black neighborhoods that another mob planned to "burn out the Negro sections" that evening. Many African Americans in Springfield prepared for self-defense against mob action. In this instance the rumors were well founded.[22] In an account of the riot, a Springfield correspondent of the Cleveland *Gazette* reported:

> Every section of the city, in which there were any number of our people, was organized for determined resistance to any mob that might molest them. Former soldiers of the World War were of especial service in forming the backbone of the various organizations. As on the preceding nights, the rioters gathered to carry out their threats but the activity of the police and firemen, who were called upon to assist, kept them from invading our sections of this city where "warm receptions" were awaiting them. While the rioters were being driven from place to place downtown, the only disturbance in our sections was when Pres. B. J. Westcott of the City Commission, City Manager Parsons and Patrolman Cody were fired upon as they attempted to enter the S. Yellow Springs St. district to assure our people that they would be protected. Fortunately, they were not hit. The firing was caused by fear of raids by auto parties. The officials were of course not known at the time the firing was done.[23]

Also, during that evening of March 11, Springfield city officials asked Ohio Governor Harry L. Davis to send in the state militia. Shortly, Ohio National Guardsmen arrived in Springfield and order was restored quickly. Subsequently, forty black and white men were fined for participation in the riots, and several were bound over to the grand jury for possessing concealed weapons and one for carrying dynamite.[24]

Racial outbreaks comparable to that in Springfield did not occur in other Ohio cities, but racial tension occasionally did become evident in parts of the state. In 1921, for example, it was rumored that whites were preparing to attack African Americans in Newburgh Heights, located just southeast of Cleveland.[25] The decennial census showed that

Newburgh Heights was an all-white town the year before. In 1927 the "mob spirit" was fanned to a "fever heat" in Dayton after the death of a city policeman who was killed in a battle between white policemen and certain African Americans resisting arrest. According to a Dayton observer "prejudiced whites and the police made it more or less uncomfortable, for several days, for all our residents of this city."[26] In response to this situation, leading African American citizens of Dayton, including the local NAACP branch president, publicly expressed their disapproval of crime. In a statement addressed to Dayton's director of public safety, they declared: ". . . [W]e stand for law and order."[27] Subsequently, Roy Freeman was arrested, tried, convicted and sentenced to death for the murder of the Dayton patrolman. However, at a second trial, this black man's conviction was overturned on the grounds that it was based in part on a confession obtained by means of "third degree" police methods.[28]

Ohio daily newspaper reporting about blacks contributed to the growth of white intolerance during the 1920s. Across the state daily newspapers exhibited disrespect for African Americans through the use of racial identification terms that were degrading or offensive to black people. The Ohio daily press rarely mentioned African Americans except in news about social problems, for instance, in crime stories often with racially inflammatory headlines. While generally presenting an undesirable image of African Americans, the press fostered a stereotype of the black male as dangerous, violent, and immoral. A scholarly survey made in 1920 showed that coverage of African Americans in Columbus' three major newspapers neglected commendable conduct and gave undue publicity to anti-social behavior, usually under "glaring headlines."[29] A scholarly study done in 1924 revealed that vice and crime was the theme of 55.7 percent of the items about African Americans in The Columbus Evening Dispatch, The Ohio State Journal, and The Columbus Citizen. It classified some articles in these dailies as "flippant and ridicule of Negroes."[30] Such reporting surely elevated color awareness in Ohio.

Large and nearly all-black districts formed in Cleveland, Cincinnati, and Columbus as residential segregation increased during the 1920s. While such major black districts did not evolve elsewhere in Ohio during the decade, African Americans were more residentially concentrated and isolated in Dayton, Toledo, and other Ohio cities in 1930. Racial discrimination and economic circumstances still prevented the general diffusion of black populations in Ohio cities. African Americans usually were barred from white residential districts in the state's cities; consequently, enlarged black populations concentrated in Ohio urban districts housing previously established black neighborhoods. Existing black residential areas expanded and new ones formed on streets and avenues between old black neighborhoods. In the wake of this trend, all-black neighborhoods were larger and whole urban districts were predominantly black for the first time. In Cleveland, during the 1920s, many new black neighborhoods formed east of East 55th Street, where few African Americans resided during World War I. Meanwhile, west of East 55th Street, Cleveland's old black areas in the vicinity of Central and Scovill Avenues expanded and came together. In 1930 African Americans in Cleveland, with few exceptions, lived in an East Side sector that ran east to west from East 105th Street to the Cuyahoga River and north to south from Euclid Avenue to Woodland Avenue. (See map 3.) In Cincinnati the old African American residential sections in the West End near the river expanded, especially northward into districts that had been predominantly white in 1920. This settlement pattern created a larger predominantly black south to north corridor near the western edge of Cincinnati's river basin. While most African Americans lived in the inner city West End in 1930, there were black settlements in several Cincinnati suburbs. These included a large black middle class section in Walnut Hills. Also, blacks "largely populated" College Hill, Cumminsville, Lockland, and Madisonville, which were low-income suburbs. Commenting on these black residential areas in 1925, Wendell P. Dabney, noted, "Comparatively few live in white neighborhoods."[31]

In Columbus black population growth during the 1920s largely occurred in the vicinity of the city center and in areas close to manufacturing plants employing African Americans. Five noncontiguous black neighborhoods in Columbus received most of the migrants. They were located in the Southgate Addition and areas near South Seventh Street, West Goodale Street, East Fifth Avenue, and East Long Street. According to J. S. Himes's study of African American life in Columbus, "the greatest numerical and spatial growth of the Negro population took place" in and around old black sections near East Long Street. Himes stated: "Prior to 1910 the foci of Negro settlement in this section were North Third Street, both north and south of East Long Street and North Champion Avenue, north and south of Mt. Vernon Avenue. The migrants entered this community at both these foci and spread in all directions, causing the community to close in upon itself and to develop the solid Negro area we now know."[32]

The residential segregation of African Americans in urban Ohio was evidenced in 1930 census statistics. Most African Americans were concentrated in four or five of the many census districts in each large Ohio city. Cleveland was divided into 40 statistical areas for census purposes, while there were 26 census wards in Cincinnati and 19 in Columbus. Eighty-seven percent of African Americans in Cleveland were located

Map 3

Distribution of the Cleveland Negro Population, 1930.

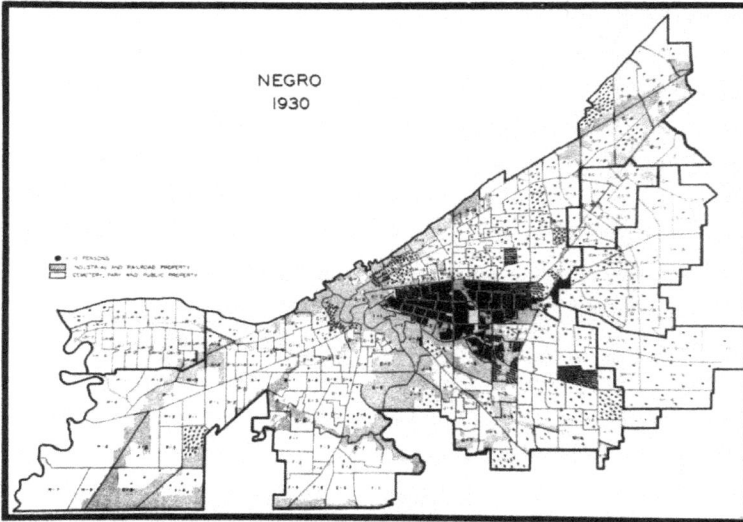

Source: Howard W. Green, *Population Characteristics by Census Tracts, Cleveland, Ohio, 1930* (Cleveland: The Plain Dealer Publishing Company, 1931). With permission of The Western Reserve Historical Society, Cleveland, Ohio.

in Statistical Areas 20–24. In Columbus, 65 percent of all African Americans lived in Wards 6, 7, 8, and 13. Sixty-three percent of Cincinnati's black population resided in Wards 15–18. (See map 4.) In smaller Ohio urban centers African Americans also were concentrated in a few census districts. Eighty-one percent of Dayton's black population resided in Wards 5, 6, and 7. One ward housed 82 percent of the African Americans in Hamilton, a small southwestern Ohio city.[33]

African American concentrations grew in Ohio's old urban residential districts because those areas experienced the departure of whites as well as the arrival of blacks. Racial bias undoubtedly affected whites departing racially integrated urban areas. But this residential mobility was a factor in the larger pattern of urban life that evolved in the United States during 1890–1930. In the nineteenth century, urban residents lived within walking distance of manufacturing areas or commercial districts inside city limits. Improvements in public transportation made it possible to work in the old urban center but reside on the city's outskirts. Prior to World War I, the proliferation of electric trolley cars especially spurred housing construction in areas beyond city centers. The emerging urban

Map 4

Census Tracts of Cincinnati Basin, 1930.

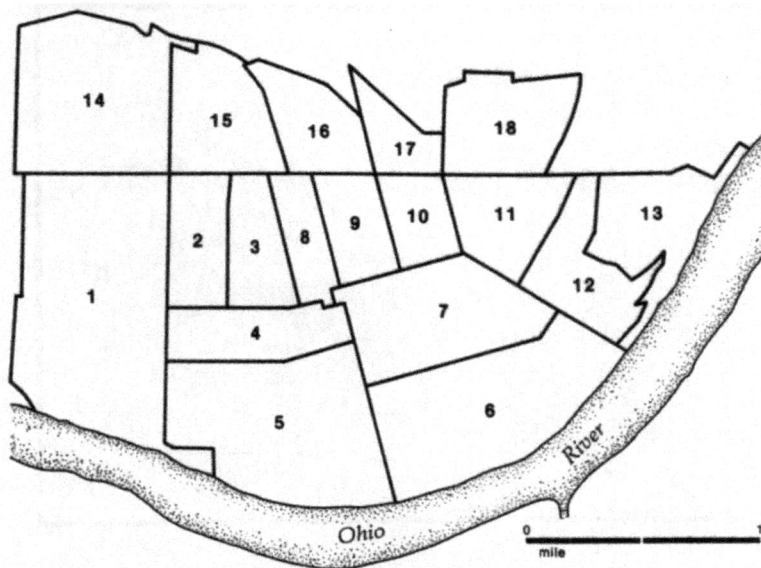

Source: Robert B. Fairbanks, *Making Better Citizens: Housing Reform and the Community Development Strategy in Cincinnati, 1890–1960* (Urbana: University of Illinois Press, 1988), p. 76.

configuration encompassed an old inner city with newer residential divisions variously located on its edges. The advantages of suburban life were evident to city dwellers, regardless of their ethnicity or color. Experience in the city center involved old buildings, crowding, noise, industrial grime and smoke. In contrast, life in new suburban housing was greener, quieter, and cleaner, while providing greater privacy and social status. Those who could afford costly suburban property moved, while low-income families remained in inner city. Decreasing in size, prewar inner city populations were disproportionately composed of southern and eastern European immigrants and African Americans. The wartime housing shortage inhibited the suburban trend. The movement accelerated in the next decade, driven by the prosperous economy, the mass production of inexpensive automobiles, and the boom in residential housing construction during the 1920s. The exodus of city inhabitants to suburban residences was a well-established pattern of residential mobility in the United States in 1930. It was impelled by various technological, economic, and social factors including racial bias.[34]

The development of the major black district in Cincinnati's River Basin occurred within the general pattern of urban change in the United States that saw movements from older to newer residential areas. The proportion of Cincinnati's total population residing in the River Basin declined from 64 percent to 20 percent between 1870 and 1930.[35] After the Civil War, Cincinnati's West End residents were mostly members of the city's older white families, some of which were quite wealthy. Near the end of the nineteenth century these families began to move into the city's hilltop suburbs. Subsequently, eastern and southern European immigrants occupied their former residences. In the 1920s these immigrant families followed earlier residents of the West End en masse to the hilltop areas. In turn, blacks and some white hill people from West Virginia and Kentucky entered their vacated old dwellings.[36] Similar demographic changes occurred in other Ohio cities. In Columbus before 1890, the West Goodale Street district residents were of Welsh, Irish, and German origins; although some were immigrants, they were mainly old stock. Once many Italian immigrants settled in the West Goodale Street section, these older white residents began an exodus in earnest, often selling their property to African Americans. Over the course of the war period and the twenties, the predominantly black areas in the West Goodale District became "larger and more solidly Negro."[37] Also, many Russians, Rumanians, and Italians who lived in separate ethnic districts on Cleveland's East Side moved elsewhere during the 1920s, making residential space for African Americans.[38]

Undoubtedly, racial prejudice was among the motives that gave impetus to the departure of whites from old urban districts in Ohio in the 1920s. In reference to this phenomenon in Cincinnati, local weekly editor Wendell P. Dabney wrote: "In every locality, as Negroes increase, the whites diminish. Before the black invasion, the whites retire and disappear as snow 'neath the rays of the rising sun."[39] Dabney suggested that whites moved in order to avoid black neighbors. While surely true, this was an oversimplification of the exodus. The whites moved from older residential sections that had been intensively used by different demographic groups. The fact that by the 1920s these areas were already "rapidly decaying" was one causal factor in the movement.[40] Also, by this time many of the white residents of these older deteriorating sections had acquired the financial resources to enable them to obtain better housing in the more prestigious suburbs. Sometimes whites moved to suburbs from all-white inner city neighborhoods. Referring to Columbus in 1922, Urban League official Nimrod B. Allen said, "the desire of white people, with means to live in the fashionable suburban sections, causes sales of homes to Negroes over the protest of their white neighbors who object to living next to Negroes."[41] The arrival of African Americans into such older residential areas certainly stimulated the exodus of whites.

The out-migration of whites and in-migration of blacks during the 1920s created predominantly black census districts in Cincinnati, Cleveland, and Columbus. In 1920 Africans Americans were the majority in only one Ohio ward, Cincinnati's Ward 18, where blacks were just over half the population. In 1930 blacks were 73 percent of the population in Columbus' 7th ward, 78 percent in Cincinnati's 16th ward, and 72 percent in Cincinnati's 18th ward. In Cleveland, African Americans were 72 percent of the people in Statistical Area 23, while that figure was 70 percent in Area 24. Also in 1930, significant black majorities existed in the combined populations of two or more adjacent census districts in each of Ohio's three largest cities. African Americans were 63 percent of the population in Cincinnati's Wards 15–18, 62 percent in Columbus' Wards 6 and 7, and 56 percent in Cleveland's Statistical Areas 21–24.[42]

Predominantly African American census wards did not form in the less populous Ohio cities, but residential segregation proceeded there on a smaller spatial scale during the 1920s. In these cities, the proportion of blacks grew in those wards where blacks were concentrated in the past. In 1930 African Americans were 40 to 44 percent of the population in Springfield Ward 7, Dayton Ward 7, and Toledo Ward 8. Akron, Canton, Hamilton, and Youngstown each contained one ward where blacks were from 10 to 25 percent of the ward population.[43]

During the 1920s, the unwillingness of whites to reside near African Americans was a constant factor causing the development of major black districts in Cincinnati, Cleveland, and Columbus and further residential concentration of African Americans in Ohio's other urban centers. Overtly and covertly, whites attempted to confine African Americans to less desirable residential areas and to maintain other places exclusively for whites. Individual whites who owned homes in racially exclusive neighborhoods usually declined to rent or sell them to African Americans. Customarily, white banks would not make mortgage loans to blacks for the purchase of houses in those areas. Realty companies and newspaper advertisements reserved some residential property for whites only. White neighborhood improvement associations campaigned to exclude or remove black residents in their locales. Sometimes, physical harassment and violence were employed to force black families to vacate their recently purchased houses in previously all-white neighborhoods.

Ralph G. Harshman, who was a contemporary observer of Columbus' housing color line in 1920–1921, said, ". . . [T]here seems to be an unwritten law which says exactly where they [African Americans] shall reside. And while it does not always work, yet in the majority of cases it is very effective." Also, according to Harshman, during the years 1919 through 1921, major Columbus newspapers carried many real estate company advertisements indicating that blacks "need not make application as the companies will not sell to them."[44] Local Urban League officer Nimrod B. Allen also witnessed the real estate color line in Columbus early in the decade and commented on issues involving business and institutional properties there. Allen wrote: "The Long Street Improvement Association, composed of white businessmen . . . uses its influence to keep colored people from purchasing property on this street."[45] He mentioned another East Long Street property issue, this one at 18th Street, where the black Centenary Methodist Episcopal congregation planned to construct a church edifice very close to a new white church (Welch Presbyterian). Allen reported: "There are being put forth strong efforts by the white people interested to prevent the erection of this church for Negroes."[46]

Organized campaigns to exclude blacks from white neighborhoods were started in northern and southern Ohio as well as in Columbus during the 1920s. These anti-black efforts existed in Ohio's major cities and in its smaller ones. White property owners established racially exclusive neighborhood associations in reaction to the presence of new black residents in formerly all-white areas. Some of these residential streets were in inner-city districts encompassing old black neighborhoods where the number of dwellings was insufficient to accommodate local African Americans. But other such all-white neighborhoods were in suburbs whose amenities attracted black and white families that could afford suburban real estate. The white neighborhoods associations were conceived as permanent organizations with central councils and committees. Supported by hundreds of members, these associations adopted formal programs containing strategies to accomplish racial exclusion and raised money to finance their agendas.

In the Cleveland area, white neighborhood associations tried to bar African Americans from the city's eastern suburbs. During the 1920s Cleveland's African American residential areas expanded eastward from the deteriorating old Central Avenue black neighborhoods near downtown. Only well-to-do families lived in the black enclaves furthest to the east. But Cleveland Heights and Shaker Heights, affluent white suburbs near the East Side, were almost racially exclusive early in the decade.[47]

White property owners organized when an African American purchased property in the exclusive Wade Park section of Cleveland bordering on Cleveland Heights. Dr. Charles Garvin, who was a physician and

World War I veteran, acquired property in Wade Park during the summer of 1925. The property was purchased by a white person and transferred to Mrs. Garvin, under her maiden name, after the previous owner refused to sell it to an African American. When this transfer became public knowledge, representatives of the Wade Park property owners met with Dr. Garvin and tried to induce him to sell the property. Dr. Garvin refused and stated that he intended to construct a house on the property and live in it. On September 20, 1925, about two hundred Wade Park residents held a meeting for the purpose of preventing the Garvins from occupying their house, which was then under construction. They established a formal organization and elected officers. Various speakers presented information about Dr. Garvin's purchase and opposed residence in the area by African Americans. Also, a committee was created and instructed to seek the cooperation of Cleveland's African American leaders in finding a solution to the dispute. Representatives of the Wade Park property owners, African American professional leaders, and the local church federation met two days later. Black attorneys Alexander H. Martin and Clayborne George firmly supported Dr. Garvin's decision to retain his property and live in his house once it was constructed. A representative of the Federated Churches of Cleveland said that the conferees should consider intelligence and character rather than color as they attempted to resolve the issue. The meeting was adjourned without agreement.[48]

In October the Wade Park neighborhood council formally approved a scheme designed to generally exclude African Americans from the area. Members of the Wade Park association resolved to restrict the sale of property to Caucasians only. The association formed a committee instructed to investigate the backgrounds of potential buyers of land and houses in Wade Park. Residents were requested to remove the "For Sale" signs from their property until the scheme was in operation. Also, it was decided to collect money to be used for the purchase of property in the neighborhood that might be bought by African Americans. The amount to be contributed by each member was set at about one quarter of the annual property tax.[49]

Acting on racial motives, white property owners in Shaker Heights also formally organized in 1925 after Dr. Edward A. Bailey, a physician, and banker Howard Murrell bought Shaker Heights properties on Huntington Drive and Fairmount Boulevard, respectively. Some four hundred property owners established the Shaker Heights Protective Association, which took steps to draft and implement a restrictive covenant against property sales to African Americans. Newton D. Baker, former Cleveland mayor and former secretary of war under

President Wilson, played a leading role in the Shaker Heights Protective Association.[50]

In 1926 white residents in Dayton founded the West End Improvement Association in reaction to racially changing residential patterns within the Dayton city limits. Dayton's West End was composed of essentially separate white and black residential areas. Prompted by overcrowding and inadequate shelter in old black neighborhoods, some African Americans sought accommodations elsewhere in the West End. For example, black residents of shack villages called "Tin Can Alley" and "Tin Town" looked for better housing. In response, the West End Improvement Association undertook a program promoting racial segregation in housing and public schools. The association intended to use realtors, creditors, inducements, and threats to accomplish its ends. As a requirement of membership, all white members of the association, some five thousand in number, agreed not to sell, lease, or rent their property to African Americans. In the association's plan certain streets in the West End were to be designated for whites only or for blacks only, black children were to be removed from Roosevelt High School, and new elementary and junior high schools were to be constructed in black areas. According to the association's program, real estate dealers who allowed blacks to purchase West End property in designated white areas were to have their names published and to be boycotted by association members. The association also intended to make arrangements ensuring that Dayton's banks and its loan associations would restrict credit for African Americans seeking mortgage loans. An implicit threat against African Americans was made in the association's statement that blacks who agreed to the association's program were to be promised peace and protection. Evidently to appease African Americans, the association advocated the construction of a community center in a black area.[51] Some black business and professional men supported the association's program in exchange for the association's promise of aid in securing a community house for African Americans, but the black ministers of Dayton made a public statement expressing their opposition to the racially restrictive scheme.[52]

The West End Improvement Association's "for white only" meetings were held in Dayton's Roosevelt High School. The announcement of the association's meeting on July 13, 1927, read: "Are we going to let the Negro take the West Side? This is for you to decide. Don't wait until the Negro moves next door! All white residents of the west side should attend this meeting."[53] African American spokespersons in Dayton contacted school officials and protested this practice. Subsequently, the Dayton Board of Education responded to it affirmatively and the association was prohibited from using the high school building for its meetings.[54]

Sometimes persons who found better housing outside Ohio's black districts were subjected to physical harassment during the 1920s. In Cleveland suburbs angry mobs tried to make black residents leave previously all-white areas. In 1924 white mobs forced the Arthur Hill family to leave their recently purchased home in Garfield Heights. The village mayor refused the Hills police protection on the grounds that the Garfield Heights authorities could not afford to pay for it. He also said that the Hills "had no right to buy such a nice place."[55] The family of Dr. Edward A. Bailey was harassed in a variety of ways after moving into Shaker Heights. The perpetrators attempted to burn the Bailey's garage, threw stones at windows, and fired gunshots at their house. The family chauffeur fired at one of the vandals. When Dr. Bailey sought protection from Shaker Heights officials, a police guard was stationed at the house. The policemen searched members of the family and their servants for concealed weapons every time they left the house and again when they returned.[56] Given this treatment the Baileys left Shaker Heights.[57]

Dr. Charles Garvin and his family faced vandalism and violence as African American newcomers to a racially exclusive area on Cleveland's far East Side. The Garvins moved into their newly constructed Wade Park home on December 31, 1925. Several days later a vandal painted "KKK" in large letters across the front of the house. Cleveland's police department made an investigation following Dr. Garvin's report of the incident.[58] At the end of January 1926, the explosion of a homemade bomb damaged the Garvin house. Following the explosion, Mrs. Garvin observed several men running from the scene. Afterwards, a police detail was assigned to guard the Garvin property.

Meanwhile, Dr. Garvin was appointed as assistant surgeon in the genito-urinary surgery department at Western Reserve University's School of Medicine and at Lakeside Hospital.[59] Early in July a second attempt was made to bomb the Garvin house. Again the police investigated the incident and provided protection.[60] The resulting anguish experienced by the family was expressed by Dr. Garvin's sister, who wrote: "I was worried nearly half to death over the trouble my . . . brother is having. . . . . His wife was very brave the first time and may be now, but it is a terrible position to be placed in."[61] Despite the harassment, which eventually subsided, the Garvins remained in their Wade Park home.[62]

Throughout the decade whites occasionally mounted physical resistance when Ohio's neighborhoods changed racially. In 1929 the family of Ozie Benson bought a house in one of Toledo's white immigrant neighborhoods. Once the Bensons moved into the residence, all their windows were broken and an attempt was made to burn their dwelling. The former owner, a white person, was threatened with mob violence because he sold the property to an African American.[63]

The segregation of African American students in Ohio schools was greater in 1930 than it was ten years earlier. African American enrollments increased and sometimes became predominant in urban school districts with neighborhoods where blacks were arriving and whites were leaving. Nineteenth century state law still prohibited all-white or all-black schools that were based on public policy. Wholly white schools nevertheless existed across Ohio usually because all children in their districts were whites. While not found in northern Ohio, there were entirely African American public schools in central and southern Ohio. All-black schools, opened earlier, continued to exist in Columbus, Cincinnati, and Dayton during the decade, while new ones were established in Cincinnati and Springfield. Racially integrated public schools increasingly placed black students in separate classes, claiming that the placements were made on the basis of scholastic achievements and not on race. Although racial separation widened, Ohio schools with few exceptions operated within state laws, and students regardless of color were admitted to schools in their districts. Yet racial discrimination was common in Ohio's racially mixed schools. White parents, students, and teachers harbored prejudiced views of African Americans. Black teachers were not assigned to instruct white students, except in some northern Ohio schools. When schools became predominantly African American, their curricula often were made less academically rigorous.

Racial segregation of public school students widened in all Ohio regions during the 1920s. Throughout the state, schools became predominantly black in school districts that were being densely settled by African American families. In Cleveland, black students were enrolled in 63 of that city's 142 public schools in 1924.[64] The other 79 Cleveland public schools undoubtedly were all white. These racially integrated and all-white institutions in Cleveland evidently mirrored the racial characteristics of their respective school districts. Enrollments in some Cleveland schools became predominantly black as racial demographics of school districts changed. For example, practically all of the students attending Outhwaite School and Rutherford B. Hayes School in 1927 were African Americans.[65] At the end of the decade, almost all black junior high students in Cleveland attended four schools, and most Cleveland Central High School students were African Americans.[66] Black students became more concentrated in some neighborhood schools, but public schools throughout Cleveland admitted students living in their respective districts regardless of color. In 1930 integrated faculties as well as student bodies still existed in Cleveland schools. Over

100 African American teachers were employed in Cleveland schools, including some predominantly white ones.[67] Yet, as late as 1926, only one black teacher was assigned to a Cleveland school above the elementary level.[68]

Likewise the Columbus public school system was racially integrated during the 1920s when racial separation grew in some of its schools. Black students attended 56 of Columbus' 58 public schools in 1921. The predominantly white schools in Columbus each enrolled at least two African American students. Black pupils were the majority at two Columbus schools in 1921.[69] One of them was located in a school district with boundary lines that had been racially gerrymandered before World War I. Referring to this Champion Avenue School in 1922, local Urban League officer Nimrod B. Allen wrote: "Being in a Negro district it is theoretically not a Negro school but is officered entirely by Negro teachers, with the exception of a manual training teacher, and all the pupils are Negroes. Any white child who lives in that section may attend another school if he wishes. This school has a Junior High Department."[70] Later, another Columbus school became predominantly black as the African American population grew on the city's East Side. The Columbus school board employed black principals and teachers to staff the three schools with large African American enrollments.[71] Consequently, the number of black teachers in Columbus rose from 27 to 58 between 1920 and 1930.[72]

The number of completely separate schools for African Americans grew in central and southern Ohio during the 1920s. All were placed in or near black neighborhoods, were staffed by African Americans, and enrolled black students only. The locations and staffing of these institutions signaled that local school authorities meant them for African Americans. But, black students not residing within the district boundaries of these schools were not required to attend them. Those founded before 1920 included Cincinnati's Douglass School and Harriet Beecher Stowe School, Dayton's Garfield School Annex, and Columbus' Champion Avenue School.

All-black schools existed only in southern and central Ohio and were more common in Cincinnati than elsewhere in the state. Paralleling enrollment growth in Cincinnati's all-black schools, the number of black teachers in that city rose from 83 to 163 between 1920 and 1930.[73] A large school edifice was constructed to accommodate the rising number of black students. The new Harriet Beecher Stowe School building, dedicated in 1923, housed a new all-black junior high school as well as an all-black elementary school. In prior years black students finishing the elementary grades could only enter racially mixed junior high schools in Cincinnati. Black students seeking admission to Stowe School exceeded its seating capacity shortly after it opened. In 1925 the Stowe pupils in the overflow were taught at the Jackson Colony, a school annex located on West Fifth Street in a nineteenth century school building with seating for 600 students. At that time, Principal Jennie D. Porter supervised 80 teachers at the Stowe School as well as the 23 teachers and the assistant principal at the Jackson annex. In 1925 Stowe School had 3,080 pupils, more than any other Cincinnati school whether black, white, or integrated. Meantime, Principal Francis M. Russell and 31 teachers were in charge of Douglass Elementary School, housed in a main edifice seating 800 pupils and in portable buildings with seats for 180 more. Ostensibly, black students in Cincinnati could choose to attend one of these all-black public schools or a racially mixed school. Meanwhile, Superintendent William J. Decatur and nine teachers conducted vocational and scholastic work at the Colored Industrial School of Cincinnati. This private trade school graduated almost 600 students between 1914 and 1926.[74]

All-black schools also existed in Dayton and in smaller central and southern Ohio towns and cities during the decade. Some of these schools were based on overtly racial policies that were in violation of Ohio law against school segregation. In Dayton, African Americans were excluded from the Garfield Elementary School building. Starting in the previous decade, Garfield School's black students and faculty were assigned to a separate annex building.[75] In 1925 decisions in Ohio courts found this practice to be unlawful. Subsequently, in 1926, a school bond issue in Dayton provided funds for the construction of an elementary school in a wholly African American school district of that city.[76] In central Ohio, the Springfield school board's policies were in accord with state law until 1922, when it approved an experiment in racial segregation. Only black students and staff were assigned to Springfield's Fulton Elementary School during 1922–1923. Ohio courts eventually barred this racial policy at Fulton School. In southern Ohio, black schools existed in very small towns with relatively large African American populations. African Americans formed residential concentrations in Lockland and Wyoming, located just north of Cincinnati in Hamilton County. In each of these towns about a fifth of the people were African Americans in 1930. The total population then was 5,703 in Lockland and 3,767 in Wyoming. In 1925, small black schools in these towns employed African American principals and faculty, with six teachers in Lockland and four in Wyoming.[77]

Increasing racial segregation also occurred within Ohio's racially integrated schools during the 1920s. In some mixed schools, special classes enrolled only black children whose families had recently migrated from the South. Southern states generally provided inadequate schooling for African American students. Consequently, a high percentage of the migrant children had not made educational achievements in accordance with their age or grade levels by Ohio public school standards. Apparently, diverse motives influenced the authorities who reacted to the problem of educational retardation among migrant children. Some local school officials made legitimate efforts to raise the educational achievements of the migrant children. Others merely used the situation to rationalize separate classes for black students from the South. Irrespective of motives, their responses to the educational problems of the migrant pupils commonly led to greater racial segregation. At about mid-decade, elementary schools in various Ohio regions started separate classes for black students whose ages and grade levels did not match as required. In southern Ohio, for example, this practice was initiated in Dayton's Willard School and in Hamilton County's Woodlawn School in 1924. In northern Ohio, such classes were introduced in Mansfield's Bowman School in 1925 and in Cleveland's Outhwaite and Rutherford B. Hayes Schools in 1927.[78]

The racial attitudes of whites contributed to the widening color divide in Ohio public schools in the 1920s. White reactions to integrated schools usually ranged from hostility to indifference, but some whites supported laws against school segregation. Anti-black biases of many white educators, parents, and children adversely affected race relations in mixed schools. As earlier, there was greater white acceptance of integrated schools in Cleveland than in central and southern Ohio cities. In Cleveland some black teachers taught white students, and a black board of education member voted on citywide school policy issues at the end of the decade. After the number of black students enrolled in Cleveland schools grew substantially, black community activists declared that African Americans were entitled to representation on the city's board of education. When school board vacancies occurred in October 1926 and April 1929, organized campaigns urged the appointment of an African American to the board. Both of these movements failed, although the latter effort involved several hundred people, black and white. The goal was achieved when Mary E. Martin won a Cleveland school board seat in the general election, November 1929. Mrs. Martin, the wife of attorney Alexander H. Martin, was a graduate of Cleveland's Central High School and the Cleveland School of Education. Her qualifications for the post included teaching experience in Alabama, Arkansas, and Cleveland schools.[79]

African Americans, nevertheless, were not fully represented in the

Cleveland Public School system. Further, color bias and hostility to racial integration existed in Cleveland schools. Blacks were underrepresented in Cleveland's school administration, and with exceptions black teachers were not employed above the elementary level. Color prejudice was expressed in the Cleveland junior high school that employed David Pierce, who was a white teacher and an active member of the local NAACP branch. Black pupils comprised almost 3 percent of enrollment in Pierce's school; however, his classes were entirely composed of white students. Pierce observed race relations at his school and reported the racial attitudes of its students, teachers, and parents in 1923. He surveyed his classes asking questions, for example, concerning the desirability of mixed schools. He learned that approximately half of the students were "decidedly prejudiced." The other half "felt the problem required intelligent and thoughtful consideration." This group included "a small number in favor of equal rights for Negroes."[80] Answers given by Pierce's students revealed that ". . . colored children were only too frequently snubbed and subjected to insults from their white classmates."[81] Similarly, Pierce observed that "in some instances" teachers taught racial "antagonism."[82]

Objections to school integration during the 1920s were even more common among whites in southern and central Ohio than in Cleveland. Commenting on Cincinnati schools in that decade, local black weekly editor Wendell P. Dabney said: "The whites generally favor separate schools. Regarding Negroes as inferior, they deplore any association with them. . . ."[83] A study of racial attitudes in Columbus schools found that opposition to school integration was widespread among white teachers and parents of school age children. In 1920–1921, sociologist Ralph G. Harshman made a survey that included 80 white parents chosen at random. All of those who replied objected to racial integration in the schools. All 20 of the black parents interviewed approved integration.[84] Of the 130 Columbus teachers who responded to Harshman's survey, only 15 favored racial integration in the schools. The white bias against mixed schools was broad in Columbus and elsewhere in the state, but there was no documented effort to legalize segregated schools in Ohio during the 1920s. Columbus public schools were conducted within the state law prohibiting color line school policies. Harshman observed: ". . . [T]here is absolutely no restriction in regard to mingling" in racially mixed Columbus public schools.[85]

Racially integrated public schools were still commonplace in Ohio cities in the 1920s; however, demographic trends and other extralegal factors at work during the decade increased the probability that an African American student would be enrolled in an all-black class in a predominantly black school or in a school composed only of African Americans. Schools that were mainly devoted to African American students often gave greater attention to vocational goals than academic ones. In Cleveland the local NAACP branch president asserted: ". . . to all intents and purposes Outhwaite and R. B. Hayes Schools are segregated schools with distinctive curricula that [do] not make fair allowance for advancement to Junior High and Senior High in the course of time."[86] Many students advanced from the elementary classes to the junior high program in the all-black Harriet Beecher Stowe School in Cincinnati. The Stowe School, however, was especially well equipped for vocational training. The generally well-appointed Stowe building contained rooms for domestic art, domestic science, catering, laundry, sewing machines, print shop, cabinet making, woodworking, and house construction.[87]

Higher education in Ohio also was affected by prejudice, but racial integration existed in at least a dozen Ohio colleges and universities during the 1920s. They were located in every region of the state. Akron University, University of Cincinnati, The Ohio State University, Ohio University, and University of Toledo were among the public institutions enrolling black students. African Americans also attended private schools, including Case Institute of Technology, Oberlin College, Ohio Northern University, Ohio Wesleyan University, Otterbein College, Western Reserve University, and Wittenberg University.[88] At least one private Ohio college openly maintained a for-white-only policy. The Western College for Women at Oxford was "exclusively for white women" according to information that a college official sent to the National Association for the Advancement of Colored People.[89] As in the past, African Americans composed the faculty and student body of Wilberforce University near Xenia.

The status of African Americans in Ohio's integrated colleges and universities remained substantially unchanged during the decade, but some color line breakthroughs were made. For example, in 1924 an African American was awarded an electrical engineering degree at The Ohio State University, which previously discouraged African Americans attempting to enter its engineering programs.[90] In 1928 Ohio State University student Bernard Young, Jr. was named managing editor of the *Ohio State Lantern*. This appointment made Young the first African American to hold such a position on a student newspaper at an integrated university in the United States.[91] An Inter-Racial Council was formed at The Ohio State University. In 1930 its publication, called the *Bulletin,* carried an article giving an explicit account of race relations across the university. It reported that African Americans were represented in the football and track programs, but that black athletes felt excluded from the basketball and baseball teams. Excepting in the engineering and medical schools, the faculty exhibited "little prejudice" against black students. While "theoretically" welcome to participate in parties and open houses, the article stated: "The Negro students have made no effort to enter into the social life of the white students." Some campus organizations admitted blacks, while others did not. Departmental and religious groups were open to all. According to this survey: "Some honoraries, such as Pi Lambda Theta, are closed to Negroes, while Phi Beta Kappa admits them. The same is true of the official student organizations. The Scarlet Mask . . . is closed to both Negroes and Jews." No African Americans were members of the Inter-Fraternity Council, the Student Senate, the Women's Student Government Association, or the Men's Glee Club. African Americans, in small numbers, were members of the YMCA, YWCA, the Women's Glee Club, and the Choral Society. The article concluded: "Nearly all the colored students live several miles from the University and have to travel by street car. Since they cannot go to their rooms between classes, they flock in large numbers to Pomerene Hall, the Library, and Ohio Union. Some white students have complained of this but the reason is obvious. No dormitories are open to the girls on campus nor to the men in the community. Both of the campus cafeterias are open to all, but the restaurants in the community off campus are closed to Negroes. State Theater does not admit Negroes to its shows."[92]

Racial discrimination at The Ohio State University received considerable attention from African Americans in the state and nation in 1930. William Bell, a starting tackle on the football team, was not permitted to travel with the team to Baltimore to play in the football game with the United States Naval Academy. Members of the black community charged the university with bowing to racial prejudices of white Southerners in refusing to allow Bell to play in the game. In not taking Bell to Baltimore, The Ohio State University president held: "The university is endeavoring to protect him from [the] unpleasant experience of probable race discrimination manifested in a southern city."[93] Bell, who was a graduate of Akron's East High School, eventually was named to the All Big Ten football team and the Associated Press All American team.[94]

Compared to earlier decades, more African Americans were enrolled in and graduated from Ohio's colleges and universities. In 1928, 250 African Americans were enrolled at The Ohio State University, 64 at Oberlin College, 49 at Western Reserve University, and 40 at the University of Cincinnati.[95] During 1920–1929, Ohio academies were recorded in The Crisis's annual listing of colleges and universities that awarded degrees to blacks. These listed Ohio institutions graduated few African Americans per year, often just one person, but in one instance 24 African Americans obtained degrees from the same university in a single year. Several black students at the University of Cincinnati, The Ohio State University, and Western Reserve University earned graduate and professional degrees including M.A., M.D., D.D.S., and LL.B.[96]

One of these African American university graduates was Cincinnati native Jennie D. Porter. She was the daughter of William Porter, who became remarkably affluent as Cincinnati's first black undertaker, and Ethlinda Porter, a Cincinnati public school teacher. Jennie D. Porter began a teaching career after graduation from the largely white Hughes High School and the Cincinnati Normal School. Later she enrolled in the University of Cincinnati, where she earned the B.S. in 1923, the M.A. in 1925, and the doctorate in education in 1927. Meanwhile, she was principal of the Harriet Beecher Stowe School.[97]

Also among the African Americans earning advanced degrees in the twenties was Clay E. Hunter, a Tennessee native, who was reared on his family's prosperous farm near Yellow Springs in southwestern Ohio. Hunter graduated from Wilberforce University with an A.B. in 1917 and then saw combat in Europe as a second lieutenant, 92nd Division, United States Army. He received the LL.B. from The Ohio State University's law school in 1923, after which he practiced law in Columbus and then in Cincinnati.[98]

During the 1920s racial segregation was still more extensive in private churches in Ohio than in public educational facilities governed by state law. In 1920 the institutional lives of black and white church people already were almost wholly separate. African Americans did not attend white churches with rare exceptions. As in the previous decade, some white congregations moved to suburban edifices from church buildings in the vicinity of black neighborhoods, thereby widening the physical gap between themselves and African Americans. For example, old St. Paul's Church at Seventh and Smith Streets in Cincinnati was vacated by whites and acquired by the black congregation of Calvary Methodist Episcopal Church in 1925.[99] A small proportion of Ohio's black churches were affiliated with white Protestant denominations or the Roman Catholic church. The actual number of these churches increased a bit after 1916.[100]

Occasionally in Ohio, white Protestants and Catholics devoted new or existing church buildings to Christian work among African Americans. In 1922 Catholic authorities in Cleveland made a separate African American parish called Our Lady of the Sacrament and erected a church building there. White churches which were in proximity to black residential areas experienced declining memberships as whites moved away. Consequently, new black congregations formed in some existing churches affiliated with white religious bodies. For example, a few old Catholic churches welcomed African Americans. In 1925 the Archbishop of Cincinnati announced that Holy Trinity Church near West Fifth and Seventh Streets was open to African Americans. Similarly, in 1922 the Lutheran Synodical Conference of America founded the "Colored Lutheran Emanuel Church" at Cutter and Betts Streets in Cincinnati.[101]

In Ohio most black church people and pastors were affiliated with separate African American denominations, mainly the National Baptist Convention and African Methodist Episcopal church. In 1926, 81 percent of Ohio's black churches belonged to black denominations. Also, black and white clergymen continued to maintain separate professional organizations in Ohio cities during the 1920s. African American pastors composed the Baptist Ministerial Alliance in Cincinnati and the Baptist Ministers' Alliance in Cleveland.[102]

Occasionally in the 1920s a black member was included in a white pastors' association because it was affiliated with a nationwide white denomination containing some separate black congregations. The Reverend Edmund H. Oxley, for example, was a member of the Cincinnati Clericus, an organization of white ministers of the Episcopal Church. The Reverend Oxley was Rector of St. Andrews Episcopal Church, serving an affluent black congregation. A native of Trinidad, West Indies, Oxley possessed outstanding credentials when he came to Cincinnati in 1912. He graduated from Howard University (B.A., B.D., and honorary D.D.), and Harvard University (S.T.B.) and won oratorical prizes at both institutions. While an active minister in the 1920s, Oxley was also a graduate student in the philosophy department at the University of Cincinnati. Racially mixed ministers' association like the Cincinnati Clericus were rare in Ohio.[103]

Limited interracial contact also occurred within Ohio's citywide church federations during the decade. Interracial committees functioned within the Federated Churches of Cleveland and the Toledo Council of Churches. The Cincinnati church federation included an interracial committee and a "Colored Department" with committees that were devoted to African American concerns and that were composed of black members.[104]

During the 1920s, as in the past, the color line was most divisive in Ohio's private social life. Blacks and whites were almost wholly separate in the conduct of private social life in churches and other established community institutions. Racial separation was the rule in Ohio's great variety of sorority and fraternal associations, social clubs, civic organizations, and women's clubs, as seen elsewhere in these pages.[105] There still was some mixing of blacks and whites in public life, but racial separation in public accommodations was wider than ever.

The heightened race consciousness of whites affected race relations in Ohio's public places during the 1920s. Even prior to World War I, public accommodations in Ohio tended to exclude or segregate African Americans. This trend accelerated during the wartime black migration and continued through the following decade. In 1930, outside of black districts, few Ohio public accommodations admitted African Americans on an equal basis. The growth of racial discrimination in public places occurred across the state from Cincinnati to Cleveland. In his brief essay on "Prejudice in Public Places" written in 1926, local black weekly editor Wendell P. Dabney commented on changing white attitudes in Cincinnati. He recalled earlier times prior to World War I when some African Americans patronized a wide variety of Cincinnati's restaurants, saloons, and theaters. "In late years, however," Dabney noted, "the prejudice has grown by leaps and bounds until now . . . colored citizens generally receive welcome, consideration or courtesy in but very few places of public welfare or entertainment."[106] Racial exclusion was practiced at Cincinnati's principal theaters, all located outside black neighborhoods. Still referring to Cincinnati in 1926, Editor Dabney reported: "There are a number of smaller picture houses on West Fifth Street whose prejudice against admission of colored patrons has been removed by the scarcity of white patrons and consequent diminution of box office receipts."[107] As in the past, African Americans used streetcars in Cincinnati, but not without occasional experiences of racial friction.[108]

In Columbus public transportation was available to African Americans, but racial discrimination was common in that city's public places. In 1920–1921, sociologist Ralph G. Harshman interviewed managers and employees of public accommodations in Columbus and observed their public conduct. Regarding racial contacts on East Long Street's public transport, Harshman noted: "The street car motormen and conductors report there is much dissatisfaction registered by the regular car patrons concerning the mingling that is necessary in the street cars."[109] In 1922 local Urban League official Nimrod B. Allen made similar observations and explained: "Both the whites and black people use principally the Long Street car and occasionally there has been race friction on this car which if sober judgment had not come into play might have caused serious embarrassment to the city. This race tension is being relieved by automobile busses that are operated on a parallel street and are patronized by a large proportion of white people who live east. The busses do not discriminate against Negroes."[110] However, color lines commonly existed in Columbus' hotels, theaters, restaurants, parks, swimming pools, and other public places. Blacks were welcome in a few of the smaller hotels in Columbus, but Harshman reported: "The leading hotels . . . namely Deshler, Neil, Southern, Chittenden, Hartman, Virginia, Jefferson, Columbus and Norwich will not cater to Negroes in any regard. The contention of the managers is that they [African Americans] keep the respectable white patrons away."[111] The public and commercial parks in Columbus were open to African Americans; however, blacks who visited them were exposed to racial discrimination, for example, the swimming pools and dance halls were "closed" to black people.[112] Columbus' approximately two dozen motion picture theaters all admitted African Americans. The few motion picture houses located in black neighborhoods did not require racially segregated seating. The other Columbus theaters required black patrons to sit in designated sections, usually in the rear or in the balcony. These sections were conspicuously marked by signs reading "'Reserved,' 'No White Patrons in This Section,' 'For Our Colored Friends,' or just 'Please.'"[113] The Columbus vaudeville theaters drew various color lines. Keith's refused admittance to African Americans, while the Broadway admitted black people on a segregated basis. The Hartman and the Lyceum, the city's two legitimate theaters, admitted African Americans but required separate seating.[114] After observing race contacts in Columbus retail stores, Harshman reported that blacks were "free to enter all the stores of the city with the exception of a few exclusive shops," but black patrons received less "attention and consideration" than white ones in most Columbus stores owned by whites.[115] African Americans were refused service in most of the Columbus restaurants.[116] Such flagrant racial discrimination in Columbus' public places continued through the decade.[117]

Racial discrimination in public accommodations increased in Cleveland during the 1920s. The color line, however, was less uniform in Cleveland than in Cincinnati and Columbus. Ohio's nineteenth century abolitionist heritage was stronger and more influential in northern Ohio than in the state's central and southern regions. In Cleveland, consequently, many whites wished to maintain at least a semblance of racial justice and many blacks were inclined to challenge color lines. Accordingly, Cleveland's public accommodations more often welcomed blacks than those in central and southern Ohio cities. The color line, nevertheless, grew more extensive in Cleveland during the decade. The racial policies of Cleveland hotels varied. In 1929 a representative of the local NAACP branch observed: "The hotel situation has changed here [Cleveland] with changing terms and management. No hotel admits a policy of exclusion and yet we have reports of refusals. At the same time we hear of instances where accommodations are afforded without question."[118] Dr. Robert R. Moton, Booker T. Washington's successor as president of Tuskegee Institute, was one person who had difficulty in obtaining satisfactory hotel accommodations in Cleveland. Dr. Moton was invited to speak to the Cleveland Chamber of Commerce in 1923. The Hotel Statler was willing to give him a room provided that he "take his meals in it." Subsequently, after a protest was made, the Hollenden Hotel accommodated Dr. Moton on satisfactorily terms.[119] Similarly, Jane E. Hunter, general secretary of Cleveland's Phillis Wheatley Association, was refused elevator service in the Statler hotel in 1926. Officials of the Cleveland Community Chest Fund invited her to address them in the Statler's rooms. She refused to use the hotel's freight lift and eventually was allowed to go on the passenger elevator. The hotel manager first ordered all other occupants from the regular elevator and then escorted her to the meeting. According to the Cleveland *Gazette* the Community Chest officials "expressed heart-felt sympathy when Miss Hunter finally arrived, in tears, in their rooms in the hotel."[120] Similarly, in 1928 the Cleveland Hotel excluded Dr. James W. Eichelberger, Jr. of Chicago. While preparing to attend the International Council of Religious Education's Cleveland convention, Dr. Eichelberger had made a room reservation. The Cleveland Hotel refused to give him the room when he arrived.[121]

The color line was also uneven in Cleveland's restaurants, theaters, parks, and swimming pools during the 1920s. Racial discrimination was commonplace, but not universal, in Cleveland restaurants at decade's end. Most of the restaurants with color line policies flatly refused service to African Americans. Others discouraged African American patronage by overcharging blacks for food. Some required blacks to pay a service charge not required of white patrons.[122] Racial segregation was practiced in the Stillman, the Allen, and many other Cleveland theaters.[123] Ostensibly the Cleveland municipal parks and swimming pools were open to all regardless of race, but blacks who attempted to patronize the pools, for example, the one at Woodland Hills Park, met violent reactions by white patrons.[124] Color lines still existed in the city's commercial parks. As always, Luna Park refused admittance to African Americans, except on specified days.[125]

In the 1920s there were documented instances of racial discrimination in the public places of smaller Ohio cities, including Akron, Toledo, and Zanesville. Several South Main Street restaurants in Akron practiced blatant racial discrimination. In the windows of these establishments were signs that carried such declarations as "We Cater Only to

White Trade" and "Colored People Served in Sacks Only, Please Don't Sit Down."[126] During a given year in Toledo there were dozens of recorded cases of racial discrimination in restaurants, stores and other public accommodations.[127] Racial lines were imposed in Zanesville; for example, blacks were excluded from a new addition to the Greenwood Cemetery in that small city located east of Columbus.[128] Color lines undoubtedly existed in public places in all Ohio population centers during the decade.

In summary, the color line in urban Ohio was more discriminatory than ever in the 1920s, which saw total black population reaching all-time highs in Ohio cities. The twenties experienced the climax of a decades-long nationwide trend of increasing intolerance of people who were foreign born or unlike Anglo-Saxon Protestants. The isolation of African Americans in the larger society was greater than ever in each Ohio region, and this was most clearly evident in patterns of residential segregation from Cleveland to Cincinnati. Exclusion and segregation by color were not absolute, but they were the norm, and black-white contacts in every Ohio region were less common than earlier. Blacks and whites generally took different routes on life's many avenues, from birth in separate medical facilities to death and burial in separate cemetery allotments. This essentially was an informal and unofficial racial caste system in many respects comparable to the legal ones existing in southern states possessing Jim Crow laws requiring segregation of blacks and whites from cradle to grave. The color line was less uniform in Ohio than in southern states. It was still relatively less unyielding in northern Ohio than in the state's other regions because Ohio's nineteenth century regional pattern of black-white relations persisted through the 1920s. Ohio's color line, unlike the South's, did not disenfranchise African American voters. The color line was different in important respects north and south of the Mason-Dixon Line; nevertheless, in Ohio as well as in southern states it dictated that blacks and whites lead largely separate lives, undermined the physical and spiritual welfare of many black people, and generally denied African Americans freedom of choice and equality of opportunity in the larger society. The following chapters demonstrate that black Ohioans in local communities became more active and effective in confronting the color line's effects in the twenties.

CHAPTER SIX

New Leadership and Welfare Work

B lack Ohioans in the 1920s persisted in the effort to assist African American newcomers, who were exposed to poverty, substandard housing conditions, and other kinds of social problems that were characteristic of life in the neighborhoods of older urban districts, before as well as after African Americans settled in them. The agenda for this effort was set before 1920 and its concerns remained much the same; however, the struggle on the social welfare front was different in character and magnitude in the twenties than in the teens. Organizations providing coordinated leadership were central to the social work movement in Ohio throughout the twenties. This was lacking in the teens until almost the end of the decade when it appeared only in Cleveland, Cincinnati, and Columbus in the form of National Urban League–like local welfare associations. Each association established its organizational structure, identified problems, and formed programs addressing them while little time for implementation remained at decade's end. This new coordinated leadership became the norm in many Ohio cities during the twenties with the founding of more local affiliates of the National Urban League. Social work was conducted on an unprecedented scale in the twenties as local welfare associations enlarged their bureaucracies and forged links with newly founded social service institutions. These welfare associations and their many affiliated institutions operated with greater funding and provided broader services than ever before.

In the teens and twenties different emphases were given to specific social services provided by National Urban League affiliates and their cohorts. When the wartime migration was in progress, high priorities were given to vocational training and assisting searches for jobs and inexpensive shelter. While these were continued after 1920, new emphasis was given to social programs in the twenties that had been much less prominent in Ohio earlier. Those intended to improve public health were an example. Other programs given new attention in the twenties were those that provided arenas suitable for socially sanctioned activities. These efforts brought a previously unseen proliferation of black neighborhood centers that possessed facilities for recreation, meetings, and other community activities. Prior to 1920 such all-black facilities were rare. In some Ohio cities they could be found in buildings of black branches of the Young Men's Christian Association or the Young Women's Christian Association, whose facilities were open to members only. In the twenties, new black neighborhood centers were opened and maintained in African American churches, in all-black schools, and in buildings with links to Urban League affiliates. Rare before 1920, black institutional churches providing various kinds of secular community services multiplied in the twenties.

The nature of the struggle to overcome urban problems in black neighborhoods was more uniform across Ohio in the 1920s than in any previous decade. This altered the regional pattern of black-white relations in Ohio that first appeared early in the nineteenth century. In accord with the pattern's regional variations, black social service institutions were more often found in southern and central Ohio than in northern Ohio prior to 1920. In the period 1915–1920, for instance, many such black establishments existed in Cincinnati, while there were only two in Cleveland. At the same time, in Cleveland both blacks and whites were served at some social service facilities, for example, at a YMCA branch, while in Cincinnati blacks were excluded from institutions of this kind serving whites. In the twenties, the trend in northern Ohio was toward separate facilities. For instance, a black YMCA branch, a black community house, and a black maternity home were opened in Cleveland then. These changes accompanied increasing urban black population, changing white attitudes, and new African American leadership in northern Ohio.

African American welfare organizations largely sought to ease the problems of migrants in Ohio. They were intended to assist other needy persons as well. The welfare organizations emphasized assistance in the areas of employment, housing, health, and crime prevention. They also wished to enlarge educational and recreational opportunities and generally improve race relations. These were goals of the National Urban League's Ohio affiliates, whose numbers grew during the decade. Prior to 1920 Urban League units existed in Columbus, Cleveland, and Youngstown. In 1930 the Urban League records also noted affiliates in

Akron, Canton, Cincinnati, and Warren.[1] Ohio's Urban League affiliates enhanced their administrative structures and extended their services during the decade. In 1921 the Columbus Urban League hired an
executive secretary in the person of Nimrod B. Allen, who was a trained
social worker and a former executive secretary of Columbus' black
Spring Street YMCA.[2] Also, the Columbus Urban League organized
auxiliary agencies including the Friendly Service Bureau, Colored Big
Brothers, and Colored Big Sisters. The Friendly Service Bureau, established in 1925, worked in cooperation with the police department to
prevent juvenile delinquency among African American youth.
Similarly, the Big Brothers and Big Sisters were initiated in 1926 for the
purpose of providing adult guidance to "semi-delinquent" youngsters.[3]
Also, in the 1920's, Cleveland's Urban League affiliate hired an industrial secretary in charge of industrial and employment activities.[4] The
Urban League of Canton opened a Community House in 1923. The
house was a center for welfare work and recreational activities and a
headquarters for social groups.[5]

The Cincinnati Negro Civic Welfare Association's structure and
activities also expanded during the 1920s. Although no formal affiliation existed, Cincinnati's black welfare association was implicitly related to the National Urban League, according to historian Andrea Tuttle
Kornbluh.[6] Its aims, form, and work largely reflected those of the league.
By mid-decade, the Negro Civic Welfare Association had grown to
include Executive Secretary James H. Robinson, a board of directors, ten
committees, and many cooperating social agencies. Among the directors
were blacks in various professions and businesses and locally prominent
whites, most notably a member of former President William Howard
Taft's family, Charles P. Taft, II. The Welfare Association's Economics
Committee was interested in developing thrift, home ownership, and
industrial welfare. Its Civics Committee was charged with promoting
good race relations, citizenship, and character. The association's com-
mittees included Housing and Health, Relief and Institutional Care,
Child Welfare, Recreation, and Education. In 1925, the Negro Civic
Welfare Association described itself as "a clearing house and coordinat-
ing agency sponsoring the Negro social work of the city as a whole."[7]
About thirty Cincinnati social agencies cooperated with the Negro
Civic Welfare Association. Most were citywide agencies such as the
American Red Cross, Associated Charities, Catholic Charities, and
Better Housing League. A dozen of them possessed institutional facilities
devoted to social work among African Americans.[8]

Black welfare associations in Ohio cities cooperated with a range of
local African American welfare institutions such as homes for the young

and aged poor, YMCA and YWCA facilities, shelters for working women, and maternity homes. While most were founded earlier, some black social work facilities opened in the 1920s. Among them were Cleveland's Mary B. Talbert maternity home and Cincinnati's Shoemaker Health and Welfare Center.[9] Ohio's African American welfare institutions still operated on small budgets, but they were better funded during the 1920s. Philanthropic support improved somewhat in that prosperous time. In Cincinnati, the Negro Civic Welfare Association reported that local black social work was supported not only by important white philanthropists but by hundreds of black contributors to the local Community Chest.[10] After raising $500,000 in contributions earlier in the decade, in 1928 Cleveland's Phillis Wheatley Association erected a new nine-story edifice to replace its small home for employed young women.[11] Prominent black Clevelander George A. Myers rated the achievements of Cleveland's Phillis Wheatley Association and Negro Welfare Association in 1926. The Wheatley Association, he concluded, was "doing excellent work, but [was] circumscribed by reason of inadequate facilities," while still in its old building.[12] Myers held that the good services done by the Negro Welfare Association were "practically negligible" when compared to the need for its assistance.[13] His assessment would have applied equally well to the general spectrum of organizations concerned with the welfare of African Americans in urban Ohio. Across the state organizations confronted the various social problems affecting black migrants. The fraction of aid seekers who came within their purview undoubtedly benefited. But these organizations lacked the financial resources, physical space, and staff necessary to assist many other needy people.

In Ohio during the 1920s vocational training and employment services were provided by Urban League affiliates and various institutions devoted to African Americans. Urban League representatives further developed contacts with industrial and commercial employers and urged them to hire African Americans. The high percentage of job applicants placed by the Cleveland Negro Welfare Association declined once the wartime labor shortage eased in 1919. Its placement record remained relatively good in the prosperous 1920s until the demand for labor dipped in the manufacturing sector in 1927. Although most blacks were employed in unskilled work, the Cleveland Negro Welfare Association placed six black personnel workers and eight black foremen in Cleveland area industrial establishments in 1920.[14] This Cleveland Urban League affiliate was especially helpful to migrants seeking employment. Almost two-fifths of the job applicants placed by the Cleveland Negro Welfare Association in 1923 had been in the city only two months.[15] In 1924, the

Cleveland Urban League had about 9,300 job applicants and succeeded in placing 43 percent of them. Some employment gains were made during 1925–1928 when Urban League affiliates in Akron, Canton, and Columbus carried out "industrial campaigns" promoting the hiring of African Americans. A national director of the Urban League took a hand in Ohio as the job market for blacks soured. T. Arnold Hill, who directed the league's Department of Industrial Relations, visited Akron in 1928. There he met officers of several rubber companies and asked them about the job security of black rubber company employees and opportunities for prospective black job applicants.[16]

Many kinds of African American institutions in Ohio conducted activities meant to promote employment in the 1920s. These included schools, churches, children's homes, working women's shelters, and maternity homes. In 1926, the privately endowed Colored Industrial School of Cincinnati had graduated 597 students in its 12-year existence. Vocational training was commonly stressed in public schools whose students were largely or all African Americans, for example, Cincinnati's Stowe School and Columbus' Champion Avenue School. In rare instances black churches pursued employment missions. Cincinnati's St. Andrews Episcopal Church offered a free employment bureau and a day nursery for employed mothers. Sometimes job training and placement services were provided in institutions whose clients were black females. One of these was Cincinnati's Home for Colored Girls, which admitted children ages 8 to 16. Employment assistance was given in shelters for unwed mothers, including the Evangeline Home in Cincinnati and the Talbert Home in Cleveland.[17] In such institutions black females were trained in household work and placed in domestic jobs. These employment programs were influenced by the fact that most whites would hire black women only in service-oriented positions. For example, 86 percent of the employed black females in Cleveland were in service occupations in 1929. The most active employment agency for black females in Ohio was located in Cleveland at the Phillis Wheatley Association's home for employed single black women. PWA leaders worked constantly in the 1920s to enhance their domestic training and employment services.[18] Wages paid for domestic labor were very low; consequently, even late in the decade, the Phillis Wheatley Association could not entirely meet the demand for domestic workers.[19]

Ohio facilities like Cleveland's Phillis Wheatley Home served multiple purposes, but providing shelter was still their primary function in the 1920s. The Wheatley Home in Cleveland, Columbus' Home for Colored Girls, and Cincinnati's Friendship Home for Colored Girls were among Ohio institutions that only accepted employed single women as residents.[20] Likewise, shelter in black YMCA and YWCA branches was only available to employed single persons in urban Ohio. These institutions offered inexpensive rooms in well-maintained and sanitary buildings when decent housing was in very short supply for African Americans, especially for black newcomers, in Ohio cities. Undoubtedly, these few Ys and women's shelters housed only a fraction of single black working men and women needing rooms. Their capacities were small and their charges for bed and board further restricted occupancies. For example, while it charged only $1.50 a week per bed, Cincinnati's Friendship Home could only accommodate 25 female transients at a time. Cincinnati's West End YWCA Branch had enough beds for 125 residents.[21] According to a cost analysis by women's studies scholar Patricia A. Carter, employed black women with below average incomes could not afford the West End YWCA's combined weekly charges for bed and meals, although the room rent alone was relatively inexpensive.[22] In 1928, undoubtedly responding to similar circumstances in Cleveland, the Phillis Wheatley Association Board of Trustees gave women receiving below average wages a temporary room rate reduction.[23]

In urban Ohio, welfare organizations were practically impotent when faced with the shortage of decent low-cost housing available to migrants and other poor African Americans during the 1920s. New construction of low-rent houses affordable to the poor was uneconomical in the private market because building costs were inflated. Using taxpayer dollars to construct public housing for the poor, white or black, was not a viable political option at the time. White philanthropists rarely backed plans to construct inexpensive dwellings for African Americans. The concerned public, consequently, focused on ills arising from the housing shortage, especially bad living conditions and poor health. Welfare organizations generally attempted to improve existing housing conditions and prevent the spread of disease in dilapidated and unsanitary dwellings.

In Cincinnati extraordinary overcrowding existed in the River Basin areas that housed the bulk of the city's black population. Undoubtedly the housing conditions of blacks there were the worst in the state in the 1920s. Cincinnati authorities addressed this housing issue. Historians Robert B. Fairbanks and Henry Louis Taylor, Jr., however, show that Cincinnati's white housing reformers and city planners formed policies that actually perpetuated the housing shortage and the residential segregation of African Americans in the West End. In 1924 and 1925 Cincinnati approved a zoning ordinance and a comprehensive city plan proposed by local city planners and backed by the Better Housing League. Much of the river basin was placed in a zone restricted for commerce and industry. Each outlying area was zoned for a specified type of residential property. Subsequently, construction of manufacturing, mercantile, and railroad facilities continued in the river basin. This economic development required the demolition of hundreds of residences accommodating thousands of families. Meanwhile, new construction occurred in outlying areas zoned for residential use, but no new dwellings were built in river basin sections where the black population was increasing. White urban planners and housing reformers, nevertheless, asserted that their city plan would ease the housing crunch for blacks in the West End. They predicted that the river basin's white tenants who could afford higher rentals would move to newly constructed buildings in the residential zones. Consequently, vacancies would occur in river basin's existing dwellings.[24]

Actually there was an exodus of working class whites, but it was insufficient to end the Cincinnati basin's housing shortage. Most African Americans remained confined to the West End, where dwellings were generally old and substandard. The Washington Terrace Apartments for African Americans were an exception. The white-owned and quasi-philanthropic Model Homes Company constructed them on the eve of the wartime migration. Washington Terrace continued to provide African Americans desirable and sanitary accommodations at low rentals through the decade. Hundreds of black applicants seeking rooms were on the Washington Terrace waiting list in the 1920s.[25] In short, multiple factors restricted most blacks in Cincinnati to poor housing in the West End. Better housing was unaffordable. As Taylor and Fairbanks show, white housing reformers employed city planning, zoning ordinances, and building regulations to reinforce Cincinnati's residential color line. Further, the actions of white property owners, realtors, and bankers imposed this residential segregation.[26]

Constructing new low rent buildings for African American occupancy seemed unfeasible in Cincinnati; consequently, improvement of conditions in old buildings in the West End was the focus of plans to remedy the black housing dilemma in Cincinnati. The Cincinnati Negro Civic Welfare Association formed a committee on housing and health issues in the 1920s. The association cooperated with the Cincinnati Department of Health, whose commissioner identified poor housing conditions as the primary source of disease among African Americans in the city. The Welfare Association also worked with whites in the Cincinnati Better Housing League to improve the living quarters of black tenants. The Better Housing League employed four African American "visiting housekeepers" whose assignments were to instruct black tenants in good housekeeping methods and to persuade white landlords to repair existing tenements. In 1924 these female "housekeepers" made thousands of "family visits" and carried out hundreds of build-ings inspections and interviews with property owners.[27] This limited reac-tion to the housing quality problem was overshadowed by broader efforts to assist African Americans whose health was threatened by exposure to unsanitary and dilapidated housing in Cincinnati.

During the 1920s a wide spectrum of Cincinnati's public and private agencies acted to improve black health care. The Negro Civic Welfare Association usually coordinated these health related activities among African Americans. In 1924 and 1925 the Cincinnati Community Chest's financial campaigns featured African American housing and health conditions.[28] The National Negro Business League recognized Cincinnati's Negro Health Week agenda as the best in the nation in 1924. The Cincinnati health department sponsored a healthy infants contest as a Negro Health Week event in 1924. Special lectures and institutes gave Cincinnati's 17 black physicians rare opportunities for postgraduate training.[29] In 1925, for example, Cincinnati's health depart-ment, Public Health Federation, Anti-Tuberculosis League, and Graduate Nurses' Association held a Tuberculosis Institute for black doctors.[30]

In Cincinnati during the 1920s black women figured prominently both as care givers and receivers in health programs for African Americans.[31] Cincinnati was the only location in Ohio where a Sheppard-Towner grant only was used to fund care for African American mothers and babies.[32] Under the Sheppard-Towner Maternity and Infancy Act, Congress provided states with funds for local projects ulti-mately meant to lower the nation's death rates at birth.[33] Undoubtedly the Cincinnati health department was reacting to the fact that the black infant mortality rate in Cincinnati was three times that for white babies in 1922. Some of the federal funds were used to hire two African American nurses who joined three black nurses already regularly employed in the city health department. These nurses made thousands of home visits to give prenatal aid or provide health care to infants or preschoolers. Health clinics for new mothers were held at Douglass and Stowe Schools for African Americans. Also, a nurse regularly visited the African American Day Nursery at St. Andrews Episcopal Church. The racial disparity in the death rates of mothers and infants was still large in 1925 when the Cincinnati project ended, but the gaps were smaller. A 1926 study showed that the mortality rate for black infants in Cincinnati was a bit less than two times that for white babies.[34]

Meantime in the 1920s maternity homes and shelters for unwed mothers existed in Ohio and other states. In Cincinnati and Cleveland, the Salvation Army operated small refuges for single mothers that accepted African Americans. The Army's Evangeline Home in Cincinnati was maintained solely for black women. Most mothers admitted there were 21 years or younger, many near puberty. They were given religious instruction and training in child-care, housework, and sewing. The Salvation Army assisted new mothers in searches for jobs and "boarding homes" for their infants. In 1925 the Evangeline Home had provided charity service to about 36 mothers and 24 babies annually since opening in 1917. Meanwhile, the home had almost as many private outpatients and annually delivered about five babies to married mothers. Nineteen black physicians had served on the Evangeline Home's volunteer medical staff by 1925.[35]

When the decade began, separate institutions for blacks, like the Evangeline Home, were more common in Cincinnati than in Cleveland. In 1920 the Crittenton Home was one of the three maternity homes in Cleveland, all based on charitable and philanthropic support. It was linked with the national Florence Crittenton mission, which sponsored maternity facilities in several states. Admission of all regardless of religion or color was the stated policy of the Crittenton Home. In practice through 1930, however, no black woman was ever admitted to the Crittenton Home. The only Cleveland maternity home that actually received black women was the Salvation Army Rescue Home, whose patients were largely whites. The Rescue Home regularly admitted black women but usually not more than five at a time.[36] In 1925 the Salvation Army stopped practicing racial integration at its Cleveland Rescue Home. Between 1917 and 1924 this institution's Kinsman Road location changed from a white ethnic area to a largely black neighborhood. Salvation Army authorities then proposed that the Army's Cleveland Branch establish another maternity shelter modeled after the Army's Evangeline Home for black women in Cincinnati. The proposal was based on the fact the racial demographics on Kinsman Road had changed and on the assumption that it was unwise to accommodate black and white women together. The Cleveland Federation of Colored Women and the Cleveland Welfare Federation backed the proposed black maternity shelter. Consequently, in 1925 the Mary B. Talbert Home for unwed black mothers was opened in the old Rescue Home edifice after the white women were transferred to a shelter elsewhere in the city. Expectant mothers under care at the Talbert Home were given spiritual guidance and vocational training only suitable for jobs in domestic service. Its staff included black medical students interning in obstetrics. The Talbert Home also served private outpatients who were delivered by black physicians.[37]

In Cleveland during the 1920s there were sporadic bursts of interest and concern about housing and health issues in black neighborhoods, for example, in 1928 when Cleveland's municipal and civic leaders discussed these issues publicly. Early in April, E. J. Gregg, one of Cleveland's black city councilmen, began to focus public attention upon substandard housing conditions in black districts. He discussed the subject in interviews that were published in the city's daily newspapers.[38] This was a theme that resonated with municipal officials in Cleveland's public health administration. During the Progressive Era, Cleveland and many cities across the nation had established municipal health departments. Meantime, city councils in many states had formed health and sanitation committees that became forums for addressing citywide health issues.[39] In this context, Louis Petrach, the white chairman of the Cleveland city council's committee on health and sanitation, took a special interest in the matter that Councilman Gregg raised. Petrach noted that scores of dilapidated buildings, which had been repeatedly condemned by the city, had neither been improved nor demolished. Petrach advised the council to call for greater enforcement of fire and sanitation ordinances and employment of several more sanitation department inspectors.[40]

In May 1928, a white civic group, the Cleveland Women's Civic Association, adopted a resolution demanding that the city take action on these housing problems and related concerns. Selected association members toured the African American districts. Afterwards, Mrs. Eva L. Griffin, Women's Civic Association president, stated: "I am shocked beyond words. I had no idea such conditions could exist in a supposedly enlightened city. The district is a breeding place for disease and crime."[41] At the minimum, the women's association demanded that the city strictly enforce building and sanitation ordinances.[42]

In June, Cleveland's city council housing committee met to discuss housing and health concerns with representatives of several civic and welfare organizations, including the Cleveland Anti-tuberculosis League and the Negro Welfare Federation, the city's National Urban League affiliate. The outcome of the meeting was a decision to make a thorough investigation of housing and health conditions in the Third Police Precinct, which was largely occupied by African Americans. The study was to be made by a select panel appointed by the city council's housing and health committee.[43] This interest and activity brought more thorough enforcement of city codes on housing and sanitation later in the summer. A large number of condemned buildings were demolished by the order of the city at this time. However, no attempt was made to provide housing for those who had lost their living quarters as a result of this demolition. The city found it necessary to station police to guard the debris of the demolished buildings to prevent the homeless from using it to construct shacks.[44]

In Columbus, as well as in Cincinnati and Cleveland, the health issue was pushed to the fore by the intractable shortage of affordable housing for poor African Americans. As elsewhere, health education campaigns in the black community were the basic means to improve the group's substandard health. For example, the Columbus Urban League annually sponsored National Negro Health Week through the 1920s. Among its activities, the Columbus Urban League's Department of Health and Housing distributed health education literature, presented health lectures, and encouraged people to take physical examinations and immunization shots and to use dental clinics and other health facilities.[45]

In Ohio during the 1920s, as earlier, African Americans recognized that vice and crime, like disease itself, were especially contagious in urban slums where impoverished people lived in overcrowded houses. African American civic leaders accused Ohio municipal authorities of turning a blind eye at vice activities in the most downtrodden black districts. Reportedly prostitutes walked the streets, narcotics were peddled, and speakeasies and gambling houses operated openly in Cincinnati's West End. Early in 1923 concerned African Americans living there formed ad hoc committees and held meetings dealing with the crime issue. At least six hundred people attended these meetings on crime and law enforcement. Committees representing the concerned black citizens called upon the Cincinnati mayor three times urging him, evidently to no avail, to crack down on vice conditions in the West End.[46] In Cleveland the African American weekly *Gazette* periodically reported that gambling, prostitution, illicit-alcohol sales, and drug dealing were conducted "brazenly" in the city's largely black Third Police Precinct and castigated police authorities for allowing vice activities to flourish there. Following *Gazette* Editor Harry C. Smith's lead, black critics of these vice operations in Cleveland occasionally campaigned for more effective law enforcement. For example, in December 1927 "businessmen, taxpayers and citizen residents of the Central Ave. district" petitioned Cleveland officials for greater police protection in the Third Police Precinct.[47]

Meantime, Ohio's large municipalities did employ black police officers who were usually detailed as patrolmen in predominantly black police precincts. At least for a time, some Ohio police department's apparently believed that more black policemen were needed to patrol growing black neighborhoods in their cities. The number of black police officers in Cleveland more than tripled to 22 when Cleveland's black population growth boomed between 1910 and 1920. The Columbus Police Department regularly hired African Americans for two decades after 1903. The number of black police officers in Columbus rose from

12 in 1920 to 18 in 1923. Usually Columbus' black officers patrolled beats in largely black districts located on the city's East Side and in "Flytown." No more African Americans joined the Columbus police force after 1923, and with attrition the number of its black officers declined to 13 at decade's end. Cleveland employed 10 fewer black officers in 1930 than in 1920. Likewise, there were fewer black policemen in Cincinnati and Toledo in 1930 than ten years earlier.[48]

Welfare association programs in urban Ohio were aimed at reducing delinquency and crime problems affecting African Americans in the 1920s. Impoverished young people living in vice-ridden slum districts were especially vulnerable to the seductive aspects of illicit activities. In Cincinnati about 25 percent of the male juvenile delinquents were black in 1924, a proportion much larger than the black ratio in the city's population. In response, Cincinnati's Negro Civic Welfare Association worked in cooperation with the Hamilton County Juvenile Court and the Juvenile Protective Association. A black worker was employed to assist the Juvenile Court in adjudicating African American delinquency cases.[49] Likewise, disproportionate numbers of African American juveniles and adults were arrested in Columbus. The Columbus Urban League used its Colored Big Brothers and Colored Big Sisters programs to curtail juvenile delinquency among African Americans. Under these programs troubled youngsters were given mentors who provided general adult guidance and help with specific problems. Also, the Columbus Urban League cooperated with the Columbus police department in 1925 when it opened the Friendly Service Bureau, a crime prevention agency headed by a black police officer.[50]

These anti-crime and anti–juvenile delinquency programs in Ohio cities were manifestations of a larger National Urban League plan to shape the behavior of black migrants in the urban North. Starting in the previous decade, the Urban League informed black migrants from the South about values and public conduct approved by the white middle class in the North. Racial uplift efforts in this period to promote middle class values in African American urban life are the subjects of current scholarly inquiry.[51] The Urban League's instruction in proper middle class behavior covered the spectrum of personal conduct in cities. For example, thriftiness in personal affairs and reliability and efficiency on the job were valued. Loud talk and raucous behavior on streetcars and in public places were disapproved. In this way, prosperous blacks in northern cities intended to aid the poor migrants' adjustment to city life. But their motives also were self-serving. Blacks in the business and professional classes in northern cities sometimes thought that the disapproved behavior of poor black migrants intensified white prejudice against all African

Americans.[52] In 1926, for example, black journalist Wendell P. Dabney noted that wealthy and educated African Americans were not admitted to Cincinnati's public accommodations as in the past and suggested: "the conduct of low class Negroes has a lot to do with the rise of prejudice."[53] Black weekly editor Harry C. Smith editorialized against loafers on Cleveland streets who yelled and cursed in the presence of women and children.[54] Likewise, Columbus Urban League Executive Secretary Nimrod B. Allen suggested that "thoughtful citizens" in black Columbus were concerned about possible trouble because the prime African American business block on East Long Street had "become the rendezvous for 'hangers-out' both night and day" and that persons passing by were "forced at times to walk off the sidewalk."[55] Subsequently, the Columbus Urban League "worked 'to control and improve the behavior and conduct of Negroes in the streets and other public places in the Negro community.'"[56] Meanwhile, Cincinnati's Negro Civic Welfare Association designated committees to promote citizenship, character building, and thrift.[57] Similarly, Cleveland's Urban League affiliate launched "thrift campaigns" in the 1920s.[58]

African American welfare associations and black institutions worked to engage poor migrants in commonly approved social activities in the 1920s. They provided alternatives to socializing on street corners or in saloons, gambling houses, and the like. Multi-purpose African American community centers with social halls, meeting rooms, and recreational facilities existed in large Ohio cities. Most were founded in the previous decade, especially in response to the wartime black migration. These community center activities were expanded during the 1920s. Ohio Urban League affiliates reorganized or enlarged their social betterment programs. The league's Community House in Canton, opened in 1923, was a center for recreational activities and a meeting place for social groups as well as a headquarters for welfare work.[59] In 1927 the Columbus Urban League established the Northwest Community Center in the Sellsville area of greater Columbus.[60] The Cleveland Negro Welfare Association social program was centered in its own Community House for a couple of years. The house's services were like those in a standard YMCA facility. Evidently to avoid duplication, this Urban League affiliate transferred the community center's activities to the building of a black YMCA that opened on Cleveland's East Side in 1921.[61]

"Ys" were active and growing social centers in black urban neighborhoods across Ohio in the 1920s. For example, Cleveland's relatively new black branch moved to a bigger building in 1923 and became known as the Cedar Avenue YMCA.[62] In Cincinnati, the Ninth Street YMCA increasingly involved black youngsters in its social and recreational programs. Its swimming pool and gymnasium with running track were available to men and boys, as were its bowling alleys and billiard tables. Separate club and meeting rooms were available to men and boys. The Ninth Street YMCA sponsored indoor basketball and volleyball contests and outdoor baseball games. The percentage of boys in the Ninth Street YMCA membership doubled between 1917 and 1925. Similarly, Cincinnati's West End YWCA Branch reported that its "Girl Reserves" program included 269 members in 11 clubs and that 5,868 attended recreational events in 1925.[63] Springfield's Center Street YMCA and Akron's Perkins Street YMCA were important black social and recreational centers in Ohio cities with smaller African American populations.[64] The "Y's" social programs were related to their underlying religions missions. Cincinnati's Ninth Street Branch, for example, reported: "The YMCA is an instrument of the church used to bring boys and young men under Christian influence."[65]

The black church in Ohio was more likely in 1930 than in 1915 to directly conduct social service programs like those associated with "Ys." On the eve of the wartime migration, Ohio's black churches generally were not prepared or equipped to assist needy black newcomers. As in ages past, black churches in Ohio were most concerned with the spiritual welfare of their members. They were much less focused on the physical and secular needs existing outside the church's traditional sphere. There were very few black institutional churches of the sort that formed in some white Protestant denominations in the wake of the late nineteenth century Social Gospel Movement, which asserted the responsibility of Christians to improve social welfare. Prior to World War I, the Episcopal denomination established black settlement houses in Columbus and Dayton with the support of separate black and white Episcopal churches in those cities.[66] Meanwhile, a couple of affluent black Baptist congregations in Cleveland and Springfield built new churches in the institutional style including rooms for recreational and social purposes as well as usual religious ones.[67] Other black congregations joined this movement during and after World War I. In Cincinnati the St. Andrews Episcopal congregation adopted a community service mission ahead of other black churches. St. Andrew's new edifice included a parish hall and social center. In 1925 many other black congregations in Cincinnati conducted social betterment programs, supporting their own playgrounds, gymnasiums, and bathing facilities. At mid-decade, for instance, the Antioch Baptist congregation built a new church with social hall and library, gymnasium and shower, and dining room with a kitchen.[68] Also, a number of black congregations in Cleveland, especially in Baptist churches, became more active in nontraditional community service during the 1920s.[69]

Everywhere in Ohio, black institutional churches tended to have large and financially generous congregations. Evidently these black churches mainly offered recreational and social services to their own members. But a few regularly reached out to nonmembers in the black community who needed aid, especially migrants. Cleveland's Antioch Baptist and Cincinnati's St. Andrew's Episcopal surely were the state's most notable black churches providing community services to a broad clientele. Antioch Baptist Church was heading programs to assist orphans and to decrease juvenile delinquency in Cleveland when the wartime migration started. Antioch Baptist extended its community service activities in the 1920s, for example, by founding a Social Service Center and opening a recreational facility in a separate building.[70] Meantime in Cincinnati, St. Andrew's Episcopal Church housed community services including a job placement office, a day nursery, and a branch of the Cincinnati Settlement School of Music. St. Andrew's also was involved in community service through its pastor's leadership roles in several Cincinnati social welfare organizations. The Reverend Edmund H. Oxley was a director or trustee of Cincinnati's Negro Civic Welfare Association, Juvenile Protective Association, and Evangeline Home for unwed mothers.[71]

Social service activities in black churches grew during the 1920s; however, black ministers who were as active in social welfare work as The Reverend Edmund H. Oxley were still exceptional in Ohio at mid-decade. Church critics noted that funds available for community welfare programs were limited by rising church indebtedness accompanying the purchase or construction of church edifices at the time.[72] In Cincinnati black journalist Wendell P. Dabney noted that black churches were losing their hold on the young and suggested that too many black ministers were out of touch with practical concerns in the black community.[73] In 1926 Dabney advised Cincinnati's black ministers and church members to unite "on a progressive, ameliorative program, or else in a few years there will be many empty churches and far greater financial stringency."[74] In order to succeed in the future, Dabney said, the black minister would have to make the church "a community center" and do practical things to aid the poor.[75]

African American schools in Cincinnati also functioned as neighborhood social centers in the 1920s. Black principal Francis M. Russell made Douglass Elementary School a locus of black neighborhood activities in Cincinnati shortly before the advent of the black wartime migration. Douglass School, built in 1910, housed a public library branch, a parents' club, and an auditorium where various community events were staged.[76] Douglass School also conducted social activities in the 1920s, some in its neighborhood clubroom and others in a separate community house on the school grounds. Cincinnati's Harriet Beecher School, dedicated in 1923, sponsored a similar community activities program. Meanwhile, "St. Ann's School and Social Center for Colored" welcomed African Americans of any faith, but mainly served the black congregation of St. Ann's Catholic parish church in Cincinnati.[77]

Some black community centers in Ohio exhibited characteristics atypical of black social centers in the state during the 1920s. Toledo's Frederick Douglass Recreational Center, founded in 1919, initially was modeled after the YMCA and served young men, but had no Y affiliation. The Douglass Recreational Center also welcomed young women, starting in 1921, and later gained financial backing from the Toledo Community Chest.[78] Cincinnati's Washington Terrace Community Center was unique in Ohio. This community center was a facility of the Model Homes Company that owned the Washington Terrace Apartments. The center reflected the philosophy and idealistic aims of this quasi-philanthropic private company. It wanted to maintain low rent and sanitary apartments for African Americans within the context of an ideal ethnic community. The Washington Terrace Community Center's rooms in the apartment complex were especially arranged for social and recreational activities. For example, in 1925 these rooms were meeting places for five women's clubs, a youth band, and the Washington Terrace Welfare Association.[79]

In conclusion, it can be argued that the movement in the 1920s to address social welfare issues in Ohio's black urban neighborhoods was relatively successful because its achievements were notably greater in this decade than in any earlier one. This was the first full decade of new leadership by local organizations that coordinated black social work conducted in Ohio cities. This leadership style evolved and spread to additional cities, and new black social service facilities were established. Black social work funding and programs were enlarged or broadened. In 1930, unlike ten years earlier, separate programs aiding black migrants and promoting black community betterment were a significant presence in urban centers of every Ohio region. Individual lives were improved through the social work of Ohio's Urban League affiliates, black YMCA and YWCA branches, churches, and schools. Other persons benefited from the various services of new community centers and new public health facilities in black neighborhoods and from homes for black single working women, dependents, and unwed mothers. The accomplishments in this struggle grew out of the willingness of African Americans in Ohio's cities to address local social issues. Black Ohioans working locally in the twenties were active participants in the struggle to alleviate the symptoms of urban ills. Black social work programs in each city were managed and staffed by African American local residents. The record shows that African American neighborhoods in Ohio were neither merely passive victims of urban pathologies nor merely passive recipients of white philanthropy.

It must be concluded, as well, that the social service gains made in Ohio's black neighborhoods in the 1920s were not nearly great enough to match the size of community needs. The struggle with urban problems was decidedly more advanced in this decade than in the past; however, innumerable black newcomers and other needy African Americans in Ohio received no assistance from social service programs because their funds, facilities, and staffing were insufficient. Combined private organizations, some for blacks and others for whites, did not have the means to eliminate the social ills that had been endemic to urban slums in the United States since the mid-nineteenth century. These problems were still present in Ohio's cities in 1930. City center areas, some black and others white, still were occupied by numbers of impoverished newcomers whose health was threatened because they were overcrowded in ramshackle and unsanitary housing located in old high-crime districts. African Americans comprised more of the needy in Ohio's inner-city areas in 1930 than in the previous decade. Prior to 1920 mostly European newcomers and their families occupied Ohio's urban slums and experienced their problems of poverty, disease, poor housing, and crime. During the twenties in Ohio, working class white ethnic families with means relocated from slums to the suburbs. Meanwhile, the color line restricted African Americans to Ohio's troubled old urban neighborhoods. In these circumstances, black Ohioans increasingly organized to address equal rights issues as well as social welfare matters.

CHAPTER SEVEN

New Leadership and Equal Rights Struggles

The 1920s presented the greatest challenge to the African American equal rights struggle in Ohio since the nineteenth century. Racial discrimination and segregation reached new levels as the floodwaters of white intolerance crested during the twenties, after rising for decades. African Americans in Ohio, upon seeing color bars rise, elevated the struggle in city after city. The decade's African American rights efforts were mainly local in nature, each being mounted by local residents and aimed at the local color line. Equal rights advocates in Ohio occasionally practiced statewide cooperation on wider issues. There were also exceptional instances of intervention in Ohio by the leadership of the national civil rights movement. Local differences in the strength and characteristics of equal rights activities existed from city to city. Equal rights work was decidedly most vigorous, extensive, and effective in the cities of northern Ohio, especially Cleveland. These efforts in northern Ohio were in accord with the relatively strong spirit of equal rights advocacy which was part of the region's heritage going back to the early nineteenth century when the Western Reserve area was a hotbed of abolitionism. This is the clearest evidence of the persistence through the twenties of the nineteenth century regional race-relations pattern in which the protest tradition was strongest in northern Ohio and weakest in southern Ohio. During the twenties equal rights efforts were stepped up in southern and central Ohio; however, in those regions the work of addressing social welfare concerns received higher priority than attempts to directly challenge color bias. In all Ohio regions the leadership of the equal rights struggle changed during the twenties. The old guard leadership was in decline and in its last decade. It was composed of aging individuals trained in nineteenth century patronage politics. They figuratively passed the gavel to a younger set of organized leaders. Prior to decade's end, a new leadership in the form of organizations pressing for equal rights displaced the old leadership that depended upon the political influence of individuals to obtain redress of grievance. This occurred as the National Association for the Advancement of Colored People (NAACP) reached maturity.

NAACP officials in Ohio were mainly employed in professions, while few were in white-collar occupations and still fewer in business.[1] In Cleveland lawyers generally served as NAACP president in the 1920s, and most executive committee members were professionals.[2] In 1920 the NAACP's president in Columbus, Edward L Gilliam, was a clergyman, and its secretary, S. T. Kelly, was an attorney.[3] The Springfield branch's officers in 1922 included two attorneys, a dentist, and a physician.[4] Nonprofessionals were more prominent in NAACP leadership in Cincinnati than elsewhere in Ohio. Contractor and builder Charles R. Davis was one of the Cincinnati branch's dominant figures in its early years. In the mid-twenties, Pullman porter instructor Charles E. A. Hunt was a vice president of the Cincinnati NAACP, and federal post office clerk Courtland Lewis served as the branch's secretary.[5]

Historian Joe William Trotter, Jr. argues that the black professionals' assumption of community leadership roles was an aspect of a linkage between their class and black working people at this time. Black professionals had a stake in the well-being of black workers because their professional incomes essentially were drawn from clients coming from within the African American community then. In exchange for this, the black working people accepted and benefited from the leadership services of black professionals. Trotter finds this mutual reliance of the professional class and the working class existing among African Americans in the coal mining areas of southern West Virginia in the period 1915–1930. A similar mutuality of interest existed in Ohio cities where African American professionals, who relied on black clients, often supplied the leadership for NAACP branches and many kinds of black community institutions.[6]

The NAACP grew stronger in Ohio during the 1920s, but its gains were not made steadily throughout the decade, nor were they evenly distributed geographically. The continuing black migration to Ohio was important to the NAACP's growth and success in the state. The ensuing black population growth enlarged the NAACP's pools of potential black dues-paying members and contributors. Also, black newcomers to the state invigorated the NAACP leadership in Ohio. The state's NAACP leaders often belonged to black families of long standing in

Ohio. Yet black migrants were well represented among Ohio branch officials by 1930. For example, Clayborne George and Charles W. White arrived in Cleveland during the 1920s, and they were Cleveland NAACP presidents successively in that decade.[7] The Reverend Samuel A. Brown joined the Cincinnati NAACP leadership shortly after he came to that city in 1923 to take the pulpit of the Mt. Carmel Presbyterian Church.[8] Also, Ohio branches were strengthened by the rising visibility of their parent body, NAACP National Headquarters in New York City. In addition, an NAACP branch's constitutional structure generally ensured the continuation of its formal organization from year to year. In contrast, the NAACP's counterparts in the past were comparatively weak and susceptible to disintegration because they conducted anti–color line protests as loose coalitions of individuals and not as organizations.[9] NAACP causes in the twenties were emboldened by the spirit of the "New Negro" that had arisen during and after World War. I. This spirit derived from black "Soldiers of democracy" who returned from Europe declaring, in W. E. B. Du Bois' words, "Make way for Democracy! We saved it in France, and . . . we will save it in the United States of America, or know the reason why."[10]

NAACP branch strength varied considerably across Ohio during the twenties. The strongest NAACPs were located in northern Ohio. Protest against racial injustice was traditionally greatest in the state's northern section and comparatively weak in central and southern Ohio where racial customs more closely approximated those of southern states. NAACP branches serving Ohio's three major black urban populations were potentially the strongest in the state. The great numbers of African Americans in Cincinnati, Cleveland, and Columbus gave NAACP branches in those cities the best opportunities to build membership size, achieve financial strength, and mount protest activity.

Indeed, the most successful Ohio NAACP branch did represent Ohio's largest black urban population. The Cleveland NAACP was decidedly the most active branch in Ohio. It acted on the widest range of racial discrimination issues. These included a real estate company's unfair practices, harassment of new black residents in white neighborhoods, and color biases in public places such as restaurants, theaters, schools, and hospitals.[11] Evidently, an Ohio branch's vitality was influenced more by its regional location in the state than by local demographic factors. Some northern Ohio branches serving relatively small black populations were more vigorous than those in southern and central Ohio cities with larger numbers of African Americans. In Toledo, the local NAACP maintained a vigorous campaign to raise local public support for the Dyer anti-lynching bill, which was under consideration in the

United States Congress.[12] This was part of a nationwide NAACP effort seeking federal action against the lynching of black men, an outrage which had reached grotesque proportions in the United States, especially in the South. The Toledo NAACP made numerous protests against the color line in local public accommodations.[13] Also, it sustained a successful six-year campaign to end objectionable treatment of African Americans in Toledo daily newspapers.[14] Working in another small black community in northern Ohio, the Akron NAACP was active through the decade; for example, it took a public stand against the Ku Klux Klan and opposed local restaurant color lines.[15] The Cincinnati NAACP occasionally made its presence felt, but its protests were conducted on a relatively narrow front. The most notable work of this southern Ohio branch was its opposition to the Ku Klux Klan. The Cincinnati NAACP, for instance, was directly involved in efforts to kill a Klan-endorsed bill that was introduced in the Ohio legislature at mid-decade. In central Ohio, it was the Columbus Urban League not the Columbus NAACP that took an early initiative against this Klan-backed measure. This central Ohio NAACP generally was less vigorous than its Cincinnati counterpart.[16]

Ohio's NAACP branches generally became more vigilant against racial discrimination during the 1920s; nevertheless, vigorous action by local branches was the exception rather than the rule. Typically an Ohio NAACP branch experienced periods of activity when community interest and membership increased. These were preceded and succeeded by periods during which community interest declined and the branch showed little vitality.[17] The Cincinnati branch, for instance, was dormant for a time in the twenties. In 1926 black weekly editor Wendell P. Dabney said that the Cincinnati NAACP "in its early days had a large and loyal membership" but added, "Interest in it gradually died. . . ."[18]

The Cleveland NAACP was the most consistently active Ohio branch; however, even it was not uniformly vigorous throughout the 1920s. The Cleveland branch in the early twenties was described by one of its prominent members as being "in a very bad way."[19] Improvements started in 1922 and continued through the decade as the Cleveland branch regularly conducted successful campaigns to raise membership and dues income.[20] Meanwhile, it occasionally launched special fund-raising drives. Early in 1926 the Cleveland NAACP collected a thousand dollars in a campaign to raise money for the national office's Legal Defense Fund. Walter W. White and Robert W. Bagnall of the national headquarters visited Cleveland to build interest in the campaign.[21] Later in 1926 the Cleveland branch carried on a determined two-week membership drive with an ambitious goal of three thousand members.

Volunteers canvassed the community seeking members. Director of Branches Bagnall hosted a dinner for campaign workers and met with various community organizations. As an incentive, organized groups that included two hundred fifty NAACP members were to be rewarded with one free trip to the NAACP Annual Convention. The local black clergymen's association cooperated by naming May 30 "NAACP Sunday." The campaign resulted in over five hundred new members and more than one thousand dollars in dues.[22] Local leaders were convinced that the Cleveland NAACP should raise its activity level still further. The following year, 1927, Branch President Charles W. White announced that the "adoption of a more aggressive attitude toward all forms of segregation and discrimination in Cleveland" was necessary.[23] The Cleveland Branch did become more vigorous, most notably in its effort to end racial discrimination at City Hospital. By the end of the decade the Cleveland NAACP was the most active branch of the organization in Ohio.[24]

The voluntary character of local NAACP offices was a factor causing branch activity levels to vary over time and place. Ohio branches were not administered by paid executive secretaries during the 1920s.[25] Management of local NAACP affairs was entirely in the hands of volunteers willing to serve as branch officers. The availability of talented volunteers for branch leadership undoubtedly was very much subject to chance. In that respect fortune was not even handed through the years or across different branches in Ohio. In addition to other advantages, the Cleveland branch was especially fortunate to attract many black volunteers with outstanding abilities for NAACP leadership. Attorneys Clayborne George and Charles W. White were among the Cleveland branch's very able and effective African American leaders. George, a Virginia native, arrived in Cleveland at the opening of the decade with law degrees earned at Howard University and Boston University. A native of Tennessee, White came to Cleveland in the mid-twenties as an alumnus of Fisk University and Harvard Law School. Shortly the two attorneys opened a law office together. Upon settling in Cleveland, each had quickly become active in the local NAACP. George and White each served three-year terms successively as branch president during 1924–1929.[26] The association's national officers recognized their abilities. For example, the NAACP's New York headquarters consulted these Cleveland attorneys about allegations of racial segregation in another northern Ohio city.[27] A remarkable portion of the Cleveland NAACP's black officers, including executive committee members, possessed considerable aptitude and acuity in politics. This undoubtedly was beneficial to the branch in areas of government and politics. For instance, attorney

Harry E. Davis often acted for the Cleveland NAACP and gave it legal counsel, especially early in the decade.[28] Davis, a native Clevelander and son of a locally prominent black family, was repeatedly elected to the state legislature during the twenties.[29] Other successful political activists included Dr. E. J. Gregg and attorneys Clayborne George and Lawrence O. Payne, all Cleveland NAACP executive committee members in 1928.[30] George and Gregg won Cleveland city council seats in 1927, and Payne was elected to the council in 1929.[31]

Together Ohio's NAACP branches made the association a force for civil rights unlike any seen in the state before 1920. Perhaps taken singly, every NAACP branch in Ohio experienced shortcomings in the twenties. In 1923 black weekly editor Harry C. Smith asserted that "drawbacks" of NAACP branches in Cleveland and other Ohio cities inhibited their membership growth. These negatives, according to the editor, were first, that a high percentage of the local branches' income was used to pay the national officers' salaries; second, "the abject failure of local branches . . . to be of real service" to their black constituencies; and third, poor management of their major activities.[32] Undoubtedly, at times these were issues for many NAACP locals in Ohio, but as was his editorial custom, Smith used hyperbole in characterizing them. Collectively the Ohio branches and the NAACP's New York headquarters addressed the Ohio color line along a wide front, especially in areas of education and public accommodations. Some branches resisted the Ku Klux Klan and attempts by whites to exclude blacks from all-white neighborhoods. Some Ohio NAACPs stood up to objectionable press coverage of African Americans and questioned police racial policy. Ohio branches fought racial discrimination in public places of various kinds ranging from hospitals to the cemeteries. Such places included the schools, restaurants, hotels, theaters, and swimming pools. The NAACP employed a variety of political and public advocacy tactics against racial bias in Ohio. These included direct negotiations with the offending parties and press releases designed to influence public opinion. Also, court suits against racial bias were filed, and legislators were lobbied in the interest of equal rights. Likewise, specific equal rights views were advocated in the political arena and in general elections when racial justice was at stake. Each of these devices was used by at least a fraction of the Ohio branches; conversely, each Ohio NAACP usually employed only a few of these measures.

The NAACP's national organization contributed to the effectiveness of its branches in Ohio. However, the NAACP's national headquarters ordinarily was not involved in Ohio branch affairs during the 1920s. National officials usually came to Ohio to promote local branch membership campaigns or to raise money for projects of the national organization but rarely to assist local efforts to combat racial bias.[33] The color line in northern and western states was not the NAACP's highest priority in the twenties. The national office was most concerned about the proliferation of lynching and about southern state laws requiring racial segregation and causing the disfranchisement of black voters. Ohio NAACP branches forwarded to the national office a portion of their dues receipts and money from special fund drives. In that way NAACP branches outside the South expressed their support for the national office's priorities and helped finance its activities including a much-publicized campaign for a federal anti-lynching law.[34] In the twenties the NAACP developed a national reputation as a cogent voice for racial justice, and that strengthened local branches in Ohio and elsewhere. A branch's pronouncements and efforts against racial bias carried added weight because it was an agent of this nationally reputed organization that might itself enter the local dispute.

During the 1920s, the NAACP's newer organized approach displaced but did not entirely eliminate the older individualistic types of responses to color line issues. Old-style racial protest was occasionally practiced in Ohio through the twenties. Prior to World War I African American individuals usually led protests against racial bias. These leaders presumed to speak and act for black constituencies. Generally respected for their integrity and accomplishments in the professions or business, they were socially and politically well connected to influential persons, both blacks and whites. These leaders generally were experienced in the patronage system common to American political parties in the late nineteenth century. Notable party activists, blacks as well as whites, were rewarded at some point in time, for example, with appointments to public offices or political party positions. Such black leaders belonged to age groups that reached maturity in the 1880s or 1890s and that formed the older generations after 1900.

While few in number, these elder black leaders in Ohio employed the individualistic nineteenth century style of racial protest into the 1920s. Most influential among them was George A. Myers, affluent proprietor of the prestigious Hollenden Hotel barbershop in Cleveland. Myers' influence was built on a foundation laid in the 1890s, when he was closely associated with fellow Clevelander and Republican party boss Mark Hanna. Myers' role at the Republican national convention in 1896 was instrumental in leading black delegates to support William McKinley, who was nominated and elected President. At that time Myers developed a state and national network of personal ties with prominent blacks and whites that he maintained through the balance of his life. Black journalist Ralph W.

Tyler of Columbus also used the older black protest style into the twentieth century. Tyler was one of Myers' early political friends. Another elder
black protest leader was William S. Scarborough, who distinguished himself first as a professor and then as president at Ohio's Wilberforce
University. Among others, Wendell P. Dabney, editor of the Union in
Cincinnati, and Harry C. Smith, editor of the Gazette in Cleveland, perpetuated through the twenties the traditional African American form of
racial protest by prominent individuals. Tyler, Scarborough, Dabney, and
Smith, as well as Myers, were associated with patronage politics in the
Ohio Republican party. Each once accepted a Republican appointment to
a federal or a state position, excepting Myers, whose private business was
preferable to an insecure political job.[35]

The 1920s witnessed the last hurrah for the generation of African
American protest leaders in Ohio whose careers began in the previous
century. Arguably, the volume of their activity against racial discrimination in the twenties was greater than that in earlier times. They were
freer to speak against the color line because, no longer employed as political appointees, their careers were less at stake in these latter years.
Undoubtedly, these few black elders also were inspired by the spirit of
"the New Negro" that called for racial justice in recognition of the
African American role in the World War. Nevertheless, their era ended
in the 1920s because only few of these notable black elders lived long
after 1930. Ralph W. Tyler of Columbus died in 1921, Wilberforce
University President Emeritus Scarborough in 1926, and George A.
Myers of Cleveland in 1930. In addition, most of the prominent African
Americans in Myers' early network of Ohio political friends were gone
by decade's end. Republican politico Charles Cottrill of Toledo, for
example, died in 1924.[36] Black author Charles W. Chesnutt's influence
with the white authorities, which was sometimes brought to bear on
color line issues in Cleveland, ended with his death in 1932. Chesnutt's
personal ties and influences were much derived from his national reputation as a significant novelist.[37]

Prominent African Americans like George A. Myers, who sometimes
took individual action against the Ohio color line, were motivated by
general principles requiring the enforcement of equal rights for the good
of all African Americans. Specific personal grievances impelled some
other African Americans in Ohio to confront the color line singly. For
instance, African Americans who personally encountered racial discrimination in public accommodations sometimes filed suits in Ohio courts.
Similarly, some African Americans took informal grassroots action when
they were personally affected by a specific color line grievance. For
example, black parents in Dayton objected when racial segregation was

practiced in their children's school. In the 1920s, while black persons of various backgrounds acted individually, the Ohio color line was most broadly challenged by organizations, usually affiliated with the NAACP.

Anti-Klan campaigns constituted the most widespread African American struggles against racial discrimination and intolerance in Ohio during the 1920s. In cities across the state African Americans opposed the Ku Klux Klan, which advocated white supremacy and gained white Protestant adherents early in the twenties. Ohio's NAACP branches often figured prominently in local efforts to counter Klan agendas. Shortly after the Ku Klux Klan was organized in Cincinnati, the local NAACP branch formed a committee to oppose it. In April 1921 representatives of the Cincinnati NAACP met with the city's mayor and personally requested him to "use all means in his power to suppress the Klan" in Cincinnati.[38] In response the mayor "promised to use the full force of the police department in case of lawlessness on the part of members of the Klan" and issued a statement to the local press that strongly condemned that organization.[39]

Since the Ku Klux Klan stood for the superiority of white Protestants, substantial anti-Klan sentiment existed in the northern Ohio cities with sizable Catholic, Jewish, and black populations. A storm of protest ensued in Cleveland when a Klan chapter was organized there in July 1921.[40] In the subsequent month, Cleveland's mayor and city councilmen were "bombarded" with anti-Klan protests from Catholics, Jews, and African Americans. A resolution condemning the Klan was introduced in the Cleveland City Council by Jewish Councilman Jacob Stacel and seconded by African American Councilman Thomas Fleming. Cleveland Mayor William S. Fitzgerald spoke in favor of this anti-Klan resolution, which the Council unanimously passed.[41] Although it continued to exist there, the Ku Klux Klan remained insignificant in Cleveland during the decade.[42]

Similar anti-Klan sentiment was expressed in Akron, another multiethnic manufacturing center in northeastern Ohio. Klan opponents objected to plans for an upcoming Klan meeting in Akron on May 24, 1922. The meeting, featuring "King Kleagle" Charles L. Harrod of Columbus, was to be part of the Klan's 1922 recruiting campaign in Akron. Critics objected to plans to hold this Klan meeting on public property, in the Akron Armory. Local Catholic, Jewish, and African American organizations, including the Akron NAACP, complained to public authorities. In response to letters of protest, Ohio Governor Harry L. Davis acted to prevent the Klan from using the armory. Afterwards the Klan secured a substitute meeting-place, a Baptist Church in Akron. The Klan's Akron meeting plans finally were blocked by a court injunction issued at the request of George W. Thompson, who was the secretary of the African American YMCA branch in Akron.[43]

African Americans across Ohio opposed legislation promoted by the Ku Klux Klan. At mid-decade, bills outlawing racial intermarriage were introduced in the Ohio, Iowa, and Michigan state legislatures. State Representative George H. Roberts of Youngstown introduced the Ohio measure in February 1925. His House Bill No. 218 prohibited ministers from marrying white persons to individuals of other races and required a fine and imprisonment for violators.[44] Shortly after its introduction, black weekly editors Wendell P. Dabney of the Cincinnati *Union* and Harry C. Smith of the Cleveland *Gazette* covered this Klan issue and urged their readers to fight the proposed legislation against racial inter-marriage.[45] A Columbus correspondent of the Cleveland *Gazette* stated a basic argument used against the bill. He wrote:

> The thing that most concerns our people [about] the introduction of the [inter-marriage] bill is the fact that as a law it would harm our girls and women most! Those who would be so unfortunate as to be taken advantage of by any white youth or man could not compel him to give her child a name, which only marriage can do. More, . . . down would go the moral status of the race because it is deter-mined most largely . . . by our women. . . .[46]

The racial intermarriage bill eventually was referred to the judiciary committee in the Ohio House of Representatives, where it encountered substantial opposition from equal rights groups and others.[47] Cleveland's African American State Representative Harry E. Davis organized dele-gations to speak against the bill at its hearing before the judiciary com-mittee on March 4, 1925. Representatives of various NAACP branches in Ohio appeared before the committee. They included the Reverend H. C. Kingsley of Cleveland and a Cincinnati delegation headed by editor Dabney. The Ohio State University Sociology Professor Herbert A. Miller, a white liberal, made a committee appearance and spoke against the intermarriage bill at the request of the Columbus Urban League. Mahoning County State Representative Mrs. C. J. Ott (white) also advised the committee to oppose the measure.[48] Other opponents who were unable to give testimony in Columbus used the postal and wire services to convey their views to the committee. Samuel T. Kelly, who was the Akron NAACP branch president, opposed the Roberts bill in a telegram to the judiciary committee chairman.[49] Klan opponents were victorious. The Roberts bill was permitted to die in committee.[50] Ku Klux Klan power peaked in the Midwest before this bill was introduced in the Ohio House. After national Klan leader D. C. Stephenson was convicted of second-degree murder in 1925, Klan support in the region faded away rapidly. The Ohio Klan was disintegrating in 1926, and by the end of the decade it was inconsequential in the state.[51]

Greater efforts were made to break color lines in Ohio's public accommodations during the 1920s than in the past; however, racial bias of that kind still was not commonly challenged. Most often action was taken against racial discrimination practiced at restaurants and less frequently against that found at theaters, stores, and swimming pools. Occasionally protest was directed at racial practices on a streetcar, at a cemetery, or another sort of public accommodation. In many of these cases the local NAACP took action through negotiations with the managers of discriminatory facilities or through legal assistance to plaintiffs in anti-discrimination court suits. Sometimes such legal action was initiated without the NAACP's involvement. In a few instances, a prominent black elder, who was not affected personally, attempted to achieve redress of the grievance through use of political influence.

As in the past, public accommodations color lines were more frequently protested in northern Ohio than downstate. In exceptional instances, African Americans in southern Ohio moved against racial discrimination existing in public places there. For example, in 1921 Mrs. Beulah Smith sued Cincinnati's traction company and was awarded five hundred dollars in damages because a conductor addressed her with a racial epithet and ejected her from a streetcar.[52] Likewise, on rare occasions, courts suits were filed against public accommodations in Columbus in central Ohio; the defendants were restaurants and other downtown commercial establishments that commonly refused service to African Americans.[53] *The Crisis*, published by the NAACP, reported a central Ohio protest mounted by a small black community in Zanesville, located east of Columbus. Local African Americans complained to the Zanesville City Council after the Greenwood Cemetery's white officials refused to sell lots in a new addition to blacks.[54]

The volume and the scope of activities against color proscriptions in public accommodations were greatest in northern Ohio cities, especially Cleveland, Toledo, and Akron. In Cleveland individual activists and the NAACP continued a long tradition of African American protest against color lines in that city. In 1921 Cleveland NAACP president William R. Green objected to a recently initiated municipal police policy of not issuing arrest warrants for persons who violated the Ohio law against racial discrimination in public accommodations. In response to Green's protest, Cleveland Mayor William S. Fitzgerald ordered the appropriate officials to rescind the policy.[55] Actions against commercial enterprises in

Cleveland usually targeted restaurants that treated blacks unequally. Civil rights suits were filed against Cleveland restaurant proprietors regularly through the twenties. Plaintiffs won some of these cases, some were lost, and some were settled out of court.[56] The Cleveland NAACP, which assisted in five restaurant cases in 1924, was only sometimes involved in this litigation.[57] Often the filers of suits against restaurants were black professionals, especially lawyers, who were especially interested in the enforcement of the state civil rights law. Attorney Chester K. Gillespie, for example, wrote: ". . . Isadore B. Cohen of the Delicafe Co., 45 Public Square, on September 2, refused to serve me a meal, stating that by doing so he would injure his trade. This was at 2:00 P.M. At 3:00 P.M. the flying squadron of the Cleveland police department was taking him to jail."[58] Subsequently, Cohen was fined fifty dollars in municipal court, and later in common pleas court his wife, the actual owner of the establishment, was fined five hundred dollars under the Ohio civil rights law. Gillespie explained: "I concern myself a great deal with these cases because I feel it my duty to make an example of some of these idiots who persist in deliberately violating your Ohio Civil Rights Law. If we people, who are supposed to know the procedure in such cases, do not take adequate action, we can hardly expect others of our people to make any effort to have their civil rights respected."[59]

African Americans sometimes protested color lines at places of public entertainment and recreation in Cleveland. In 1924 Cleveland NAACP negotiators persuaded the management of Loews' Ohio Theater to admit African Americans.[60] Despite organized protest, however, racially segregated seating still was required at many Cleveland theaters including the Stillman and the Allen.[61] Also in 1924, the Cleveland NAACP obtained corrective action by Brookside Park officials following an instance of racial discrimination at the park's swimming pool. Prominent African Americans took the lead when racial disturbances occurred at a Cleveland municipal park swimming pool in the summer of 1927. White patrons reacted violently when blacks tried to use the pool at Woodland Hills Park. Upon the request of George A. Myers and other leading black citizens of Cleveland, city officials promised to provide police supervision of the Woodland Hills pool to prevent further racial incidents there.[62]

Local NAACP branches usually were at the forefront in public accommodations disputes in Toledo and Akron. In 1920 the Toledo Branch of the NAACP filed twenty-four civil rights suits involving racial discrimination in restaurants, stores and other public accommodations and "secured satisfaction" in eighteen of them.[63] Late in the decade, the Akron Branch of the NAACP took action against blatant racial discrimination in several South Main Street restaurants of that city.[64] The Akron NAACP's objections induced proprietors of these restaurants to remove "whites only" signs from their windows in 1928.[65]

In the 1920s African Americans in Ohio expressed concerns about offensive treatment of blacks in the state's daily newspapers. Press coverage of blacks naturally varied in character from one paper to another and from city to city, but blacks were disrespected in newspapers across Ohio in the twenties. Objectionable references to blacks in Ohio newspapers and complaints about them had nineteenth century antecedents. In 1926 black weekly editor Wendell P. Dabney noted: "Nearly fifty years ago the [Cincinnati] *Enquirer* had writers on its staff who were much addicted to using opprobrious terms and epithets concerning the Negro."[66] A delegation of black citizens met with *Enquirer* owner John R. McClean to discuss the unfair reporting. According to Dabney, "He promised that it would not occur again and 'it didn't.'"[67] In contrast, throughout the 1920s all four major Columbus dailies regularly associated blacks with disapproved behavior, especially vice and crime, and sometimes subjected African Americans to ridicule.[68]

Complaints made by blacks affected how African American news was treated in some northern Ohio daily newspapers. The major Cleveland dailies became fairer toward blacks between 1915 and 1930. Undoubtedly, this trend reflected criticism of their racial reporting. Over decades, certain notable black citizens of Cleveland monitored the Cleveland dailies and called attention to their racial abuses. In the century's second decade, black weekly editor Harry C. Smith regularly publicized this issue in the Cleveland *Gazette*. Cleveland daily newspapers then commonly used such terms as "negress," "darky" and even "nigger" and the word "Negro" without capitalization. In addition, the daily press occasionally carried cartoons ridiculing African Americans.[69] The Cleveland dailies also emphasized crime news involving African Americans and published "scare-headline" front-page articles about blacks.[70] The *Plain Dealer* was less offensive to African Americans than its leading competitors. But even the *Plain Dealer* occasionally used objectionable terms.[71] Letters protesting unfair news treatment of African Americans sometimes were sent to newspaper officials. The *Plain Dealer* reacted to these letters most sympathetically. In 1913, for example, upon receiving Harry C. Smith's complaint that his newspaper had used the term "darky," the *Plain Dealer*'s managing editor explained that he had not known that the word was objectionable and said the *Plain Dealer* "would not willingly use a word or do a thing which even by innuendo might do injury or bring in any degree into disrepute so worthy a class of our population."[72] Thereafter, insulting references to blacks nevertheless occasionally appeared in the *Plain Dealer*. Responding to another such complaint from Harry C. Smith in 1919, the managing editor found it necessary to explain: "in a paper with as many departments as the *Plain Dealer* and with the . . . shifting of the staff . . . , these things will occasionally happen. The best we can do is to keep everlastingly on the job. . . ."[73] Influential black Clevelander George A. Myers also surveyed the Cleveland dailies and once received assurances from *Plain Dealer* General Manager Elbert H. Baker that his newspaper would not use insulting references to blacks, but even in the 1920s there were occasional abuses. In 1929, Myers wrote Paul Bellamy, the *Plain Dealer*'s chief editor, to complain that the words "negress" and "darky" appeared recently in his newspaper.[74] In reply, Bellamy welcomed complaints from African American readers and said that newspapers ordinarily should not make racial distinctions, except in such matters as "race uplift."[75]

Also in northern Ohio, the Toledo NAACP sustained a successful six-year campaign against objectionable treatment of blacks in Toledo daily newspapers. In 1920 representatives of the Toledo branch discussed the matter in meetings with local newspaper editors. Another Toledo NAACP committee, formed in 1923, obtained pledges from the editors of the three leading Toledo dailies that their newspapers would not make offensive references to African Americans.[76] Then in 1926 each of these newspapers adopted common rules governing news items about African Americans. They agreed, for example, not to emphasize racial identities, not to report color in a headline, never to use "Negress" or "Black," and always to capitalize "Negro."[77]

Public school policies were the subjects of the most intensive civil rights protests conducted by African Americans in Ohio cities during the 1920s. These actions escalated in response to a racial trend in Ohio schools. As the number of black students grew during the wartime migration and afterwards, Ohio public schools increasingly placed black students in special classes in separate rooms, sometimes in ones located outside regular school buildings. In justification of these practices, public school administrators generally asserted that black students were classified according to scholastic achievement and not color. In comments on such policies, public school officials often mentioned that these special classes were initiated at the request of local black citizens. Indeed some African Americans held that freedom from racial antipathy and sincere commitment to the success of black pupils could exist only in classrooms of black students taught by black instructors. In addition, black teachers possessed a vested interest in classes composed of black students. Excepting some Cleveland schools with racially mixed staffs and students, Ohio public schools only employed black faculty to teach black students. Strong proponents of equal rights for African Americans, nevertheless, insisted on the enforcement of the nineteenth century Ohio law prohibiting racial segregation in the state's public schools.

Protests charging racial segregation in Ohio public schools proliferated in the twenties and touched every region of the state. Public school racial issues were raised at Cleveland, Shaker Heights, and Mansfield in the northern area, at Woodlawn and Dayton in the southern section, and at Springfield in central Ohio. In some instances an affected black parent acting singly took the initiative. Sometimes aggrieved black parents acted in association, and sometimes interested black citizens formed leagues opposing local school policies affecting black students. The NAACP often was involved in these Ohio school segregation issues, but the character of its participation was not uniform from city to city. Protest tactics and devices employed in the Ohio school segregation controversies varied from place to place, but they included petitions, court actions, public meetings, fund raising drives, and publicity in black weeklies. In a couple of these instances, protestors used direct action tactics in the form of school boycotts.

Active critics of racial discrimination expected and demanded that the Cleveland public schools maintain their traditionally high standard of fairness to African Americans. During the 1920s, as in the past, public school racial integration was greater in Cleveland than anywhere else in Ohio. Prominent black individuals, including journalist Harry C. Smith, and the local NAACP kept watch against the introduction of color line school policies in Cleveland. For example, a protest was mounted in 1925 when Cleveland schools initiated a new practice of requiring students to designate their race and religion on certain questionnaires. In reply to the complaints, the Cleveland Board of Education voted to discontinue that race labeling policy.[78] In 1927 the Cleveland NAACP received reports that racial segregation had been introduced at Outhwaite and R. B. Hayes Schools. NAACP branch president Charles W. White raised the issue in a letter to Cleveland Superintendent of Schools Robert G. Jones.[79] The superintendent immediately replied: ". . . the basis of selection of pupils in these schools [Outhwaite and Hayes] is that of age only. That is, they are designed for pupils who are at least three years behind that point in their school work where age would naturally place them."[80] Cleveland's leading African Americans generally were convinced of the good intentions of the local public school officials charged with growing numbers of black students who previously attended inferior schools in southern states. Black weekly editor Smith, who was the most consistent and strident opponent of Jim Crow practices in

Ohio, expressed general satisfaction with school superintendent Jones' fairness on the race issue.[81]

Cleveland NAACP leaders, also, were concerned in a dispute about racial practices at a school in Mansfield, located about eighty miles southwest of Cleveland. In September 1925 attorney Harry E. Davis, a Cleveland NAACP activist, alerted the NAACP's national headquarters that a civil rights problem was developing there. He indicated that the Mansfield Board of Education, in reaction to "a large influx of Southern children," was preparing to provide "separate classrooms for colored children" which were unprecedented in that city's schools.[82] Attorney Davis registered a protest with the Mansfield school board and advised the NAACP's national office to do the same.[83] Although opposed to the new policy, the Mansfield NAACP branch was not at the forefront of protest against it. Instead the Good Citizenship League, a black local organization, actually took the lead. In August 1925 the Good Citizenship League sent to the Mansfield Board of Education a petition opposing plans for separate classes composed of black students.[84] In reply, the school board said that after "carefully considering" the petition it reaffirmed its intention to place "retarded colored children" under the "instruction of two colored teachers," enabling the pupils to "make up their school credits" and rise to their proper grade levels.[85]

As these events foreshadowed, separate classes for black students were conducted at Mansfield's Bowman Street School during the1925–1926 school year. The Good Citizenship League acquired the services of Toledo attorney B. Harrison Fisher (white), evidently anticipating continuation of this Bowman School policy in the following year. In August 1926 attorney Fisher protested the separate classes in a letter to Mansfield Superintendent of Schools Henry H. Helter. In response, the school superintendent denied that there was ever any intention to introduce "the principle of segregation of colored pupils" and asserted, "The organization of classes of colored children of the Bowman School was effected for the express purpose of helping and benefiting the colored children, a few of whom were slow and many of whom were far retarded behind the grades to which their ages and abilities would place them."[86] Superintendent Helter promised: " . . . colored children in the Bowman School who are up to grade . . . will be allowed to remain in the white classes and those in the colored classes who made rapid progress will be allowed to join the white pupils in their grade as speedily as they catch up to grade."[87] Helter's reply stated plans for the upcoming year to employ three black teachers and add domestic and manual training to the academic work already in the separate curricula for black pupils. Practical training of that sort was not available to white students in Mansfield. [88]

Bowman Street School maintained separate classes of black students through the 1930–1931 scholastic year, when Cleveland attorneys Clayborne George and Charles W. White visited Mansfield and made a thorough investigation of the school situation there. In an elaborate report of their findings sent to the NAACP's national office, these former Cleveland NAACP presidents discussed the controversy's larger social context and its nuances. Mansfield was a northern Ohio industrial city with a population of about 33,000 in 1930. Mansfield's black population was then about 900, up from 249 in 1920 and from 105 in 1910.[89] One entrepreneur, one physician, three clergymen, and three public school teachers largely constituted the business and professional group in this small black community. Most black employees in Mansfield worked for a steel company, and some were in domestic occupations. The city's largest employers included the Empire Steel Company and a state reformatory. Most African Americans in Mansfield were migrants from the South who arrived during the last decade and a half. Persons interviewed by George and White all said that racial discrimination and segregation increased in the city during that migration period. Black newcomers to Mansfield tended to be residentially clustered, but the older black households were widely distributed over the city. In 1930 color lines existed at all Mansfield restaurants, theaters, and other public accommodations. The exclusively black classes at Bowman School were initiated in that setting.[90]

The investigation of the Mansfield public school system conducted by Charles W. White and Clayborne George found no evidence of racial discrimination in any of its eleven schools, excepting Bowman. Black students were enrolled in most of the system's schools and participated in junior high and high school athletics and other extracurricular activities. Bowman School enrolled about 800 students including about 100 African American pupils. The investigators from Cleveland interviewed Bowman School's three black female instructors, all college graduates.[91] They concluded that all three were "capable, one of them being an unusually able teacher, and they would be assets to the school system without segregation."[92] Attorneys White and George learned from the Bowman School principal, through a personal interview, that many of his students were children belonging to white immigrant families and to native white migrant families from the Appalachian South who tended to achieve below their expected grade levels. They suffered language barrier and educational retardation problems, respectively, but the school did not give them special and separate remedial classes.[93] Reporting other indications of racial bias, White and George noted that the Bowman School's black pupils were confined to three rooms, were not permitted to enter other rooms and were not allowed to leave the building until the white students were dismissed. However, no racial discrimination existed in the rest rooms or on the playgrounds.[94] Black students who finished at Bowman School were enrolled in junior high school without difficulty.[95]

The Good Citizenship League's campaign against public school color lines in Mansfield was handicapped because the city's African Americans were not united behind it.[96] Although a segment of the Mansfield black community joined the school protest, Charles W. White and Clayborne George concluded: "segregation has the open endorsement of a part of the colored population; and probably the lethargic acquiescence of a majority of it."[97] One of their sources said that a black employee in a city hall patronage job was an early advocate of separate classes for black students at Bowman School. According to that source, he was motivated by the possibility that his daughter might be employed as a Bowman teacher, as she eventually was once black students were placed in separate rooms. Mansfield employed no black teachers until that time. White and George noted that the teachers themselves had a financial stake in the existence of Bowman's separate classes. Many local African Americans with no personal interest in the matter supported the segregated classes because they meant jobs for black teachers. The black investigators from Cleveland also learned that black parents, being much pleased by the black teachers' work, were uncooperative in protests against Bowman School policies. The black teachers' appeal was so great, George and White discovered, that some black parents wished to transfer their children from one racially integrated school to Bowman's segregated classes.[98] In this context Mansfield NAACP officials were ineffectual; however, according to White and George, they were "most perturbed" about the segregated classes and wanted their elimination.[99] The local NAACP lacked the benefits of leaders with professional training. Mansfield's few black professionals did not include a lawyer. In larger Ohio cities NAACP officials were largely black professionals, but the Mansfield branch president and vice president were black steel mill workers. Mansfield whites, nevertheless, were responsible for Bowman School's racial practices. An exclusively white Parent Teachers Association was opposed to racial mixing in Bowman School, and its white officials were intransigent in the face of protest.[100]

New public school policies affecting African Americans also were protested in southern Ohio during the 1920s. Woodlawn, a hamlet of less than one thousand population, was located in Hamilton County about ten miles north of downtown Cincinnati. In 1924–1925, a Woodlawn school placed black students in special classes under black

teachers, apparently on the grounds that the pupils were behind academically. Unaided by organizations, a lone family disputed the practice in
court, making a determined but eventually fruitless effort. Meanwhile,
the Cincinnati NAACP was aware of the Woodlawn situation and
reported to its national office on the case's progress. William Phillips, a
parent of black students in the special classes, requested a local common
pleas court to issue a writ of mandamus ordering Woodlawn officials to
admit his children to regular classes. The common pleas court declined
to issue the order after holding that the special classes were not racially
discriminatory. Phillips then carried the issue to a court of appeals, which
sustained the decision of the lower court. Finally in March 1925 the
Ohio Supreme Court dismissed Phillips' appeal to that body.[101]

Meanwhile, larger protests against public school color lines were made
in Dayton, one of the major southern Ohio cities with sizable black populations. In 1924 black migrant children attending Dayton's Willard
Elementary School were placed in special classes on the grounds that
their educational achievements did not correspond to their age or grade
levels. The African American students were assigned to basement rooms
in the Willard building and were required to use the rear exit. In
response, offended fathers and mothers of the black children formed the
Parents Protective Association, which drafted and sent a protest statement to the Dayton Board of Education. When the Dayton school board
ignored its objections, the Parents Protective Association organized and
implemented a student boycott of Willard School that was 95 percent
effective for over two months. While parents initiated this action, the
NAACP in Dayton kept abreast of the Willard School controversy and
informed its national office. Consequently, NAACP Assistant Secretary
Robert W. Bagnall was sent from the national office to Dayton with
instructions to assist the parents' efforts. Bagnall and various local black
leaders conducted a series of meetings sympathetic to the parents' action.
The meetings raised several hundred dollars in contributions to their
cause. It was publicized through articles in the NAACP's *Crisis* and in
the Cleveland *Gazette*, which was circulated across Ohio. Then an
attempt was made to secure arbitration of the issue with the assistance of
a local judicial official. In the end, however, the arbitration failed to
resolve the differences between the parents and the Dayton Board of
Education.[102]

Opponents of racial segregation in the Dayton public school system
then focused their attention upon Garfield Elementary School. In 1925
the Garfield School was comprised of a main brick building used exclusively by white teachers and children and two frame annex buildings
used exclusively by black teachers and children. Black students were

required to attend the annex school and were not permitted to receive instruction with white students in the main building.[103] The Dayton Board of Education established the separate facility at Garfield School about ten years earlier when a segment of Dayton's black community requested it.[104]

Early in 1925 a black parent initiated action against Dayton public school officials who required his child to attend Garfield School's annex facility for black students only. Earl Reese requested the school's principal to admit his son to classes in Garfield's main building. When the principal refused this request, Reese hired a lawyer and entered a mandamus suit in the local common pleas court. He requested the court to issue a mandamus writ that would compel the Dayton Board of Education to admit his son to the main building of the Garfield School.[105] After several months of inaction on the suit by the common pleas court, Reese requested and received a dismissal of the case. He then filed a similar suit in the local court of appeals.[106] Assistant Secretary Bagnall was in touch with the Reese case in its early stages and reported the matter to NAACP headquarters in New York City.

Prominent black citizens of Dayton were seriously divided on the Garfield School issue. Some professional men and women, especially doctors, dentists, and teachers, opposed Earl Reese's court suit and supported the Board of Education's policy at Garfield School. Those in accord with the Dayton school board were organized in a group called the Hand of Ethiopia. Local black opponents of Reese's legal efforts mainly based their stance upon the contention that the black teachers at Garfield School would lose their positions if the annex classes for black pupils were abolished by court order. The Dayton school board's action toward the black teachers made that argument credible. The board officials implied that they would not use black teachers in integrated classes. They held up the reappointment of the black teachers for the next academic year pending the outcome of the Reese case. The school board officials reasoned that if they were reappointed and the courts ruled in favor of Reese, the black teachers would have to be paid full salaries although their services would not be used in court-ordered integrated classes. Eventually the black faculty members were appointed as substitute teachers and thus were paid a substantially lower salary, although they taught full time during the school year 1925–1926. Reese's supporters argued that the Dayton Board of Education was using the African American teachers as a "club" to force them to drop their attempt to integrate Garfield School. Earl Reese's legal efforts received moral and financial support from the local NAACP branch, the black Alpha Phi Alpha fraternity, and a group representing black parents of school children. The Dayton school board chose to regard Reese's opponents as being reflective of majority opinion on the issue in Dayton's African American population.[107]

The Dayton Board of Education filed a demurrer to Earl Reese's mandamus suit in the court of appeals. The board's demurrer claimed that separate classes for black students were formed because some black pupils at Garfield School exhibited "backwardness." The appeals court overruled the demurrer, reasoning that the "discretion of the board of education . . . does not permit segregation purely on the basis of race or color."[108] Earl Reese died a few days before this decision in his favor. Carrie Reese, his wife, stayed in the legal fight. The board appealed the previous decision to the Ohio Supreme Court, which unanimously affirmed the ruling of the Montgomery County Court of Appeals.[109] This legal victory for the equal rights cause did not reverse the trend toward greater de facto racial segregation in the local public schools. In 1926, only months after the Reese case ended, a school bond issue in Dayton provided funds for the construction of an elementary school in an almost all-black district of the city.[110]

Central Ohio was the locus of a civil rights campaign against an all-black public school established in the early1920s contrary to Ohio civil rights legislation. Springfield, a city of about 60,000, was located on the National Road west of Columbus. About 7,000 black people comprised about 12 percent of that city's population. The proportion of African Americans was larger in Springfield than in most Ohio urban centers. African Americans inhabited every Springfield district, and black pupils attended each of the city's public schools. However, over half of Springfield's black population was concentrated in two of the city's seven census wards, and schools in those wards enrolled most of the city's black students. Springfield's black society included a variety of churches, an Odd Fellows chapter, a YMCA branch, a NAACP branch, and several other black community organizations. Members of the black business and professional classes in Springfield, who tended to be socially active, included entrepreneurs, lawyers, physicians, dentists, and clergymen, but in 1920 no public school teachers. In-migration and population increases in the previous decade enlarged the social and economic life of African Americans in Springfield. As in other Ohio cities, growing white intolerance accompanied black demographic changes in Springfield. Among manifestations of this trend in Springfield were a race riot in 1921, the rise of the local Ku Klux Klan, and increased white support for resegregation of public schools.[111]

What eventually came to be known as the Springfield Fulton School controversy arose in that setting. The dispute's origins owed much to the white supremacy views held by Springfield Superintendent of Schools George E. McCord. He was opposed to racial mixing in schools and publicly admitted his membership in the Ku Klux Klan in the wake of this school controversy.[112] Black teachers played a role in events ultimately leading to the dispute. They applied for teaching positions in the local school system and were denied employment. The Springfield Board of Education refused to hire the African American teachers on the grounds that there was no all-black school in the city. The board seemed to imply that it would employ an African American staff if such a school existed. In consequence, a group of Springfield's socially prominent black women secured two hundred signatures on petitions favoring the establishment of a black school with black teachers. After these petitions were presented to school officials, counter-petitions containing about twelve hundred signatures were submitted to the Board of Education. This seemed to stop the movement for an all-black school. But, in May 1922 Superintendent McCord announced that a black principal and twelve black teachers had been hired and assigned to Fulton School in order to implement an "experiment of an all-colored school" during the following academic year. School officials asserted that the local black citizens desired a separate school. When the 1921–1922 school years ended, all white students living in the Fulton School District were assigned to other schools.[113]

Opposition to the new Fulton School policy quickly took shape. The Springfield Branch of the NAACP met, formed a special committee, and eventually petitioned the local school officials. The Springfield Board of Education was unmoved by the NAACP's objections. This led to the creation of the Civil Rights Protective League, a black organization formed solely to fight local school segregation. Its most visible activity was a sustained public demonstration at Fulton School. The league prompted a student boycott of the Fulton School. Approximately one hundred local black women formed a pool of demonstrators, some of whom regularly picketed the school from September to December 1922. Occasionally, black men joined the regular pickets. The boycott was so effective that no more than about fifty of the approximately three hundred black students enrolled in Fulton School ever attended classes during this period. Also, the Civil Rights Protective League sponsored regular weekly meetings that were sometimes addressed by notable out of town speakers, including editor Harry C. Smith of the Cleveland *Gazette*. In addition, the league raised funds and hired attorneys to challenge the school board's racial practices. League attorneys filed a common pleas court suit requesting that the Springfield Board of Education be enjoined from making Fulton School an all-black institution contrary to state law. In autumn 1922 the common pleas court issued a temporary restraining order against the school board's action, and in January 1923 the same court issued a permanent injunction against the operation of Fulton School as a racially segregated institution. The school board appealed the decision, and the legal issue was ended when a court of appeals dismissed the case early in 1924.[114]

The campaign against racial segregation at Fulton School lacked the full and undivided backing of Springfield's black citizenry. African Americans supporting the school board largely belonged to a faction led by pastors of two affluent black churches in the city. Leading opponents of the Fulton School policy like its backers were socially prominent African Americans; for example, Charles S. Johnson, the Civil Rights Protective League's president, was the Champion Chemical Company plant supervisor.[115] The league bore the brunt in the anti-segregation fight with the Springfield Board of Education. The local NAACP's part in the dispute was practically invisible to the public. Protest meetings, boycott activities, fund raising, and judicial actions were conducted under the league's banner. Nevertheless, the NAACP's national head-quarters and some of its local officers participated in the cause. Among the key league activists were several local NAACP officials including black attorneys George W. Daniels and Sully Jaymes, the branch president. Daniels and Jaymes were chosen to serve on the league's legal staff. Their legal activity in the court dispute was done in the name of the league, not the NAACP.[116]

NAACP correspondence reflected that organization's restrained participation in the Fulton School controversy during 1922–1923. In September 1922 George W. Daniels telegraphed W. E. B. Du Bois in New York City requesting NAACP aid. The telegram identified Daniels as legal advisor to the league and did not record his NAACP title. In reply Director of Branches Robert W. Bagnall offered Daniels the assistance of NAACP field secretary Mrs. Addie Hunton. At the same time, Bagnall wrote local NAACP president Jaymes inquiring about the Springfield branch's efforts to date and advising it to organize and lead civic organizations in the cause. Bagnall further advised that the next step should proceed to a court injunction.[117] In answer to Bagnall, the branch president claimed that the local NAACP and the league were "working joint-ly," for instance, "pooling . . . [their] financial interests" and using "a joint committee" to choose speakers for the public protest meetings.[118] Some league backers were critical of the Springfield NAACP, charging that it did not help enough in the protest.[119] Branch president Jaymes took a different view. Early in 1923 he complained: ". . . we do not feel that the Home Office has been showing the proper regard for the work we have been doing here."[120] Addressing his complaints to the NAACP director of branches, Jaymes cited lack of publicity in the *Crisis* about the Fulton School issue. Jaymes was then reminded that Director Bagnall spoke to a mass meeting in Springfield and advised leaders there in May 1922 near the start of the school controversy. Also, Bagnall explained that unavoidable circumstances permitted the *Crisis* to give the dispute only a little attention.[121]

Protests against school racial policies barely slowed the growth of racial separation in Ohio public schools, a statewide trend that was most pronounced in central and southern Ohio during the twenties. In Springfield, as in Dayton, a court decision against an all-black institution did not preclude the eventual development of a nearly all-black school. Springfield officials retained none of Fulton School's black teachers for the 1923–1924 school year, when the city again employed only white teachers. Subsequently, white students attended Fulton School, but in time its enrollment was increasingly African American and eventually predominantly black.[122] As the decade ended, however, all-black public schools existed in only two major Ohio cities, Columbus and Cincinnati. There was no sustained protest or legal action against racial practices at Columbus' Champion Avenue School or at Cincinnati's Douglass and Stowe Schools, although each enrolled black students only. There was a dispute of sorts involving the Champion Avenue School in Columbus. This institution was an elementary school with a "Junior High School Department." Early in the decade, Columbus Urban League official Nimrod B. Allen noted, "An additional building to be used by this Junior High is being bitterly opposed by groups of Negroes."[123] Any objection to color lines at Douglass and Stowe Schools evidently was forestalled because their popularity was widespread among Africans Americans in Cincinnati. Their black principals and teachers were widely respected, and their facilities were valued as important black community centers.[124]

Civil rights protest aimed at Ohio's public universities was exceptional in the 1920s. The state universities freely admitted African Americans, but in varying degrees color lines existed in their social life and extracurricular activities. Late in the decade, African American students raised an equal rights issue concerning Ohio University at Athens in southern Ohio. They said that Ohio University had a rule that discriminated against the admission of black applicants from southern states whose universities barred African Americans. The alleged regulation excluded from admission to Ohio University all students who were not eligible for admission to a university in their own states. Black students at Ohio University, who wanted the rule eliminated, asked the

Columbus Urban League's executive secretary and others to assist their cause.[125] In March 1929 Cleveland's African American state representative and leading black citizens of Columbus and Dayton appeared at a meeting of the Ohio General Assembly's joint finance committee and protested against the regulation.[126]

Public hospitals in Ohio, like state universities, were rarely the objects of civil rights protests in the twenties. Hospital racial practices in Ohio raised a color line paradox. Black patients were admitted to Ohio public hospital charity wards, but these rooms often were racially segregated. Generally black physicians, interns, and nurses were barred from public hospital staffs. Black doctors, consequently, could not treat paying black patients in these public medical centers. When private hospitals also were unavailable to black physicians, their black patients underwent childbirth, surgery, and other medical procedures in facilities not meeting hospital standards. Given racial exclusion at public institutions, black physicians often saw private hospitals as potential means to improve their black patients' medical care and enhance their medical practices at the same time. Yet African American doctors and patients generally lacked the resources to make full-fledged private hospitals financially viable. Private black hospitals in financial need could survive only with outside assistance from white philanthropy or local government. But black hospitals accepting such funding then became publicly financed institutions for blacks only. These hospitals were possible targets for anti–racial segregation protests. This was the color line dilemma facing black doctors lacking proper hospital facilities. In Cincinnati and Columbus, African American physicians founded black hospitals that existed for a time in the twenties. These hospitals encountered no significant protests. But in Cleveland, attempts to establish a black hospital were blocked by opponents charging that it would be a Jim Crow institution. The Cleveland instance was unusual in the state and the nation. Increasingly since the late 1980s, scholarly studies of black hospitals and medicine in the United States have called attention to the history of black hospitals in many cities in states of the South and North.[127]

The color line was pervasive in Cincinnati hospitals in the twenties. The tax-supported Cincinnati General Hospital's charity wards admitted African Americans on a segregated basis. No black physicians, interns, or nurses were appointed to this city hospital's staff.[128] In 1925 Cincinnati Health Commissioner W. H. Peters reported: "Not many beds [for blacks] . . . are available in private hospitals."[129] At about the same time, Mary L. Hicks conducted a hospital survey in Cincinnati and found that about 85 percent of the city's black patients were cared for in General Hospital.[130] The Hicks hospital survey also noted: "In numerous instances, Negro physicians, failing to obtain accommodations for their patients in the hospitals, have kept those patients in their homes to the definite disadvantage of the patients."[131] In addition, Health Commissioner Peters observed: "We have no training school for colored nurses and the colored physicians have no opportunity for postgraduate medical work or bedside instruction in the wards of any hospitals."[132]

A group of black physicians in Cincinnati founded Mercy Hospital in order to compensate for the exclusive practices of the city's hospitals. The facility was meant to provide care for paying black patients, professional advantages for black doctors, and training for black nurses. The physicians in the hospital group committed themselves to support the institution financially. In 1925 all of the black doctors associated with Mercy Hospital were young men in their thirties or twenties. Numbering about ten, they were largely newcomers to Cincinnati who came after the start of the wartime black migration. Half of them came to Cincinnati early in the decade with recently earned doctorates from black medical schools. Mercy Hospital's physicians possessed M.D.s mainly from Meharry Medical College, Nashville, Tennessee, but a couple were graduates of the medical school at Howard University in Washington, D.C. These were the only black medical schools still existing in the country by 1923.[133] Most black doctors practicing at Cincinnati's Mercy Hospital had served postgraduate internships, for example at Kansas City General Hospital in Missouri and Freedman's Hospital in Washington, D.C.[134] These internships were at black hospitals financed with tax revenues or philanthropic funds.[135]

Their earlier experiences with black colleges, medical schools, and hospitals, undoubtedly, inclined some young black physicians on the Mercy Hospital staff to participate in the development of black organizations and institutions in Cincinnati. In addition to founding Mercy Hospital, some of these black doctors established a black medical association in Cincinnati and formed a chain of pharmacies owned and operated by African Americans. Prominent among these physicians was Dr. E. B. Gray, who was Mercy Hospital's chief of staff and president of the Model Drug Company, owner of local drug stores. At age thirty-five, Dr. R. P. McClain served as Mercy Hospital's manager, as the Model Drug Company's secretary, and as a member of the black Ninth Street YMCA's management committee. At age twenty-eight, Dr. R. Eugene Clark was Mercy Hospital's secretary of staff and president of the Cincinnati Medical Association.[136]

Cincinnati's Mercy Hospital was open for the greater part of the 1920s, but its existence was troubled all the while. Its bed capacity was limited, and it could not qualify as a hospital under the "accepted usage of the term hospital."[137] Mercy Hospital's thirty-three beds were too few to meet state requirements for nursing school accreditation, and that curtailed applications for its nurses' training program. Chronic income shortages were most damaging. Fund raising efforts were made, but they proved to be insufficient. For example, staff physicians sponsored an annual benefit that solicited donations for Mercy Hospital.[138] By the end of the decade Mercy Hospital had succumbed to financial difficulties.[139]

Civil rights protest was not a factor in the private black hospital's demise. Black weekly editor Wendell P. Dabney, Cincinnati's most outspoken critic of Jim Crow policies, opposed racial separation at public hospitals, but not at private ones. Objecting sarcastically to the lack of protest against color lines at Cincinnati's municipal hospital, Dabney said: "The patients, black and white, get about the same treatment, but the colored are segregated and the segregation is received by colored citizens here with the complacence usually accorded by them to such indignities."[140] Apparently, he saw Mercy Hospital as an inoffensive black private business like a newspaper, bank, or insurance company. The issue changed late in the decade after private fund raising failed to keep Mercy Hospital open. In 1929 a group of black physicians sought the establishment of a tax-supported hospital to care for African Americans. Opponents of racial segregation complained bitterly about this hospital proposal. Editor Dabney maintained that "the establishment of a city Negro hospital would mean the final barring of all Negro patients" from Cincinnati General Hospital.[141] He added: ". . . if the Negro doctors haven't the courage or wisdom to gain entrance into a place for which they are taxed [General Hospital] why should others condone their cowardice and bow to an undemocratic custom and perpetuate prejudice by submission to a racial wrong?"[142] Dabney was vehement about this hospital effort, but there was no organized opposition to it. Nevertheless, the proposal of a tax-funded black hospital in Cincinnati went unrealized. Undoubtedly, this was not a high priority of Cincinnati officials responsible for appropriating municipal funds in 1929–1930.

In the early 1920s, the hospital situations of African Americans in Columbus and Cincinnati shared some common factors. Alpha Hospital in Columbus was the counterpart of Cincinnati's Mercy Hospital. Black physicians were excluded from practice in other Columbus hospitals, which likewise denied African Americans opportunities for nurses' training.[143] Racial segregation was not the rule in the charity wards of the city's hospitals; however, few white doctors with "respectable" patients, evidently paying ones, would treat African Americans, according to contemporary observers.[144] In this context, Alpha Hospital was established as a private medical facility for the city's African Americans. Costing

$23,000 to construct, its building was located on East Long Street in Columbus' black business district. The hospital's black founders, Drs. W. A. Method and R. M. Tribbitt, were associated with a group of recent migrants from the South that Columbus Urban League official Nimrod B. Allen praised for invigorating black institutional and business life in Columbus. Respectively, Method and Tribbitt were chairman and vice chairman of the black Spring Street YMCA's management committee, and Method also was a Columbus Urban League board member. Their private hospital venture was short lived. By 1922 their institution was reorganized as the Alpha Hospital Association, a social agency that evidently was eligible for financial aid from the city's charitable funding agencies. The Hospital Association provided a nurses' training program open to African Americans.[145] This evolution of the Alpha Hospital occurred without any notable criticism from opponents of racially segregated institutions in Columbus. The city's black protest heritage was not strong. Furthermore, this tradition in Columbus lost perhaps its loudest voice with the death of Ralph W. Tyler in the midst of the Alpha Hospital developments. Tyler, an old-style black leader with political patronage connections, was an active opponent of color line practices in Columbus during the years just prior to his death in 1921.[146]

Anti–color line protests overshadowed and thwarted the efforts of black hospital promoters in Cleveland during the twenties. Effective counteraction against efforts to found publicly supported black institutions was a long-established custom in Cleveland. It was a force that black hospital advocates were unable to match.[147]

The establishment of a hospital staffed by black doctors was proposed repeatedly in Cleveland in the 1920s. Local black physicians unsuccessfully attempted to advance the idea in 1920–1921 and 1925.[148] Again during 1926–1927, black physicians were prime movers of campaigns promoting a black hospital in Cleveland. Unlike the earlier movements, these were highly organized, sustained over time, and conducted in the midst of much public controversy. The Cleveland Hospital Association solicited money in 1926 to fund its black hospital proposition, and in 1927 it was reorganized as the Mercy Hospital Association (MHA). Association officers and advocates were prominent members of Cleveland's black community, including Dr. Charles H. Garvin, a staff member at Cleveland's Lakeside Hospital, and entrepreneur Herbert S. Chauncey. The MHA hired a publicity agent and disseminated a handbill advocating a "Negro Manned Hospital," while its promoters solicited funds during "open forum meetings" at black churches. The campaign raised some funds; however, the MHA experienced financial problems and went defunct in July 1927.[149]

Lack of broad-based support foreshadowed the collapse of the MHA from its inception. The hotly debated Mercy Hospital issue in black Cleveland was neatly summarized by local NAACP president Charles W. White, who wrote: "On the one hand it [Mercy Hospital] is being bitterly opposed as a self-inflicted bit of Jim Crowism. On the other hand it is being espoused as a very much needed institution for the training of Negro physicians and nurses who at the present time have no such facilities for training anywhere in Cleveland." White added: "Its opponents fear that the effect would be to close the doors tighter in existing institutions against colored people; its proponents insist just as positively that it would not. . . ."[150] Heading the opposition were elder black Clevelanders, notably George A. Myers, editor Harry C. Smith, and clergyman Horace C. Bailey. They addressed their prominent black and white contacts who were capable of influencing public opinion. These included the Cleveland city manager, Cleveland daily newspaper editors, and black ministers associations. The anti-MHA campaign also was conducted in the daily press and in black weeklies. This determined opposition to the MHA was the crucial factor in its demise.[151] The opponents' efforts prevented Mercy Hospital boosters from gaining endorsements from Cleveland's black organizations and financial support from philanthropic white sources like the Cleveland Community Chest. The local NAACP, Urban League, and black ministers associations refrained from endorsing or opposing the Mercy Hospital proposal, evidently wishing to avoid internal divisiveness.[152]

Later in the decade, the central hospital issue for African Americans in Cleveland concerned color lines in the city's municipal hospital. There was another debate about an African American staffed hospital, but it was upstaged by protests against racially exclusive practices at Cleveland City Hospital. The Cleveland NAACP initiated a campaign against the municipal hospital late in 1927. A broad variety of African American organizations and individuals adopted this cause. Eventually the protesters included representatives of the Universal Negro Improvement Association and the Phillis Wheatley Association. Also represented in this movement were influential black elders like George A. Myers, recently elected black city council members, and black weekly newspapers. The City Hospital protest was conducted in various forums including editorials in the black press, correspondence with municipal officials, debates in city council chambers, and political campaigns in municipal elections.

The Mercy Hospital controversy in 1927 raised awareness in Cleveland that black interns and prospective nurses were not admitted to hospital training programs in the city. Mercy Hospital's proponents argued that their proposal would create these professional opportunities for blacks, while its opponents retorted that City Hospital should make them available to African Americans. This debate made others aware of these hospital issues. After discussing the matter, the interracial committee of the Cleveland Area Church Federation concluded that internships and nurse's training for African Americans should exist in a Cleveland facility, but not necessarily at City Hospital. Responding to the Church Federation's interest in positions for black interns and nurse trainees in October 1927, Cleveland City Manager William R. Hopkins promised to authorize a study of pertinent hospital practices in municipalities outside Ohio. He indicated that Cleveland City Hospital's racial policies in future would reflect its findings. Director of Public Health and Welfare Dudley S. Blossom then selected members of a hospital investigating committee that toured several cities including Chicago, St. Louis, New York City, and Washington. They found that predominantly white hospitals with intern and nurses' training programs open to blacks were very exceptional. Reporting in December 1927, Blossom's investigating committee chose not to recommend the admission of black interns and nurses to the City Hospital staff. This recommendation was in accord with the preponderance of advice received by committee members from medical personnel at hospitals on their tour.[153]

Meanwhile, in fall 1927 the Cleveland NAACP and other parties were in the early stages of a campaign to open the City Hospital's intern and nurses' training programs to African Americans.[154] Early in November the Cleveland NAACP initiated its own inquiries about the treatment of blacks in hospital training programs outside Ohio. The influential elder black politico George A. Myers shortly voiced his concerns about City Hospital color lines in a series of letters to City Manager William R. Hopkins with whom he was well acquainted. Starting in December 1927, this elaborate correspondence continued for over two months. In short, Myers reaffirmed his opposition to a separate hospital for blacks and advised the city official to end all racial discrimination at the municipal hospital.[155] On January 31, 1928, the city manager indignantly denied the accusation of racial bias when he made his first and only reply to Myers letters on this subject. Also, Hopkins expressed incredulity as to how Myers could oppose additional hospital facilities for African Americans, which the city manager said were sorely needed.[156]

Echoing this view in June 1928, new councilman E. J. Gregg, a black physician, announced his intention of introducing in the Cleveland City Council a resolution providing for the formation of a City Hospital branch on the East Side "to take care of the poor of that district," which housed the greater part of Cleveland's black population.[157] Several days later Councilman Gregg introduced his hospital resolution with the endorsement of City Manager William R. Hopkins. Opponents of the defunct Mercy Hospital campaign immediately rejected the Gregg resolution, and the *Gazette* denounced it as "Jim Crow hospital scheme."[158]

The exclusion of blacks from the Cleveland City Hospital medical staff ended few weeks later. In July 1928 Dr. John H. McMorries became the first African American to receive a Cleveland municipal hospital appointment as a staff physician. An experienced doctor, McMorries had acquired undergraduate and medical degrees from Howard University in Washington, D.C., where he also interned at Freedman's Hospital. Dr. McMorries possessed twelve years' tenure on the staff of Cleveland's Lakeside Hospital, a private facility in a local university hospital group.[159] Other African Americans on the Lakeside Hospital staff were Dr. Charles H. Garvin, a distinguished urologist, and Dr. Stanley Brown, a graduate of Western Reserve University Medical School in Cleveland. Although he was a Cleveland resident, Dr. Brown served his internship at Freedman's Hospital in Washington, D.C. because internships in Cleveland were unavailable to blacks. In 1928 two other black doctors were affiliated with the private University Hospital System in Cleveland.[160] Editorializing in the *Gazette*, Harry C. Smith characterized Dr. McMorries' appointment to the City Hospital staff as an unsatisfactory attempt to placate those who were attempting to open the public hospital to black interns and nurse trainees.[161]

Dr. McMorries' appointment did not forestall the anti–color line campaign against Cleveland City Hospital. In fall 1928 Cleveland NAACP President Charles W. White requested the city's director of public health and welfare to remove the barriers against black nurse trainees and interns at City Hospital. But, Director Dudley S. Blossom replied that he had no authority to act in this area.[162] An investigation of Cleveland City Hospital in December 1928 was the next move to advance the cause of the municipal hospital's critics. An investigating committee was composed of a diverse array of Cleveland's black civic leaders. They included two new city councilmen, attorney Clayborne George and physician E. J. Gregg, and representatives of the local NAACP and UNIA.[163] The investigating committee had previous knowledge that the municipal hospital was not open to black interns and nurse trainees. But upon visiting City Hospital, the committee learned that the hospital did not employ blacks in any capacity.[164] This fact was particularly galling to local African Americans because blacks were employed, some in quite responsible positions, in other local medical facilities. These included St. Luke's, St. Vincent's (Charity), Lakeside, Huron Road, and Mt. Sinai Hospitals and Cleveland Clinic, all private institutions.[165]

During their Cleveland City Hospital visitation, the investigating committee's members observed segregation of black patients.[166] The investigators publicized their findings in a published letter of Clayborne George and E. J. Gregg to the editor of the Cleveland *Plain Dealer*. They announced that the committee "found bold and flagrant segregation" in three of the hospital's thirty-five divisions.[167] The senior nurses of these three divisions told the committee that as long as they had held their positions patients had been separated by race in their divisions, except when it was inconvenient to do so.[168] Investigating committee representatives also called upon City Manager Hopkins to discuss the hospital segregation findings. In January 1929 Hopkins stated, "it was not the intention of the City to segregate patients on account of color."[169] The city manager then issued an order stating that patients were not to be segregated by race at City Hospital.[170]

During 1929 black interns, nurse trainees, and nurses still were absent from Cleveland City Hospital and protests against these remaining color lines continued through the year. In March the Reverend Russell S. Brown took a stand on this issue. He was one of Cleveland's three black city councilmen at that time. Brown announced his intention to introduce in the city council a resolution designed to end racial discrimination in the municipal hospital unless city administrators took action toward this end.[171] Administrative officials made no such moves, and Councilman Brown bided his time. In summer 1929 color bias at the municipal hospital became a personal concern to the Reverend Horace C. Bailey, former pastor of Antioch Baptist Church in Cleveland. In league with other local black elders, he had worked against the Mercy Hospital proposal as a matter of principle. But family interests impelled the Reverend Bailey when his granddaughter was twice refused admission to the nurses' training school of City Hospital that summer.[172] He contemplated court action in order to win admission for his granddaughter and gave the story to the local black press.[173]

Meanwhile in 1929, Dr. E. J. Gregg, a black member of the Cleveland City Council, continued to advocate the establishment of an East Side branch of the City Hospital, staffed by African Americans. In April, for example, Councilman Gregg spoke of the need for this hospital branch in a statement addressed to a meeting of Cleveland's black Baptist pastors.[174] Many local black physicians favored the councilman's proposal to place a municipal hospital branch in Cleveland's East Side African American district.[175] In Cleveland's black community, criticism of Gregg's hospital idea was more widespread than the opposition to the Mercy Hospital proposal made earlier. The latter did not include the Cleveland NAACP. Many local NAACP leaders had seen Mercy

Hospital as a private black facility. The difference between that kind of institution and a black municipal hospital branch was apparent to the Cleveland NAACP leadership, which formed a consensus and took an unequivocal stand against Councilman Gregg's proposition. Explaining the local branch's views, Cleveland NAACP President Charles W. White said that NAACP principles did not require opposition to a private black hospital or city hospital branch with a racially integrated staff and clientele. But the NAACP could not approve a racially segregated municipal institution. White declared: "We stand against a branch of City Hospital which, whether intended or not, will eventuate in a short while into what to all intents and purposes is a Negro branch of City Hospital."[176]

The hospital branch issue was not permitted to obscure the civil rights campaign against Cleveland City Hospital in 1929. The East Side branch hospital matter was on the Cleveland City Council's agenda late in the year. Its opponents used the ensuing debate to focus public attention on the municipal hospital's color lines. At this time, the campaign against racial discrimination at City Hospital possessed the backing of a diverse, large, and still growing body of black civic leaders in Cleveland. On November 11, 1929, the city administration recommended to city council that three hundred fifty thousand dollars of a proposed $1 million tax levy be appropriated for an East Side branch of City Hospital. The recommendation was introduced in council in ordinance form and referred to the finance committee.[177] On November 19 this bond question was discussed at a finance committee hearing that became a forum for civil rights protest. African Americans who were present at this committee debate argued that the city should not finance an East Side hospital branch. Among them were Councilmen Russell S. Brown and Claybourne George, NAACP President Charles W. White, the Reverend Horace C. Bailey, and Phillis Wheatley Association Executive Secretary Jane E. Hunter. While admitting that hospital facilities were needed, they refused to support a city hospital branch on the East Side while the interns' and nurses' training programs at City Hospital were closed to African Americans.[178] The protest campaign against hospital color lines won a victory when the question of financing the branch hospital with municipal bonds was permitted to die quietly in the finance committee.[179]

During 1927 through 1929 African Americans persistently opposed Cleveland City Hospital color lines. In the wake of these sustained efforts, the Cleveland City Council decided to racially integrate the municipal hospital's professional training programs. On November 25, 1929, Councilman F. W. Walz, an octogenarian white physician, introduced a resolution in city council designed to end racial discrimination at the municipal hospital.[180] Advising reliance on the Walz resolution, African American Councilman Russell S. Brown persuaded Harry C. Smith and others to postpone their planned court action against City Hospital for not admitting the Reverend Horace C. Bailey's granddaughter to its nurses' training program.[181] In a unanimous vote on January 13, 1930, the Cleveland City Council did pass the Walz resolution requiring municipal officials to "give all citizens the right to receive training as internes [sic] and nurses at City Hospital in accord with the provisions of the U.S. Constitution and the law of the State of Ohio."[182]

The racial integration of Cleveland City Hospital occurred in a political context. Politics was involved in hospital issues concerning African Americans in Cleveland from 1927 through 1930. For example, the municipal hospital's African American critics entered the political arena in 1927 when they tried to persuade city officials to eliminate City Hospital color lines. African Americans in groups, most notably the NAACP, raised political pressure on the city manager by urging him to remedy the hospital's inequities. Meantime black individuals like George A. Myers, seeking the same end, employed old-style politics that relied on networks of acquaintances with influential civic leaders. During the Cleveland municipal elections in fall 1927, another political dimension was added to this sort of lobbying. The general election ballot carried a proposition to approve a bond issue to raise funds for Cleveland City Hospital. Its black critics urged African Americans to vote no on the hospital bond proposition in protest against the City Hospital's racially exclusive practices. This was the public stance of the Cleveland NAACP and most of Cleveland's prominent black ministers. Also, local black weeklies, *The Call*, *The Post*, and *The Gazette*, editorialized against the bond issue. The hospital bond proposition was defeated, and there was a heavy vote against it in the city's black wards. Shortly afterwards, George A. Myers warned the city manager that African American support for his administration was being seriously undermined by the City Hospital's racial practices.[183]

As noted, starting in 1928 black council members used the Cleveland City Council as a platform to protest against municipal hospital color lines. African Americans obtained unprecedented influence on the Cleveland City Council following the November 1929 municipal elections. Three African Americans were elected to the council that year. They were attorneys Claybourne George and Lawrence O. Payne and dentist Leroy Bundy. Each one had made a campaign pledge to fight against racial exclusion at City Hospital. Also, after the 1929 election the white city council members were evenly split along party lines. In

January 1930 the African American councilmen joined the Republican caucus, giving it the majority in council. Councilmen George, Payne, and Bundy demanded that City Hospital color lines be eliminated and the African American share of Republican party patronage appointments be enlarged. Once given such assurances, the black councilmen agreed to vote with Republican council members on key issues. As promised, City Hospital admitted African Americans to its nursing school, beginning in September 1930. An African American intern was appointed to the City Hospital staff for the first time in summer 1931.[184] Clearly, politics had its place in the remarkable African American campaign for equal rights in Cleveland's municipal hospital. The next chapter considers partisan politics' role in the larger equal rights struggle in Ohio during the twenties.

In summary, the struggle for equal rights in Ohio challenged inequities in most areas along the color line in the 1920s. Protests usually involved local efforts to overcome local instances of color bias found in restaurants, hotels, theaters, residential housing, daily newspapers, public schools, hospitals, cemeteries, and other public places. The most adamant and effective assertions of equal rights in the state came from African Americans in northern Ohio cities in the twenties, as in past generations. Occasionally, the struggle went statewide as African American equal rights advocates in many Ohio cities worked in a common cause, for example, opposition to the Ku Klux Klan in the state.

The equal rights struggle in the 1920s came at a pivotal time in the long African American protest tradition in Ohio. It borrowed tactics from the past, adapted them, and used them in ways that set precedents for the future. Ohio NAACP branches made public protests in the newspaper press, courtrooms, legislative halls, and election campaign forums. Protests had been made in these same arenas in the nineteenth century. The NAACP adaptation gave organizational backing to such protests, which were conducted in the previous century by black individuals possessing political influence. The NAACP, while leading the way in the twenties, was not alone in the equal rights struggle in Ohio. Clevelander George A. Myers and a few other elder black leaders kept alive the traditional leadership style, which died with them early in the next decade. Also, in a few instances concerned black neighbors assembled ad hoc community associations and organized mass demonstrations, for example, the student boycott mounted by black parents objecting to racial segregation at Dayton's Willard School in 1924. These were nontraditional tactics in Ohio's equal rights struggle in the twenties, but they became antecedents of the direct action strategy commonly employed at the height of the Civil Rights Movement in the early 1960s.

The advocacy of equal rights for African Americans sometimes was successful in Ohio, but the color line in the state remained about as rigid as ever in 1930. The significance of protest then was not about winning or losing specific contests concerning rights; instead, its importance lay in how the contests were conducted. New leadership was established in the equal rights struggle. It practiced and developed tactics drawn from an old and less-organized African American protest tradition. This relatively new NAACP form of organized protest came of age in Ohio and elsewhere, making the twenties an important decade in the formation of the twentieth century Civil Rights Movement in the state and the nation.[185]

CHAPTER EIGHT

Toward Black Political Independence

During the 1920s partisan politics remained an important arena of the African American struggle against the color line in Ohio. Politics and elections still determined whether office holders were more or less sympathetic to the principle of equality before the law regardless of color. Political actions still shaped legislative measures and other governmental actions that were either contrary to that equality principle or in accord with it. In Ohio the Republican party remained more supportive of African American political interests than the Democratic party. The decade, however, saw an acceleration of the Republican party's long retreat from its position in the Reconstruction Period as vigorous champion of equal rights for African Americans. The Ohio Republican party, for example, was much less inclined in the 1920s to choose African Americans for significant political patronage jobs and as the party's nominees for public offices. Also, reflecting the GOP's changing stance on civil rights, the Ku Klux Klan was more likely to back Republican candidates than Democratic ones in Ohio and surrounding states. This Republican trend also was evident in national politics. For instance, Republicans, who held majorities in Congress, declined to enact federal anti-lynching legislation demanded by the NAACP. Undoubtedly, the flood of white intolerance in the twenties influenced these Republican developments in the state and nation.[1]

The vast majority of Ohio's rank and file black electorate voted for Republican candidates from the Reconstruction Period through the 1920s. However, there were more independent black Republicans in Ohio during the twenties than in earlier decades. The Republican party alienated unprecedented numbers of black Republican political leaders.

Old as well as young black Republican politicos criticized their party for failure to provide blacks with adequate shares of patronage employment and nominations. In protests against these failures, black Republicans increasingly entered primary and general elections without Republican party endorsements. Also, independent black Republicans opposed Republican candidates who were regarded as unsympathetic to the rights of African Americans, notably those identified with the Ku Klux Klan. Often these black independents were veterans of Ohio Republican party politics. While calling attention to Republican shortcomings towards African Americans, they acted individually and in traditional political factions. In addition, nonpartisan organizations representing African American viewpoints, especially the NAACP, sometimes voiced opinions that were at least implicitly critical of Republican candidates or issue positions in Ohio elections. This developing black protest in the political venue, as in others, was imbued with the spirit of "the New Negro" that grew out of the black military experience in World War I. Furthermore, black political protest in Ohio was emboldened by the growing electoral clout of African Americans. The number of black voters in Ohio increased, particularly in urban centers, as accelerated black in-migration enlarged Ohio's African American population. Disaffection with the Republican party was expressed in national, state, and local elections conducted in Ohio. While most independent black Republican leaders protested from within the Republican party, some eventually affiliated with the Democratic party or a third party.[2]

Early in this period, dissident black Republicans in Ohio criticized Republican party patronage policies as unfair to African Americans. Black politicians in Ohio were involved in the patron-client relationships typical of "the spoils system" in United States politics since the age of Andrew Jackson. In patronage politics, the political party rewarded partisan voters and party workers who contributed to its electoral success. Party workers were arrayed at various hierarchical levels depending on whether they were engaged in precinct, ward, municipal, county, state, or presidential politics. When political rewards were given, each politico in the structure, whether black or white, was at the same time both a client receiving favors and a patron dispensing them. Among the patrons' favors were public jobs, nominations for appointive and elective public offices, and political party positions.[3]

Black as well as white bosses figured in old urban political machines that still were significant aspects of Ohio's municipal politics and government after 1914. Precedents establishing African American roles in Ohio patronage politics were set in the nineteenth century. Perhaps, William Thompson was the original black municipal ward boss in Ohio.

"Bill" Thompson formed an early friendship and political association with George B. Cox, who ultimately became the Republican party "boss" in Cincinnati. During the 1880s, according to black newspaperman Wendell P. Dabney, Thompson was "a colored man who had a big saloon and a tremendous following at the polls" in Cincinnati's West End African American precincts.[4] Cox's early success in the West End owed much to Thompson's support and to his role as an organizer of the inter-racial pro-Republican Blaine Club. In reward, Thompson was elected to the Ohio House of Representatives and appointed as a member of the Republican state executive committee.[5] Early in the twentieth century, Alexander "Smoky" Hobbs was a black Republican ward boss in Columbus. Evidently, Hobbs' campaign efforts for the party were reward-ed by lax law enforcement against his notorious saloon that doubled as an opium den.[6] In Cleveland black saloonkeeper Albert D. "Starlight" Boyd was a cog in the political machine of Maurice Maschke, who was the Cuyahoga County Republican party chairman. Boyd's saloon received little police interference, although illicit incidents were fre-quent at his public house.[7]

As in decades past, black politicos and voters in the 1920s often were assigned menial political patronage jobs in municipal government. In each major Ohio city African Americans constituted a disproportionate number of those in public service occupations who were employed as laborers, doorkeepers, and watchmen. Relatively few blacks were employed in other public service positions in Ohio, for example, in police and fire departments. In most major Ohio cities, the number of black police officers declined during the twenties because black police-men were not replaced when they left their departments. In 1920 no fire department employed an African American in a large Ohio city. In 1930, 9 blacks were employed in Ohio fire departments: 4 in Cleveland, 4 in Columbus, and 1 in Cincinnati. Each of these departments employed hundreds of whites.[8]

Black Ohioans who were prominent in statewide and presidential pol-itics typically were businessmen and professionals. They were esteemed in African American society and respected by politically powerful whites. Hollendon Hotel barbershop proprietor George A. Myers of Cleveland was the most influential African American political figure in Ohio as the nineteenth century closed. Into the 1920s, the Republican party's appointments and endorsements of African Americans in Ohio were often made upon Myers' recommendations. Myers' influence ini-tially derived from the fact that he was a close friend and political confi-dant of Clevelander Mark Hanna, the Ohio Republican boss whose machinations were instrumental to President William McKinley's rise in national politics. Content to exercise power off stage, Myers never used his connections to obtain office for himself; however, he often was an Ohio delegate to Republican national conventions before World War I.[9] Myers died in 1930, and he was survived by few high-ranking black Republicans of his generation in Ohio. Ralph W. Tyler of Columbus, Charles Cottrill of Toledo, William S. Scarborough of Wilberforce University, and others died in the twenties and earlier.[10]

During 1915–1930, African Americans in Ohio experienced a relative dearth of Republican patronage appointments in state and federal government. Ohio's black Republicans had received a number of notable appointments during 1880–1914. Examples include membership on The Ohio State University Board of Trustees (Peter H. Clark), collector of the customs at Honolulu (Charles Cottrill), and auditor in the United States Navy Department (Ralph W. Tyler).[11] A black Democrat, Dr. Joseph L. Johnson of Columbus, served as minister to Liberia during Democrat Woodrow Wilson's terms as President.[12] Such remarkable appointments, which were declining in the teens, were awarded to very few black Republicans in Ohio after 1922. During 1915–1930, as earlier, African American Republicans appointed to state and federal posts typically were highly educated and well trained professionals. Attorney Robert Barcus of Columbus was appointed special counselor in the office of the Ohio attorney general in 1919. Barcus, a Howard University alumnus, had been admitted to practice in the United States District Court, Southern District in 1913.[13] Wilberforce University President Emeritus William S. Scarborough was a United States Department of Agriculture research assistant, and attorney A. Lee Beaty of Cincinnati was an assistant in the office of the United States District Attorney for Southern Ohio.[14] Dr. Aubrey Lane of Cincinnati, who possessed an Ohio State University degree in veterinary medicine, became Ohio's state veterinarian.[15] Each received his appointment in 1921–1922. Baptist pastor E. W. Curry of Springfield was appointed in 1929 to head a special Negro section of the Parole and Probation Division of the State Welfare Department.[16] Meantime, lesser state government patronage traditionally assigned to African Americans included several clerkships, such as enrolling clerk of the state senate, and numerous menial jobs such as porter in the Statehouse.[17]

In view of the fact that the black electorate loyally backed the Republican party, African Americans expected Republican leaders in government to appoint a fair number of well-qualified African Americans to substantial public jobs. African Americans criticized Republican officials when they failed to give blacks full recognition in this way. In 1916, for example, independent black Republicans across the state called public attention to the small number of appointments given to African Americans by Republican Governor Frank B. Willis. A. D. Male, a successful black dairy farmer of central Ohio, publicly complained that under Willis African Americans received only "a few minor appointments that no well-posted, energetic Colored man could afford to accept. . . ."[18] Alluding to the Republican debt owed to black voters, The Reverend Carl W. Haskell of Columbus asserted that it was time for the party "to be paying something far more than it has in late years on that debt."[19]

In Ohio the most sustained manifestation of independent black Republican activity in the 1920s occurred in statewide politics. Black Clevelander Harry C. Smith filed as a candidate in each statewide Republican primary election during the decade. He was a veteran journalist, and his newspaper had regularly supported Republican candidates for public office. Over the decades Smith had been active in Republican patronage politics. He had served three terms in the Ohio legislature in the 1890s and sponsored a public accommodations law and an anti-lynching act. Smith was a staunch and consistent advocate of equal rights for African Americans; he often used acerbic language when criticizing persons accused of limiting those rights. Smith ran energetic campaigns seeking the Republican nomination for secretary of state in 1920 and for governor in 1922, raising considerable interest among black voters. Smith again was a candidate for the gubernatorial nomination in the 1924, 1926, and 1928 primary elections. All of his candidacies created forums to criticize the party. They were devices to make the state's Republican leaders conscious of the growing black vote and pressure them to equitably distribute patronage favors to African Americans.[20]

Growing independence of black Republicans also was seen in general elections conducted in Ohio during the 1920s. Black Republicans criticized both state and national Republican leaders for their Party's regressive treatment of African American interests. However, this criticism still was limited because few African American voters saw the national Democratic party as a safe option. Democrats in the White House and in Congress tended to be much influenced by Negrophobes in their party's southern wing.

African American distrust of the national Democratic party was reinforced early in the decade when Ohio Democratic leaders exploited racial fears. During the 1920 campaign the Ohio Democratic state committee issued two lengthy circulars that expressed anxiety about the growing migration of southern Negroes into Ohio, warned that Negroes were seeking social equality, and implied that a vote for the Republican state ticket was a vote for "Negro domination."[21] The "A Timely

Warning" circular concluded: "Men and women of Ohio, rally to the ballot box and give such a verdict as forever will rid Ohio of this menace to yourselves and your children."[22] Also in 1920, some Ohio opponents of Republican presidential candidate Warren G. Harding played a race card undoubtedly intended to undermine his support from white voters. It was rumored that Harding had Negro forebears.[23] The possibility that Harding had African ancestors certainly did not damage his popularity with black voters.

The 1920 Republican presidential campaign in the Ohio general election was notable for the absence of black insurgency. Black Republicans very largely rallied around Warren G. Harding, an Ohio native. The Harding campaign made extraordinarily strong appeals to black voters, stressing "Equal Opportunity" for instance.[24] A black veteran of the women's suffrage movement in Cleveland, Lethia Fleming, was appointed to membership on the national women's advisory board of the Republican party.[25] The women's suffrage amendment to the United States Constitution became effective in this election.[26] Harding received virtually uniform support from the state's black Republican leaders.[27] They included the dissident black weekly editor Harry C. Smith, who wrote a widely circulated pro-Harding pamphlet addressed to African Americans.[28]

Black Republican leaders in Ohio and in other states asserted greater independence in statewide general elections following President Warren G. Harding's death in office. Independent black Republicans criticized some Republican nominees for president and governor and campaigned against them, sometimes in cooperation with their Democratic party opponents. The most cogent criticism concerned Ku Klux Kan issues and questions about the racial fairness of Republican candidates. This trend developed through 1928, and a few black Republican leaders switched allegiance to the Democratic party at decade's end.

In Ohio the level of black Republican political protest rose in 1924. Leading black Republicans from across the state, meeting in Columbus, petitioned Ohio party officials to return to past practice and include a black delegate in the Ohio delegation to the 1924 Republican National Convention to be held in Cleveland. When this request was denied, a number of those advocating a black delegate started a movement to organize Ohio's independent black Republicans. Convention officials did appoint prominent black Clevelanders to a committee in charge of local arrangements for black delegates from other states. Eventually, editor Harry C. Smith and other African Americans in Cleveland formed a long list of demands and urged the out-of-state black delegates to present them to the convention's platform committee. This group, for instance, wanted the Republican platform to advocate enactment of fed-eral anti-lynching legislation and repudiation of the Ku Klux Klan.[29] The black delegates' actual platform proposals were almost completely reject-ed. The Ku Klux Klan issue was ignored at this Republican National Convention that nominated Calvin Coolidge for President.[30]

Many prominent black Republicans across the state were alienated by the failure of Coolidge Republicans to act on matters of concern to African Americans. Some opposed the Republican nominee and occa-sionally supported his rivals. In northern Ohio, for example, Clevelander Harry C. Smith's black weekly repeatedly criticized President Coolidge and published information favorable to Democratic presidential candi-date John W. Davis and to the Progressive party candidate Robert M. LaFollette. Davis made statements sympathetic to racial fairness, while LaFollette made a clear-cut condemnation of the Ku Klux Klan. Some black Clevelanders organized the Independent Colored Voters League of Cuyahoga County, which vigorously campaigned for LaFollette in north-eastern Ohio cities.[31] In central Ohio, an Emancipation Day ceremony speaker urged African Americans in Springfield to vote independently.[32] At Ohio University in the state's southern hills, a small group of politi-cally independent black students formed a John W. Davis Club and cam-paigned for the Democratic candidate.[33] Despite defections, other promi-nent black Republicans in Ohio remained regular and actively cam-paigned for Coolidge, who carried Ohio in a national election landslide for the Republican presidential candidate.

During the 1920s Republican candidates for governor in Ohio and in Indiana drew criticism from black Republican insurgents. In 1924 the Cleveland *Gazette* stated that the Ku Klux Klan endorsed Ohio Republican candidate Harry L. Davis and that Davis did not deny it. *Gazette* editor Harry C. Smith aided the Democratic candidate for Ohio governor, A. Victor Donahey, for instance, by reporting Donahey's state-ment that he would give Ohioans an honest government "without prej-udice as to race, color or creed."[34] In neighboring Indiana the black elec-torate of Marion County voted Democratic for the first time after inde-pendent black Republicans in Indianapolis mounted a highly organized protest against the Klan-endorsed Republican state ticket in 1924.[35]

The Klan remained an issue in Ohio's 1926 election campaigns. Black independents from thirty-four Ohio counties attending a meeting in Columbus formed a nonpartisan league of African American voters, head-ed by Clevelander Dr. E. J. Gregg.[36] Many African Americans opposed Republican nominee for governor Myers Y. Cooper, believing he was anti-black. Black weekly editor Harry C. Smith refused to give Cooper his edi-torial endorsement. In a letter of explanation to a Republican campaign official, Smith charged that the Klan backed Cooper and that he drew the color line in his real estate business transactions.[37] According to a black Democrat in Columbus, the state Democratic campaign committee circulated one hundred thousand copies of this letter in Ohio prior to the election.[38] Smith concluded that black voters gave Donahey "the balance of votes" which ensured his re-election.[39] A Columbus observer reported that members of Ohio's "Colored Democratic Clubs" voted for the Democratic candidates out of party preference.[40]

Myers Y. Cooper again was the Republican candidate for Ohio governor in 1928. Editor Smith reiterated his accusation that Cooper discriminated against blacks.[41] He published an open letter written by a black teacher at Cincinnati's Douglass School, who charged Cooper with using pressure tactics and harassment to drive her and her sister out of a house that they had purchased in an area in which Cooper's real estate firm owned much property.[42] Editor Smith advised his readers to vote for the Democratic gubernatorial candidate, Martin L. Davey.[43] However, many African American voters stayed with the Republican candidate.[44] Republican Cooper was elected governor of Ohio, undoubtedly benefiting from Republican Herbert Hoover's landslide election as president.

The African American taboo against supporting Democratic candidates had weakened somewhat by 1928. Respected black personalities advocated black political independence and criticized the Republican party during the twenties, making opposition to it more acceptable. This evidently emboldened African Americans in Ohio who favored Democratic presidential candidate Al Smith over his Republican opponent Herbert Hoover in 1928. Some prominent black Republicans, including editor Harry C. Smith of Cleveland, continued to urge African Americans to be independent voters in the presidential election.[45] Meantime, some African Americans in each Ohio region supported the Democratic presidential candidate Al Smith. He was popular with minority groups around the country, who identified with him as a victim of intolerance. Al Smith's political enemies stirred Protestant fears of his Roman Catholic faith. Black political leaders from Springfield, Rendville, Cincinnati, Cleveland, Toledo, Columbus, and Dayton formed the Al Smith League of Colored Voters of Ohio, purportedly to promote independent voting. The league's president, Dr. Joseph L. Johnson of Columbus, was a veteran Democratic politician.[46] Some other black Ohioans supporting Al Smith were avowedly partisan Democrats. The drift towards the Democratic party by some black politicians in Ohio also was seen in other states. In July 1928 the National Colored Democratic Association staged its national convention in Cleveland and nominated Al Smith for president. Black Clevelanders

Walter L. Brown and Peter Boult held posts in the association's national committee structure.[47] Such expressions of black political independence from the Republican party did not basically change the African American voting pattern in the presidential election. Republican Herbert Hoover was elected with the assistance of most black voters, but Al Smith received more African American support at the polls than was usual for a Democratic candidate.[48]

Demonstrations of African American independence from the Republican party were made in Ohio's municipal elections in large and small urban centers during the 1920s. Black Republicans ran for election to local offices in each region of the state. Usually, the black candidates campaigned as independents after having failed to obtain Republican endorsements in the primaries. These independent candidacies increased in number as the decade passed.

The few African Americans in smaller Ohio urban centers who ran for local offices rarely won in this period, especially after 1920. William Goode was elected in 1915 to the city council of Bridgeport, located on the Ohio River in eastern Ohio's Belmont County, where blacks were about 5 percent of the approximately 4,000 population.[49] In 1919 Washington Courthouse resident John T. Oatmeal was elected justice of the peace of Fayette County, located in southwestern Ohio.[50] Arthur Johnston was elected to the town council of Miles Heights, a small community near Cleveland, where he was a foreman in the Cuyahoga County highway department. Johnston became council president because he received more votes than any other council member. This put him in line to succeed the incumbent mayor in the event of the latter's incapacity. Upon the incumbent's death in 1929, Arthur Johnston became mayor of Miles Heights. African Americans constituted about one-third of the population there.[51] Black candidates in the twenties unsuccessfully ran for public offices in smaller Ohio cities including Elyria, Springfield, and Zanesville. Robert W. Pulley of Elyria, for one, was a candidate for sheriff in northern Ohio's Lorain County in 1922.[52]

Prior to 1910 African Americans were not elected to city councils in Ohio's large urban centers with one exception.[53] In Columbus, during the period 1881–1912, several African Americans were elected to the city council and the board of education from a predominantly black ward. But in 1912 the Columbus city charter was revised to provide for the election of councilmen and school board members at large rather than by wards. No African American was elected to municipal office in Columbus during the remainder of the decade. About a half dozen black candidates campaigned unsuccessfully for public office in Columbus and Franklin County during the twenties.[54]

The most sustained and effective black Republican insurgent movements in municipal politics were carried out in Cincinnati and Cleveland, which contained the largest black populations in the state. Both used municipal election forms giving the black vote visibility. In Cincinnati black Republicans expressed growing dissatisfaction with the Hamilton County Republican organization because it did not embrace African American candidates for election to county offices as it had in the past. The Republican party did not support a black candidate for the Cincinnati City Council in 1921.[55] Some black Republican leaders consequently threatened to back a white independent mayoralty candidate while charging that the Republican party was ungrateful for the consistently Republican black vote.[56] Many black voters evidently supported the independent white candidate for mayor in 1921.[57] In 1922 the county Republican organization broke a long tradition by failing to nominate a black candidate for any county office.[58] Local black leaders vociferously objected, for example, during an African American political meeting held at Cincinnati's Metropolitan Baptist Church.[59] Subsequently, the local Republican organization apparently attempted to mollify alienated black Republicans. Black weekly editor Wendell P. Dabney was promoted to paymaster of Cincinnati after having served as assistant paymaster since 1907. Dabney shortly resigned his post in protest against the fact that his salary had not been increased to correspond with his higher rank. During the 1924 election Dabney advised others to join him in declaring independence of the Republican party.[60]

In 1925 Cincinnati began to conduct municipal elections on the basis of proportional representation, making it theoretically possible for African Americans to be represented in the city council in proportion to the number of black voters in Cincinnati.[61] The local Republican organization, however, did not endorse black candidates for council seats. In response, Dr. E. Duval Colley, a black physician, launched a highly visible protest candidacy for a Hamilton County congressional seat in 1926.[62] Likewise, in 1927 Cincinnati police department detective Frank A. B. Hall ran as an independent Republican candidate for city council after being denied a regular Republican nomination. A local newspaper observed, "for the first time the colored voters partly concentrated on a member of their own race."[63] Two African Americans, George W. B. Conrad and Hall, contested for council seats as independent Republicans in 1929. At a campaign meeting, black attorney A. Lee Beaty condemned local Republicans for denying African Americans fair recognition and asserted: "Either George Conrad or Frank Hall must teach them to respect us."[64] Hall received more votes in 1929 than he had in 1927. The Republican party in Cincinnati apparently learned the lesson of Hall's candidacies; it backed Hall for a city council seat in 1931, and he was elected.[65]

Black independence in Ohio's local politics was most evident in Cleveland, where African American grievances against the Republican party were different from those in other Ohio cities. Black Clevelanders obtained some Republican nominations and were elected to some public offices though the twenties, in contrast to events elsewhere in Ohio. African Americans in Cleveland were aggrieved that blacks did not receive a more significant share of Republican endorsements for public offices and political patronage jobs. Also, many blacks in Cleveland were disaffected from the Republican party by the belief that local Republican authorities were responsible for the neglect of municipal services in black residential areas.

Early in the twenties, progressive African Americans in Cleveland criticized the record of black city councilman Thomas W. Fleming, who represented Cleveland's Ward Eleven. Fleming had served several terms on the Cleveland City Council, 1910–1920.[66] He was a politico of the old-style patronage politics at the municipal level. Fleming repeatedly ran for council with the endorsement of Maurice Maschke, boss of the Cuyahoga County Republican organization. Black saloonkeeper A. D. Boyd headed the Republican machine in Ward Eleven and effectively delivered its votes to Fleming and Maschke, election after election. Councilman Fleming's black critics in the twenties asserted that he voted according to the wishes of Maschke and gave little attention to conditions in his ward or to the concerns of African Americans in Cleveland. At the urging of progressive African Americans in Ward Eleven, black weekly editor Harry C. Smith ran as an independent opposing Fleming in the city council elections of 1921. Smith received endorsements from several black churches and many black organizations in Ward Eleven, including the Baptist Ministers' Conference and the Council of Colored Women. Following Fleming's election victory, his progressive black critics acted to provide alternative representation; they formed a group called the Central Body to pressure the city administration for such things as better streetcar service and street repairs in Ward Eleven.[67]

During the 1920s, especially in the latter half of the decade, black candidates for elective and appointive offices were more successful in Cleveland than in Ohio's other major urban centers. This success reflected the extraordinary concentration and growth of the black voting population in certain wards on Cleveland's East Side. The increasing black voter strength in these wards was effective in elections because Cleveland's election procedures were not designed to exclude African Americans from local offices. During the decade, Cleveland adopted a complicated system of election districts containing wards and a version of proportional representation that encouraged independent black candidates to seek municipal offices. Initiatives taken by independent black candidates also contributed to the political success of African Americans in Cleveland. Generally these independent candidates represented a new-style politics tied to special interest organizations, particularly the NAACP, rather than to networks of friends associated with established party patronage politics. After witnessing exhibitions of political insurgency by black Republicans, the Cuyahoga County Democratic organization apparently saw its chance to win the black vote or some larger fraction of it. As the decade closed, the Republican and Democratic political machines in Cleveland were competing for the black vote. Each party nominated black candidates for public offices and sometimes favored African Americans for political appointments.

In 1925 and 1927 several African Americans ran for public offices in Cleveland's municipal elections. In the 1925 city council elections, two black independent candidates opposed Councilman Thomas W. Fleming in Cleveland's Third District, and black attorney Clayborne George ran in the Fourth District. Only Councilman Fleming, whom the Republican Party backed, was elected.[68] By 1927 Cleveland's growing black constituency was able to elect three African American City Council members. Attorney George and Dr. E. J. Gregg, a physician, were elected to the council in 1927 as independent Republicans, and once more Councilman Fleming was reelected with a Republican endorsement. Although they identified themselves as independent Republicans, Councilmen George and Gregg entered the city council's Democratic caucus. They were expected to receive the support of the Democratic minority in council on measures which they sponsored.[69] Prior to the election, Cuyahoga County Democratic Executive Committee Chairman W. B. Gongwer had approved Gregg's candidacy. This was the first time in history that the Democratic party endorsed an African American for the Cleveland City Council.[70] Gongwer and the Democrats also endorsed the candidacy of African American attorney William R. Green, who campaigned unsuccessfully in 1927 as an independent candidate for Cleveland municipal court judge.[71]

In 1928 the three African Americans on the Cleveland City Council were in a position to affect the outcomes of close votes on council issues, and this, undoubtedly, gave local Democratic leaders further incentive to win black political support. For example, the council was evenly divided about which candidate would receive an appointment to the Cleveland Civil Service Commission. The Republicans wanted black attorney Harry E. Davis, who was a member of the Ohio House of

Representatives and a legal adviser to the local NAACP. Councilman E. J. Gregg spoke and voted against Davis' appointment on grounds that Davis could be of greater service in the state legislature than on the commission. Councilmen Thomas W. Fleming and Claybourne George voted for Davis, who was appointed with the votes of thirteen of the twenty-five council members. In January 1928 Harry E. Davis became the first black member of the Cleveland Civil Service Commission.[72] Thereafter, county political boss Gongwer intensified the local Democratic organization's appeal to Cleveland's black voters. In the summer of 1928 Gongwer appointed forty-two African Americans as precinct committeemen in Cleveland's Eleventh, Twelfth, and Eighteenth Wards. Consequently, all the Democratic precinct committeemen in Wards Eleven and Twelve were blacks, although some of their Republican counterparts in the same Wards were whites.[73]

In 1929 the Cuyahoga County Republican organization headed by Maurice Maschke was embarrassed when City Councilman Thomas W. Fleming was indicted and convicted for soliciting and accepting a bribe to use his influence on the council toward the passage of special legislation.[74] Some local daily newspapers sharply criticized boss Maschke and his Republican associates. One editorialized: ". . . Maschke stands responsible for the conditions which have made Tom Fleming what he is."[75] The Republican organization subsequently backed for the vacancy an African American candidate of unquestioned character. Dr. Russell S. Brown, pastor of the Mt. Zion Congregational Church, was experienced in welfare work, scholarship, and teaching. Although he was not identified with any political faction, Brown was a local NAACP activist. He was elected by the votes of the fourteen white Republicans and two black members on the city council.[76] The Cleveland Plain Dealer's editor described the choice of Dr. Brown as "a good selection."[77] Thereafter, African American Councilmen Gregg and George attended the city council's Republican caucus.[78]

Buoyed by recent successes, numerous black candidates entered the Cleveland municipal elections in 1929. Public school teacher Mary B. Martin was a Cleveland school board incumbent who had been appointed to fill a vacated seat. In 1929 she ran and was elected to serve a term of her own on the Cleveland Board of Education.[79] Several black candidates for the Cleveland City Council displayed considerable independence from the Republican party. Some campaigned as independents, while others were identified with major and minor parties. Again, three African Americans were elected to a city council balanced along party lines, giving the black members significant political clout. County Democratic boss W. B. Gongwer endorsed Dr. James A. Owen for city council in the 1929 election, marking only the second time the Democrats backed a black council candidate.[80] Councilman Claybourne George evidently ran as a regular Republican. Councilman E. J. Gregg and attorney Chester K. Gillespie associated their candidacies with the Progressive Government Committee (for the city manager plan). Lawrence O. Payne and Dr. Leroy Bundy were independent candidates. Bundy and Payne were elected to the Cleveland City Council and Councilman George was reelected.[81] Attorney Payne was an assistant prosecutor in the Cleveland municipal courts, 1924–1929, and an associate of Thomas W. Fleming when the latter was a city councilman.[82] Dr. Bundy was reared and professionally trained in Cleveland. Later, when practicing dentistry in Illinois, he was charged and ultimately acquitted of criminal offenses allegedly committed during the East St. Louis race riot in the summer of 1917. After returning to Cleveland, he possessed the political advantage of very high name recognition because his litigation was much publicized.[83]

When the newly elected Cleveland City Council met in January 1930, its three black members were in a position to decide important issues facing that body because its white members were evenly divided by their party affiliations. Eleven were Democrats and eleven were Republicans. Councilmen Bundy, George, and Payne used their political clout effectively. The replacement of William R. Hopkins as city manager was the council's prime concern early in the year. The black councilmen met and negotiated with the council's white Republicans and with Republican Daniel E. Morgan, who wished to succeed Hopkins. After obtaining political commitments from him, Bundy, George, and Payne cast deciding votes in Council that elected Morgan. True to his commitments, City Manager Morgan took steps to racially integrate Cleveland City Hospital and to increase the number of African Americans with appointments to municipal offices, including the city clerk's office.[84]

In the 1920s the Republican party was less inclined to nominate and elect black candidates for the Ohio General Assembly than it was prior to World War I, when there were sometimes three black Republican members of the Ohio House of Representatives per term.[85] No more than one African American sat in the Ohio legislature during 1915–1930. Cincinnatian A. Lee Beaty was elected to the Ohio House of Representatives from Hamilton County in 1916 and reelected in 1918.[86] The Hamilton County Republican ticket included black nominees for state legislature in elections during 1916–1920. Franklin County (Columbus) Republicans nominated, but failed to elect, black candidates for the legislature in 1918, 1920, and 1922.[87] Thereafter, only in

Cuyahoga County (Cleveland) were black Republicans nominated and elected to the Ohio legislature in the twenties. A black Republican from Cleveland served in the Ohio House of Representatives in every term of the legislature during the decade. Attorney Harry E. Davis won a state representative nomination in the Cuyahoga County Republican primary election, and he was elected to the state House of Representatives in 1920, 1922, 1924, and 1926. Davis faced African American competitors in some of those primaries. His African American successor was another loyal Republican party member, attorney Perry B. Jackson, who ran and was elected as a Cuyahoga County Republican nominee for the state legislature in 1928. Meantime, black Democrat Peter Boult failed to win endorsement as a Cuyahoga County Democratic candidate for the general assembly in 1928.[88]

During 1915–1930, Ohio's African American state representatives, all accomplished attorneys, acted to advance the principle of equal rights regardless of color; this followed precedents set by Ohio's nineteenth century black state legislators. Hamilton County (Cincinnati) State Representative A. Lee Beaty (1917–1920) sponsored a measure strengthening the nineteenth century Ohio law that provided penalties for racial discrimination in public accommodations. Ohio NAACP branches and black organizations and individuals across the state lobbied for the passage of Beaty's bill. When it died in committee, members of the Colored Women's Republican Club in Columbus and many African Americans blamed the Ohio legislature's Republican majority.[89]

Cuyahoga County State Representatives Harry E. Davis (1921–1928) and Perry B. Jackson (1929–1930) vigilantly watched for anti-black measures and fought such bills. In 1923, for instance, Davis succeeded in challenging a proposal to amend and weaken Ohio's nineteenth century anti–mob violence act.[90] In 1925 Davis cooperated with others in preventing the passage of a bill against racial intermarriage that the Ku Klux Klan wanted.[91] He sponsored legislative measures intended to advance the cause of equal rights for African Americans. In 1921, for example, Davis introduced a resolution that would have put the Ohio legislature on record as favoring a federal "investigation of peonage conditions in the South" that exploited the black workers.[92] Representative Perry B. Jackson also guarded the interests of the state's black constituency; for instance, he successfully opposed a racial identification requirement in a 1929 state senate bill on Ohio election code revision.[93]

As previously indicated, the character of black politics in Ohio changed substantially in the 1920s. Nonpartisan organizations became more prominent in the political sphere than individual black politicians who were tied to partisan networks. Civil rights and race organizations often used political devices to influence public opinion and affect governmental decision-making in favor of their causes. Such associations sponsored political meetings, circulated petitions and issued press statements on political issues, and endorsed partisan candidates. In one notable instance such groups opposed the appointment of a United States Supreme Court nominee. During the twenties, the most visible organizations in Ohio's black politics were the NAACP and the Universal Negro Improvement Association. The black leadership trend toward political independence was advanced by both of these organizations.

The Universal Negro Improvement Association (UNIA) was a black separatist body founded in the previous decade by Marcus Garvey, a West Indian immigrant. Garvey advocated black economic self-sufficiency, unity, and pride. In the postwar period, his message gained extensive support among African American masses nationwide.[94] Divisions of Garvey's organization were founded in Cincinnati, Cleveland, Akron, and other Ohio cities. Garvey addressed Ohio audiences several times during the early twenties. He appeared in Akron and in larger cities.[95] His Cleveland addresses in December 1922 were described as "well attended."[96] When he gave a speech in September 1923, members of the Cleveland UNIA Division "and its many friends packed the church to the doors."[97] Early in the decade Cleveland Division Number Fifty Nine of the UNIA held its meetings in Haltworth's Hall and Liberty Hall. In 1923 the Cleveland UNIA began a campaign to raise thirty-five thousand dollars to purchase a headquarters building.[98] Likewise, the UNIA made an impact in Cincinnati, especially after Marcus Garvey spoke there in February 1921. The Cincinnati membership of Garvey's organization was eventually 8,000 according to William Ware, a social worker who formed the Cincinnati UNIA chapter late in 1920.[99] Black weekly editor Wendell P. Dabney noted that the Garvey movement "had a large following" in Cincinnati and that its George Street headquarters were "always thronged with its adherents."[100]

Political action was required to achieve some UNIA goals. For example, the association wished to shape United States foreign policy respecting Africa. The Cleveland unit's political programs undoubtedly exemplified like activities in Ohio's other UNIA divisions. Early in 1924 the Cleveland UNIA circulated petitions requesting the President and Congress to support "the creation of an independent Negro Republic in Africa."[101] This effort in Cleveland was a part of a national campaign of the UNIA to secure six million signatures on such petitions.[102] In March 1924 the Cleveland organization held a meeting celebrating the return of UNIA delegates who had toured Europe and Africa "in the interest of the repatriation of Africa."[103] In the spring of the same year, the Cleveland Division heard an address by a national UNIA official on the topic "Reclamation of Africa by Negroes of Western Civilization."[104]

UNIA divisions in Ohio emphatically advocated black political independence in the 1920s. Across the decade, UNIA leaders criticized the Republican party and approved black independent candidates. Eventually the Ohio UNIA backed a Democratic ticket. Cincinnati Division President William Ware expressed the Ohio Garveyites' viewpoint at a 1927 UNIA political meeting. He asserted: "The Negroes' lamentable condition here [Cincinnati] is largely caused by sticking to preachers and the Republican Party. Many of them go to the Republican campaign managers, get about fifty dollars . . . and say, solemnly, my church is with you."[105] Ohio UNIA bodies took independent stands in elections. For example, the Cleveland UNIA endorsed Harry C. Smith as an independent black candidate for Cleveland city council in 1921.[106] The Cincinnati UNIA cosponsored a political meeting addressed by Harry C. Smith when he was a gubernatorial candidate in the 1922 Republican primary election.[107] In 1927 Garvey's Cincinnati organization supported the ticket of the Charter party, a local third party.[108] In 1928 delegates attending the UNIA's state convention in Ohio backed the Democratic presidential candidate, Al Smith.[109]

The achievement of NAACP goals in the 1920s often required that civil rights organization to engage in politics, broadly conceived. A large part of the NAACP's agenda was composed of activities meant to influence public opinion and governmental action in support of racial equality in law. The NAACP also was involved in politics narrowly defined as party rivalry. It took positions in popular elections and sometimes in political patronage disputes. The NAACP avoided formal identification with a specific party and thereby incidentally advanced the independent voting trend then developing among African Americans. For example, in 1924 the NAACP's central office encouraged NAACP members across the country to vote for candidates on the basis of their merits rather than on their party affiliation. This was in reaction against Republican President Calvin Coolidge's negative record on racial issues. The NAACP's *Crisis* took an independent stance by publishing a symposium on the relative merits of the presidential candidates in 1924. Speakers representing the NAACP were sent to various parts of the nation to promote this independent view. NAACP Secretary James Weldon Johnson, for instance, urged blacks in Springfield, Ohio, to vote independently and vote against any candidate who was a member of or was supported by the Ku Klux Klan.[110]

Increasing NAACP political activity in Ohio during the twenties peaked in the 1930 general elections. The NAACP led a highly publicized and thorough campaign against a Republican nominee for the United States Senate. The campaign focused on Roscoe C. McCulloch, an incumbent United States senator from Ohio. He had voted for confirmation of the appointment of Judge John J. Parker of North Carolina as an associate justice of the United States Supreme Court. The NAACP and others charged that Judge Parker had exhibited anti-black behavior earlier in his career and thus opposed his appointment to the court by President Herbert Hoover.[111] Senator McCulloch received "an avalanche of pleas from his Negro and white constituents" asking that he vote against Judge Parker's confirmation, but he voted for confirmation anyway.[112] Parker lost the Senate vote, giving the NAACP a remarkable victory.

NAACP leaders at the local, state, and national levels subsequently conducted a campaign in Ohio to prevent Senator McCulloch's reelection in 1930. In May the Cleveland NAACP branch president wrote that he was using every opportunity to have black organizations in Cleveland go on record in opposition to McCulloch.[113] In Columbus, NAACP membership leaped with the occurrence of "rally after rally" opposing McCulloch's reelection.[114] The NAACP's national leaders, apparently sensing an African American revolt in Ohio, decided to make the defeat of Senator McCulloch a test of black voting potential. In the run-up to the election, the NAACP established a state conference of local NAACP branches in Ohio to coordinate the future general activities of the local branches. In the short term, this state conference was used to coordinate a statewide NAACP campaign seeking McCulloch's defeat. Branch delegates meeting in Columbus voted unanimously to oppose his election.[115] Headed by C. E. Dickinson, the state conference mailed thousands of anti-McCulloch materials, including postcards and sample ballots.[116] The black political revolt in Ohio was described and promoted in a *Crisis* article by Walter White, acting secretary of the NAACP, who observed: "The revolt is especially to be seen among the younger and more progressive Negroes of Ohio."[117] White and W. E. B. Du Bois, editor of the *Crisis*, addressed Ohio audiences just prior to the election.[118]

The 1930 election results were gratifying to Roscoe McCulloch's opponents. Ohio Democrat Robert J. Bulkley was elected to the United States Senate. The factors causing McCulloch's defeat included the prohibition issue and the poor economic conditions, but the black vote was influential. One scholar reported: "The colored districts of Cleveland, Toledo, Akron, Columbus, and Canton went to McCulloch's

Democratic opponent by margins of from 50 to 86 percent, while many voters in these districts refrained from voting for United States Senator."[119] The anti-McCulloch campaign evidenced several notable developments in Ohio's black politics during the twenties. Its leadership practiced a new politics tied to associations representing group interests rather than to the old politics that was derived from patronage networks. The campaign's magnitude reflected demographic changes that enlarged and concentrated the body of black voters in numbers sufficient to constitute the balance of power in a close election race. Finally, the anti-McCulloch campaign was a remarkable climax of insurgent activity ensuing from the expansion of black political independence during the twenties.

Knowledge of politics is required for a full understanding of the struggle against the Ohio color line in the 1920s because much of it occurred in political and governmental arenas. The voting places in Ohio and other northern states were untouched by the color line, in contrast to the polls in many southern states where racially biased enforcement of voting laws practically disenfranchised African Americans. Arguably, the possession of the franchise by African Americans in states like Ohio was the most important difference between the racial system of the North and that of the South in the 1920s. Different means were used to draw the color line in the North and South, but both regions countenanced extensive racial segregation and discrimination in practically every category of social and economic life. African Americans in Ohio held the ballot, however, which was a tangible symbol of citizenship rights desired by black migrants who departed from southern states with hopes of finding greater possibilities and better lives in the North. African Americans in locales across Ohio voted and participated in politics, acknowledging the value of this right. In short, access to political and governmental processes was available and essential to African Americans who challenged the Ohio color line in the twenties.

The color line existed in the North's political realm, nevertheless, and its effects became more exclusive in Ohio's politics in the 1920s. The Republican party failed to roundly condemn the Ku Klux Klan and generally tended to ignore equal rights issues in the twenties, although it was once the political champion of that cause. The Republican party in Ohio was less inclined than in the past to include African Americans when it chose candidates for appointive and elective offices. Instead of accepting this quiescently, black political leaders in Ohio protested Republican racial policies throughout the decade. A growing body of independent black Republican politicians challenged their party in local, state, congressional, and presidential elections throughout the decade. The party's leadership was regularly criticized for failure to reciprocate the loyalty that black voters gave to the Republican party. Black Republicans often expressed dissatisfaction by running for public offices without the backing of the Republican party.

The historical literature on early twentieth century African American politics often underplays evidence revealing such disaffection of black Republicans in the twenties and focuses on events in the thirties that contributed to the shift of the African American bloc vote from the Republican party to the Democratic party. The traditional literature suggests that black voter solidarity with the Republican party suddenly cracked and crumbled in the 1936 presidential election. African Americans benefited from the newly established policies of President Franklin D. Roosevelt and the New Deal. Undoubtedly, this was the immediate cause of the split; however, studies of black politics in Ohio and Indiana indicate that the break with the Republicans in the thirties occurred along fault lines that appeared earlier. Many black Ohioans in the twenties were at the same time alienated from the Republican party and unable to switch allegiance by voting for Democrats because they were seen as representing the party of the Jim Crow South. President Roosevelt altered that image of the Democratic party, creating a viable alternative for black Ohioans who had been alienated by the Republican party in the twenties.[120]

Political scientist Martin Kilson argues that the style of African American politics changed in the early twentieth century. Clearly, the twenties was the end of an era in Ohio for a style of black political leadership that grew out of the patron-client political system that was basic to state and national politics in the United States during the nineteenth century. In this old American system, political influence was traded like a commodity in exchanges among political leaders stationed at various ranks in a hierarchical network of individual political relationships. The individual at each level gained a measure of power and influence in the public sphere. This national political system was reshaped during the era of Progressive reform prior to World War I. Political factions composed of influential individuals were overshadowed in politics by a broad assortment of "special interest groups" that used organizations to influence party policy and public action. African American political leadership in Ohio and elsewhere changed with the times.[121] In the twenties, organizations of special interest to African Americans in Ohio, especially NAACP branches, were more effective in mustering political influence than were the few remaining elderly black political leaders who had been schooled in nineteenth century politics.

Conclusion

This book discusses the changing experiences of Ohio's black urban communities during 1915–1930, but it is mainly about the color line. Such studies focusing on the past's color lines surely can contribute to understanding of the black experience, but historians must produce additional works that focus on life within Ohio's black communities, rather than on black-white relations; otherwise, comprehension of the African American past will remain incomplete. Kimberly L. Phillips' recent book centering on social-economic class themes within Cleveland's black community helps fill that need.[1] Likewise, Steven C. Tracy's recent volume illuminates the rich history of blues music in Cincinnati.[2] Andrew Cayton's new one-volume Ohio history brings alive early twentieth century black cultural history in pages devoted to the lives, times, and literature of black writers with Ohio experiences who ultimately gained national literary reputations: Charles W. Chesnutt, Paul Lawrence Dunbar, Chester Himes, and Toni Morrison.[3]

Vital social and cultural life existed within black communities, but outside, the color line was always lurking. Ohio's noted black literary figures all addressed it in their works. The color line ran through the music sphere as well. Blues music was one of various musical genres with African roots existing in the United States at this time. The blues was most often performed in nightspots and other places in black districts. Working class blacks valued blues music and identified with it. The sounds of the blues may have been attractive to middle class whites and blacks, but their sensibilities were offended when the blues used rough street words or lyrics about sex, drink, or drugs. Middle class folk, regardless of color, appreciated and enjoyed other music drawing on Africa, like spirituals and jazz, so long as the accompanying lyrics were acceptable by middle class standards. Across the United States the general public in the 1920s heard musical sounds echoing Africa in vaudeville and motion picture houses and at home on radio and on record players.[4]

A Cincinnati blues singer in the 1920s was limited to venues such as local speakeasies. Meantime, a wider audience was possible for John, Jr., Herbert, Harry, and Donald Mills, who were born in Piqua, Ohio, where their father was a barber. Their songs were in tune with middle class sentiments, and their singing performances were entertaining and seductive combinations of harmony and a new jazz sound influenced by their father's barbershop quartet and black church music. Starting late in the twenties when they were still teenagers, the African American brothers toured on the midwest vaudeville and tent circuit and broadcast on Cincinnati's WLW radio station. After moving to New York City, the Mills Brothers gained nationwide and life-long fame starting in 1931–1932 when they made big-selling records, performed on national radio broadcasts, and appeared in a motion picture with show business celebrities including Kate Smith, Cab Calloway, and Bing Crosby.[5]

There were statewide dimensions of the Ohio color line and the shadow it cast on the African American experience in the years 1915–1920. Rising intolerance reached new plateaus in every Ohio region, and at the same time local people everywhere stiffened resistance to the color line. This Ohio evidence shows that the segregation of blacks and whites in the social-economic life of this northern state often rivaled that in former slave states of the South where segregation laws, enacted since 1890, required the separation of blacks and whites practically from birth to death. The imposition of segregation in Ohio was less visible and more difficult to challenge on legal grounds than in the South because blacks and whites in Ohio were separated mainly by private acts of racial discrimination and extralegal means. This undoubtedly explains why leaders of the national civil rights movement and historians gave less attention to northern states, like Ohio, than to southern ones when addressing Jim Crow society in this period.

The statewide African American experience in Ohio included, in addition to increased white hostility, black migration to cities, enlargement of black urban populations, growth of black urban community life, and establishment of new organizations confronting urban social welfare and equal rights issues. Each of these was a long-term development that took modern shape in the period 1890–1930, although each had antecedents in the more distant past. These developments took shape in their early stages from the 1890s through 1915, as historian David A. Gerber shows.[6] Evidence for the period 1915–1930 indicates that these trends accelerated significantly during World War I and reached climaxes in the twenties. For example, black migration boosted Cleveland's African American population from 8,448 in 1910 to 71,899 in 1930. Together, the culmination of these trends in the twenties was the formation of an African American "metropolis" in each of three Ohio urban centers located across the state from the Ohio River to Lake Erie. Large all-black districts within Cleveland, Cincinnati, and Columbus in 1930 possessed many of the characteristics of a city, populations in the tens of thousands and broad ranges of modern urban institutions, economic, social, and cultural in nature. Black populations in other Ohio cities, such as Akron, Dayton, Toledo, and Youngstown, moved toward "metropolis" status but did not reach it by 1930.[7]

This Ohio discussion speaks to several themes prominent in the generations-long and scholarly discourse about early twentieth century black experiences in the nation. Scholarship has produced an extensive literature on the development of all-black urban districts in the United States then and on associated historical trends including black migration to urban centers. Studies conducted from the late 1890s through the 1940s were largely produced by social scientists including sociologists, political scientists, and economists. Each focused on African Americans in an urban center and on race relations mainly in the current time.[8] Historians entered this scholarly endeavor in a major way during the 1960s and 1970s with the emergence of the ghetto school. These historians added greater temporal perspectives by emphasizing the years between 1865 and 1915 that saw developments presaging the rise of all-black urban districts in the United States during the period 1915–1930.[9] Historian Joe William Trotter's insightful essay surveying this literature is recommended to interested readers. In much of the early scholarship based on the "ghetto model," Trotter observes, African American migrants often seemed to be inert figures directed by uncontrollable historical phenomena.[10]

The experiences of black and white urban dwellers were altered but not controlled by historical forces that shaped the modern United States. This Ohio research supports the scholarly arguments holding that white immigrants and black migrants in the nation's cities exercised free will and influenced events. A generation of United States immigration historians, writing since 1960, revealed that European immigrants and their progeny created functional and enduring ethnic subcultures. Earlier immigration scholars often had viewed white ethnics largely as victims of social disorganization in slum districts. The post-1960 scholarship clarified the importance of kinship and community as means that white ethnics effectively used to deal with urban-industrial life in the United States. The reader may consult historical geographer David Ward's careful 1989 survey covering much of the literature on immigrants and the city, 1840–1925.[11] In the late 1980s and 1990s, Joe William Trotter, Kimberley L. Phillips, and other historians researching black migration to urban centers found that kinship and friendship ties enabled black migrants to actively cope with life in urban-industrial society. They changed the focus of study from black ghetto development to black working-class formation and analyzed the black urban migration as a social process connected to the migrants' social and cultural origins in the rural South. Such studies emphasizing the race, class, and gender perspective showed that ordinary black migrants were not merely problematical pawns moved about by historical forces on the chessboard of urban-industrial life but were instead active players who shaped their own lives.[12]

The framing of this Ohio analysis calls special attention to the complexities and the ambiguities of urban life intersected by the color line. It discusses both color line issues and black community themes in many cities. The variety of black experiences is evident when seen from this broad perspective. Narrower views are found in the traditional scholarly literature composed of single-city studies focusing either on race relations or on black community formation. Black urban experiences in the early twentieth century were notably different from place to place. Among the scholars recently calling attention to these nationwide variations are Kenneth L. Kusmer, Henry Louis Taylor, Jr., and Joe William Trotter, Jr.[13]

This Ohio study demonstrates that the character of race relations and the shapes of black communities varied from city to city and from region to region within a single state. It shows that in Ohio there were clear regional differences in the intensity of racial intolerance and the strength of protest. The color line was most uniform in southern Ohio and somewhat less so in central Ohio; it was more yielding in northern Ohio than elsewhere in the state. De facto racial segregation in public places, for example, was less common in cities of the northern region than those to the south. The Playhouse Settlement in Cleveland, for instance, was open to whites and blacks, while no such social institution in Cincinnati and Columbus was open to all. A black physician was appointed to a medical staff with white doctors in a major hospital system in Cleveland, while citywide hospital medical staffs in Cincinnati and Columbus were all white. Among many other instances of such regional variations, only northern Ohio's Cuyahoga County (Cleveland) elected black candidates to seats in the state legislature in the twenties.[14]

The strength of protest against the color line was greater in northern Ohio than in other regions. The struggle for equal rights was carried on in cities throughout Ohio, but it was conducted in distinctive ways in the state's southern and central regions because levels of racial hostility were comparatively higher there. Student boycotts protesting public school segregation in Dayton and Springfield, for instance, reflected the fact that all-black schools only existed in southern Ohio and central Ohio. Racial intolerance grew in northern Ohio, although it remained less intense there than elsewhere in the state. Nevertheless, protest against racial injustice in Ohio was more recurrent, insistent, and widespread in scope in the north than in regions to the south. The Cleveland *Gazette*, for instance, was decidedly the most persistent and strident voice of African American protest in Ohio. Only its editor, Harry C. Smith, advised African Americans to possess "a U.S. Army Riot Gun" as a means of defense against possible attacks by white rioters.[15] Also, the most active NAACP branches in Ohio were located in northern cities, particularly Cleveland.[16]

Why was African American protest strongest in northern Ohio in the period 1915–1930? Why was white intolerance greatest in southern Ohio then? The answers offered in this study are in accord with the findings of scholars, notably David A. Gerber, who see continuities in nineteenth and twentieth century African American history in the Midwest. Early in the nineteenth century, the cultural and social values of the southeastern states and northeastern states were transplanted in southern Ohio and northern Ohio respectively. A pro–equal rights and anti-slavery viewpoint then common in northeastern states, especially in New England, took root in northern Ohio. Meantime attitudes of racial intolerance generally found in the southern slave states became embedded in southern Ohio. These developments were influenced by the sectional origins of the white and black settlers and their regional settlement patterns in Ohio. The initial black settlers from slave states were most populous in Ohio's southern region. This Ohio regional race-relations model was shaped in the early decades after 1800. Color line customs and protest traditions established from south to north in Ohio then evolved through the nineteenth century and were perpetuated to 1930 and beyond.[17]

Ohio findings affirm a standard thesis in black urban history that was set forth by scholars in the 1960s ghetto school who held that racial intolerance was the catalytic agent in developments that shaped patterns of black urbanization. Ohio research also informs the arguments saying that unique local circumstances, aside from the color line, were factors making black community formation different from city to city. Scholars such as Kenneth L. Kusmer (1986) and Henry Louis Taylor, Jr. (1993), while accepting the standard theory about the importance of race relations, argue that city building processes and "structural forces" in an urban center also impacted the black community formation there.[18]

This Ohio analysis indicates that the differences in the shapes of black urban communities, in some respects, are attributable to local demographic, spatial, and economic factors that were peculiar in each city. Historian Joe William Trotter, Jr. asserts that the Great Migration's impact on a city varied from place to place in the United States with an urban center's evolving economic structure and its standing among the nation's range of cities.[19] Black populations grew in urban centers with booming industrial-commercial activities and stagnated or shrank in cities with less expansive or faltering economies. Census figures for major Ohio cities support this interpretation. Black urban populations in Ohio varied greatly in magnitude. The state's largest black communities were in Ohio's biggest and most prosperous cities, Cleveland, Cincinnati, and Columbus. Black population size in an Ohio urban center generally was related to that city's place in the ranking of Ohio cities listed according to total population. Central Ohio's Springfield was an outstanding example of a city not greatly impacted by the black migration in this period. Springfield, which prospered before 1900, did not keep economic pace with major Ohio cities in the twentieth century. Springfield's black population was substantial in 1910 and comprised a relatively large proportion of the city's total population. Springfield in the twenties was smaller in total population than Akron, Toledo and most of the other large Ohio cities, and after 1920 the African American population growth rate in Springfield began to fall sharply.[20]

Black urban population growth rates in the Great Lakes region, arguably, were related to the nature of a city's economy and the ethnic composition of its workforce. Historian Emma Lou Thornbrough finds that black urban populations in Indiana increased at especially fast rates in several industrial cities including Gary, South Bend, and Fort Wayne. Similarly, the African American growth rate was high in Detroit, Michigan.[21] The Ohio cities with notably rapid rates of increase were Akron, Toledo, Youngstown, and Cleveland. Remarkably, the numbers of African Americans in Cleveland grew 751 percent between 1910 and 1930. All of these Great Lakes area urban centers shared some common characteristics. They were industrial cities with comparatively large white foreign-born populations and with relatively small numbers of African Americans in 1910. They were more dependent on white foreign-born labor than other cities; consequently, labor shortages there were greater when immigration was severely curtailed during World War I and after. This exigency forced industries to end racial exclusion policies and to employ African Americans. The small black populations grew rapidly in these circumstances, evidently because industrial job opportunities for African Americans were greater in these cities than elsewhere.[22]

Unique local topography was a factor in the development of a distinctive black residential pattern in each Ohio city. Sometimes natural barriers, like rivers, influenced the shapes of boundaries encompassing black neighborhoods or districts. The Cuyahoga River formed a residential color line in Cleveland separating the nearly all-black districts on the city's East Side and the practically all-white West Side. Land formations or their absence figured in decisions about the locations of all-black settlements. This was an aspect of the Cincinnati area's distinctive black residential pattern, which included African American hilltop settlements that were like distant satellites of the black residential districts in the extraordinarily crowded river-basin West End where most African Americans resided. Cincinnati possessed much less flat land than its urban peers in the state because it was the only major Ohio city located along the Ohio River Valley. Cincinnati residents occupied the low land of the river basin and the surrounding hilltops that were often naturally separated by small valleys or ravines. While the outlying hilly areas were mainly white, there were a few separate black settlements on hilltops, for example, at West College Hill and in areas north of Lockland. Local and outside realtors and investors selected these isolated sites and initiated low-cost housing developments for African Americans.[23]

Differences within black society added to the complexity of African American urban life in each city early in the twentieth century. Recent scholarship provides interpretations that point to the existence of this diversity across the United States and call attention to distinctions of class, gender, and culture in black urban life. This study shows that these distinctions were in play within the African American society of each large Ohio city.

The social-economic stratification of African American society, which had existed for generations, was reshaped in urban industrial centers after 1915. Historians interested in this development produced a body of literature, which grew significantly after 1990, emphasizing the importance of black working class formation and black migration to industrial centers in such disparate locations as California, Illinois, Ohio, Pennsylvania, Virginia, and West Virginia.[24] The valuable Ohio analysis is Kimberley L. Phillips, *Alabama North: African-American Migrants, Community and Working Class Activism in Cleveland, 1915–1945* (1999). A new class of black industrial workers took shape in Ohio cities when the numbers of African Americans employed in industrial occupations rose sharply. This came during and after World War I with the modification of racially biased employment practices in local factories, mills, plants, and railroad facilities. The growth of this class was greatest in Ohio industrial centers, particularly Cleveland, that were most adversely affected when the wartime curtailment of immigration eliminated the supply of white foreign-born laborers. The great majority of adult African Americans in Ohio cities were employed in low-paying industrial jobs and domestic work. The black business and professional classes were relatively small, but in Ohio cities during this period there were extraordinary rates of increase in the numbers of black ministers, teachers, lawyers, physicians, dentists, and entrepreneurs of many kinds.[25]

In an important regional analysis of color and class in this period, historian Joe William Trotter, Jr. asserts that the black industrial workers and the small black elite class in southern West Virginia were linked together by social-economic circumstances; he explains that reciprocity was the key element in this relationship. Black professionals depended on black industrial working class clients as the sources of their income in a color line society. In turn, the black industrial working class usually relied on black professionals to supply its leadership in matters of protest, politics, and institutional life.[26] This mutual reliance became fully characteristic of the relationship between these two black population groups in Ohio cities in the period 1915–1930, when the clientele of black professionals became almost wholly African American. Black entrepreneurs and professionals in Ohio often served white patrons or clients in the generation prior to World War I. This became increasing rare as the hardening of the Ohio color line accelerated after 1915. During this period in urban industrial Ohio, black lawyers, physicians, social workers, ministers, and newspaper proprietors most often were at the head of protest activities and in the leadership of social and political organizations in African American neighborhoods. These activities were in the interests of the lower and upper levels of black society. The efforts of the black elite to uplift black working people were based on more than altruism. Through service in these leading positions black professionals acquired additional prestige, status, and sometimes income as well, when the leadership involved paying jobs in private institutions and in government service. Meanwhile in Ohio, many African American workers in industrial and domestic occupations patronized black business places and black professionals using income earned from companies and other sources located in the larger economy beyond black neighborhoods.[27]

Often people at the bottom and at the top of African American urban society experienced starkly different lifestyles in Ohio and elsewhere, notwithstanding the reciprocal relationship between the two black populations. Historian Georgina Hickey's recent study (2003) illuminates the complexities of this relationship by examining the functions and inequities of class in black Atlanta.[28] In Ohio cities, black working people and the black elite often lived in separate neighborhoods that were sharply different in character. In Cincinnati, for instance, George Street was a black working class neighborhood situated in the city's tenderloin where bawdy houses and vice activities were permitted by authorities at the start of the wartime black migration. George Street was located in the densely populated black working class West End district, which contained old industrial, commercial, and residential buildings, usually crowded tenement houses or other multi-family dwellings. Walnut Hills, in contrast, was the address of many in Cincinnati's black business and professional classes. Located just outside the river basin's industrial districts, Walnut Hills was a residential area with spacious single-family dwellings and a mix of black neighborhoods and white ones.[29]

African American social and cultural life in Ohio cities, likewise, varied greatly from class to class. African Americans in business and the professions often were members of black congregations that owned fine traditional church edifices in residential neighborhoods. Ohio's black elite formed elaborate organized structures of formal social life including fraternal lodges and social clubs, many owning their clubhouses or lodge halls. In contrast, many black working people attended church services in rented storefront quarters in downtown areas. Socially approved leisure activities at the bottom of black society in urban Ohio often were informal in nature, for instance, involving people with close kinship and friendship ties meeting in their homes, in nearby streets, or in neighborhood community centers.[30]

Complexities in African American society and in life along the color line involved important distinctions of gender, as well as class differences. Studies on black urban history generally agree that gender made a great difference in the amount of social-economic opportunity available in Midwest cities.[31] In accord with that scholarship, this research finds that in Ohio cities employment opportunities were less limited for black men than for black women, who encountered both gender limits and color barriers in the job market. Consequently, only the least desirable and lowest paying jobs were open to black working women. Black women in the period 1915–1930 were excluded from men's occupations, such as industrial jobs, and hired for traditional women's work, excepting the World War I years. The severe wartime labor shortages forced Ohio industry to temporarily lower color and gender barriers and employ black women for work in factories, plants, and railroad yards. Most of these wartime occupational gains were lost in the twenties, when men were available for industrial work. As in prewar times, in the postwar decade large proportions of black women employed in Ohio cities were in domestic work. Meantime, white employers following the color line hired only white women for clerical and retail store positions.[32]

Employment and life experiences were notably different for black women in the working and the professional classes. Some black women in each large Ohio city were employed in professions approved for women in this period, including teaching, social work, and nursing. This employment usually was with institutions or facilities that catered to African Americans. Professional opportunities for African Americans were greater in the cities with larger numbers of racially separate institutions. Professional employment opportunities for black women, in education for example, were affected by the color line and its regional variations from southern Ohio to northern Ohio. Black public school educators in Cincinnati taught only in all-back schools. No all-black public schools existed in Cleveland, and some African American teachers there were assigned to schools with white and black students. Consequently, a significantly larger number of black female public school teachers were employed in Cincinnati than in Cleveland. An African American female was principal of an all-black Cincinnati public school. None of the public school principals in Cleveland was black, but an African American woman was elected to the Cleveland school board in the twenties. The leadership and service roles of black female social workers were important to African American institutional life in urban Ohio. But, gender lines also were evident in this area of institutional and civic leadership. Generally, black women were the supervisors and staff members of social work and care institutions in African American neighborhoods. Black male professionals and entrepreneurs usually served as officers and board members of major black community organizations, particularly the NAACP branches and Urban League affiliates.[33]

Black women in Ohio participated in African American civic affairs and provided community leadership in distinctive ways. African American women with ties to the black elite developed an infrastructure of sororities, church groups, social clubs, and charity associations. Many were affiliated with the African American Ohio Federation of Women's Clubs. Charity work in the black community and promotion of racial uplift were common dimensions of black women's organizations, which otherwise varied much in aims and activities. Women at the bottom and the top of black society were active in organized religion, making up large proportions of black church congregations. Black women managed and staffed black branches of the Young Women's Christian Association in Ohio. The reader may note that historian Evelyn Brooks Higginbotham (1993), in a groundbreaking book, focuses on the important leadership roles of African American women in black Baptist congregations during the period 1880–1920. Local and state women's auxiliaries and the Woman's Convention were formed within the framework of what was then the largest black denomination in the United States, the National Baptist Convention, U.S.A. These organizations became platforms to voice the distinctive views of black women. Early in the twentieth century, the Woman's Convention sponsored many kinds of local community betterment projects and entered the political arena in support of women's suffrage.[34] Specialized Ohio studies on this and other gender themes are needed.

The organized voices of African American women in Ohio were heard in partisan politics and in protests during the period 1915–1930. Clevelander Lethia Fleming, for instance, was a veteran women's suffrage activist and a member of the national Republican party's black women's advisory board in 1920. Wilberforce University instructor Hallie Q. Brown led Republican Calvin Coolidge's presidential election campaign among black women in 1924. She was a prominent official in the National Federation of Negro Women's Clubs early in the twenties. Undoubtedly, most black women as well as black men voted Republican in this period; however, some black female and black male Republicans objected to that party's color line practices. The Colored Women's Republican Club in Columbus became the Colored Women's Independent Political League in 1919. The affiliation change was a protest against the Republican Party's failure to back the passage of an equal rights bill in the Ohio legislature. This was an early expression of black independence from the Republican party in Ohio, which became more common in the twenties than in the teens.[35]

Gender lines clearly were evident in African American political and protest activities. African Americans chosen for public offices rarely were females. NAACP branch officers and trustee board members mostly were black men, while black women only occasionally held such posts. Cleveland Juvenile Court probation officer L. Pearl Mitchell, for instance, was a Cleveland NAACP executive committee member in 1928.[36] Black men were most prominent in the usual protest venues, courtrooms, legislative halls, and executive offices. Notably, black women took featured roles in street demonstrations and student boycotts in Ohio, which were less traditional protest forms and uncommon in this period. For example, scores of black women in Springfield, Ohio, made up a pool of demonstrators who walked picket lines for months in 1922 to back a student boycott protesting racial segregation in the local public school system.[37]

African American life in urban Ohio was made still more complex by the fact that black class and black gender groupings each were divided into newcomers and old residents. Most black migrants possessed a southernness mirroring the culture of the South. In recent years, scholarship on black migration has revealed the continuity of southern culture in African American centers of the North. Darlene Clark Hine asserts that southern black women living in the Midwest perpetuated a broad range of the South's cultural values, for example, with respect to food preparation, menus, home remedies, religious practices, family ties, and speech patterns.[38] Did such cultural distinctions arise from the social isolation of southern newcomers in the North's African American societies? Kenneth L. Kusmer argues that there is evidence showing that black natives of the North and South were much "integrated" in African American institutions, excepting some churches.[39]

Perhaps excepting Columbus, evidence in Ohio mostly supports Kusmer's assertion. According to J. S. Himes, southern newcomers in the black wartime migration "were anathema to the old residents" in Columbus. "This resentment created a rift in the Negro community which manifested itself in every phase of Negro life, and remains even today a source of tension in some quarters," Himes wrote in 1941 when he was director of research for the Columbus Urban League. Himes was explicit, pointing to "the often chilly welcome" that newcomers received in some of Columbus' black churches, social clubs, lodges, and "many other groups."[40] Northerners and southerners commonly interacted in Cleveland's African American institutions. Contemporary black sociologist Kelly Miller, nevertheless, made critical remarks about the attitudes and reactions of old black residents of Cleveland, whom he characterized as unwelcoming to black migrants from the South. Shortly after visiting Cleveland, Miller composed a report on "Negro Migration" that several black weeklies published in July 1923. Miller said that as the black migration from the South accelerated, the old black Clevelander stood "bewildered as he felt the foundations of his former privileges shaking beneath him." Local black weekly editor Harry C. Smith wrote that Miller's remarks about Cleveland were in error and that old black residents of the city did not "'at first oppose the in rushing tide,'" as Miller claimed. Smith, one of city's longtime black citizens, praised the old black Clevelanders, asserting that they "were the ones who made possible the favorable conditions of *all kinds* sought by those of color who constituted the inrush to Cleveland."[41]

Culture consciousness undoubtedly existed among African Americans in Ohio during this period. Frequently it was easy to recognize the identity of black newcomers or black southerners in urban Ohio. There was great awareness and much public discussion among African Americans of the presence in Ohio of black migrants from the South. As the forgoing comments illustrate, African American natives of Ohio were at least somewhat ambivalent about black migrants coming to the state from the South. Many old black residents in every Ohio city manifested humane concern and community spirit by coming to the assistance of black migrants making the adjustment to a different life experience in Ohio. Black newcomers were welcome often, if not always, in Ohio's existing African American institutions. At the same time there was a measure of concern that the black migration was bringing adjustment pains and different cultural values that might adversely affect established black residents of Ohio. "A Colored Citizen of Elyria," Ohio, provided a telling illustration of this ambivalence. In a 1920 letter to the Cleveland *Gazette*'s editor, he reported that local church records showed that "about 500 of our people" settled in Elyria, located just west of Cleveland, after "coming from the South." He wrote: "Some of them purchased homes but many had to be taken into the homes of our good citizens who made them welcome," adding that all were welcome in this small city's two African American churches, one Baptist and the other Methodist Episcopal. But he indicated that there were concerns, stating: "Some of the new arrivals are not what they should be and are making it harder for our good people here."[42] This letter from Elyria showed a mix of caring and anxiety about black migrants from the South that was found in African American urban communities across Ohio.

This dual response to black migrants was one of the many ambiguities arising from the Ohio color line. Another was the mixed answer to the question of how best to deal with color line problems and to promote racial uplift. Black activists who engaged in public protest saw the violation of citizenship rights as the greatest concern. Others focused on urban social problems that were complicated by the color line and used racially separate social work institutions to address these ills. Advocates of black social work sometimes were criticized for furthering racial segregation and racial proscription preferred by many whites. Black citizenship rights proponents sometimes were perceived as insensitive when they charged that the racially separate institutions caring for needy blacks were a threat to the equal rights cause.

Black activists who were principally concerned with social work had different views and strategies than those largely interested in civil rights issues; but, usually in these years, members of neither activist group took a doctrinaire or absolutist position in favor of racial integration or racial separation. In every Ohio region, leading African Americans generally approved racial separation in some circumstances. Even the black Ohioans who were most inclined to protest color line grievances did not object to separate activities and organizations conducted by African Americans, if they were privately financed and voluntary. Harry C.

Smith, a founder of the Cleveland NAACP, surely was the loudest voice of protest in Ohio. The pages of his weekly, *The Gazette*, blasted racially exclusive practices consistently and continuously for decades. Yet Smith approved black private organizations, institutions, and enterprises, like his own African American newspaper business. For example, early in his political career Smith founded Cleveland's Afro American Republican Club.[43] Likewise, black weekly editor Wendell P. Dabney, who was an early leader of the Cincinnati NAACP, commonly published biting criticism of blacks who accommodated to racial exclusion imposed by whites. Nevertheless, he was a member of a black men's club and a stockholder in black corporations. Also, Dabney was on the board of directors of Cincinnati's Home for Colored Girls and Negro Civic Welfare Association.[44] The NAACP in Ohio was a generally effective agent of protest against various kinds of racial discrimination, but it did not uniformly oppose racial separation. Many members of Ohio NAACP branches even were disinclined to oppose publicly supported schools and hospitals for blacks because that would imply criticism of the black professionals who staffed them. In consequence, for example, the local NAACP branches played marginal roles in the anti-segregation campaigns at Springfield's Fulton School and Mansfield's Bowman Street School in the twenties.[45]

Racial exclusion and discrimination, however, were objectionable to the broad spectrum of the state's leading African Americans, again regardless of region, during 1915–1930. The exclusion of African Americans from public places was a grievance to all because it denied blacks access to the benefits obtainable in public venues and generally violated state law, as well as denying individual blacks the freedom of choice available to whites. Even the black Ohioans who were most identified with racially separate organizations and institutions occasionally protested color line grievances. The Marcus Garvey movement emphatically advocated a separatist strategy for advancing African American interests, but its organizations in Ohio sometimes protested racially exclusive practices. Cleveland's Universal Negro Improvement Association was represented on a committee of local black civic leaders investigating racial discrimination at Cleveland City Hospital in 1928.[46] Also in Cleveland, Phillis Wheatley Association Executive Secretary Jane E. Hunter was best known for her management of a separate shelter for black single women and not for racial protest. But in 1929 Jane E. Hunter and other prominent African Americans appeared before the Cleveland City Council to oppose a hospital bonds issue because the municipal hospital excluded black interns and nurse trainees.[47] National Urban League affiliates in Ohio principally were devoted to improving the welfare of needy African Americans, but at times their leaders expressed concern about color line issues. Columbus Urban League Executive Secretary Nimrod B. Allen asked an Ohio State University sociology professor to give testimony opposing a bill against racial inter-marriage that was being considered by the state legislature in 1925.[48] Similarly, the existence of racial bias in Cincinnati concerned African American social worker James H. Robinson, who became the executive secretary of Cincinnati's Negro Civic Welfare Association. Robinson emphasized that prejudice and racial discrimination were fundamental to the social problems affecting blacks when he reported the findings of his survey of Cincinnati's black community to the city's Council of Social Agencies in 1919.[49]

The activities of other black Ohioans also showed that concerns about social problems and opposition to civil rights violations were not mutually exclusive. Dr. Charles H. Garvin, a black physician in Cleveland, was undaunted in claiming his citizenship rights in the larg-er society while supporting separate black organizations promoting the social and economic advancement of African Americans. Garvin, a staff urologist at Lakeside Hospital, once was the only African American on the medical staff of Cleveland's private hospital system. In 1925 he pur-chased a home in an all-white residential area of Cleveland. The Garvin family stayed in it despite severe harassment, including a bombing. At the same time, Garvin joined other black doctors to form the Cleveland Medical Reading Club. He advocated the establishment of a private black hospital in Cleveland. In his lifetime, Garvin was active in the Cleveland affiliates of both the Urban League and the NAACP.[50] In Cincinnati, Lizzie Branch and her husband possessed the means to reside in an affluent largely black suburb, Walnut Hills. Much of her time was spent in church and women's club work. She, like Garvin, supported racial organizations with different immediate aims and opposing strate-gies. But all were meant to ameliorate the conditions of African Americans in the long run. In 1926, according to her biography, Lizzie Branch was "prominent in the Y.W.C.A., N.A.A.C.P., U.N.I.A., and every movement for racial uplift."[51]

Ideally, disparate African Americans would unite to counter instances of racial discrimination. Such unity was not always realized, but civil rights issues in Ohio often did unify African Americans repre-senting different approaches to color line problems. Perhaps the most eloquent expression of this ideal in Ohio at the time was made in the words of George A. Myers, Cleveland's most influential black elder. On occasions, Myers made alliances with an old political foe when civil rights issues were at stake. Black weekly editor Harry C. Smith and

Myers were affiliated with different factions of the Republican party in Ohio. In many respects, the two men were opposites. Myers was a friend of Booker T. Washington prior to the war, and his style in some ways reflected that of the famous Tuskeegean. Congeniality was Myers' hallmark, and it brought him warm acquaintanceships with important figures in government and business who visited his Hollenden Hotel shop. When Myers used his influence in the interest of African Americans, he did so out of public view. His letters to powerful acquaintances stated protests in a genteel and courteous rhetoric. In contrast, Harry C. Smith was a founder of the Cleveland NAACP. He favored public protest, especially in his Cleveland *Gazette*. The editor's style often was abrasive, and his racial protest rhetoric was deliberately bombastic. Their differences notwithstanding, they sometimes made common cause, for example, in the campaign against Cleveland's municipal hospital color lines during the twenties. Smith fired editorial broadsides against municipal officials responsible for Cleveland City Hospital's racial policies. In private correspondence, Myers alerted Cleveland City Manager William R. Hopkins that the municipal hospital issue was causing his administration to lose the black vote. Perceiving this as a political threat, Hopkins was offended and accused Myers of having "gone over to Harry Smith bag and baggage." In reply Myers explained that his views and actions concerning civil rights had not changed. Myers wrote: "For Mr. Smith I hold no brief, he is as you know and others, perfectly competent to take care of himself. But for your enlightenment I wish to say that we have never trained together politically. . . . The same conditions exist today. But when any Negro was or is unjustly discriminated against or deprived of his manhood rights, we have always been, as all Negroes should be, as one in their defense."[52] Arguably, Myers' sentiment was widespread among black Ohioans at the end of the twenties.

Documents for the period 1915–1930 reveal the many complex dimensions of black urban life in the shadows of Ohio's color barriers. No theme stands out more clearly than the role of local people in the struggle against the Ohio color line. Out-of-state personalities rarely participated in equal rights and social work activities in Ohio. Affiliates of national associations were present in the state, but they owed their vitality to local African American leadership. Again and again, the record shows that the struggles in Ohio were conducted by African American local residents in cities from Cleveland to Columbus to Cincinnati and from Toledo to Springfield to Dayton. White intolerance had mounted, and the aims of the struggle were unrealized when this period ended. The evidence, however, proves that black Ohioans were more organized and effective in confronting the realities of the Ohio color line in 1930 than in 1915. Equal rights and social work organizations achieved maturity in Ohio cities in these years. This was important to the struggle in the future because these organizations consequently were prepared to be the principal vehicles of the civil rights movement in Ohio at crucial times after mid-century.

APPENDIX

Tables

Table A1

Number and Percentage of Blacks and Whites in Ohio by State
Population and Urban Population, 1910–1930.

	Number			Percent of Total Population		
	1910	1920	1930	1910	1920	1930
The State						
Total	4,767,121	5,759,394	6,646,697	100.0%	100.0%	100.0%
Black	111,452	186,187	309,304	2.3%	3.2%	4.7%
White	4,654,897	5,571,893	6,331,136	97.6%	96.7%	95.3%
Urban						
Total	2,665,143	3,677,136	4,507,371	100.0%	100.0%	100.0%
Black	82,282	155,975	271,972	3.1%	4.2%	6.0%
White	2,582,143	3,519,910	4,229,930	96.9%	95.7%	93.8%

Source: *Census 1930: Population* 3, p. 457.

Table A2

Black Population in Ohio Cities, 1910–1930.

City	1910	1920	1930
Akron	657	5,580	11,080
Cincinnati	19,639	30,079	47,818
Cleveland	8,448	34,451	71,899
Columbus	12,739	22,181	32,774
Dayton	4,842	9,025	17,077
Springfield	4,933	7,029	8,249
Toledo	1,877	5,691	13,260
Youngstown	1,936	6,662	14,522

Source: *Census 1910: Population* 3, p. 418; *Census 1920: Population* 3, pp. 797–809; *Census 1930: Population* 3, pp. 535–36.

232

Table A3

Number and Percentage Increase of Black Professionals, by Ohio City, Occupation, and Year.

	Clergy*			Percentage Increase		Lawyers			Percentage Increase	
	Number					Number				
	1910	1920	1930	1910–1920	1920–1930	1910	1920	1930	1910–1920	1920–1930
Cincinnati		91	127		39.6%	4	8	6	100.0%	00.0%
Cleveland		73	121		65.8%	11	10	38	00.0%	280.0%
Columbus		59	101		71.2%	7	14	16	100.0%	14.3%
Dayton		27	53		96.3%		4	5		25.0%
Toledo		20	39		95.0%	1	1	6	00.0%	500.0%

	Physicians			Percentage Increase		Teachers			Percentage Increase	
	Number					Number				
	1910	1920	1930	1910–1920	1920–1930	1910	1920	1930	1910–1920	1920–1930
Cincinnati	14	16	17	14.3%	6.3%	35	83	163	137.1%	96.4%
Cleveland	8	27	41	237.5%	51.9%	27	71	101	163.0%	42.3%
Columbus	13	19	27	46.2%	42.1%	20	27	58	35.0%	114.8%
Dayton	10	11	11	10.0%	00.0%	2	14	24	600.0%	71.4%
Toledo	4	4	7	00.0%	75.0%	1	10	10	900.0%	00.0%

Source: *Census 1910: Occupation Statistics* 4, pp. 548, 459, 550, 552, 606; *Census 1920: Occupations* 4, pp. 1082, 1086, 1089, 1094, 1244; *Census 1930: Occupations* 4, pp. 1283–96.
*Not given in *Census 1910*.

Table A4

Court Suits Alleging Ohio Public Accommodations Law Violations, 1914–1919.

	Restaurant Suits			Theatre Suits		
	Cases	Won	Lost	Cases	Won	Lost
Akron	1	1	0	1	0	1
Columbus	1	1	0			
Cleveland	5	3	2	1	1	0
Fostoria	1	1	0			
Springfield	1	1	0	1	0	1
Total	9	7	2	3	1	2

Source: Compiled by the author from reports in *Gazette* and *Crisis* about public accommodations suits. *Gazette* Editor Harry C. Smith, who had informants across the state, was ever alert to such suits and probably reported all that came to his attention. See *Gazette*, Jan. 31, 1914; March 18, 1914; July 24, 1915; Aug. 14, 1915; Feb. 17, 1917; March 3, 1917; April 28, 1917; May 12, 1917; Dec. 15, 1917; July 27, 1918; Nov. 2, 1918; May 3, 1919; June 14, 1919; Oct. 25, 1919; and *Crisis* 8 (July 1914), p. 115; 14 (July 1917), p. 145; 15 (Jan. 1918), p. 144.

Notes

Notes to Introduction

1. George C. Wright, *Racial Violence in Kentucky, 1865–1940: Lynchings, Mob Rule, and "Legal Lynchings"* (Baton Rouge: Louisiana State University Press, 1990); Joe William Trotter, Jr., *Coal, Class, and Color: Blacks in Southern West Virginia, 1915–1932* (Urbana: University of Illinois Press, 1990); John Dittmer, *Local People: The Struggle for Civil Rights in Mississippi* (Urbana: University of Illinois Press, 1994); Adam Fairclough, *Race & Democracy: The Civil Rights Struggle in Louisiana, 1915–1972* (Athens: University of Georgia Press, 1995); Fon L. Gordon, *Caste & Class: The Black Experience in Arkansas, 1880–1920* (Athens: University of Georgia Press, 1995); Joe William Trotter, Jr. and Eric Ledell Smith, eds. *African Americans in Pennsylvania: Shifting Historical Perspectives* (University Park: The Pennsylvania State University Press, 1997); Paul A. Ortiz, "'Like water covered the sea': The African American Freedom Struggle in Florida, 1877–1920" (Ph.D. Diss., Duke University, 2000); Emma Lou Thornbrough, *Indiana Blacks in the Twentieth Century*, ed. by Lana Ruegamer (Bloomington: Indiana University Press, 2000); Larissa M. Smith, "Where the South Begins: Black Politics and Civil Rights Activism in Virginia, 1930–1951," (Ph.D. Diss., Emory University, 2001); Stephen G. N. Tuck, *Beyond Atlanta: The Struggle for Racial Equality in Georgia, 1940–1980* (Athens: University of Georgia Press, 2001); Bobby J. Donaldson, "New Negroes in a New South: Race, Power, and Ideology in Georgia, 1890–1925" (Ph.D. Diss., Emory University, 2002).

2. David A. Gerber, *Black Ohio and the Color Line 1860–1915* (Urbana: University of Illinois Press, 1976).

3. Charles F. Kellogg, *NAACP: A History of the National Association for the Advancement of Colored People* (Baltimore: Johns Hopkins Press, 1967); Dittmer, *Local People*.

4. Examples are: W. E. B. Du Bois, *The Philadelphia Negro: A Social Study* (1899, reprint, New York: Schocken Books, 1967); Chicago Commission on Race Relations, *The Negro in Chicago: A Study of Race Relations and a Race Riot*, written by Charles S. Johnson (Chicago: University of Chicago Press, 1922); E. Franklin Frazier, *The Negro Family in Chicago* (Chicago: University of Chicago Press, 1932); and St. Clair Drake and Horace R. Cayton, *Black Metropolis: A*

Study of Negro Life in a Northern City (reprint, New York: Harcourt Brace, and World, 1970; original, New York: Harcourt Brace and Company, 1945).

5. Gilbert Osofsky, *Harlem, The Making of a Ghetto: Negro New York, 1890–1930* (New York: Harper & Row, 1966); Allan H. Spear, *Black Chicago: The Making of a Negro Ghetto* (Chicago: University of Chicago Press, 1967); David M. Katzman, *Before the Ghetto: Black Detroit in the Nineteenth Century* (Urbana: University of Illinois Press, 1973); and Kenneth L. Kusmer, *A Ghetto Takes Shape: Black Cleveland, 1870–1930* (Urbana: University of Illinois Press, 1976).

6. Peter Gottlieb, *Making Their Own Way: Southern Blacks' Migration to Pittsburgh, 1916–30* (Urbana: University of Illinois Press, 1987); James R. Grossman, *Land of Hope: Chicago, Black Southerners, and the Great Migration* (Chicago: University of Chicago Press, 1989); Trotter Jr., *Coal, Class, and Color* (1990); Earl Lewis, *In Their Own Interests: Race, Class, and Power in Twentieth Century Norfolk* (Berkeley: University of California Press, 1991); Kimberly L. Phillips, *Alabama North: African-American Migrants, Community and Working Class Activism in Cleveland, 1915–1945* (Urbana: University of Illinois Press, 1999); Shirley Anne Wilson Moore, *To Place Our Deeds: The African American Community in Richmond, California, 1910–1963* (Berkeley: University of California Press, 2000); Paul L. Robinson, "Class and Place with the Los Angeles African American Community, 1940–1990" (Ph.D. Diss., University of Southern California, 2001).

7. Albert S. Broussard, *Black San Francisco: The Struggle for Racial Equality in the West, 1900–1954* (Lawrence: University of Kansas Press, 1993); Daniel Crowe, *Prophets of Rage: The Black Freedom Struggle in San Francisco, 1945–1969* (New York: Garland, 2000); Marvin Dunn, *Black Miami in the Twentieth Century* (Gainesville: University Press of Florida, 1997); Gretchen C. Eick, *Dissent in Wichita: The Civil Rights Movement in the Midwest, 1954–72* (Urbana: University of Illinois Press, 2001); Mark R. Schneider, *Boston Confronts Jim Crow, 1890–1920* (Boston: Northeastern University Press, 1997); Randal M. Jelks, "Race, Respectability, and the Struggle for Civil Rights: A Study of the African American Community of Grand Rapids, Michigan, 1870–1954" (Ph.D. Diss., Michigan State University, 2001); Bernadette Pruitt, "For the Advancement of the Race: African-American Migration and Community Building in Houston, 1914–1945" (Ph.D. Diss., University of Houston, 2001); Mary S. Sacks, "'We cry among the skyscrapers': Black People in New York City, 1880–1915" (Ph.D. Diss., University of California, Berkeley, 1999); Josh A. Sides, "Working Away: African American Migration and Community in Los Angeles from the Great Depression to 1954," (Ph.D. Diss., University of California, Los Angeles, 1999); Nikki M. Taylor, "'Frontiers of Freedom': The African American Experience in Cincinnati, 1802–1862" (Ph.D. Diss., Duke University, 2001).

8. Kenneth L. Kusmer, "The Black Urban Experience in American History," in *The State of Afro-American History, Past, Present, and Future*, ed. Darlene Clark Hine (Baton Rouge: Louisiana State University Press, 1986), 111; Henry Louis Taylor, Jr., "City Building, Public Policy, the Rise of the Industrial City, and Black Ghetto-Slum Formation in Cincinnati, 1850–1940," in *Race and the City: Work, Community, and Protest in Cincinnati, 1820–1970*, ed. Henry Louis Taylor, Jr. (Urbana: University of Illinois Press, 1993), 157, 179.

9. Richard B. Sherman, *The Republican Party and Black America: From McKinley to Hoover, 1896–1933* (Charlottesville: University of Virginia Press, 1973). The outstanding study of black voter realignment covers the period 1928–1940: Nancy J. Weiss, *Farewell to the Party of Lincoln: Black Politics in the Age of FDR* (Princeton: Princeton University Press, 1983).

Notes to Chapter 1

1. United States Department of Commerce, Bureau of the Census, *Fourteenth Census of the United States Taken in the Year 1920: Population, 1920, Composition and Characteristics of the Population by States* 3 (Washington, D.C.: Government Printing Office, 1922), 768.
2. James H. Robinson, "The Negro Migration," *Social Service News: "A Magazine of Human Helpfulness"* 1, no. 7 (July 1917): 100.
3. *Cleveland Plain Dealer*, Oct. 19, 1916, in *The Gazette* (Cleveland), Oct. 28, 1916.
4. *Cleveland Plain Dealer*, Aug. 4, 1917, 5.
5. *Gazette*, June 10, 1916.
6. *The Crisis* 14 (June, 1917): 86.
7. *Gazette*, May 12, 1917.
8. Lee Williams, "Newcomers to the City: A Study of Black Population Growth in Toledo, Ohio, 1910–1930," *Ohio History* 89 (Winter 1980): 10–11; Toledo *Blade*, May 23, 1917.
9. *Gazette*, Aug. 31, 1918.
10. Ibid., April 27, 1918.
11. Ibid., March 15, 1919.
12. Ibid.
13. *Gazette*, June 10, 1916; *Crisis* 12 (July 1916): 143; John Hope Franklin and Alfred A. Moss, Jr., *From Slavery to Freedom: A History of African Americans* (New York: McGraw Hill, 2000), 376.
14. *Crisis* 16 (Sept. 1918): 238.
15. Ibid. 12 (July 1916): 116.
16. *Gazette*, April 29, 1916; *Crisis* 12 (June 1916): 63.
17. Williams, "Newcomers to the City," 11.
18. William Franklin Moore, "Status of the Negro in Cleveland" (Ph.D. Diss., The Ohio State University, 1953), 38.
19. Richard Clyde Minor, "The Negro in Columbus, Ohio" (Ph.D. Diss., The Ohio State University, 1936), 42.
20. Wendell P. Dabney, *Cincinnati's Colored Citizens: Historical, Sociological and Biographical* (Cincinnati: The Dabney Publishing Company, 1926), 197.
21. Julian Krawcheck, "The Negro in Cleveland, A History, 1809–1963," reprint from *Cleveland Press*, May 27–31 and June 1, 1963, PA Box 297, 1, Ohio Historical Society Archives/Library, Columbus.
22. Moore, "Status of the Negro in Cleveland," 38.
23. *Crisis* 12 (July 1916): 142.
24. *Gazette*, Nov. 24, 1917.
25. Williams, "Newcomers to the City," 10–11; Toledo *Blade*, June 1, 1917.

26. Letter of Lamar T. Beman to Geo. Welts Parker, May 9, 1917, in *Gazette*, May 26, 1917.

27. Ibid., Aug. 10, 1918.

28. George E. Haynes, "The Opportunity of Negro Labor," *Crisis* 18 (Sept. 1919): 237.

29. *Gazette*, April 27, 1918, Jan. 25, 1919, March 15, 29, 1919.

30. Peter Gottlieb, "Rethinking the Great Migration: A Perspective from Pittsburgh," *The Great Migration in Historical Perspective: New Dimensions of Race, Class, and Gender*, ed. Joe William Trotter, Jr. (Bloomington: Indiana University Press, 1991), 74.

31. Emmett J. Scott, *Negro Migration during the War* (New York: Oxford University Press, 1920), 6–7.

32. Gottlieb, *Making Their Own Way*; Grossman, *Land of Hope: Chicago*; Trotter Jr., *Coal, Class, and Color*; Earl Lewis, *In Their Own Interests*; Phillips, *Alabama North*.

33. United States Department of Commerce, Bureau of the Census, *Thirteenth Census of the United States Taken in the Year 1910: Population, 1910, Reports by States, With Statistics for Counties, Cities and Other Civil Divisions, Nebraska-Wyoming, Alaska, Hawaii, and Porto Rico*, 3 (Washington, D.C.: Government Printing Office, 1913), 418; *Census 1920: Population*, 3: 797–809; United States Department of Commerce, Bureau of the Census, *Negroes in the United States 1920–1932* (Washington, D.C.: Government Printing Office, 1935), 9, 12,15, 32, 62–63.

34. Bureau of the Census, *Census 1910: Population* 3: 418; *Census 1920: Population* 3: 797–809; *Negroes in the United States 1920–1932*, 9, 12, 15, 32, 62–63.

35. Gerber, *Black Ohio*, 280.

36. Letter to Mary E. Jackson, who made an industrial survey of Negro women for the National Board of the Young Women's Christian Association, in Mary E. Jackson, "The Colored Woman in Industry," *Crisis* 17 (Nov. 1918): 12.

37. Ibid., 14 (July 1917): 143.

38. See Cleveland Negro Welfare Association's annual report for 1918, *Gazette*, Feb. 1, 1919.

39. Williams, "Newcomers to the City," 7.

40. Scott, *Negro Migration during the War*, 126.

41. *Gazette*, May 5, 1917.

42. Ibid., May 12, 1917.

43. Ibid., Aug. 18, 1917.

44. Scott, *Negro Migration during the War*, 126; *Cleveland News*, Aug. 11, 1917.

45. George E. Haynes, "Negroes Move North," *Survey*, 42 (Jan. 4, 1919): 459.

46. Williams, "Newcomers to the City," 12; Toledo *Blade*, May 23, 1917, July 17, 1917.

47. Williams, "Newcomers to the City," 11; *Crisis* 12 (June 1916): 63; Krawcheck, "The Negro in Cleveland."

48. Scott, *Negro Migration during the War*, 126; Williams, "Newcomers to the City," 17.

49. Robert B. Fairbanks, *Making Better Citizens: Housing Reform and the Community Development Strategy in Cincinnati, 1890–1960* (Urbana: University of Illinois Press, 1988), 59–60.

50. *Cleveland Plain Dealer*, Aug. 4, 1917, and *Cleveland News*, Aug. 11, 1917, noted in Scott, *Negro Migration during the War*, 126.

51. Williams, "Newcomers to the City," 15–17.

52. *The Columbus Evening Dispatch*, Aug. 1, 1917, 9.

53. See a Cincinnati example, in *Cincinnati: A Guide to the Queen City and Its Neighbors*, compiled by the Workers of the Writers' Program of the Work Projects Administration in the State of Ohio (Cincinnati: The Wiesen-Hart Press, 1943), 225.

54. Williams, "Newcomers to the City," 16–17; *Cleveland Plain Dealer*, Aug. 13, 1918, 7; *Gazette*, Aug. 17, 1918.

55. Ibid., June 2, 1917.

56. *Cleveland Plain Dealer*, Aug. 13, 1918, 7; *Gazette*, Aug. 17, 1918.

57. Kusmer, *A Ghetto Takes Shape*, 166–67.

58. Williams, "Newcomers to the City," 15–16.

59. Maldwyn A. Jones, *American Immigration* (Chicago: University of Chicago Press, 1974), 132–33.

60. See chapters on "The New Immigrants" and "Ethnic Mobility" in Leonard Dinnerstein and David M. Reiners, *Ethnic Americans* (New York: Harper & Row, 1982).

61. For Toledo examples see Williams, "Newcomers to the City," 12, 15.

62. *Columbus Dispatch*, Aug. 1, 1917, noted in Scott, *Negro Migration during the War*, 128–29.

63. Ibid.

64. *Gazette*, Aug. 4, 1917. Municipal officials in the South as well as the North feared that poor housing conditions in black neighborhoods could affect a city's general public health. Steven J. Hoffman, "Progressive Public Health Administration in the Jim Crow South: A Case Study of Richmond, Virginia, 1907–1920," *Journal of Social History* 35 (Fall 2001): 175–194.

65. "Negro Health and Race Relations," *Cincinnati Sanitary Bulletin* 8, no. 4, Oct. 14, 1925, 1, Cincinnati Historical Society Library.

66. J. S. Himes, Jr., "Forty Years of Negro Life in Columbus, Ohio," *The Journal of Negro History* 27 (April, 1942): 149; Kusmer, *A Ghetto Takes Shape*, 221–22.

67. Kevin J. Mumford, *Interzones: Black/White Sex Districts in Chicago and New York in the Early Twentieth Century* (New York: Columbia University Press, 1997), passim; Dinnerstein and Reiners, *Ethnic Americans*, 56; Gerber, *Black Ohio*, 269, 281–82, 283–87, 388, 424, 425, 430, 432; Zane L. Miller, *Boss Cox's Cincinnati: Urban Politics in the Progressive Era* (New York: Oxford University Press, 1968), 10–11; Dabney, *Colored Citizens*, 147–49, 153–70, 398–99; Spear, *Black Chicago*, 25; Katzman, *Before the Ghetto: Black Detroit*, 172; Osofsky, *Harlem*, 14–15; Scott, *Negro Migration during the War*, 126.

68. See discussion of vice in Kusmer, *A Ghetto Takes Shape*, 48, 49–50, 51, 111, 177–78, 220–21.

69. *Gazette*, April 1, 1916.

70. Ibid., Nov. 14, 1917, March 2, 1918, Oct. 11, 1919, June 12, 1920.

71. Ibid., Sept. 15, 1917.

72. *Cleveland Plain Dealer*, Aug. 1, 1917; Scott, *Negro Migration during the War*, 126.

73. Miller, *Boss Cox's Cincinnati*, 10–11.

74. Dabney, *Colored Citizens*, 167.

75. Ibid., 167–70.

76. Ibid., 167.

77. Ibid.

78. Ibid., 147. For Illinois examples of such changing neighborhoods, see Cynthia M. Blair, "Vicious Commerce: African American Women's Sex Work and the Transformation of Urban Space in Chicago, 1850–1915" (Ph.D. Diss., Harvard University, 1999).

79. Himes, Jr., "Forty Years of Negro Life in Columbus," 149.

80. Gerber, *Black Ohio*, 107, 428–29.

81. Njeru Murage, "Making Migrants an Asset: The Detroit Urban League-Employers Alliance in Wartime Detroit, 1916–1919," *Michigan Historical Review* 26 (Spring 2000): 67–93.

82. Kusmer, *A Ghetto Takes Shape*, 190–91; United States Department of Commerce, Bureau of the Census, *Thirteenth Census of the United States Taken in the Year 1910, Volume IV, Population 1910, Occupation Statistics* (Washington, D.C.: Government Printing Office, 1914), 547–51 and *Fourteenth Census of the United States Taken in the Year 1920, Volume IV, Population 1920, Occupations* (Washington, D.C.: Government Printing Office, 1923), 1081–90.

83. Kusmer, *A Ghetto Takes Shape*, 191.

84. Gerber, *Black Ohio*, 310–11.

85. Henry L. Suggs, *The Black Press in the Middle West, 1865–1985* (Westport: Greenwood, 1996).

86. Dabney, *Colored Citizens*, 197–98.

87. Ibid., 116–19, 188, 190; Gerber, *Black Ohio*, 381.

88. Kusmer, *A Ghetto Takes Shape*, 194; Russell H. Davis, *Black Americans in Cleveland From George Peake to Carl B. Stokes, 1796–1969* (Washington, D.C.: Associated Publishers, 1972), 203; Gerber, *Black Ohio*, 381.

89. Ibid.; *Crisis* 14 (May 1917): 26; *Gazette*, Aug. 22, 1925.

90. *Ohio State Monitor* (Columbus), Sept. 9, 1918, May 22, 1920.

91. *Census 1910: Occupation Statistics* 4: 547, 459, 550; *Census 1920: Occupations* 4: 1082, 1086, 1089.

92. Kusmer, *A Ghetto Takes Shape*, 192–193.

93. Quoted in Scott, *Negro Migration during the War*, 127.

94. Kusmer, *A Ghetto Takes Shape*, 192–93.

95. Dabney, *Colored Citizens*, 267, 270, 301, 312–13, 351.

96. Gerber, *Black Ohio*, 297–98; Kusmer, *A Ghetto Takes Shape*, 192.

97. *Census 1920: Occupations* 4: 1083, 1086, 1089.

98. Wm. A. McWilliams, *Columbus Illustrated Record, 1919–1920* (Columbus, OH: W. A. McWilliams, Publisher, 1920), 105, 107, 111.

99. Gerber, *Black Ohio*, 298.

100. Kusmer, *A Ghetto Takes Shape*, 191–92; *Census 1910: Occupation Statistics* 4: 548, 459, 550, 552, 606; *Census 1920: Occupations* 4: 1082, 1086, 1089, 1094, 1244.

101. Gerber, *Black Ohio*, 434–437; United States Department of Commerce, Bureau of the Census, *Religious Bodies 1916, Part I, Summary and General Tables* (Washington, D.C.: Government Printing Office, 1919), 570.

102. Milton C. Sernett, *Bound for the Promised Land: African American Religion and the Great Migration* (Durham: Duke University Press, 1997).

103. *Gazette*, March 15, 1919.

104. Kusmer, *A Ghetto Takes Shape*, 207.

105. Gerber, *Black Ohio*, 436; McWilliams, *Columbus Illustrated Record, 1919–1920*, 5.

106. *Census 1910: Occupation Statistics* 4: 548; *Census 1920: Occupations* 4: 1082.

107. Kusmer, *A Ghetto Takes Shape*, 208.

108. Dabney, *Colored Citizens*, 338.

109. Kusmer, *A Ghetto Takes Shape*, 208, 209.

110. David T. Beito, *From Mutual Aid to Welfare State: Fraternal Societies and Social Services, 1890–1967* (Chapel Hill: University of North Carolina Press, 2000).

111. Jones, *American Immigration*, 135–36; Gerber, *Black Ohio*, 158–65; Charles Wesley, *The History of the Prince Hall Grand Lodge of Free and Accepted Masons of the State of Ohio, 1849–1960* (Wilberforce, Ohio: Central State College Press, 1961), 149–236.

112. Kusmer, *A Ghetto Takes Shape*, 206–207; McWilliams, *Columbus Illustrated Record, 1919–1920*, 99, 101.

113. Anne B. Allen, "Sowing the Seeds of Kindness—and Change: A History of the Iowa Association of Women's Clubs," *Iowa Heritage Illustrated* 83 (Spring 2002): 2–13; Wanda A. Hendricks, *Gender, Race, and Politics in the Midwest: Black Club Women in Illinois* (Bloomington: Indiana University Press, 1998); Ann Meis Knupfer, *Toward a Tenderer Humanity and a Nobler Womanhood: African American Women's Clubs in Turn of the Century Chicago* (New York: New York University Press, 1996); Khadijah Olivia Turner Miller, "Everyday Victories: The Pennsylvania State Federation of Negro Women's Clubs, Inc., 1900–1930: Paradigms of Survival and Empowerment" (Ph.D. Diss., Temple University, 2001).

114. Kusmer, *A Ghetto Takes Shape*, 105–6, 206–7; Phillips, *Alabama North*, 166–67; McWilliams, *Columbus Illustrated Record, 1919–1920*, 97, 99, 101, 103; Gerber, *Black Ohio*, 309, 441–43; Krawcheck, "The Negro in Cleveland;" Helen M. Chesnutt, *Charles Waddell Chesnutt, Pioneer of the Color Line* (Chapel Hill: University of North Carolina Press, 1952), 61; Herbert M. Morais, *The History of the Negro in Medicine* (New York: Publishers Company, 1969), 52–57, 68–69.

115. Kusmer, *A Ghetto Takes Shape*, 209.

Notes to Chapter 2

1. William Hagan, *American Indians* (Chicago: University of Chicago Press, 1969), 121–50; James S. Olson and Raymond Wilson, *Native Americans in the Twentieth Century* (Provo: Brigham Young University Press, 1984).

2. Jones, *American Immigration*, 249, 265.

242 NOTES TO CHAPTER TWO

3. August Meier and Elliott Rudwick, *From Plantation to Ghetto* (New York: Hill and Wang, 1970), 178–88; C. Vann Woodward, *The Strange Career of Jim Crow*, (New York: Oxford University Press, 1955). 83–86, 87, 97–102.

4. Kusmer, *A Ghetto Takes Shape*, 54.

5. Jones, *American Immigration*, 260, 266–67.

6. Richard Hofstadter, *The Age of Reform: From Bryan to F. D. R* (New York: Knopf, 1972), 175–84.

7. Gary Gerstle, *American Crucible: Race and Nation in the Twentieth Century* (Princeton: Princeton University Press, 2001); Matthew Pratt Guterl, *The Color of Race in America, 1900–1940* (Cambridge: Harvard University Press, 2001); John Higham, *Strangers in the Land: Patterns of American Nativism, 1860–1925* (New Brunswick: Rutgers University Press, 1988).

8. Kenneth T. Jackson, *The Ku Klux Klan in the City* (New York: Oxford University Press, 1970), passim.

9. Jones, *American Immigration*, 268–274.

10. Meier and Rudwick, *From Plantation to Ghetto*, 193, 217–22.

11. Kusmer, *A Ghetto Takes Shape*, 171.

12. Nimrod B. Allen, "East Long Street," *Crisis* 25 (Nov. 1922): 12; *Cincinnati: A Guide to the Queen City*, 225.

13. Kusmer, *A Ghetto Takes Shape*, 162.

14. Robert B. Fairbanks, "Cincinnati Blacks and the Irony of Low-Income Housing Reform, 1900–1950," in *Race and the City*, ed. Taylor, Jr., 196; Bureau of the Census, *Census 1910: Population* 3: 427; *Census 1920: Population* 3: 797–809; *Negroes in the United States 1920–1932*, 800.

15. Gerber, *Black Ohio*, 291–292; Roderick Duncan McKenzie, "The Neighborhood: A Study of Local Life in the City of Columbus, Ohio," *American Journal of Sociology* 27 (Sept. 1921): 153–155; Mary Louise Mark, *Negroes in Columbus* (Columbus: The Ohio State University Press, 1928), 15–29.

16. Cincinnati Wards 3, 4, 6, 15, 16, 17, 18. Cleveland Wards 11 and 12. Columbus Wards 6, 7, 8, 9. *Census 1920: Population, 1920* 3: 799–800, 801, 803–4.

17. Taylor, Jr., "Black Ghetto-Slum Formation in Cincinnati," in *Race and the City*, ed. Taylor, Jr., 163.

18. *Census 1910: Population* 3: 426–27; *Census 1920: Population* 3: 799–800, 801.

19. Toledo's ward 11 was 19 percent black. Ibid., 3: 803–4, 807–8; Williams, "Newcomers to the City," 12.

20. Stephen Grant Meyer, *As Long as They Don't Move Door: Segregation and Racial Conflict in American Neighborhoods* (Lanham: Rowan & Littlefield, 2000).

21. Report of the Cleveland Branch of the National Association for the Advancement of Colored People, April 25, 1914, Ohio Correspondence, Cleveland, Branch Files (Container 157), Papers of the National Association for the Advancement of Colored People, Manuscript Division, The Library of Congress, Washington, D.C.

22. *Gazette*, July 3, 1915.

23. Williams, "Newcomers to the City," 13.

24. Ibid.

25. Kusmer, *A Ghetto Takes Shape*, 167.

26. *Cleveland Plain Dealer*, Aug. 13, 1918, 7; *Gazette*, Aug. 17, 1918.

27. Ibid.

28. Fairbanks, "Cincinnati Blacks and the Irony of Low-Income Housing Reform," in *Race and the City*, ed. Taylor, Jr., 196–97.

29. Bureau of the Census, *Religious Bodies 1916*, 570; Gerber, *Black Ohio*, 438–39; McWilliams, *Columbus Illustrated Record, 1919–1920*, 103; Kusmer, *A Ghetto Takes Shape*, 208, 209; Dabney, *Colored Citizens*, 373, 375–76.

30. See Chapter 1, endnotes 110–14.

31. Gerber, *Black Ohio*, 13, 263–66.

32. Ibid.

33. *Crisis* 17 (Nov. 1918): 35; *Gazette*, Sept. 28, 1918.

34. Ibid., Nov. 22, 1919.

35. Gerber, *Black Ohio*, 265.

36. Ibid., 266–67.

37. Ibid; Allen, "East Long Street," 14; Minor, "The Negro in Columbus, Ohio" 152; *Which September*, The Education Committee, The Vanguard League (Columbus, Ohio, 1944), 9 in Thomas Baker Jones, "An Analysis of the Interracial Policies and Practices of the Group Work Agencies in Columbus, Ohio" (Ph.D. Diss., The Ohio State University, 1947), 17–18; Himes, Jr., "Forty Years of Negro Life in Columbus," 139; Eric L. Johnson, "A History of Black Schooling in Franklin County, Ohio, 1870–1913" (Ph.D. Diss., The Ohio State University, 2002).

38. Gerber, *Black Ohio*, 266–67; McWilliams, *Columbus Illustrated Record, 1919–1920*, 44.

39. Gerber, *Black Ohio*, 450–451; Walter McKinley Nicholes, "The Educational Development of Blacks in Cincinnati from 1800 to the Present" (Ph.D. Edu. Diss., University of Cincinnati, 1977), 137, 139.

40. Gerber, *Black Ohio*, 451; Nicholes, "Educational Development of Blacks in Cincinnati," 139, 140, 141.

41. *Crisis* 11 (March 1916): 219; *Gazette*, Feb. 5, 1916.

42. Eric Anderson and Alfred A. Moss, Jr., *Dangerous Donations: Northern Philanthropy and Southern Education* (Columbia: University of Missouri Press, 1999); Suellen Hoy, "Illinois Technical School for Colored Girls: A Catholic Institution on Chicago's South Side, 1911–1953," *Journal of Illinois History* 4 (Summer 2001): 103–22.

43. Dabney, *Colored Citizens*, 355.

44. *Crisis* 17 (Nov. 1918): 35.

45. *Gazette*, April 21, 1917, May 5, 1917.

46. Franklin and Moss, Jr., *From Slavery to Freedom*, 181; Eugene H. Roseboom and Francis P. Weisenburger, *A History of Ohio* (Columbus: The Ohio State Archaeological and Historical Society, 1961), 300.

47. *Crisis* 8 (July 1914): 129, 132.

48. Ibid.

49. McWilliams, *Columbus Illustrated Record, 1919–1920*, 44.

50. Ferguson was the first African American to win this honor. *Crisis* 11 (Dec. 1915): 61.

51. *Gazette*, March 31, 1917.

52. *The Ohio State Journal* (Columbus), March 11, 1917, in ibid., March 17, 1917.

53. See the July issues of *Crisis* for the years 1914–1919; Ronald E. Butchart, "Mission Matters: Mount Holyoke, Oberlin, and the Schooling of Southern Blacks, 1861–1917," *History of Education Quarterly* 42 (Spring 2002): 1–17.

54. Gerber, *Black Ohio*, 257–63.

55. Dabney, *Colored Citizens*, 145.

56. Ibid., 146.

57. *Crisis* 15 (Jan. 1918): 144; *Gazette*, March 27, 1915, May 12, 1917.

58. Chas. S. Sutton, Enrolling Clerk of the State Senate, in ibid., April 10, 1915.

59. *The Union* (Cincinnati) in ibid., Oct. 25, 1919.

60. See table A4 for references to court suits alleging discrimination by restaurants.

61. Gerber, *Black Ohio*, 259–63.

62. Kusmer, *A Ghetto Takes Shape* 178–79.

63. Report of the Cleveland Branch of the National Association for the Advancement of Colored People, April 25, 1914, Cleveland, Ohio Correspondence, Cleveland, Branch Files (Container 157), NAACP Papers.

64. Gerber, *Black Ohio*, 260–62.

65. *Gazette*, May 3, 1919; Aug. 9, 16, 1919; Krawcheck, "The Negro in Cleveland."

66. *Gazette*, Sept. 6, 1919.

67. See William M. Tuttle, Jr., *Race Riot: Chicago in the Red Summer of 1919* (Urbana: University of Illinois Press, 1996); Elliott M. Rudwick, *Race Riot at East St. Louis, July 2, 1917* (Carbondale, IL: Southern Illinois University Press, 1964); Arthur I. Waskow, *From Race Riot to Sit-in: 1919 and the 1960s* (Garden City, NY: Anchor Books, 1967); Brian Butler, *An Undergrowth of Folly: Public Order, Race Anxiety, and the 1903 Evansville, Indiana, Riot* (New York: Garland, 2000); Mark Bauerlein, *Negrophobia: A Race Riot in Atlanta, 1906* (San Francisco: Encounter, 2001); Roberta Senechal, *The Sociogenesis of a Race Riot: Springfield, Illinois, in 1908* (Urbana: University of Illinois Press, 1990); Christopher P. Bettinger, "Strange Interludes? A Sociological History of American Race Rioting, 1900–1996" (Ph.D. Diss., University of Michigan, 1999); Marilyn K. Howard, "Black Lynching in the Promised Land: Mob Violence in Ohio, 1876–1916" (Ph.D. Diss., The Ohio State University, 1999); Stacy P. McDermott, "'An Outrageous Proceeding': A Northern Lynching and the Enforcement of Anti-Lynching Legislation in Illinois, 1905–1910," *Journal of Negro History* 84 (Winter 1999): 61–78.

68. *The New York Times*, Aug. 31, 1916, 1.

69. *Gazette*, Sept. 9, 1916, Oct. 7, 1916.

70. Ibid., Oct. 7, 14, 1916.

71. Ibid., Oct. 7, 14, 1916.

72. *Crisis* 14 (May 1917): 9; *Gazette*, Sept. 30, 1916, Dec. 2, 9, 30, 1916, Feb. 3, 1917.

73. Ibid., June 16, 1917; Kusmer, *A Ghetto Takes Shape*, 185.

74. Carter G. Woodson, *The Negro in Our History* (Washington, D.C.: The Associated Publishers, 1947), 511; letter of N. C. A. Rayhouser to Editor *Gazette*, Sept. 10, 1917, *Gazette*, Sept. 15, 1917.

75. Himes, Jr., "Forty Years of Negro Life in Columbus," 150–51

76. Williams, "Newcomers to the City," 13.

77. *Gazette,* April 19, 1919.

78. Ibid., July 5, 1919, Aug. 2, 1919; letter of O. W. Childers to Friend Smith, Aug. 11, 1919, ibid., Aug. 16, 1919.

79. J. D. Barnhart, "The Southern Influence in the Formation of Ohio," *Journal of Southern History* 3 (Feb. 1937): 40–42; Robert E. Chaddock, *Ohio before 1850: A Study of the Early Influence of Pennsylvania and Southern Populations in Ohio* (New York: Columbia University Press, 1908), 31–46; David Carl Shilling, "Relations of Southern Ohio to the South during the Decade Preceding the Civil War," *Historical and Philosophical Society of Ohio Quarterly* 8, no. 1 (1913): 3–62; Roseboom and Weisenburger, *A History of Ohio,* 114–15; Gerber, *Black Ohio,* 9–14.

80. Chaddock, *Ohio before 1850,* 31–46.

81. Roseboom and Weisenburger, *History of Ohio,* 114–115.

82. Gerber, *Black Ohio,* 9–14; Nikki M. Taylor, "'Frontiers of Freedom': The African American Experience in Cincinnati, 1802–1862" (Ph.D. Diss., Duke University, 2001).

83. Barnhart, "Southern Influence in the Formation of Ohio," 40–42; Shilling, "Relations of Southern Ohio to the South during the Decade Preceding the Civil War," 6–15, 27.

Notes to Chapter 3

1. Gerber, *Black Ohio.*

2. Ibid.; Kusmer, *A Ghetto Takes Shape,* 3–113.

3. Gerber, *Black Ohio,* 433–67.

4. Hofstadter, *Age of Reform,* 203–12; Weiss, *National Urban League,* 2–28.

5. The National Urban League technically was formed with the consolidation of three organizations in 1911, but the League traditionally traces its birth to 1910 and its antecedents in that year. Franklin and Moss, Jr, *From Slavery to Freedom,* 354–55, and see Weiss, *National Urban League,* 29–46

6. Jessica I. Elfenbein, *The Making of a Modern City: Philanthropy, Civic Culture, and the Baltimore YMCA* (Gainesville: University Press of Florida, 2001); Stephanie Y. Felix, "Committed to Their Own: African American Women Leaders in the YWCA. The YWCA of Germantown, Philadelphia, Pennsylvania, 1870–1970." (Ph.D. Diss., Temple University, 1999); Wanda A. Hendricks, "Child Welfare and Black Female Agency in Springfield: Eva Monroe and the Lincoln Colored Home," *Journal of Illinois History* 3 (Summer 2000): 86–104; Lillian Taiz, *Hallelujah Lads & Lasses: Remaking the Salvation Army in America, 1880–1930* (Chapel Hill: University of North Carolina Press, 2001); Judith Weisenfeld, *African American Women and Christian Activism: New York's Black YWCA, 1905–1945* (Cambridge: Harvard University Press, 1997).

7. Gerber, *Black Ohio,* 21, 166, 449–50.

8. Dabney, *Colored Citizens,* 394.

9. Ibid., 396.

10. Ibid., 216–17, 396, 397.

11. Ibid., 211; *Crisis* 11 (March 1916): 219.

12. Dabney, *Colored Citizens*, 218.

13. Ibid., 397.

14. Ibid., 210–11.

15. Ibid., 216–17.

16. Ibid., 211; *Crisis* 11 (March 1916): 219; Gerber, *Black Ohio*, 447–48.

17. Dabney, *Colored Citizens*, 218.

18. *Cincinnati: A Guide to the Queen City*, 292; Jacob G. Schmidlapp, printed pamphlet, *Low Priced Housing for Wage Earners* (New York: National Housing Association Publications, 1919), 1 (Box 62, Folder 18), Cincinnati Model Homes Company Records, 1912–1977, Cincinnati Historical Society Library, Cincinnati.

19. *Cincinnati: A Guide to the Queen City*, 292–93.

20. Dabney, *Colored Citizens*, 387.

21. *Crisis* 18 (Aug. 1919): 194.

22. Dabney, *Colored Citizens*, 387; Jacob G. Schmidlapp, untitled paper, Cincinnati, Nov. 6, 1919 (MSS VF4124), Jacob Godfrey Schmidlapp Papers, Cincinnati Historical Society Library, Cincinnati.

23. Gerber, *Black Ohio*, 166, 446–48.

24. McWilliams, *Columbus Illustrated Record 1919–1920*, 115; Himes, Jr., "Forty Years of Negro Life in Columbus," 148; *Crisis* 17 (March 1919): 246; Gerber, *Black Ohio*, 446–47.

25. Himes, Jr., "Forty Years of Negro Life in Columbus," 149; McWilliams, *Columbus Illustrated Record 1919–1920*, 83.

26. Himes, Jr., "Forty Years of Negro Life in Columbus," 149; McWilliams, *Columbus Illustrated Record 1919–1920*, 103.

27. Ibid., 99.

28. *Crisis* 9 (Dec. 1914): 61; Kusmer, *A Ghetto Takes Shape*, 148–52; Gerber, *Black Ohio*, 455–58; Davis, *Black Americans in Cleveland*, 191–97; Laura Tuennerman-Kaplan, *Helping Others, Helping Ourselves: Power, Giving, and Community Identity in Cleveland, Ohio, 1880–1930* (Kent: Kent State University Press, 2001).

29. Jane E. Hunter, *A Nickel and a Prayer* (Cleveland: Elli Kani Publishing Company, 1940), 105; Annual Report for the Year 1923, The Phillis Wheatley Association, Cleveland, 4, Ohio Historical Society Archives/Library, Columbus; *Gazette*, June 18, 1932; Krawcheck, "Negro in Cleveland"; Chesnutt, *Charles Waddell Chesnutt*, 262; Kusmer, *A Ghetto Takes Shape*, 149–51; Gerber, *Black Ohio*, 390–92, 457–58; Adrienne Lash Jones, *Jane Edna Hunter: A Case Study of Black Leadership, 1910–1950* (Brooklyn: Carlson Pub., 1990), 35–58; Virginia R. Boynton, "Contested Terrain: The Struggle Over Gender Norms for Black Working-Class Women in Cleveland's Phillis Wheatley Association, 1920–1950," *Ohio History* 103 (Winter-Spring 1994): 5–22; Phillips, *Alabama North*, 88–96.

30. Chesnutt, *Charles Waddell Chesnutt*, 263.

31. Ibid.; Kusmer, *A Ghetto Takes Shape*, 216–17; Gerber, *Black Ohio*, 458.

32. Dabney, *Colored Citizens*, 216–17.

33. Kusmer, *A Ghetto Takes Shape*, 149–51; Gerber, *Black Ohio*, 391–92, 457–58.

34. McWilliams, *Columbus Illustrated Record, 1919–1920*, 97.

35. Dabney, *Colored Citizens*, 210, 218.

36. McWilliams, *Columbus Illustrated Record, 1919–1920*, 115; Andrea Tuttle Kornbluh, "James Hathaway Robinson and the Origins of Professional Social Work in the Black Community," in *Race and the City*, ed. Taylor, Jr., 213–14.

37. Toure Reed, "'Helping negroes to help themselves': Middle Class Reform and the Politics of Racial Order, 1910–1950" (Ph.D. Diss., Columbia University, 2002).

38. Hazel Carby, "Policing the Black Woman's Body in an Urban Context," *Critical Inquiry* 18 (Summer 1992): 741–46.

39. Kusmer, *A Ghetto Takes Shape*, 151; Davis, *Black Americans in Cleveland*, 195–96.

40. *Gazette*, May 3, 1919, Dec. 20, 1919.

41. Himes, Jr., "Forty Years of Negro Life in Columbus," 149; McWilliams, *Columbus Illustrated Record 1919–1920*, 83.

42. Dabney, *Colored Citizens*, 397.

43. McWilliams, *Columbus Illustrated Record, 1919–1920*, 115; Dabney, *Colored Citizens*, 210–11; Patricia A. Carter, "Housing the Women Who Toiled: Planned Residences for Single Women, Cincinnati 1860–1960," *Ohio History* 103 (Winter–Spring 1996): 55–56.

44. *Cincinnati Enquirer*, May 26, 1917, 2.

45. Fairbanks, *Making Better Citizens*, 29.

46. Similar domestic agendas existed in other states. See Nina E. Banks, "Steadying the Husband, Uplifting the Race: The Pittsburgh Urban League's Promotion of Black Female Domesticity during the Great Depression" (Ph.D. Diss., University of Massachusetts, 1999)

47. Kornbluh, "James Hathaway Robinson," *Race and the City*, ed. Taylor, Jr., 230.

48. Negro Welfare Association, "Aims and Perspective" and "Record of Service [1925] in Dabney, *Colored Citizens*, 222–23; Kornbluh, "James Hathaway Robinson," in *Race and the City*, ed. Taylor, Jr., 215–16.

49. "Service Report of the Negro Civic Welfare Committee of the Council of Social Agencies (Development thru two years)," typescript (Box 29, Folder 9), Urban League of Greater Cincinnati Papers, Cincinnati Historical Society Library; Dabney, *Colored Citizens*, 223; Kornbluh, "James Hathaway Robinson," in *Race and the City*, ed. Taylor, Jr., 221.

50. The Columbus Urban League, "Twenty Years of Service in the Field of Social Work for Negroes and Inter-race Relations 1917–1937"[Columbus: Columbus Urban League, 1937], PA Box 534, 44, Ohio Historical Society Archives/Library, Columbus, 2; "The Columbus Urban League: An Inventory of Its Papers in the Ohio Historical Society (Manuscript Department), Ohio Historical Society, Columbus, Ohio, 1969," Ohio Historical Society Archives/Library, Columbus, 4; McWilliams, *Columbus Illustrated Record, 1919–1920*, 121.

51. *Gazette*, Dec. 22, 1917, Jan. 12, 1918; Scott, *Negro Migration during the War*, 127.

52. Kusmer, *A Ghetto Takes Shape*, 255.

53. *Cleveland Plain Dealer*, Aug. 4, 1917, 5; *Gazette*, Aug. 11, 1917.

54. Kusmer, *A Ghetto Takes Shape*, 255.

55. *Gazette*, Dec. 22, 1917, Jan. 12, 1918; Scott, *Negro Migration during the War*, 127.

56. Ibid., 126

57. Ibid.; *Cleveland Plain Dealer*, Aug. 4, 1917, 5; *Gazette*, Aug. 11, 1917.

58. Ibid., Dec. 22, 1917, Jan. 12, 1918; Scott, *Negro Migration during the War*, 127; Kusmer, *A Ghetto Takes Shape*, 255.

59. *Gazette*, Feb. 1, 1919.

60. Ibid., Dec. 14, 1918, Feb. 15, 1919, March 1, 1919, May 17, 1919.

61. Dabney, *Colored Citizens*, 220; Kornbluh, "James Hathaway Robinson," in *Race and the City*, ed. Taylor, Jr., 211, 225, fn. 2.

62. Kusmer, *A Ghetto Takes Shape*, 255; Davis, *Black Americans in Cleveland*, 199; *Gazette*, Dec. 22, 1917, Jan. 12, 1918; Scott, *Negro Migration during the War*, 127.

63. Kusmer, *A Ghetto Takes Shape*, 255; Dabney, *Colored Citizens*, 227; Kornbluh, "James Hathaway Robinson," in *Race and the City*, ed. Taylor, Jr., 221.

64. McWilliams, *Columbus Illustrated Record, 1919–1920*, 121; "Columbus Urban League: An Inventory of Its Papers," 6.

65. Ohio Federation for Uplift Among Colored People, *Are You With Us?* Cleveland, 1918 (Printed pamphlet), Ohio Historical Society Archives/Library, Columbus; Scott, *Negro Migration during the War*, 128.

66. Kellogg, *NAACP*, 9–30, 31.

67. *Crisis* 17 (April 1919): 284–85.

68. Gerber, *Black Ohio*, 465; Kusmer, *A Ghetto Takes Shape*, 259.

69. Ibid., 261.

70. McWilliams, *Columbus Illustrated Record, 1919–1920*, 103.

71. *Crisis* 17 (April 1919): 284–85.

72. Dabney, *Colored Citizens*, 188.

73. Kusmer, *A Ghetto Takes Shape*, 260–61.

74. *Gazette*, Jan. 27, 1917, June 9, 23, 1917, Oct. 20, 1917, Jan. 12, 1918.

75. *Crisis* 12 (June1916): 88; *Gazette*, June 3, 1916.

76. Ibid., June 28, 1919.

77. Ibid., Dec. 28, 1918.

78. Letter of Chas. S. Sutton, Enrolling Clerk of the Ohio Senate, to *Gazette*, ibid., April 10, 1915.

79. Ibid., May 5, 1917.

80. Ibid., May 3, 1919, Aug. 9, 16, 1919; Krawcheck, "The Negro in Cleveland."

81. *Census 1910: Population* 3: 423; *Census 1920: Population* 3: 790.

82. *Gazette*, Jan. 18, 1919.

83. Ibid.

84. Ibid.

85. Ibid.

86. Ibid., April 3, 1915.

87. Ibid.

88. Letter, March 29, 1915, ibid.

89. *The Moving Picture World*, March 27, 1915, in ibid.

90. Letter, March 30, 1915, in ibid., April 3, 1915.

91. Letter to Hon. Newton D. Baker, April 1, 1915, in ibid., April 10, 1915.

92. Letter, April 8, 1915, in ibid., April 17, 1915.

93. Letter of Newton D. Baker, Mayor, to Hon. Harry C. Smith, April 12, 1915, in ibid., April 17, 1915.

94. Letter to Frank B. Willis, July 7, 1915, in ibid., July 17, 1915.

95. Letter of Mrs. John R. Rudd, Chas. D. Swayne, W. Forest Speaks, Publicity Committee, Springfield Branch NAACP, to Harry C. Smith, June 10, 1915, in ibid., June 19, 1915; *Crisis* 10 (Oct. 1915): 293.

96. *Gazette*, June 19, 1915.

97. Ibid.; *Crisis* 10 (June 1915): 86.

98. Letter to Harry C. Smith, July 9, 1915, in *Gazette*, July 17, 1915.

99. Kellogg, *NAACP*, 142–45; Goodwin Berquist and James Greenwood, "Protest Against Racism: 'The Birth of a Nation' in Ohio," in *Rhetoric of the People*, ed. Harold Barrett (Amsterdam: Rodopi, N. V., 1974), 221–40.

100. *Gazette*, October 2, 1915.

101. Ibid.

102. Ibid.

103. Ibid.

104. Ibid.

105. Ibid., Jan. 15, 1916.

106. Turner's opinion was published in ibid., Jan. 22, 1916.

107. Ibid.

108. Ibid., Feb. 19, 1916.

109. The Epoch Producing Corporation v. The Industrial Commission of Ohio, et al., *Ohio State Reports* 95 (1916): 400–401.

110. *Gazette*, Feb. 10, 1917.

111. Letter to W. B. Gongwer, Feb. 3, 1917 (copy), in George A. Myers Papers, Manuscript Division, Ohio Historical Society Archives/Library, Columbus, Ohio.

112. Letter of W. B. Gongwer to Governor James M. Cox (copy), enclosed in letter of W. B. Gongwer to George A. Myers, Feb. 5, 1917, Myers Papers.

113. *Crisis* 14 (May 1917): 26.

114. Ibid.

115. *Gazette*, Feb. 24, 1917.

116. *Cleveland Plain Dealer*, March 30, 1917, 10; *Gazette*, April 7, 1917.

117. Ibid.

118. Ibid., May 12, 1917.

119. Ibid., April 14, 1917.

120. Letter of William Stevenson to Roy Nash, Feb. 19, 1917, and letter of William Stevenson to Roy Nash, April 7, 1917, in Cincinnati, Branch Files (Container 155), NAACP Papers.

121. *Gazette*, Feb. 3, 1917; *Ohio House Journal* 107 (1917): 114.

122. *Gazette*, Feb. 24, 1917; *Ohio House Journal* 107 (1917): 148.

123. Ibid., 280.

124. Letter of William Stevenson to Roy Nash, Feb. 19, 1917, in Cincinnati, Branch Files (Container 155), NAACP Papers.

125. *Gazette*, March 3, 1917; *Dayton News*, Feb. 21, 1917, 6.

126. *Ohio House Journal* 107 (1917): 506, 562, and 685.

127. *Ohio Senate Journal* 107 (1917): 616, 640.

128. *Gazette*, March 31, 1917.

129. Ibid.

130. Ibid.

131. See Letter of Harry C. Smith to Governor James W. Cox, Sept. 23, 1918, in ibid., Sept. 28, 1917.

132. Letter of Charles E. Morris, Secretary to the Governor, to Harry C. Smith, September 30, 1918, in ibid., Oct. 5, 1918.

133. Ibid., July 14, 1917.

134. Ibid., Oct. 11, 1919.

135. Ibid., Aug. 31, 1918.

136. *Crisis* 18 (Nov. 1919): 350; *Gazette*, Oct. 11, 1919.

137. Ibid., Aug. 2, 1919.

138. *Cleveland News*, Aug. 4, 1919, 1.

139. *Gazette*, Aug. 9, 1919.

140. "Race Riots and Their Remedy," *The Independent* 99 (1919): 223.

141. *Cleveland Plain Dealer*, May 2, 1919, 2.

142. *The Cincinnati Enquirer*, Sept. 7, 1919, Section 2, 20.

143. *Gazette*, Sept. 20, 1919.

144. Ibid., Oct. 11, 1919.

145. *New York Times*, Oct. 7, 1919, 2; *Gazette*, Oct. 25, 1919.

146. Mark Ellis, *Race, War, and Surveillance: African Americans and the United States Government during World War I* (Bloomington: Indiana University Press, 2001); Wray R. Johnson, "Black American Radicalism and the First World War: The Secret Files of the Military Intelligence Division," *Armed Forces and Society* 26 (Fall 1999): 27–53; Theodore Kornweibel, Jr., *"Investigating Everything": Federal Efforts to Control Black Loyalty during World War I* (Bloomington: Indiana University Press, 2002).

147. Niki L. M. Brown, "'Your patriotism is of the purest quality': African American Women and World War I" (Ph.D. Diss., Yale University Press, 2002).

148. Arthur Barbeau and Florette Henri, *The Unknown Soldiers: Black American Troops in World War I* (Philadelphia: Temple University Press, 1974), passim; Lowell Dwight Black, *The Negro Volunteer Militia Units of the Ohio National Guard, 1870–1954: The Struggle for Military Recognition and Equality in the State of Ohio* (Manhattan, Kansas: Military Affairs/Aerospace Historian Publishing, 1976), 260–66, 269–307; William W. Giffin, "Mobilization of Black Militiamen in World War I: Ohio's Ninth Battalion," *The Historian* 40 (Aug. 1978): 686–703.

149. These figures are from the Mobilization Division of the Provost Marshal General's Office (December 16, 1918), Emmett J. Scott, *The Negro American in the World War* (Chicago: Homewood Press, 1919), 68; James Mennell, "African Americans and the Selective Service Act of 1917," *Journal of Negro History* 84 (Summer 1999): 275–87.

150. Roseboom and Weisenburger, *A History of Ohio*, 337.

151. Scott, *The Negro American in the World War*, 131; *Gazette*, Feb. 16, 1918.

152. The names and addresses of these officers were listed in Scott, *The Negro American in the World War*, 471–81 and in *Gazette*, Oct. 27, 1917.

153. Ibid., Jan. 12, 1918, May 4, 1918.

154. "Address of President William S. Scarborough upon the opening of the

academic year 1918–1919 at Wilberforce University, September 17, 1918," *The Wilberforcian*, 1, no. 6 (March, 1919), Carnegie Library, Wilberforce University, Wilberforce, Ohio.

155. Scott, *The Negro American in the World War*, 334–36.

156. Ibid., 477.

157. *Gazette*, Sept. 1, 1917.

158. Scott, *The Negro American in the World War*, 287.

159. Ibid., 448; Charles H. Williams, *Sidelights on Negro Soldiers* (Boston: B. J. Bimmer Company, 1923), 122; and *Gazette*, July 27, 1918.

160. George A. Myers to Newton D. Baker, July 22, 1916, George A. Myers to Elbert H. Baker, May 4, 1917 (copies), Ben W. Hough, Ohio Adjutant General, to Chief, Militia Bureau, August 11, 1916 (copy), Elbert H. Baker to Ohio Governor James M. Cox, June 29, 1917 (copy), Myers Papers; Harry E. Davis and George A. Myers to Newton D. Baker, July 26, 1916, Item No. 2438152, Index to General Correspondence of the Adjutant General's Office 1890–1917 (microfilm), M-698, Location 10–22–1, Roll No. 866, National Archives, Washington, D.C.; Charles W. Chesnutt to Newton D. Baker, July 24, 1916 (copy), Charles W. Chesnutt Papers, Fisk University Library, Nashville, Tennessee; Newton D. Baker to Charles W. Chesnutt, July 31, 1916 (copy), Document File, No. 2414738, Files of the Adjutant General's Office, War Department Records, Record Group 94, National Archives; Newton D. Baker to Woodrow Wilson, July 7, 1917 (copy), Newton D. Baker Papers, Manuscript Division, Library of Congress, Washington D.C.; *Cleveland Plain Dealer*, Aug. 3 and 7, 1917; *Ohio State Journal*, Aug. 3, 1917; Ohio Adjutant General's Department, Special Orders, 1917, No. 148, Aug. 4, 1917, and No. 155, Aug. 17, 1917, Ohio Historical Society Archives/Library.

161. *Gazette*, Sept. 8, 1917; *Cleveland Plain Dealer*, Sept. 5, 1917; *Montgomery Advertiser*, Sept. 5, 1917.

162. *Gazette*, Dec. 15, 29, 1917, May 18, 1918; Barbeau and Henri, *Unknown Soldiers*, 79; 372nd Infantry Files, World War I Organization Records, Case 22, Drawer 3, Box No. 4299, National Archives, Washington, D.C.; *Cleveland Advocate*, Dec. 15, 22, 29, 1917, Jan. 12, 1918; Ohio Adjutant General's Department, Special Orders, 1918–1919, No. 34, June 10, 1918.

163. Scott, *The Negro American in the World War*, 239.

164. War Correspondent Ralph W. Tyler, *Gazette*, Nov. 23, 1918; *Union* (Cincinnati), Nov. 23, 1918.

165. See detailed accounts of the record of the 372nd Regiment in Scott, *The Negro American in the World War*, 239–55; Williams, *Sidelights on Negro Soldiers*, 229–40; *Gazette*, March 1, 1919; *Cleveland Plain Dealer*, Feb. 23, 1919, 1, 2.

166. *Wilberforcian* 1, no. 6 (March 1919).

167. Franklin and Moss, Jr., *From Slavery to Freedom*, 374–75.

168. *Crisis* 17 (Dec. 1918): 84.

169. Letter of C. E. Dittmer, Publicity Director of the Ohio War Savings Committee, to Hon. Harry C. Smith, Nov. 9, 1918, *Gazette*, Nov. 16, 1918.

170. Scott, *The Negro American in the World War*, 116, 284.

171. W. E. B. Du Bois of the NAACP later criticized him for not telling about the military's discrimination against black soldiers in Europe. *Crisis* 18 (July 1919): 130; see William G. Jordan, *Black Newspapers and America's War for*

Democracy, 1914–1920 (Chapel Hill: University of North Carolina Press, 2001).

172. Such houses were located in Youngstown, Dayton, Cincinnati, Columbus, and Cleveland. Williams, *Sidelights on Negro Soldiers*, 88–89, 122; Scott, *The Negro American in the World War*, 387; *Gazette*, Feb. 16, 1918, Oct. 19, 1918.

173. Franklin and Moss, Jr., *From Slavery to Freedom*, 402.

174. Letter to George Myers, Dec. 21, 1918, Myers Papers.

175. Giffin, "Mobilization of Black Militiamen in World War I," 686–703; Jordan, *Black Newspapers and America's War for Democracy*, passim.

176. *Gazette*, Jan. 18, 1919.

177. James T. Patterson, *America in the Twentieth Century: A History* (New York: Harcourt, Brace Jovanovich, 1976); Nancy Cohen, *Reconstruction of American Liberalism, 1865–1914* (Chapel Hill: University of North Carolina Press, 2002).

Notes to Chapter 4

1. Osofsky, *Harlem;* Spear, *Black Chicago.*

2. Drake and Clayton, *Black Metropolis.*

3. Zane L. Miller and Patricia M. Melvin, *The Urbanization of Modern America: A Brief History* (San Diego: Harcourt, Brace Jovanovich, 1987).

4. Bureau of the Census, *Negroes in the United States 1920–1932*, 9, 62, 63.

5. Ibid., 9, 15.

6. Letter of J. E. Neal to N. B. Allen, Aug. 5, 1923, Columbus Urban League Papers, Ohio Historical Society Archives/Library, Columbus.

7. Ibid.

8. Gottlieb, "A Perspective from Pittsburgh," in *Great Migration in Historical Perspective*, ed. Trotter, Jr., 69–70.

9. *Crisis* 21 (Jan. 1921): 132; Himes, Jr., "Forty Years of Negro Life in Columbus," 149.

10. Ralph Garling Harshman, "Race Contact in Columbus, Ohio" (M.A. Thesis, The Ohio State University, 1921), 26.

11. Figures obtained from officials of the mills and employment agencies in Youngstown. *Gazette*, Dec. 9, 1922.

12. Ibid., June 9, 1923.

13. Ibid., March 8, 1924.

14. Himes, Jr., "Forty Years of Negro Life in Columbus," 152.

15. George A. Myers, "Answer to Questionnaire from [Cleveland] Chamber of Commerce Committee on Immigration and Emigration," 1926 (copy), Myers Papers.

16. *Gazette*, Oct. 29, 1927; Minutes of the Board of Trustees, Dec. 8, 1927, Urban League of Cleveland Papers, Western Reserve Historical Society Archives/Library, Cleveland, Ohio.

17. Williams, "Newcomers to the City," 18.

18. Dabney, *Colored Citizens*, 382.

19. Fairbanks, *Making Better Citizens*, 63.

20. The League added: "The houses in the suburbs [African American areas] are not so congested and are of a better type, including many more single family houses with yards and fairly good conveniences." Dabney, *Colored Citizens*, 382.

21. See Lendell Charles Ridley, "A Study of Housing Conditions Among Colored People of Columbus, Ohio" (M.A. Thesis, The Ohio State University, 1920); Hew-Yi Cheng, "A Housing Study of the Negro of the City of Columbus, Ohio" (M.A. Thesis, The Ohio State University, 1925).

22. *Gazette*, April 14, 1928.

23. Dabney, *Colored Citizens*, 383.

24. Ibid.

25. Fairbanks, *Making Better Citizens*, 63, 64.

26. Letter to James Weldon Johnson, 1925, Cleveland, Branch Files (Container 157), NAACP Papers.

27. *Gazette*, Feb. 20, 1926.

28. Dabney, *Colored Citizens*, 379; "Negro Health and Race Relations," *Cincinnati Sanitary Bulletin* 8, no. 4, Oct. 14, 1925, 1.

29. Ibid.

30. Ibid., 1, 3.

31. *Gazette*, Feb. 20, 1926.

32. Bureau of the Census, *Negroes in the United States 1920–1932*, 445, 452.

33. Dabney, *Colored Citizens*, 147, 167.

34. Ibid.

35. *Gazette*, Oct. 21, 1922.

36. Speech, Cleveland, Dec. 2, 1927, in *Gazette*, Dec. 10, 1927.

37. Kusmer, *A Ghetto Takes Shape*, 220; Dabney, *Colored Citizens*, 398.

38. Columbus Urban League, *Twenty Years of Service in Social Work for Negroes and Inter-race Relations, 1917–1937*.

39. Dabney, *Colored Citizens*, 398, 399.

40. Bureau of the Census, *Negroes in the United States 1920–1932*, 558.

41. *Census 1920: Occupations* 4: 361–362; United States Department of Commerce, Bureau of the Census, *Fifteenth Census of the United States: 1930, Population, Volume IV, Occupations By States* (Washington, D.C.: Government Printing Office, 1933) 4: 1266.

42. Ibid., 1285–86.

43. Ibid., 1281, 1288–89.

44. *Crisis* 21 (Dec. 1920): 82.

45. Ibid. 20 (Oct. 1920): 290.

46. *Gazette*, Jan. 1, 1921.

47. *Census 1930: Occupations* 4: 1282, 1285, 1289.

48. Ibid., 1285–86; *Census 1910: Occupation Statistics* 4: 549.

49. Ibid. 4: 548, 549; *Census 1920: Occupations* 4: 1083, 1086, 1089; *Census 1930: Occupations* 4: 1266, 1283, 1284, 1286, 1287, 1289, 1290.

50. Myers, "Answer to Questionnaire from [Cleveland] Chamber of Commerce Committee on Immigration and Emigration," 1926 (copy), Myers Papers. See discussions of occupational status of blacks and racial discrimination in employment in Akron and Toledo in Shirla R. McClain, "The Contributions of Blacks in Akron, 1825–1975" (Ph.D. Diss., University of Akron, 1975),

176–85 and Leroy Thomas Williams, "Black Toledo: Afro-Americans in Toledo, 1890–1930" (Ph.D. Diss., University of Toledo, 1977), 194–98.

51. Allen, "East Long Street," 14.

52. Dabney, *Colored Citizens*, 141–42.

53. Myers, "Answer to Questionnaire from [Cleveland] Chamber of Commerce Committee on Immigration and Emigration,"1926 (copy), Myers Papers.

54. Bureau of the Census, *Negroes in the United States 1920–1932*, 522.

55. Dabney, *Colored Citizens*, 190, 197–98; *Gazette*, Aug. 22, 1925; Dayton *Forum*, April 11, 1930; *Ohio Recorder* (Columbus), May 1, 1927; letter of N. B. Allen to *Columbus Daily News*, Dec. 9, 1925, Columbus Urban League Papers; *Columbus Voice*, Oct. 19, 1929; *Ohio Torch* (Columbus), Oct. 1, 1928, Jan. 18, 1930; *Springfield Informer*, Nov. 1, 1928; McClain, "Contributions of Blacks in Akron, 1925–1975," 208–9.

56. Davis, *Black Americans in Cleveland*, 203, 263, 298; Kusmer, *A Ghetto Takes Shape*, 194; "Cleveland's *Call and Post*," *Crisis* 45 (Dec. 1938): 391, 404.

57. Dabney, *Colored Citizens*, 180–82.

58. *Census 1930: Occupations* 4: 1287, 1289, 1290.

59. Dabney, *Colored Citizens*, 183.

60. Ibid., 183–85.

61. Davis, *Black Americans in Cleveland*, 163; Kusmer, *A Ghetto Takes Shape*, 123; John A. Garraty's introduction in *The Barber and the Historian: the Correspondence of George A. Myers and James Ford Rhodes, 1910–1923* (Columbus: Ohio Historical Society, 1956), 126–27.

62. Charles W. Chesnutt, "The Negro in Cleveland," *The Clevelander* 5 (Nov. 1930): 6.

63. Dabney, *Colored Citizens*, 182.

64. Kusmer, *A Ghetto Takes Shape*, 193; *Census: 1930 Occupations* 4: 1286, 1292, 1295.

65. Dabney, *Colored Citizens*, 183, 241, 310–11, 322, 382, 403.

66. *Census 1910: Occupation Statistics* 4: 549; *Census 1920: Occupations* 4: 1082, 1086, 1089; *Census 1930: Occupations* 4: 1283, 1286, 1289.

67. Bureau of the Census, *Negroes in the United States 1920–1932*, 522.

68. *Census 1920: Occupations* 4: 1082, 1086, 1089; *Census 1930: Occupations* 4: 1283, 1286, 1289.

69. Kusmer, *A Ghetto Takes Shape*, 194–95.

70. Dabney, *Colored Citizens*, 209, 237.

71. Gerber, *Black Ohio*, 315–16.

72. *Crisis* 8 (May 1914): 10; *Gazette*, Jan. 26, 1918.

73. Davis, *Black Americans in Cleveland*, 243–44, 290; Myers, "Answer to Questionnaire from [Cleveland] Chamber of Commerce Committee on Immigration and Emigration," 1926 (copy), Myers Papers; Allen, "East Long Street," 16.

74. Dabney, *Colored Citizens*, 209, 237; McClain, "Contributions of Blacks in Akron, 1925–1975," 184.

75. *Crisis* 18 (Nov. 1919): 348 and 25 (Nov. 1922): 32–33.

76. Ibid. 35 (May 1928): 161.

77. Myers, "Answer to Questionnaire from [Cleveland] Chamber of

Commerce Committee on Immigration and Emigration," 1926 (copy), Myers Papers.

78. Dabney, *Colored Citizens*, 244.

79. *Census 1920: Occupations* 4: 1082, 1086, 1089; *Census 1930: Occupations* 4: 1283, 1286, 1289.

80. Alexa B. Henderson, *Atlanta Life Insurance Company: Guardian of Black Economic Dignity* (Tuscaloosa: University of Alabama Press, 1990); Robert E. Weems Jr., *Black Business in the Black Metropolis: The Chicago Metropolitan Assurance Company, 1925–1985* (Bloomington: Indiana University Press, 1996).

81. Allen, "East Long Street," 15, 16.

82. Robert C. Kenzer, *Enterprising Southerners: Black Economic Success in North Carolina, 1865–1915* (Charlottesville, University Press of Virginia, 1997).

83. Allen, "East Long Street," 16.

84. Davis, *Black Americans in Cleveland*, 244–45; Dabney, *Colored Citizens*, 209.

85. *Census 1920: Occupations* 4: 1082, 1084, 1086, 1087, 1089, 1090, 1094, 1095, 1244, 1245, *Census 1930: Occupations* 4: 1283, 1284, 1286, 1287,1289, 1290, 1292, 1293, 1295, 1296. See Margaret Jones Clark, "The Negro Pharmacist and Physician in Columbus, Ohio" (M.A. Thesis, The Ohio State University, 1929).

86. Allen, "East Long Street," 16.

87. Myers, "Answer to Questionnaire from [Cleveland] Chamber of Commerce Committee on Immigration and Emigration," 1926 (copy), Myers Papers.

88. Chesnutt, "The Negro in Cleveland," 6.

89. Dabney, *Colored Citizens*, 142.

90. Ibid., 142–44.

91. Ibid., 141.

92. Trotter Jr., *Coal, Class, and Color*.

93. Myers, "Answer to Questionnaire from [Cleveland] Chamber of Commerce Committee on Immigration and Emigration," 1926 (copy), Myers Papers.

94. Bureau of the Census, *Religious Bodies 1916*, 570, and *Negroes in the United States 1920–1932*, 547; Dabney, *Colored Citizens*, 373; *Census 1920: Occupations* 4: 1094, 1244; *Census 1930: Occupations* 4: 1283, 1286, 1289.

95. Himes, Jr., "Forty Years of Negro Life in Columbus," 147.

96. Ibid.

97. Kusmer, *A Ghetto Takes Shape*, 207, 208.

98. Dabney, *Colored Citizens*, 377.

99. Kusmer, *A Ghetto Takes Shape*, 208.

100. Himes, Jr., "Forty Years of Negro Life in Columbus," 148.

101. Dabney, *Colored Citizens*, 279, 298–99, 373.

102. Bureau of the Census, *Religious Bodies 1916*, 570, and *Negroes in the United States 1920–1932*, 547.

103. McClain, "Contributions of Blacks in Akron, 1925–1975," 193–97; Himes, Jr., "Forty Years of Negro Life in Columbus," 148.

104. Dabney, *Colored Citizens*, 415.

105. Freemasons, Prince Hall Grand Lodge of Ohio, Official Program of the

77th Annual Communication of the Most Worshipful Grand Lodge, F. and A. M. . . . Newark, Ohio, August 15, 16, 17, 18, and 19, 1926, PA, Box 714, 3; Freemasons, Prince Hall Grand Lodge of Ohio, Souvenir Programme of the Diamond Jubilee Celebration of the Most Worshipful Grand Lodge, F. and A. M. . . . to be held in Cleveland, Ohio, Aug. 10 to 15, 1924, PA, Box 714, 6; Freemasons, Prince Hall Grand Lodge of Ohio, Souvenir Programme. 76th Annual Communication of the Most Worshipful Grand Lodge, F. and A. M. . . . Canton, Ohio, August 16–22, 1925, PA, Box 714, 2, (Manuscript Department), Ohio Historical Society Archives/Library, Columbus, Ohio.

106. Davis, *Black Americans in Cleveland*, 213; Allen, "East Long Street," 14; and biographical sketches in Dabney, *Colored Citizens*, 304 and passim.

107. Allen, "East Long Street," 14; Dabney, *Colored Citizens*, 359.

108. Ibid., 415.

109. Ibid., 302, 331.

110. Bureau of the Census, *Negroes in the United States 1920–1932*, 9, 62, 63.

Notes to Chapter 5

1. *Cincinnati Enquirer*, April 27, 1924, 6, May 5, 1924, 6.

2. Fanny Fullerton Miller to Mr. Maurer, Friday, 26th 1922 (copy), Columbus Urban League Papers.

3. Jackson, *Ku Klux Klan in the City*, 237, 239, passim; Embry Bernard Howson, "The Ku Klux Klan in Ohio after World War I" (M.A. Thesis, The Ohio State University, 1951), 21–32.

4. United States Department of Commerce, Bureau of the Census, *Fifteenth Census of the United States: 1930 Population, Volume III, Part 2, Reports by States Showing the Composition and Characteristics of the Population for Counties, Cities and Townships or Other Minor Civil Divisions, Montana-Wyoming* (Washington, D.C.: United States Government Printing Office, 1932) 3: 457.

5. Jackson, *Ku Klux Klan in the City*, 9–23.

6. William D. Jenkins, *Steel Valley Klan: The Ku Klux Klan in Ohio's Mahoning Valley* (Kent: Kent State University Press, 1990); Leonard J. Moore, *Citizen Klansmen: The Ku Klux Klan in Indiana, 1921–1928* (Chapel Hill: University of North Carolina Press, 1991); M. William Lutholtz, *Grand Dragon: D. C. Stephenson and the Ku Klux Klan in Indiana* (West Lafayette: Purdue University Press, 1991); Richard K. Tucker, *The Dragon and the Cross: The Rise and Fall of the Ku Klux Klan in Middle America* (Hamden: Archon, 1991).

7. *Gazette*, Jan. 5, 1924.

8. *New York Times*, April 11, 1926, section two, 19.

9. Ibid., March 22, 1924, 12; letter of D. D. Dancy of Youngstown to Harry C. Smith, March 24, 1924, *Gazette*, March 29, 1924, April 5, 1924.

10. *New York Times*, Nov. 6, 1923, 3, Nov. 7, 1923, 3, Nov. 8, 1923, 1; *Akron Beacon-Journal*, Nov. 7, 1923, 1; Howson, "Ku Klux Klan in Ohio After World War I," 71–72.

11. *Gazette*, Nov. 15, 1924.

12. *Columbus Citizen*, Feb. 26, 1925, in Howson, "Ku Klux Klan in Ohio After World War I," 74.

13. Ibid.

14. *Crisis* 29 (April 1925): 252.

15. Howson, "Ku Klux Klan in Ohio after World War I," 74–76.

16. *Gazette*, Feb. 24, 1923.

17. *Urbana and Champaign County*, compiled by Workers of the Writer's Program of the Works Progress Administration in the State of Ohio (Urbana, OH: Gaumer Publishing Company, [c. 1942]), 106.

18. *Census 1920: Population*, 3: 792.

19. Howson, "Ku Klux Klan in Ohio after World War I," 72, 95–96; Jackson, *Ku Klux Klan in the City*, 157–60.

20. *Springfield and Clark County, Ohio*, compiled by the Workers of the Writer's Program of the Works Progress Administration in the State of Ohio (Springfield, OH: Springfield Tribune Printing Company, [1941]), 55.

21. *Gazette*, March 26, 1921.

22. Ibid.

23. Ibid.

24. Ibid.; *New York Times*, March 12, 1921, 1, March 13, 1921, 13. Coincidently, a major race riot occurred just a few months later in Tulsa, Oklahoma. Scott Ellsworth, *Death in a Promised Land: The Tulsa Race Riot of 1921* (Baton Rouge: Louisiana State University, 1982); Alfred L. Brophy, *Reconstructing the Dreamland: The Tulsa Riot of 1921: Race, Reparations, and Reconciliation* (New York: Oxford University Press, 2002).

25. *Gazette*, Sept. 3, 17, 1921.

26. Ibid., Oct. 8, 1927.

27. Ibid.

28. Ibid., March 30, 1929.

29. Harshman, "Race Contact in Columbus, Ohio," 46.

30. Prather J. Hauser, "Treatment by Columbus Daily Newspapers of News Regarding the Negro" (M.A. Thesis, The Ohio State University, 1925), 9, 51; see Sebron Basil Billingslea, "The Negro, 1901–1920, as Portrayed in the *Cincinnati Enquirer*" (M.A. Thesis, Howard University, 1950).

31. Kusmer, *A Ghetto Takes Shape*, 162–63; Dabney, *Colored Citizens*, 145.

32. Himes, Jr., "Forty Years of Negro Life in Columbus," 141–42; Mark, *Negroes in Columbus*, 16–26.

33. *Census 1930: Population* 3: 535, 536.

34. Valuable references to the literature about the impact of basic urbanization phenomena on black ghetto formation and an excellent discussion of an Ohio example are found in Taylor, Jr., "Black Ghetto-Slum Formation in Cincinnati," in *Race and the City*, ed. Taylor, Jr., 156–92.

35. Ibid., 163.

36. *Cincinnati: A Guide to the Queen City*, 224–25.

37. Mark, *Negroes in Columbus*, 19–20.

38. Kusmer, *A Ghetto Takes Shape*, 163–165.

39. Dabney, *Colored Citizens*, 145.

40. *Cincinnati: A Guide to the Queen City*, 225.

41. Allen, "East Long Street," 13.

42. *Census 1920: Population*, 1920 3: 799–800, 801, 803–804, *Census 1930: Population* 3: 535, 536.

43. Ibid., 536.

44. Harshman, "Race Contact in Columbus, Ohio," 21–22, 24.

45. Allen, "East Long Street," 13.

46. Ibid., 14.

47. Kusmer, A Ghetto Takes Shape, 165, 212–14.

48. Gazette, Sept. 26, 1925.

49. Ibid., Oct. 17, 1925.

50. Cleveland Plain Dealer, Sept. 27, 1925, 1 C; Gazette, Oct. 3, 1925; Cleveland Plain Dealer, October 29, 1925 (clipping), Cleveland, Branch Files (Container 158), NAACP Papers.

51. Dayton correspondent, Gazette, March 5, 1927.

52. Ibid., March 19, 1927.

53. Dayton correspondent, ibid., July 23, 1927.

54. Ibid.

55. "Resume of Facts in Case of Intimidation of Mr. and Mrs. Arthur Hill," enclosed in letter of Harry E. Davis to James Weldon Johnson, Sept. 15, 1924, Cleveland, Branch Files (Container 157), NAACP Papers; Crisis 29 (Nov. 1924): 20.

56. Gazette, Oct. 17, 1925.

57. Ibid., Feb. 6, 1926.

58. Ibid., Jan. 16, 1926.

59. Ibid., Feb. 6, 1926; letter of Harry E. Davis to Walter White, Feb. 8, 1926, Cleveland, Branch Files (Container 157), NAACP Papers.

60. Cleveland Plain Dealer, July 7, 1926, 1; letter of Clayborne George to Walter White, July 20, 1926, Cleveland, Branch Files (Container 157), NAACP Papers.

61. Letter of Mrs. Mable Clark to James Weldon Johnson, July 6, 1926, ibid.

62. Gazette, July 9, 1927.

63. Ibid., Sept. 21, 1929; Williams, "Black Toledo: Afro-Americans in Toledo, 1890–1930," 261–62.

64. Carlton H. Mann, Cleveland Public Schools, Division of Reference and Research, Gazette, June 21, 1924.

65. Letter of Charles W. White to R. G. Jones, March 22, 1927 (copy), Myers Papers.

66. Kusmer, A Ghetto Takes Shape, 183.

67. Proceedings Second Annual Conference of Ohio N.A.A.C.P. Branches, Sept. 25, 26, 27, 1931, Columbus, Ohio, Ohio State Conference, Branch Files (Container 151), NAACP Papers.

68. Krawcheck, "The Negro in Cleveland."

69. Harshman, "Race Contact in Columbus, Ohio," 15.

70. Allen, "East Long Street," 14.

71. Himes, Jr., "Forty Years of Negro Life in Columbus," 146.

72. Census 1920: Occupations 4: 1089, Census 1930: Occupations 4: 1289.

73. Census 1920: Occupations 4: 1082, Census 1930: Occupations 4: 1283.

74. Dabney, Colored Citizens, 110, 111,235, 244, 355; Nicholes, "Educational Development of Blacks in Cincinnati," 141, 142; Jennie D. Porter, "The Problem of Negro Education in Northern and Border Cities" (Ph.D. Diss., University of Cincinnati, 1928), 134.

75. Board of Education of School District of City of Dayton et al., v. The State, ex rel. Reese, *Ohio State Reports* 114 (1925): 188–89; Dayton correspondent, *Gazette*, May 16, 1925.

76. Dayton correspondent, ibid., May 22, 1926.

77. *Census 1930: Population* 3: 496, 498; Dabney, *Colored Citizens*, 109.

78. *Crisis* 29 (Nov. 1924): 20; *Gazette*, April 4, 1925; letter of Harry E. Davis to James Weldon Johnson, Sept. 5, 1925, Cleveland, Branch Files (Container 157), NAACP Papers; letter of R. G. Jones to Charles W. White, March 30, 1927 (copy), Myers Papers.

79. *Gazette*, Oct. 16, 1926, May 4, 1929, Nov. 16, 1929.

80. Pierce was an active member of the Cleveland NAACP Branch. David H. Pierce, "White Children and Their Colored Schoolmates," *Crisis* 26 (June 1923): 63.

81. Ibid.

82. Black students comprised somewhat less than 3 percent of the total enrollment of Pierce's school. Ibid., 64.

83. Dabney, *Colored Citizens*, 149.

84. Harshman, "Race Contact in Columbus, Ohio," 17.

85. Ibid., 15–16.

86. Letter of Charles W. White to R. G. Jones, March 22, 1927 (copy), Myers Papers.

87. Dabney, *Colored Citizens*, 235.

88. List compiled by the author from *Crisis*, August educational issues for the years 1920–1929.

89. *Crisis* 20 (July 1920): 147.

90. Ibid. 28 (July 1924): 110.

91. Ibid. 35 (Dec. 1928): 412.

92. Ibid. 37 (Aug. 1930): 264

93. Telegram of George E. Rightmire to Walter White, Nov. 5, 1930, Columbus, Branch Files (Container 162), NAACP Papers.

94. McClain, "Contributions of Blacks in Akron, 1825–1975," 191–92.

95. *Crisis* 35 (Aug. 1928): 260.

96. Statistics compiled by the author from *Crisis*, August educational issues for the years 1920–1929.

97. Dabney, *Colored Citizens*, 235, 419; see Porter, "The Problem of Negro Education in Northern and Border Cities."

98. Dabney, *Colored Citizens*, 248.

99. Kusmer, *A Ghetto Takes Shape*, 209; Dabney, *Colored Citizens*, 285, 372.

100. Bureau of the Census, *Negroes in the United States 1920–1932*, 547.

101. Kusmer, *A Ghetto Takes Shape*, 209; *Gazette*, April 15, 1922; Davis, *Black Americans in Cleveland*, 254; Dabney, *Colored Citizens*, 372, 375–76.

102. Bureau of the Census, *Negroes in the United States 1920–1932*, 547; Dabney, *Colored Citizens*, 300.

103. Ibid., 231–33.

104. Ibid., 257, 302; Davis, *Black Americans in Cleveland*, 254; Williams, "Black Toledo: Afro-Americans in Toledo, 1890–1930," 255–56.

105. See Chapter 4, endnotes 104–109.

106. Dabney, *Colored Citizens*, 145–146.

107. Ibid., 187–88.

108. *Union,* May 28, 1921.

109. Harshman, "Race Contact in Columbus, Ohio," 30–31.

110. Allen, "East Long Street," 14.

111. Harshman, "Race Contact in Columbus, Ohio," 32.

112. Ibid., 32–33.

113. Ibid., 35.

114. Ibid., 35–37.

115. Ibid., 40.

116. *Crisis* 20 (Aug. 1920): 196.

117. See letter of Mrs. J. F. Burrell to Nimrod Allen, Sept. 17, 1926, Columbus Urban League Papers.

118. Letter of Harry E. Davis to Walter White, Sept. 19, 1929, Cleveland, Branch Files (Container 157), NAACP Papers.

119. *Gazette,* March 3, 1923.

120. Ibid., June 5, 1926.

121. Ibid., Dec. 29, 1928, Jan. 26, 1929.

122. Ibid., Nov. 9, 1929, Feb. 13, 1926.

123. Ibid., June 16, 1923, April 19, 1924, May 24, 1924.

124. Letters of George A. Myers to W. R. Hopkins, City Manager, Aug. 9, 1927 (copy), Thomas W. Fleming to George A. Myers, Aug. 11, 1927, Edwin D. Barry, Director of Public Safety, to George A. Myers, April 20, 1928, Myers Papers.

125. *Gazette,* Aug. 11, 1928.

126. *The Black and White Chronicle* (Akron, Ohio), May 6, 1927 (clipping), Akron, Branch Files (Container 153), NAACP Papers; The National Association for the Advancement of Colored People, Akron Branch, Annual Report, 1928, ibid.; press release, Akron, Ohio, Nov. 30, 1928, ibid.

127. *Crisis* 19 (March 1920): 247.

128. Ibid. 19 (Feb. 1920): 213.

Notes to Chapter 6

1. Weiss, *National Urban League,* 112, 113, 164; McClain, "Contributions of Blacks in Akron, 1825–1975," 200–202.

2. "Columbus Urban League: An Inventory of Its Papers," 6.

3. Columbus Urban League, "Twenty Years of Service in the Field of Social Work for Negroes and Inter-race Relations, 1917–1937."

4. Weiss, *National Urban League,* 190.

5. *Crisis* 27 (Dec. 1923): 85.

6. Kornbluh, "James Hathaway Robinson," in *Race and the City,* ed. Taylor, Jr., 224.

7. Dabney, *Colored Citizens,* 222.

8. Ibid., 226–67; see typescript report: "Agencies at Work among Colored People in Cincinnati and Hamilton County, 1927" (Box 58, Folder 1), Urban League of Greater Cincinnati Papers.

9. Marian J. Morton, "'Go and Sin No More': Maternity Homes in

Cleveland, 1869–1936," *Ohio History* 93 (Summer-Autumn 1984): 117; Dabney, *Colored Citizens*, 218–19.

10. Ibid., 222.

11. Kusmer, *A Ghetto Takes Shape*, 257; Minutes of the Board of Trustees, Feb. 8, May 10, 1927, Phillis Wheatley Association (Cleveland, Ohio) Records, Manuscript Collections, Western Reserve Historical Society Archives/Library, Cleveland, Ohio.

12. Myers, "Answer to Questionnaire from [Cleveland] Chamber of Commerce Committee on Immigration and Emigration," 1926 (copy), Myers Papers; also see Annual Report for the Year 1923, The Phillis Wheatley Association, Cleveland, Ohio Historical Society Archives/Library; a summary of the 1924 annual report of the Association, in *Gazette*, Jan. 17, 1925.

13. Myers, "Answer to Questionnaire from [Cleveland] Chamber of Commerce Committee on Immigration and Emigration," 1926 (copy), Myers Papers.

14. *Crisis* 21 (Dec. 1920): 82.

15. *Gazette*, March 8, 1924.

16. Weiss, *National Urban League*, 181, 189, 352, fn. 48.

17. Dabney, *Colored Citizens*, 232, 355, 396–97; Morton, "'Go and Sin No More': Maternity Homes in Cleveland, 1869–1936," 134.

18. Boynton, "Contested Terrain: The Struggle over Gender Norms for Black Working-Class Women in Cleveland's Phillis Wheatley Association, 1920–1950," 12.

19. Ibid., 11; Phillips, *Alabama North*, 88–96.

20. Himes, Jr., "Forty Years of Negro Life in Columbus," 149; McWilliams, *Columbus Illustrated Record 1919–1920*, 83.

21. Dabney, *Colored Citizens*, 210, 217, 397

22. Carter, "Housing the Women Who Toiled: Planned Residences for Single Women, Cincinnati 1860–1960," 55–56, 67.

23. Boynton, "Contested Terrain: The Struggle over Gender Norms for Black Working-Class Women in Cleveland's Phillis Wheatley Association, 1920–1950," 12.

24. Taylor, Jr., "Black Ghetto-Slum Formation in Cincinnati," in *Race and the City*, ed. Taylor, Jr., 157–58, 171, 175–78; Fairbanks, "Cincinnati Blacks and the Irony of Low-Income Housing Reform," in ibid., 197–200.

25. "From information furnished by Bleecker Marquette, Executive Secretary, Cincinnati Better Housing League," in Dabney, *Colored Citizens*, 382–83; "Model Homes Company Report, Feb. 3, 1925, in ibid., 389–90.

26. Taylor, Jr., "Black Ghetto-Slum Formation in Cincinnati" and Fairbanks, "Cincinnati Blacks and the Irony of Low-Income Housing Reform," in *Race and the City*, ed. Taylor, Jr., 157, 200–201.

27. Dabney, *Colored Citizens*, 226, 411; "From information furnished by Bleecker Marquette, Executive Secretary, Cincinnati Better Housing League," in ibid., 383.

28. Ibid., 226.

29. Kristie Lindenmeyer, "Saving Mothers and Babies: The Sheppard-Towner Act in Ohio, 1921–1929," *Ohio History* 99 (Summer-Autumn 1990): 124–25; Dabney, *Colored Citizens*, 379.

30. Ibid., 379; printed program: *National Negro Health Week as Observed in Cincinnati, Ohio, April 5th to April 12th, 1925 by agencies co-operating through the Negro Civic Welfare Association, Department of the Community Chest and Council of Social Agencies* (Box 15, Folder 6), Urban League of Greater Cincinnati Papers.

31. For examples of scholarly interest in black female health issues in this period see: Darlene Clark Hine, *Black Women in White: Racial Conflict and Cooperation in the Nursing Profession, 1890–1950* (Bloomington: Indiana University Press, 1989); Jamie Hart, "African Americans, Health Care, and the Reproductive Freedom Movement in Detroit, 1918–1945" (Ph.D. Diss., University of Michigan, 1998).

32. Dabney, *Colored Citizens*, 379.

33. Lindenmeyer, "Saving Mothers and Babies: The Sheppard-Towner Act in Ohio, 1921–1929," 105, 125.

34. Dabney, Colored Citizens, 380, 381; Lindenmeyer, "Saving Mothers and Babies: The Sheppard-Towner Act in Ohio, 1921–1929," 123, 124.

35. Dabney, *Colored Citizens*, 218–19.

36. Morton, "'Go and Sin No More': Maternity Homes in Cleveland, 1869–1936," 117, 133, 142–43; Katherine G. Aiken, *Harnessing the Power of Motherhood: The National Florence Crittenton Mission, 1883–1925* (Knoxville: University of Tennessee Press, 1998).

37. Morton, "'Go and Sin No More': Maternity Homes in Cleveland, 1869–1936," 133–35.

38. *Gazette*, April 14, 1928.

39. Steven J. Hoffman, "Progressive Public Health Administration in the Jim Crow South: A Case Study of Richmond, Virginia, 1907–1920," *Journal of Social History* 35 (Fall 2001): 175–94.

40. *Gazette*, April 28, 1928.

41. *Cleveland Plain Dealer*, in ibid., May 26, 1928.

42. Ibid.

43. Ibid., July 7, 1928.

44. Ibid., July 14, 28, 1928.

45. Columbus Urban League, *Twenty Years of Service in the Field of Social Work for Negroes and Inter-race Relations, 1917–1937.*

46. Cincinnati correspondent, *Gazette*, April 14, 1923.

47. Ibid., Oct. 21, 1922, Dec. 10, 1927.

48. William M. Dulaney, "Black and Blue in America: The Black Policemen of Columbus, Ohio, 1895–1974" (M.A. Thesis, The Ohio State University, 1974), 37, 38, 39; *Census 1920: Occupations* 4: 1082, 1086, 1089, 1244, *Census 1930: Occupations* 4: 1283, 1286, 1289, 1295; Dabney, *Colored Citizens*, 139–40; W. Marvin Dulaney, *Black Police in America* (Bloomington: Indiana University Press, 1996).

49. Dabney, *Colored Citizens*, 226, 395–96, 413.

50. Columbus Urban League, *Twenty Years of Service in the Field of Social Work for Negroes and Inter-race Relations, 1917–1937*, 44–45, 46; Dulaney, "Black and Blue in America: The Black Policemen of Columbus, Ohio," 44; Myron E. Morehead, "An Evaluation of the Friendly Service Bureau in Its Crime Prevention among Negroes in the City of Columbus, Ohio, 1921–1930" (M.A. Thesis, The Ohio State University, 1935), passim. Adolescent delinquency is an ongoing scholarly interest. See Carlo J. Corea, "Racial Delinquency: Italian-American and

African-American Adolescent Identity and the Delinquency Experience, 1915–1932" (Ph.D. Diss., State University of New York, Stony Brook, 2001).

51. Current scholarly works illuminating the place of middle class values in African American urban life in this period include: Victoria W. Wolcott, *Remaking Respectability: African American Women in Interwar Detroit* (Chapel Hill, University of North Carolina Press, 2001); Davarian L. Baldwin, "Chicago's New Negroes: Race, Class, and Respectability in the Midwestern Black Metropolis, 1915–1935" (Ph.D. Diss., New York University, 2002); Toure Reed, "'Helping negroes to help themselves': Middle Class Reform and the Politics of Racial Order, 1910–1950 (Ph.D. Diss., Columbia University, 2002).

52. Weiss, *National Urban League*, 117–24, 171–73.

53. Dabney, *Colored Citizens*, 146.

54. *Gazette*, Oct. 21, 1922.

55. Allen, "East Long Street," 16.

56. Weiss, *National Urban League*, 172.

57. Dabney, *Colored Citizens*, 226.

58. Weiss, *National Urban League*, 172.

59. *Crisis* 27 (Dec. 1923): 85.

60. Columbus Urban League, *Twenty Years of Service in the Field of Social Work for Negroes and Inter-race Relations, 1917–1937.*

61. Kusmer, *A Ghetto Takes Shape*, 265–66.

62. Ibid.

63. Dabney, *Colored Citizens*, 210, 211, 395.

64. *Gazette*, March 26, 1921; McClain, "Contributions of Blacks in Akron, 1825–1975," 144, 199–200.

65. Dabney, *Colored Citizens*, 211.

66. Gerber, *Black Ohio*, 437–38.

67. Ibid., 439.

68. Dabney, *Colored Citizens*, 299, 395.

69. Kusmer, *A Ghetto Takes Shape*, 253.

70. Gerber, *Black Ohio*, 439; Kusmer, *A Ghetto Takes Shape*, 253.

71. Dabney, *Colored Citizens*, 232.

72. Gerber, *Black Ohio*, 439–40.

73. Dabney, *Colored Citizens*, 172.

74. Ibid., 173.

75. Ibid., 172–73.

76. Gerber, *Black Ohio*, 451.

77. Dabney, *Colored Citizens*, 235–36, 243–44, 395.

78. Williams, "Black Toledo: Afro-Americans in Toledo, 1890–1930," 250–53.

79. Dabney, *Colored Citizens*, 395.

Notes to Chapter 7

1. For the role of professionalism elsewhere, see: Christopher R. Reed, *The Chicago NAACP and the Rise of Black Professional Leadership, 1910–1966* (Bloomington: Indiana University Press, 1997).

2. Kusmer, *A Ghetto Takes Shape*, 261.

3. McWilliams, *Columbus Illustrated Record 1919–1920*, 103.

4. August Meier and Elliott Rudwick, "Early Boycotts of Segregated Schools: The Case of Springfield, Ohio, 1922–23," *American Quarterly* 20, no. 4 (Winter 1968): 750.

5. Dabney, *Colored Citizens*, 253, 303, 410; Gerber, *Black Ohio*, 466; letter of Courtland Lewis to R. W. Bagnall, Dec. 10, 1924, Cincinnati, Branch Files (Container 155), NAACP Papers; *Gazette*, April 4, 1925.

6. Trotter, Jr., *Coal, Class, and Color*.

7. Kusmer, *A Ghetto Takes Shape*, 262.

8. Dabney, *Colored Citizens*, 206, 252.

9. Kusmer, *A Ghetto Takes Shape*, 263.

10. *Crisis* 18 (May 1919): 14.

11. Kusmer, *A Ghetto Takes Shape*, 263.

12. Williams, "Black Toledo: Afro-Americans in Toledo, 1890–1930," 221–23.

13. *Crisis* 19 (March 1920): 247.

14. Ibid., 249, and 26 (May 1923): 24; *Gazette*, Feb. 13, 1926.

15. Report of Akron, Ohio Branch N.A.A.C.P., June 18, 1922, Akron, Branch Files (Container 153), NAACP Papers; The National Association for the Advancement of Colored People, Akron Branch, Annual Report, 1928, ibid.

16. *Gazette*, March 7, 14, 1925; letter of N. B. Allen to Dr. Herbert A. Miller, Feb. 26, 1925, Columbus Urban League Papers.

17. See the Ohio, Branch Files, NAACP Papers.

18. Dabney, *Colored Citizens*, 188.

19. *Gazette*, Jan. 6, 1923.

20. Kusmer, *A Ghetto Takes Shape*, 261.

21. *Gazette*, Jan. 16, 1926.

22. Ibid., May 15, 29, 1926, July 10, 1926.

23. Ibid., April 2, 1927.

24. Conclusion drawn from a survey of 1920s records in Ohio, Branch Files, NAACP Papers.

25. Davis, *Black Americans in Cleveland*, 319.

26. Kusmer, *A Ghetto Takes Shape*, 262.

27. Letter of John H. Bristor, Clerk, Board of Education, Mansfield, Ohio, to John H. Davis, President, Good Citizenship League, Aug. 26, 1925 (copy) in Charles W. White and Clayborne George to W. T. Andrews, Special Legal Assistant, N.A.A.C.P., Report of Investigation, Mansfield, Ohio School Situation, May 22, 1931, Mansfield, Branch Files (Container 165), NAACP Papers.

28. Kusmer, *A Ghetto Takes Shape*, 262.

29. Davis, *Black Americans in Cleveland*, 228.

30. Letter of Charles W. White to James Weldon Johnson, July 23, 1928, Cleveland, Branch Files (Container 158), NAACP Papers.

31. Davis, *Black Americans in Cleveland*, 232.

32. *Gazette*, May 26, 1923.

33. For example, the involvement of the national headquarters in the

Springfield Fulton School issue was exceptional. Letter of Robert W. Bagnall to Sully Jaymes, March 17, 1923 (copy), Springfield, Branch Files (Container 167), NAACP Papers.

34. Franklin and Moss, Jr., *From Slavery to Freedom*, 392–94.

35. Russell H. Davis, *Memorable Negroes in Cleveland's Past* (Cleveland: Western Reserve Historical Society, 1969), 28–33; Francis P. Weisenburger, "William S. Scarborough, Scholarship, The Negro, Religion, and Politics," *Ohio History* 52, no. 1 (Jan. 1963): passim; Dabney, *Colored Citizens*, 360; Gerber, *Black Ohio*, 345, 367, 400–403, 460.

36. *Gazette*, June 11, 1921, Nov. 29, 1924; Weisenburger, "William S. Scarborough, Scholarship, The Negro, Religion, and Politics," 50; Davis, *Memorable Negroes in Cleveland's Past*, 28–33.

37. Ibid., 28.

38. Report of the Cincinnati Branch N.A.A.C.P. for the Conference Year July 1, 1920, to July 1, 1921, Cincinnati, Branch Files (Container 155), NAACP Papers.

39. Ibid; Jackson, *Ku Klux Klan and the City*, 164–65.

40. *Gazette*, Aug. 6, 27, 1921.

41. Ibid., Sept. 3, 1921.

42. Ibid., March 3, 1923, June 6, 1926, July 3, 1926; *New York Times*, Oct. 25, 1924, 14, June 23, 1926, 2; Jackson, *Ku Klux Klan and the City*, 166

43. Report of Akron, Ohio Branch N.A.A.C.P., June 18, 1922, Akron, Branch Files (Container 153), NAACP Papers; *Akron Beacon-Journal*, May 23–25, 1922 in Howson, "Ku Klux Klan in Ohio after World War I," 33.

44. *Ohio House Journal* 111 (1925): 152; *Gazette*, Feb. 21, 1925; *Crisis* 29 (April 1925): 252.

45. *Gazette*, Feb. 21, 1925.

46. Ibid., March 7, 1925.

47. *Ohio House Journal* 111 (1925): 172.

48. *Gazette*, March 7, 14, 1925; letter of N. B. Allen to Dr. Herbert A. Miller, Feb. 26, 1925, Columbus Urban League Papers; Dabney, *Colored Citizens*, 206–7.

49. Telegram of Samuel T. Kelly to Hon. Justin W. Harding, March 2, 1925 (copy), Akron, Branch Files (Container 153), NAACP Papers.

50. *Gazette*, March 14, 1925; letter of Harry E. Davis to James Weldon Johnson, July 15, 1926, Cleveland, Branch Files (Container 157), NAACP Papers.

51. Howson, "Ku Klux Klan in Ohio after World War I," 72, 95–96; Jackson, *Ku Klux Klan and the City*, 159–60, 251–52.

52. *Union*, May 28, 1921.

53. *Crisis* 20 (Aug. 1920): 196.

54. Ibid. 19 (Feb. 1920): 213.

55. *Gazette*, June 4, 11, 1921.

56. Ibid., July 10, 1920, Oct. 7, 1922, July 25, 1925, Aug. 22, 1925, Sept. 5, 1925, Oct. 3, 1925, Sept. 22, 1928, Nov. 10, 1928, Sept. 21, 1929.

57. Kusmer, *A Ghetto Takes Shape*, 263.

58. Letter to Harry C. Smith, Sept. 4, 1926, *Gazette*, Sept. 11, 1926.

59. Letter to Harry C. Smith, Jan. 25, 1928, ibid., Feb. 4, 1928.

60. Kusmer, *A Ghetto Takes Shape*, 263.

61. *Gazette*, June 16, 1923, April 19, 1924, May 24, 1924.

62. Letters of George A. Myers to W. R. Hopkins, City Manager, Aug. 9, 1927 (copy), Thomas W. Fleming to George A. Myers, Aug. 11, 1927, Edwin D. Barry, Director of Public Safety, to George A. Myers, April 20, 1928, Myers Papers.

63. *Crisis* 19 (March 1920): 247.

64. *Black and White Chronicle* (Akron, Ohio), May 6, 1927 (clipping), Akron, Branch Files (Container 153), NAACP Papers; The National Association for the Advancement of Colored People, Akron Branch, Annual Report, 1928, ibid.; press release, Akron, Ohio, Nov. 30, 1928, ibid.

65. Ibid.

66. Dabney, *Colored Citizens*, 205.

67. Ibid.

68. Harshman, "Race Contact in Columbus, Ohio," 46; Hauser, "Treatment by Columbus Daily Newspapers of News Regarding the Negro," 9, 51.

69. *Gazette*, Nov. 21, 1914, Jan. 20, 1917, April 21, 1917, Jan. 11, 1918, March 22, 1919.

70. Ibid., Oct. 11, 1919.

71. Harry C. Smith to Eric C. Hopwood, Nov. 1, 1913, in *Crisis* 7 (Jan. 1914): 126–127.

72. Letter of Eric C. Hopwood to Harry C. Smith, Nov. 6, 1913, in ibid. 7 (Jan. 1914): 127.

73. Letter of Eric C. Hopwood to Harry C. Smith, *Gazette*, Jan. 11, 1919.

74. Letter of George A. Myers to Paul Bellamy, Nov. 13, 1929 (copy), Myers Papers.

75. Letter to George A. Myers, Nov. 14, 1929, ibid.

76. *Crisis* 19 (March 1920): 249 and 26 (May 1923): 24.

77. *Gazette*, Feb. 13, 1926.

78. Ibid., March 7, 21, 1925.

79. Letter of Charles W. White to R. G. Jones, March 22, 1927 (copy), Myers Papers.

80. Letter of R. G. Jones to Charles W. White, March 30, 1927 (copy), ibid. See letter of R. G. Jones to George A. Myers, March 23, 1927, ibid.

81. Blacks in Cleveland, however, were wary of discrimination in neighboring Shaker Heights' schools. *Gazette*, May 26, 1928, Oct. 24, 31, 1925, Nov. 14, 1925, June 19, 1926; letter of Harry E. Davis to James Weldon Johnson, Oct. 30, 1925, Cleveland, Branch Files (Container 157), NAACP Papers; *The Cleveland Call*, Dec. 12, 1925, (clipping), in ibid.

82. Letter of Harry E. Davis to James Weldon Johnson, Sept. 5, 1925, ibid.

83. Ibid.

84. Charles W. White and Clayborne George to W. T. Andrews, Special Legal Assistant, N.A.A.C.P., Report of Investigation, Mansfield, Ohio School Situation, May 22, 1931, 3, Mansfield, Ohio, Branch Files (Container 165), NAACP Papers.

85. Letter of John H. Bristor, Clerk, Board of Education, Mansfield, Ohio, to John H. Davis, President, Good Citizenship League, Aug. 26, 1925 (copy) in Charles W. White and Clayborne George to W. T. Andrews, Special Legal Assistant, N.A.A.C.P., Report of Investigation, Mansfield, Ohio School Situation, May 22, 1931, Exhibit B., ibid.

86. Letter to B. Harrison Fisher, Aug. 14, 1926 (copy), in Charles W. White and Clayborne George to W. T. Andrews, Special Legal Assistant, N.A.A.C.P., Report of Investigation, Mansfield, Ohio School Situation, May 22, 1931, Exhibit A, ibid.

87. Ibid.

88. Ibid.

89. *Census 1910: Population* 3: 421, *Census 1920: Population* 3: 785, *Census 1930: Population* 3: 493.

90. Charles W. White and Clayborne George to W. T. Andrews, Special Legal Assistant, N.A.A.C.P., Report of Investigation, Mansfield, Ohio School Situation, May 22, 1931, 1, 2, 7, Mansfield, Ohio, Branch Files (Container 165), NAACP Papers.

91. Ibid., 3, 5–6.

92. Ibid., 8.

93. Ibid., 5

94. Ibid., 6.

95. Ibid., 5, 6, 7.

96. Ibid., 4.

97. Ibid., 8.

98. Ibid., 4, 7.

99. Ibid., 8.

100. Ibid., 1, 4.

101. Letter of Courtland Lewis to R. W. Bagnall, Dec. 10, 1924, Cincinnati, Branch Files (Container 155), NAACP Papers. Lewis was Secretary of the Cincinnati NAACP. *Gazette*, April 4, 1925.

102. Report of Assistant Secretary Bagnall to the national headquarters of the NAACP, in ibid., Feb. 14, 1925; Dayton correspondent, ibid., Sept. 13, 20, 27, 1924, Oct. 11, 1924; *Crisis* 29 (Nov. 1924): 20.

103. Board of Education of School District of City of Dayton et al., v. The State, ex rel. Reese, *Ohio State Reports* 114 (1925): 188–89. Dayton correspondent, *Gazette*, May 16, 1925.

104. Dayton correspondent, ibid., Oct. 11, 1924.

105. Report of Assistant Secretary Bagnall to the national headquarters of the NAACP, in ibid, Feb. 14, 1925, Dayton correspondent, ibid., Jan. 24, 1925.

106. Dayton correspondent, ibid., May 16, 1925.

107. Report of Assistant Secretary Bagnall to the national headquarters of the NAACP, in ibid, Feb. 14, 1925, ibid., Jan. 24, 1925, May 16, 1925, June 20, 1925.

108. *Dayton News*, July 4, 1925, 9; *Gazette*, July 11, 1925.

109. Board of Education of School District of City of Dayton et al., v. The State, ex rel. Reese, *Ohio State Reports* 114 (1925): 188–89.

110. Dayton correspondent, *Gazette*, May 22, 1926.

111. *Census 1920: Population* 3: 806; Meier and Rudwick, "Early Boycotts of Segregated Schools: The Case of Springfield, Ohio, 1922–23," 746–51, 756–57.

112. Ibid., 747, 757.

113. *Gazette*, Sept. 16, 1922, Feb. 2, 1924; *Crisis* 26 (May 1923): 25.

114. *Gazette*, Sept. 16, 1922, Feb. 2, 1924; *Crisis* 26 (May 1923): 25; Meier and Rudwick, "Early Boycotts of Segregated Schools: The Case of Springfield, Ohio, 1922–23," 754, 756.

115. Ibid., 748–49, 751.

116. Ibid., 749, 750, 752.

117. Telegram of George W. Daniels to W. E. B. Du Bois, March 16, 1922, letters of Robert W. Bagnall to George W. Daniels, March 18, 1922 (copy), Robert W. Bagnall to Sully Jaymes, March 18, 1922 (copy), Springfield, Branch Files (Container 167), NAACP Papers.

118. Letter of Sully Jaymes to R. W. Bagnall, Oct. 4, 1922, ibid.

119. Meier and Rudwick, "Early Boycotts of Segregated Schools: The Case of Springfield, Ohio, 1922–23," 749.

120. Letter of Sully Jaymes to R. W. Bagnall, March 14, 1923, Springfield, Branch Files (Container 167), NAACP Papers.

121. Letter of Robert W. Bagnall to Sully Jaymes, March 17, 1923 (copy), ibid.

122. Meier and Rudwick, "Early Boycotts of Segregated Schools: The Case of Springfield, Ohio, 1922–23," 756, 757.

123. Allen, "East Long Street," 14.

124. Kornbluh, "James Hathaway Robinson," in Race and the City, ed. Taylor, Jr., 212–15.

125. Letter of N. B. Allen to Dr. C. C. North, April 1, 1926 (copy), Columbus Urban League Papers.

126. Gazette, March 16, 1929.

127. See: Hine, Black Women in White: Racial Conflict and Cooperation in the Nursing Profession, 1890–1950; David McBride, Integrating the City of Medicine: Blacks in Philadelphia Health Care, 1910–1965 (Philadelphia: Temple University Press, 1989); Mitchell F. Rice and Woodrow Jones, Jr., Public Policy and the Black Hospital: From Slavery to Segregation to Integration (Westport: Greenwood, 1994); Vanessa N. Gamble, Making a Place for Ourselves: The Black Hospital Movement 1920–1945 (New York: Oxford University Press, 1995).

128. Dabney, Colored Citizens, 400.

129. "Negro Health and Race Relations," Cincinnati Sanitary Bulletin 8, No. 4 (Oct. 14, 1925): 3.

130. "The Hospitalization of the Negro," From Hospital Survey by Mary Hicks, in Dabney, Colored Citizens, 390.

131. Ibid., 392.

132. "Negro Health and Race Relations," Cincinnati Sanitary Bulletin 8, No. 4 (Oct. 14, 1925): 3.

133. Todd L. Savitt, "Four African-American Proprietary Medical Colleges: 1888–1923," Journal of the History of Medicine and Allied Sciences 55 (July 2000): 203–55.

134. Mercy Hospital doctors included T. L. Berry, Lenine R. Breedlove, R. Eugene Clark, Norman E. Dunham, E. B. Gray, B. Jay Lockley, R. P. McClain, James E. Randolph, Edward J. Ross, and J. H. Wallace. Dabney, Colored Citizens, 247, 248, 251, 261, 264–65, 266, 294, 328.

135. Gamble, Making a Place for Ourselves: The Black Hospital Movement 1920–1945, xii, 9, 36.

136. Dabney, Colored Citizens, 229, 247, 262, 264, 271, 294, 327, 401.

137. See Hicks survey, ibid., 391.

138. Ibid., 266, 392.

139. Union, in Gazette, June 15, 1929.

140. Dabney, *Colored Citizens*, 400; theoretically African Americans had access to all wards in the General Hospital. See statement by Health Commissioner W. H. Peters, ibid., 380.

141. *Union*, in *Gazette*, June 15, 1929.

142. Ibid.

143. Andrew Barta, "A Sociological Survey of the East Long Street Negro District in Columbus, Ohio" (M.A. Thesis, The Ohio State University, 1933), 67.

144. Harshman, "Race Contact in Columbus, Ohio," 43.

145. Allen, "East Long Street," 14, 15–16; McWilliams, *Columbus Illustrated Record 1919–1920*, 117, 121.

146. *Gazette*, June 11, 1921; Gerber, *Black Ohio*, 460.

147. William Giffin, "The Mercy Hospital Controversy among Cleveland's Afro-American Civic Leaders, 1927," *Journal of Negro History* 61 (Oct. 1976): 327–50.

148. *Gazette*, June 12, 26, 1915, April 17, 1920, Feb. 19, 26, 1921, Jan. 17, 1925.

149. Giffin, "Mercy Hospital Controversy," 330–31, 339, 340, 345, 347; *Gazette*, April 10, 1926, May 1, 1926, Aug. 7, 1926, Feb. 5, 19, 1927, March 5, 12, 26, 1927, April 9, 1927, May 21, 1927, June 4, 11, 25, 1927, July 16, 1927; unidentified newspaper clipping headlined "Pros and Cons for the Mercy Hospital Ass. In Conference," Charles H. Garvin Papers, Manuscript Division, Western Reserve Historical Society Archives/Library, Cleveland, Ohio; Russell W. Jelliffe to Robert W. Bagnall, May 12, 1926, Cleveland, Branch Files (Container 157), NAACP Papers; Charles H. Garvin, "The Negro Physicians and the Hospitals of Cleveland," *Journal of the National Medical Association* 22 (July-Sept. 1930): 125; Mercy Hospital Association, *Does Cleveland Need a Negro Manned Hospital? Facts Are the Answer* (Printed pamphlet), Western Reserve Historical Society Archives/Library, Cleveland, Ohio; George P. Hinton to George A. Myers, April 1, 1927, Myers Papers.

150. Letter of Charles W. White to R. W. Bagnall, March 28, 1927, Cleveland, Branch Files (Container 157), NAACP Papers.

151. Giffin, "Mercy Hospital Controversy," 330–31, 336–37, 339, 340, 345, 347; Harry C. Smith to George A. Myers, Feb. 2, 8 (postcard), 19, 24, 28 (post-card), March 1, 2 (letter and postcard), 28, April 2,1927, George A. Myers to W. R. Hopkins, March 7, 1927 (copy), Myers Papers; *Gazette*, March 5, 12, 26, 1927, April 2, 1927, July 16, 1927.

152. Charles W. White to George A. Myers, March 7, 1927, Myers Papers; unidentified newspaper clipping headlined "Pros and Cons for the Mercy Hospital Ass. In Conference," Garvin Papers; *Gazette*, March 12, 26, 1927, April 2, 16, 1927, May 7, 28, 1927; Minutes of the Board of Trustees, April 7, 1927, Urban League of Cleveland Papers.

153. Minutes, Interracial Committee, June 28, 1927, October 26, 1927, Minutes, Sub-committee of Interracial Committee, Oct. 27, 1927, Cleveland Area Church Federation, Manuscript Collections, Western Reserve Historical Society Archives/Library, Cleveland, Ohio; Hospital Report, Exhibit A, Cleveland Committee Investigating the Admittance of Colored Internes [sic] and Nurses to the Staff of City Hospital, Report, Dec. 12, 1927, Western Reserve

Historical Society Archives/Library, Cleveland, Ohio; Gamble, *Making a Place for Ourselves: The Black Hospital Movement 1920–1945*, 164–68

154. Letter of Harry E. Davis to James Weldon Johnson, Nov. 1, 1927, Cleveland, Branch Files (Container 157), NAACP Papers.

155. Letters to W. R. Hopkins, Dec. 13, 29, 1927, and Jan. 26, 1928 (copies), Myers Papers.

156. Letter of W. R. Hopkins to George A. Myers, Jan. 31, 1928, ibid.

157. *Gazette*, June 30, 1928.

158. Ibid., July 7, 1928.

159. Ibid., Aug. 4, 1928.

160. Ibid.

161. Ibid., July 28, 1928.

162. Letters of D. S. Blossom to Charles W. White, Oct. 24, 1928 (copy), and Charles W. White to Dudley S. Blossom, Oct. 26, 1928 (copy), Myers Papers.

163. *Cleveland Plain Dealer*, Jan. 5, 1929, 17; *Gazette*, Jan. 12, 1929.

164. Cleveland Branch N.A.A.C.P., Annual Report of President, Nov. 21, 1929, Cleveland, Branch Files (Container 158), NAACP Papers.

165. Letter of George A. Myers to Harry C. Smith, Jan. 5, 1929, *Gazette*, Jan. 12, 1929.

166. *Cleveland Plain Dealer*, Jan. 5, 1929, 17; *Gazette*, Jan. 12, 1929.

167. Letter to the Editor, *Cleveland Plain Dealer*, ibid.

168. Ibid.

169. *Cleveland Plain Dealer*, Jan. 5, 1929, 17; *Gazette*, Jan. 12, 1929.

170. Cleveland Branch, N.A.A.C.P., Annual Report of President, Nov. 21, 1929, Cleveland, Branch Files (Container 158), NAACP Papers.

171. *Gazette*, March 16, 1929.

172. Letter of Harry C. Smith to George A. Myers, Sept. 4, 1929, Myers Papers; *Gazette*, Aug. 17, 1929.

173. Ibid., Nov. 23, 1929.

174. Letter of George A. Myers to Harry C. Smith, Jan. 7, 1929, ibid., Jan. 12, 1929; see Gregg's statement in ibid., April 30, 1929.

175. Ibid., Sept. 7, 1929.

176. Cleveland Branch, N.A.A.C.P., Annual Report of President, November 21, 1929, Cleveland, Branch Files (Container 158), NAACP Papers.

177. *Gazette*, Nov. 16, 1929.

178. Ibid., Nov. 23, 1929.

179. Ibid.

180. Ibid., Nov. 30, 1929.

181. Ibid.

182. Ibid., Jan.18, 1930.

183. Ibid., Nov. 19, 1929; letters of George A. Myers to W. R. Hopkins, Dec. 13, 29, 1927, and Jan. 26, 1928 (copies), Myers Papers.

184. *Gazette*, Jan. 18, 1930; Gamble, *Making a Place for Ourselves: The Black Hospital Movement 1920–1945*, 171; Kusmer, *A Ghetto Takes Shape*, 272–73; Davis, *Black Americans in Cleveland*, 234, 236; Thomas F. Campbell, *Daniel E. Morgan, 1877–1949: The Good Citizen in Politics* (Cleveland: Western Reserve University Press, 1966), 115–17.

185. Kenneth W. Goings, *"The NAACP Comes of Age": The Defeat of Judge John J. Parker* (Bloomington: Indiana University Press, 1990).

Notes to Chapter 8

1. Sherman, *Republican Party and Black America: From McKinley to Hoover, 1896–1933*.

2. William W. Giffin, "Black Insurgency in the Republican Party of Ohio, 1920–1932." *Ohio History* 82 (Winter-Spring 1973): 25–45.

3. Martin Kilson, "Political Change in the Negro Ghetto, 1900–1940's," in *Key Issues in the Afro-American Experience*, eds. Nathan I. Huggins, Martin Kilson, and Daniel M. Fox (New York: Harcourt Brace Jovanovich, Inc, 1971), 167–92.

4. Dabney, *Colored Citizens*, 114.

5. Ibid., 115, 119.

6. Himes, Jr., "Forty Years of Negro Life in Columbus," 137.

7. *Gazette*, March 3, 1917.

8. *Census 1920: Occupations* 4: 1082, 1086, 1089, 1094, 1244, *Census 1930: Occupations* 4: 1277, 1280, 1283, 1286, 1289, 1292, 1295, 1298.

9. Dabney, *Colored Citizens*, 209; John A. Garraty's introduction in *The Barber and the Historian: the Correspondence of George A. Myers and James Ford Rhodes, 1910–1923* (Columbus: Ohio Historical Society, 1956), xi-xxiv.

10. *Gazette*, June 11, 1921, Nov. 29, 1924; Weisenburger, "William S. Scarborough, Scholarship, The Negro, Religion, and Politics," 50.

11. Dabney, *Colored Citizens*, 209; Gerber, *Black Ohio*, 367–368;

12. Himes, Jr., "Forty Years of Negro Life in Columbus," 145.

13. *Crisis* 18 (Aug. 1919): 200.

14. Weisenburger, "William S. Scarborough, Scholarship, The Negro, Religion, and Politics," 45–46; *Gazette*, Aug. 26, 1922.

15. Ibid., April 15, 1922.

16. Ibid., April 27, 1929.

17. Ibid., Jan. 2, 1915, April 15, 1916.

18. Ibid., April 15, 1916.

19. Ibid.

20. *Cleveland Plain Dealer*, June 25, 1920, 12; *Gazette*, April 8, 1920, June 19, 1920, July 3, 10, 24, 1920, Aug. 7, 14, 28, 1920, July 1, 8, 15 22, 1922, and Aug. 5, 12, 19, 1922, June 21, 1924, June 12, 1926, Aug. 21, 1926, June 30, 1928, Sept. 28, 1928; *Cincinnati Enquirer*, April 5, 1922, 3.

21. *Gazette*, Oct. 23, 1920; *Cleveland Branch Bulletin* 1, No. 9 (Nov. 1920), Cleveland, Branch Files (Container 157), NAACP Papers.

22. New York *Times*, Oct. 22, 1920, 2.

23. Eugene H. Roseboom, *A History of Presidential Elections* (New York: The Macmillan Company, 1959), 402; see Francis Russell, *The Shadow of Blooming Grove: Warren G. Harding in His Times* (New York: McGraw-Hill, 1968), passim.

24. *Gazette*, Sept. 11, 1920.

25. Ibid.; Davis, *Black Americans in Cleveland*, 143.

26. Rosalyn Terborg-Penn, *African American Women in the Struggle for the Vote, 1850–1920* (Bloomington: Indiana University Press, 1998).

27. *Gazette*, Sept. 25, 1920; letter of Harry S. New to Scarborough, Nov. 3, 1920, William S. Scarborough Papers, Carnegie Library, Wilberforce University, Wilberforce, Ohio.

28. *Gazette*, Oct. 30, 1920, Nov. 13, 1920.

29. Ibid., May 24, 1924.

30. Ibid., June 14, 21, 28, 1924, July 5, 19, 1924; Roseboom, *A History of Presidential Elections*, 410.

31. *Gazette*, Aug. 30, 1924, Sept. 13, 27, 1924, Oct. 18, 25, 1924.

32. Ibid., Sept. 27, 1924.

33. Ibid., Oct. 4, 1924.

34. Ibid., Nov. 1, 1924.

35. Thornbrough, *Indiana Blacks in the Twentieth Century*, 50.

36. *Gazette*, Oct. 9, 1926.

37. Harry C. Smith to G. H. Townsley, Oct. 26, 1926, ibid., Oct. 30, 1926.

38. Letter of Harry C. Smith to Gov. A. V. Donahey, Nov. 6, 1926, ibid., Nov. 20, 1926.

39. Ibid.

40. Ibid., Nov. 13, 1926; letter of Earl Bloom to Harry C. Smith, Dec. 11, 1926, ibid., Dec. 18, 1926; letter of Vic Donahey to Harry C. Smith, Nov. 29, 1926, ibid, Dec. 11, 1926.

41. Ibid., Oct. 20, 1928.

42. Hettie G. Taylor to Whom It May Concern, Oct. 15, 1928, in ibid.

43. Ibid., Oct. 27, 1928.

44. Ibid., Sept. 8, 1928.

45. Ibid., March 31, 1928.

46. Ibid., Sept. 1, 1928.

47. Davis, *Black Americans in Cleveland*, 237; *Gazette*, June 16, 1928, July 21, 1928.

48. Henry Lee Moon, *Balance of Power: The Negro Vote* (Garden City, NY: Doubleday, 1948), 18; Ernest M. Collins, "Cincinnati Negroes and Presidential Politics," *Journal of Negro History* 41 (April 1956): 132.

49. *Gazette*, Nov. 20, 1915; *Census 1910: Population* 3: 422, *Census 1920: Population* 3: 789.

50. *Gazette*, Nov. 15, 1919.

51. Ibid., Feb. 2, 9, 1929.

52. Ibid., Nov. 20, 1920; July 29, 1922; Sept. 19, 1925.

53. Collins, "The Political Behavior of the Negroes in Cincinnati, Ohio, and Louisville, Kentucky" (Ph.D., University of Kentucky, 1950), 153.

54. Himes, Jr., "Forty Years of Negro Life in Columbus," 136–37, 145.

55. *Union*, Nov. 5, 1921, Nov. 19, 1921; Collins, "Political Behavior of the Negroes in Cincinnati, Ohio, and Louisville, Kentucky," 150.

56. *The Cincinnati Post*, in ibid.

57. *Cincinnati Post*, Nov. 9, 1921, 12.

58. *Gazette*, July 1, 1922.

59. *Cincinnati Enquirer*, July 20, 1922, 20.

60. *Gazette*, July 1, 1922, Aug. 26, 1922; *Crisis* 27 (Nov. 1923): 8; ibid. 29 (Nov. 1924): 13.

61. Collins, "Political Behavior of the Negroes in Cincinnati, Ohio, and Louisville, Kentucky," 150–51.

62. *Gazette*, Aug. 28, 1926.

63. *The Cincinnati Times-Star*, Nov. 10, 1927, 6; Dabney, *Colored Citizens*, 408.

64. *Gazette*, Nov. 2, 1929.

65. Collins found no evidence that Cincinnati's black voters strayed substantially from the Republicans during the decade. Collins, "Political Behavior of the Negroes in Cincinnati, Ohio, and Louisville, Kentucky," 77–78, 152–53; Cincinnati *Post*, Nov. 11, 1931.

66. *Crisis* 12 (June 1916): 67; *Gazette*, Nov. 10, 1917, Nov. 1, 1919.

67. Ibid., May 14, 1921, Oct. 29, 1921, Nov. 12, 1921; March 18, 25, 1922.

68. Ibid., Oct. 17, 1925, Nov. 7, 1925.

69. Ibid., Nov. 12, 1927, Jan. 14, 1928.

70. Ibid., Oct. 19, 1929.

71. See enclosure in letter of W. B. Gongwer to George A. Myers, May 28, 1927, Myers Papers; *Gazette*, Nov. 12, 1927.

72. Ibid., Jan. 7, 1928.

73. Ibid., Sept 1, 1928.

74. Ibid., Feb. 16, 1929.

75. *Cleveland Press*, Feb. 10, 1929, 4.

76. *Gazette*, Feb. 23, 1929.

77. *Cleveland Plain Dealer*, Feb. 19, 1929, 24.

78. *Gazette*, March 9, 1929.

79. Ibid., Nov. 9, 1929; Regennia N. Williams, "Equity and Efficiency: African American Leadership and Education Reform in Cleveland, Ohio, 1915–1940" (Ph.D. Diss., Case Western Reserve University, 2001).

80. *Cleveland Plain Dealer*, Oct. 15, 1929, 8.

81. *Gazette*, Nov. 9, 1929.

82. Davis, *Black Americans in Cleveland*, 234.

83. Ibid., 175; Kusmer, *A Ghetto Takes Shape*, 272–73, fn. 61.

84. Davis, *Black Americans in Cleveland*, 234, 236; Kusmer, *A Ghetto Takes Shape*, 272, 273.

85. See list compiled by House of Representatives Enrolling Clerk Ella M. Scriven, Columbus, Ohio, 1948, in Ernest M. Collins, "Political Behavior of the Negroes in Cincinnati, Ohio, and Louisville, Kentucky," 138–39.

86. *Ohio House Journal* 108 (1919): 1909.

87. *Gazette*, Sept. 7, 1918, Nov. 20, 1920, July 1, 1922; Minor, "The Negro in Columbus, Ohio," 180.

88. *Gazette*, Aug. 7, 1920, Aug. 7, 14, 1926, May 12, 1928, Nov. 3, 17, 1928; see *Ohio House Journal* for the twenties.

89. Dabney, *Colored Citizens*, 344–45; *Gazette*, March 15, 1919, April 26, 1919, May 10, 1919; *Ohio House Journal* 108 (1919): 113, 372–74, 418, 662, 882–83; *Cincinnati Enquirer*, Sept. 7, 1919, section 2, 20; *Crisis* 18 (July 1919): 140, 154; see Kellogg, *NAACP*, 202.

90. *Ohio House Journal* 110 (1923): 282, 1202–3; *Gazette*, April 7, 1923, May 5, 1923.

91. See references to the Ku Klux Klan in Chapter 5, endnotes 3–19.

92. *Ohio House Journal* 109 (1921): 549, 629.

93. *Gazette*, April 20, 1929; *Ohio House Journal* 113 (1929): 676.

94. E. David Cronon, *Black Moses: The Story of Marcus Garvey and the Universal Negro Improvement Association*, (Madison: University of Wisconsin Press, 1969), passim; Phillips, *Alabama North*, 186–88.

95. McClain, "The Contributions of Blacks in Akron, 1825–1975," 198–99.

96. *Gazette*, Dec. 2, 9, 1922.

97. Ibid., Sept. 29, 1923, May 31, 1924.

98. Ibid., Dec. 2, 1922, Sept. 29, 1923.

99. Dabney, *Colored Citizens*, 213–14; Joe William Trotter, Jr., *River Jordan: African American Urban Life in the Ohio Valley* (Lexington: The University Press of Kentucky, 1998), 119–20.

100. Dabney, *Colored Citizens*, 188.

101. *Gazette*, Feb. 23, 1924.

102. Ibid.

103. Ibid., March 22, 1924.

104. Ibid., April 12, 1924.

105. Reprinted from *Union*, Oct. 1927, in Wendell. P. Dabney, *Chisum's Pilgrimage and Others* (Cincinnati, 1927), 21–22.

106. *Gazette*, May 14, 1921, Oct. 29, 1921, Nov. 12, 1921.

107. Ibid., July 29, 1922.

108. Dabney, *Chisum's Pilgrimage and Others*, 21.

109. *Gazette*, Sept. 29, 1928.

110. "How Shall We Vote?" *Crisis* 29 (Nov. 1924): 12–15; *Gazette*, Sept. 27, 1924.

111. Goings, *"NAACP Comes of Age": The Defeat of Judge John J. Parker*.

112. Walter White, "The Test in Ohio," *Crisis* 36 (Nov. 1930): 373. See telegram of Charles W. White to Senator Roscoe McCulloch (copy) enclosed in letter of Charles W. White to Walter White, April 5, 1930, Cleveland, Branch Files (Container 158), NAACP Papers.

113. Letter of Charles W. White to Walter White, May 28, 1930, ibid.

114. Minor, "The Negro in Columbus, Ohio," 188.

115. Minutes of the Second Conference of the Ohio Branches of the National Association for the Advancement of Colored People, Columbus, Ohio, Oct. 5, 1930, Ohio State Conference, Branch Files (Container 151), NAACP Papers; *Gazette*, Oct. 11, 1930.

116. *Crisis* 37 (Dec. 1930): 418; letter of Geraldyne R. Freeland to Walter White, Nov. 4, 1930, Ohio State Conference, Branch Files (Container 151), NAACP Papers.

117. White, "The Test in Ohio," 374.

118. Letter of Geraldyne R. Freeland to Walter White, Nov. 4, 1930, Ohio State Conference, Branch Files (Container 151), NAACP Papers.

119. John G. Van Duesen, "The Negro in Politics," *Journal of Negro History* 21 (July 1936): 271.

120. Rita W. Gordon, "The Change in the Political Realignment of Chicago's Negroes During the New Deal," *Journal of American History* 56 (December 1969): 584; Harvard Sitkoff, *A New Deal for Blacks, The Emergence of Civil Rights as a National Issue: The Depression Decade* (New York: Oxford University Press, 1981); Weiss, *Farewell to the Party of Lincoln: Black Politics in the Age of FDR*; Karen Ferguson, *Black Politics in New Deal Atlanta* (Chapel Hill: University of North Carolina Press, 2002); Durahn A. B. Taylor, "Black Gotham: Voters, Leaders, and the Political Game in Harlem, 1928–1950" (Ph.D. Diss., Columbia University, 1999); William W. Giffin, "The Political Realignment of Black Voters in Indianapolis, 1924," *Indiana Magazine of History* 79 (June 1983): 133–66; Franklin and Moss, *From Slavery to Freedom*, 422–27.

121. Kilson, "Political Change in the Negro Ghetto, 1900–1940's," in *Key Issues in the Afro-American Experience*, eds. Huggins, Kilson, and Fox, 167–92.

Notes to Conclusion

1. Phillips, *Alabama North* (1999).

2. Steven C. Tracy, *Going to Cincinnati: A History of the Blues in the Queen City* (Urbana: University of Illinois Press, 1993).

3. Andrew R. L. Cayton, *Ohio: The History of a People* (Columbus: The Ohio State University Press, 2002).

4. Nathan I. Huggins, *Harlem Renaissance* (New York: Oxford University Press, 1973); Francis Davis, *The History of the Blues* (New York: Hyperion, 1995); Burton W. Peretti, *The Creation of Jazz: Music, Race, and Culture in Urban America* (Urbana: University of Illinois Press, 1992).

5. *New York Times*, Jan. 25, 1936, 15, July 17, 1981, C3, June 29, 1982, D23, April 14, 1989, D17.

6. Gerber, *Black Ohio* (1976).

7. Bureau of the Census, *Census 1910: Population* 3: 418 and *Negroes in the United States 1920–1932*, 9, 62, 63.

8. Examples are: Du Bois, *The Philadelphia Negro* (1899, reprint, 1967); Chicago Commission on Race Relations, *The Negro in Chicago: A Study of Race Relations and a Race Riot*, written by Charles S. Johnson (1922); Frazier, *The Negro Family in Chicago* (1932); and Drake and Cayton, *Black Metropolis* (reprint, 1970; original: New York: Harcourt Brace and Company, 1945).

9. Osofsky, *Harlem* (1966); Spear, *Black Chicago* (1967); Katzman, *Before the Ghetto: Black Detroit* (1973); and Kusmer, *A Ghetto Takes Shape* (1976).

10. Joe William Trotter, Jr., "Introduction: Black Migration in Historical Perspective, A Review of the Literature," *The Great Migration in Historical Perspective*, ed. Trotter, Jr. (1991), 13.

11. David Ward, *Poverty, Ethnicity, and the American City, 1840–1925: Changing Conceptions of the Slum and the Ghetto* (New York: Cambridge University Press, 1989).

12. Gottlieb, *Making Their Own Way* (1987); Grossman, *Land of Hope: Chicago* (1989); Trotter Jr., *Coal, Class, and Color* (1990); Lewis, *In Their Own Interests* (1991); Phillips, *Alabama North* (1999).

13. Kusmer, "The Black Urban Experience in American History," in *The State of Afro-American History*, ed. Hine (1986), 111; Taylor, Jr., "Black Ghetto-Slum Formation in Cincinnati," in *Race and the City*, ed. Taylor, Jr. (1993), 157, 179; Joe William Trotter, Jr., "Black Migration Studies: The Future," in *The Great Migration in Historical Perspective*, ed. Trotter, Jr., 147.

14. Chesnutt, *Charles Waddell Chesnutt*, 263; *Gazette*, Aug. 4, 1928; and see list in Collins, "The Political Behavior of the Negroes in Cincinnati, Ohio, and Louisville, Kentucky," (Ph.D. Diss., University of Kentucky, 1950), 138–39 and *Ohio House Journal* for the nineteen twenties.

15. *Gazette*, Aug. 2, 1919.

16. See discussion of protest tradition in Chapters 3 and 7 herein, passim.

17. Barnhart, "The Southern Influence in the Formation of Ohio," *Journal of*

Southern History 3 (Feb. 1937): 40–42; Chaddock, *Ohio before 1850,* 31–46; Shilling, "Relations of Southern Ohio to the South during the Decade Preceding the Civil War," *Historical and Philosophical Society of Ohio Quarterly* 8, no. 1 (1913): 3–62; Roseboom and Weisenburger, *A History of Ohio,* 114–15; Gerber, *Black Ohio,* 9–14.

18. Kusmer, "The Black Urban Experience in American History," in *The State of Afro-American History,* ed. Hine, 107–8; Taylor, Jr., "Black Ghetto-Slum Formation in Cincinnati," in *Race and the City,* ed. Taylor, Jr., 157.

19. Trotter, Jr., "Black Migration Studies: The Future," in *The Great Migration in Historical Perspective,* ed. Trotter, Jr., 147.

20. Bureau of the Census, *Census 1910: Population* 3: 418 and *Negroes in the United States 1920–1932,* 9, 62, 63.

21. Thornbrough, *Indiana Blacks in the Twentieth Century,* ed. by Ruegamer (2000), 35.

22. Bureau of the Census, *Census 1910: Population* 3: 418, *Census 1920: Population* 3: 797–809, *Negroes in the United States 1920–1932,* 9, 12, 15, 32, 62–63.

23. Kusmer, *A Ghetto Takes Shape,* 162–63, 166; Fairbanks, "Cincinnati Blacks and the Irony of Low-Income Housing Reform, 1900–1950," in *Race and the City,* ed. Taylor, Jr. (1993), 200; Fairbanks, *Making Better Citizens* (1988), 55, 193.

24. Gottlieb, *Making Their Own Way* (1987); Grossman, *Land of Hope: Chicago* (1989); Trotter Jr., *Coal, Class, and Color* (1990); Lewis, *In Their Own Interests* (1991); Phillips, *Alabama North* (1999); Shirley Anne Wilson Moore, *To Place Our Deeds: The African American Community in Richmond, California, 1910–1963* (Berkeley: University of California Press, 2000).

25. *Census 1910: Occupation Statistics* 4: 547–52, 605–6, *Census 1920: Occupations* 4: 361–62, 1081–90, 1093–95, 1243–45, *Census 1930: Occupations* 4: 1266, 1276–99.

26. Trotter, Jr., *Coal, Class, and Color* (1990).

27. Leadership examples in Chapters 6, 7, and 8 herein, passim. Also, see Christopher R. Reed, *The Chicago NAACP and the Rise of Black Professional Leadership, 1910–1966* (1997) and Toure Reed, "'Helping negroes to help themselves': Middle Class Reform and the Politics of Racial Order, 1910–1950 (Ph.D. Diss., Columbia University, 2002).

28. Georgina Hickey, *Hope and Danger in the New South City: Working-Class Women and Urban Development in Atlanta, 1890–1940* (Athens: University of Georgia Press, 2003).

29. Dabney, *Colored Citizens,* 145, 147, 167, 424–27; Fairbanks, *Making Better Citizens,* 62.

30. Find discussions of church activities and other social and cultural life in Chapters 1 and 4 herein.

31. Darlene Clark Hine, "Black Migration to the Urban Midwest: The Gender Dimension, 1915–1945," in *The Great Migration in Historical Perspective,* ed. Trotter, Jr., 129.

32. See evidence regarding working class and professional class women given in Chapters 1 and 4 herein.

33. Find herein examples relating to schools in Chapter 5, to Urban League

affiliates and social work institutions in Chapter 6, and to NAACP branches in Chapter 7.

34. Evelyn Brooks Higginbotham, *Righteous Discontent: The Women's Movement in the Black Baptist Church, 1880–1920* (Cambridge: Harvard University Press, 1993).

35. *Gazette*, Sept. 11, 1920, Aug. 23, 1924; Davis, *Black Americans in Cleveland*, 143; *Crisis* 18 (July 1919): 154.

36. Davis, *Black Americans in Cleveland*, 241; see branch officers listed in letterhead, letter of Charles W. White to James Weldon Johnson, July 23, 1928, Cleveland, Branch Files (Container 157), NAACP Papers.

37. See Chapters 7 and 8 herein for some other evidence about black gender roles in these areas.

38. Hine, "Black Migration to the Urban Midwest," in *The Great Migration in Historical Perspective*, ed. Trotter, Jr., 134.

39. Kusmer, "The Black Urban Experience in American History," in *The State of Afro-American History*, ed. Hine 114.

40. Himes, Jr., "Forty Years of Negro Life in Columbus, Ohio," *Journal of Negro History* 27 (April, 1942): 151.

41. *Gazette*, July 14, 1923.

42. Ibid., Oct. 9, 1920.

43. Davis, *Black Americans in Cleveland*, 139.

44. Gerber, *Black Ohio*, 466; Dabney, *Colored Citizens*, 123–26, 216, 227, 359, 400, 437.

45. See discussion in Chapter 7.

46. *Cleveland Plain Dealer*, Jan. 5, 1929, 17; *Gazette*, Jan. 12, 1929.

47. Ibid., Nov. 16, 23, 1929.

48. Letter of N. B. Allen to Dr. Herbert A. Miller, Feb. 26, 1925, Columbus Urban League Papers.

49. Kornbluh, "James Hathaway Robinson," in *Race and the City*, ed. Taylor, Jr. (1993), 217–22.

50. Davis, *Black Americans in Cleveland*, 225–26; Davis, *Memorable Negroes in Cleveland's Past*, 56; Kusmer, *A Ghetto Takes Shape*, 250–51.

51. Dabney, *Colored Citizens*, 317.

52. Letter of George A. Myers to Wm. R. Hopkins, Feb. 6, 1928 (copy), Myers Papers.

Bibliography

Manuscript Collections

Adjutant General's Office Files, War Department Records. National Archives, Washington, D.C.

Baker Papers, Newton D. Manuscript Division, Library of Congress, Washington, D.C.

Chesnutt Papers, Charles W. Fisk University Library, Nashville, Tennessee.

Cincinnati Model Homes Company Records, 1912–1977. Cincinnati Historical Society Library, Cincinnati, Ohio.

Cleveland Area Church Federation. Manuscript Collections, Western Reserve Historical Society Archives/Library, Cleveland, Ohio.

Columbus Urban League Papers. Manuscript Division, Ohio Historical Society Archives/Library, Columbus, Ohio.

Freemasons, Prince Hall Grand Lodge of Ohio. Manuscript Division, Ohio Historical Society Archives/Library, Columbus, Ohio.

Garvin Papers, Charles H. Manuscript Collections, Western Reserve Historical Society Archives/Library, Cleveland, Ohio.

Myers Papers, George A. Manuscript Division, Ohio Historical Society Archives/Library, Columbus, Ohio.

National Association for the Advancement of Colored People Records. Manuscript Division, The Library of Congress, Washington, D.C.

Ohio, Adjutant General's Department Records. State Archives, Ohio Historical Society Archives/ Library, Columbus, Ohio.

Phillis Wheatley Association (Cleveland, Ohio) Records. Manuscript Collections, Western Reserve Historical Society Archives/Library, Cleveland, Ohio.

Scarborough Papers, William S. Carnegie Library, Wilberforce University, Wilberforce, Ohio.

Schmidlapp Papers, Jacob Godfrey. Cincinnati Historical Society Library, Cincinnati, Ohio.

Urban League of Cleveland Papers. Manuscript Collections, Western Reserve Historical Society Archives/Library, Cleveland, Ohio.

Urban League of Greater Cincinnati Records. Cincinnati Historical Society Library, Cincinnati, Ohio.
World War I Organization Records. National Archives, Washington, D.C.

Government Publications

Ohio. Annual Report of the Adjutant General to the Governor of the State of Ohio, 1919. Columbus, 1921. Ohio Historical Society Archives/Library, Columbus, Ohio.
Ohio. *Ohio House Journal.*
Ohio. *Ohio Senate Journal.*
Ohio. *Ohio State Reports.*
United States, Department of Commerce, Bureau of the Census. *Thirteenth Census of the United States Taken in the Year 1910: Population, 1910, Reports by States, With Statistics for Counties, Cities and Other Civil Divisions, Nebraska-Wyoming, Alaska, Hawaii, and Porto Rico.* 3 Washington, D.C.: Government Printing Office, 1913.
———. *Thirteenth Census of the United States Taken in the Year 1910, Volume IV, Population 1910, Occupation Statistics.* 4 Washington, D.C.: Government Printing Office, 1914.
———. *Fourteenth Census of the United States Taken in the Year 1920: Population, 1920, Composition and Characteristics of the Population by States.* 3 Washington: Government Printing Office, 1922.
———. *Fourteenth Census of the United States Taken in the Year 1920, Volume IV, Population 1920, Occupations.* 4 Washington, D.C.: Government Printing Office, 1923.
———. *Fifteenth Census of the United States: 1930 Population, Volume III, Part 2, Reports by States Showing the Composition and Characteristics of the Population for Counties, Cities and Townships or Other Minor Civil Divisions, Montana-Wyoming.* 3 Washington, D.C.: United States Government Printing Office, 1932.
———. *Fifteenth Census of the United States: 1930, Population, Volume IV, Occupations by States.* 4 Washington, D.C.: Government Printing Office, 1933.
———. *Negro Population, 1790–1915.* Washington, D.C.: Government Printing Office, 1918.
———. *Negroes in the United States 1920–1932.* Washington, D.C.: Government Printing Office, 1935.
———. *Religious Bodies 1916, Part I, Summary and General Tables.* Washington, D.C.: Government Printing Office, 1919.

Newspapers

Advocate (Cleveland)
Akron Beacon Journal
Black and White Chronicle (Akron)

Chicago Tribune
Cincinnati Enquirer
Cincinnati Post
Cincinnati Times-Star
Cleveland Call
Cleveland News
Cleveland Plain Dealer
Cleveland Press
Ohio State Monitor (Columbus)
Ohio Recorder (Columbus)
Ohio Torch (Columbus)
Columbus Voice
Gazette (Cleveland)
Dayton Forum
Dayton News
Montgomery Advertiser (Alabama)
New York Times
Ohio State Journal (Columbus)
Springfield Informer
Toledo Blade
Union (Cincinnati)

Unpublished Materials

Baldwin, Davarian L. "Chicago's New Negroes: Race, Class, and Respectability in the Midwestern Black Metropolis, 1915–1935. Ph.D. Diss., New York University, 2002.

Banks, Nina Elizabeth. "Steadying the Husband, Uplifting the Race: The Pittsburgh Urban League's Promotion of Black Female Domesticity during the Great Migration." Ph.D. Diss., University of Massachusetts, 1999.

Barta, Andrew. "A Sociological Survey of the East Long Street Negro District in Columbus, Ohio." M.A. Thesis, The Ohio State University, 1933.

Bettinger, Christopher Paul. "Strange Interludes? A Sociological History of American Race Rioting, 1900 to 1996." Ph.D. Diss., University of Michigan, 1999.

Billingslea, Sebron Basil. "The Negro, 1901–1920, as Portrayed in the *Cincinnati Enquirer*." M.A. Thesis, Howard University, 1950.

Blair, Cynthia Marie. "Vicious Commerce: African American Women's Sex Work and the Transformation of Urban Space in Chicago, 1850–1915." Ph.D. Diss., Harvard University, 1999.

Brown, Nikki L. M. "'Your patriotism is of the purest quality': African American Women and World War I." Ph.D. Diss., Yale University, 2002.

Bryant, Vinnie Vanessa. "Columbus, Ohio and the Great Migration." M.A. Thesis, The Ohio State University, 1983.

Cheng, Hew-Yi. "A Housing Study of the Negro of the City of Columbus, Ohio." M.A. Thesis, The Ohio State University, 1925.

Clark, Margaret Jones. "The Negro Pharmacist and Physician in Columbus, Ohio." M.A. Thesis, The Ohio State University, 1929.

Collins, Ernest M. "The Political Behavior of the Negroes in Cincinnati, Ohio, and Louisville, Kentucky." Ph.D. Diss., University of Kentucky, 1950.

Donaldson, Bobby J. "New Negroes in a New South: Race, Power, and Ideology in Georgia, 1890–1925." Ph.D. Diss., Emory University, 2002.

Dulaney, William M. "Black and Blue in America: The Black Policemen of Columbus, Ohio, 1895–1974." M.A. Thesis, The Ohio State University, 1974.

Felix, Stephanie Yvette. "Committed to Their Own: African American Women Leaders in the YWCA. The YWCA of Germantown, Philadelphia, Pennsylvania, 1870–1970." Ph.D. Diss., Temple University, 1999.

Harshman, Ralph Garling. "Race Contact in Columbus, Ohio." M.A. Thesis, The Ohio State University, 1921.

Hart, Jamie. "African Americans, Health Care, and the Reproductive Freedom Movement in Detroit, 1918–1945." Ph.D. Diss., University of Michigan, 1998.

Hauser, Prather J. "Treatment by Columbus Daily Newspapers of News Regarding the Negro." M.S. Thesis, The Ohio State University, 1925.

Howard, Marilyn Kaye. "Black Lynching in the Promised Land: Mob Violence in Ohio, 1876–1916." Ph.D. Diss., The Ohio State University, 1999.

Howson, Embry Bernard. "The Ku Klux Klan in Ohio After World War I." Thesis, The Ohio State University, 1951.

Jelks, Randal Maurice. "Race, Respectability, and the Struggle for Civil Rights: A Study of the African American Community of Grand Rapids, Michigan, 1870–1954." Ph.D. Diss., Michigan State University, 2001.

Johnson, Eric Lamar. "A History of Black Schooling in Franklin County, Ohio, 1870–1913." Ph.D. Diss., The Ohio State University, 2002.

McClain, Shirla R. "The Contributions of Blacks in Akron, 1825–1975." Ph.D. Diss., University of Akron, 1975.

Materson, Lisa Gail. "Respectable Partisans: African American Women in Electoral Politics, 1877 to 1936." Ph.D. Diss., University of California, Los Angeles, 2000.

Miller, Khadijah Olivia Turner. "Everyday Victories: The Pennsylvania State Federation of Negro Women's Clubs, Inc., 1900–1930: Paradigms of Survival and Empowerment." Ph.D. Diss., Temple University, 2001.

Minor, Richard Clyde. "The Negro in Columbus, Ohio." Ph.D. Diss., The Ohio State University, 1936.

———. "Negro Recreation in Columbus, Ohio." M.A. Thesis, The Ohio State University, 1926.

Moore, William Franklin. "Status of the Negro in Cleveland." Ph.D. Diss., The Ohio State University, 1953.

Nicholes, Walter McKinley. "The Educational Development of Blacks in Cincinnati from 1800 to the Present." Ph.D. Edu. Diss., University of Cincinnati, 1977.

Ortiz, Paul Andrew. "'Like water covered the sea': The African American Freedom Struggle in Florida, 1877–1920." Ph.D. Diss., Duke University, 2000.

Porter, Jennie D. "The Problem of Negro Education in Northern and Border Cities." Ph.D. Diss., University of Cincinnati, 1928.

Pruitt, Bernadette. "For the Advancement of the Race: African-American Migration and Community Building in Houston, 1914–1945." Ph.D. Diss., University of Houston, 2001.

Reed, Toure. "'Helping negroes to help themselves': Middle Class Reform and the Politics of Racial Order, 1910–1950." Ph.D. Diss., Columbia University, 2002.

Ridley, Lendell Charles. "A Study of Housing Conditions Among Colored People of Columbus, Ohio." M.A. Thesis, The Ohio State University, 1920.

Robinson, Paul Langham. "Class and Place with the Los Angeles African American Community, 1940–1990." Ph.D. Diss., University of Southern California, 2001.

Sacks, Mary Sarah. "'We cry among the skyscrapers': Black People in New York City, 1880–1915." Ph.D. Diss., University of California, Berkeley, 1999.

Sides, Josh A. "Working Away: African American Migration and Community in Los Angeles from the Great Depression to 1954." Ph.D. Diss., University of California, Los Angeles, 1999.

Smith, Larissa M. "Where the South Begins: Black Politics and Civil Rights Activism in Virginia, 1930–1951." Ph.D. Diss., Emory University, 2001.

Taylor, Durahn Andrew Bernardo. "Black Gotham: Voters, Leaders, and the Political Game in Harlem, 1928–1950. Ph.D. Diss., Columbia University, 1999.

Taylor, Nikki Marie. "'Frontiers of Freedom': The African American Experience in Cincinnati, 1802–1862." Ph.D. Diss., Duke University, 2001.

Williams, LeRoy Thomas. "Black Toledo: Afro-Americans in Toledo, 1890–1930." Ph.D. Diss., University of Toledo, 1977.

Williams, Regennia Nanette. "Equity and Efficiency: African American Leadership and Education Reform in Cleveland, Ohio, 1915–1940." Ph.D. Diss., Case Western Reserve University, 2001.

Books

African Americans in Pennsylvania: Shifting Historical Perspectives. Joe William Trotter, Jr. and Eric Ledell Smith, eds. University Park: Pennsylvania State University Press, 1997.

Aiken, Katherine G. Harnessing the Power of Motherhood: The National Florence Crittenton Mission, 1883–1925. Knoxville: University of Tennessee Press, 1998.

Anderson, Eric and Alfred A. Moss, Jr. Dangerous Donations: Northern Philanthropy and Southern Education. Columbia: University of Missouri Press, 1999.

Barbeau, Arthur and Florette Henri. The Unknown Soldiers: Black American Troops in World War I. Philadelphia: Temple University Press, 1974.

Bauerlein, Mark. Negrophobia: A Race Riot in Atlanta, 1906. San Francisco: Encounter, 2001.

Beaver, Daniel R. Newton D. Baker and the American War Effort 1917–1919. Lincoln, Nebraska: University of Nebraska Press, 1966.

Beito, David T. From Mutual Aid to Welfare State: Fraternal Societies and Social Services, 1890–1967. Chapel Hill: University of North Carolina Press, 2000.

Black, Lowell Dwight. *The Negro Volunteer Militia Units of the Ohio National Guard, 1870–1954: The Struggle for Military Recognition and Equality in the State of Ohio.* Manhattan, Kansas: Military Affairs/Aerospace Historian Publishing, 1976.

Brophy, Alfred L. *Reconstructing the Dreamland: The Tulsa Riot of 1921: Race, Reparations, and Reconciliation.* New York: Oxford University Press, 2002.

Broussard, Albert S. *Black San Francisco: The Struggle for Racial Equality in the West, 1900–1954.* Lawrence: University of Kansas Press, 1993.

Butler, Brian. *An Undergrowth of Folly: Public Order, Race Anxiety, and the 1903 Evansville, Indiana, Riot.* New York: Garland, 2000.

Campbell, Thomas F. *Daniel E. Morgan, 1877–1949: The Good Citizen in Politics.* Cleveland: Western Reserve University Press, 1966.

Cayton, Andrew R. L. *Ohio: The History of a People.* Columbus: The Ohio State University Press, 2002.

Chaddock, Robert E. *Ohio before 1850: A Study of the Early Influence of Pennsylvania and Southern Populations in Ohio.* New York: Columbia University, 1908.

Chesnutt, Helen M. *Charles Waddell Chesnutt, Pioneer of the Color Line.* Chapel Hill: University of North Carolina Press, 1952.

Chicago Commission on Race Relations. *The Negro in Chicago: A Study of Race Relations and a Race Riot.* [written by Charles S. Johnson] Chicago: University of Chicago Press, 1922.

Cincinnati: A Guide to the Queen City and Its Neighbors. Compiled by the Workers of the Writers' Program of the Work Projects Administration in the State of Ohio. Cincinnati: The Wiesen-Hart Press, 1943.

Cohen, Nancy. *Reconstruction of American Liberalism, 1865–1914.* Chapel Hill: University of North Carolina Press, 2002.

Cronon, E. David. *Black Moses: The Story of Marcus Garvey and the Universal Negro. Improvement Association.* Madison: University of Wisconsin Press, 1969.

Crowe, Daniel. *Prophets of Rage: The Black Freedom Struggle in San Francisco, 1945–1969.* New York: Garland, 2000.

Dabney, Wendell P. *Chisum's Pilgrimage and Others.* Cincinnati, 1927.

———. *Cincinnati's Colored Citizens, Historical, Sociological and Biographical.* Cincinnati: The Dabney Publishing Company, 1926.

Davis, Russell H. *Black Americans in Cleveland from George Peake to Carl B. Stokes, 1796–1969.* Washington, D.C.: Associated Publishers, 1972.

———. *Memorable Negroes in Cleveland's Past.* Cleveland: Western Reserve Historical Society, 1969.

Dinnerstein, Leonard and David M. Reimers. *Ethnic Americans.* New York: Harper & Row, Publishers, 1982.

Dittmer, John. *Local People: The Struggle for Civil Rights in Mississippi.* Urbana: University of Illinois Press, 1994.

Drake, St. Clair and Horace R. Cayton. *Black Metropolis: A Study of Negro Life in a Northern City.* 1945. Reprint, New York: Harcourt Brace, and World, 1970. Original, New York: Harcourt Brace and Company, 1945.

Du Bois, William Edward Burghardt. *Dusk of Dawn, An Essay Toward An Autobiography of a Race Concept.* New York: Harcourt, Brace and Company, 1940.

Du Bois, W. E. B. *The Philadelphia Negro: A Social Study*. 1899, reprint, New York: Schocken Books, 1967.

Dulaney, W. Marvin. *Black Police in America*. Bloomington: Indiana University Press, 1996.

Dunn, Marvin. *Black Miami in the Twentieth Century*. Gainesville: University Press of Florida, 1997.

Eick, Gretchen Cassel. *Dissent in Wichita: The Civil Rights Movement in the Midwest, 1954–72*. Urbana: University of Illinois Press, 2001.

Elfenbein, Jessica I. *The Making of a Modern City: Philanthropy, Civic Culture, and the Baltimore YMCA*. Gainesville: University Press of Florida, 2001.

Ellis, Mark. *Race, War, and Surveillance: African Americans and the United States Government during World War I*. Bloomington: Indiana University Press, 2001.

Ellsworth, Scott. *Death in a Promised Land: The Tulsa Race Riot of 1921*. Baton Rouge: Louisiana State University Press, 1982.

Fairclough, Adam. *Race & Democracy: The Civil Rights Struggle in Louisiana, 1915–1972*. Athens: University of Georgia Press, 1995.

Franklin, John Hope and Alfred A. Moss, Jr. *From Slavery to Freedom: A History of African Americans*. New York: McGraw-Hill, Inc., 2000.

Ferguson, Karen. *Black Politics in New Deal Atlanta*. Chapel Hill: University of North Carolina Press, 2002.

Frazier, E. Franklin. *The Negro Family in Chicago*. Chicago: University of Chicago, 1932.

Gamble, Vanessa N. *Making a Place for Ourselves: The Black Hospital Movement 1920–1945*. New York: Oxford University Press, 1995.

Garrity, John H. *The Barber and the Historian: The Correspondence of George A. Myers and James A. Rhodes, 1910–1923*. Columbus: Ohio Historical Society, 1956.

Gerber, David A. *Black Ohio and the Color Line 1860–1915*. Urbana: University of Illinois Press, 1976.

Gerstle, Gary. *American Crucible: Race and Nation in the Twentieth Century*. Princeton: Princeton University Press, 2001.

Goings, Kenneth W. *"The NAACP Comes of Age": The Defeat of Judge John J. Parker*. Bloomington: Indiana University Press, 1990.

Gordon, Fon Louise. *Caste & Class: The Black Experience in Arkansas, 1880–1920*. Athens: University of Georgia Press, 1995.

Gottlieb, Peter. *Making Their Own Way: Southern Black's Migration to Pittsburgh, 1916–30*. Urbana: University of Illinois Press, 1987.

The Great Migration in Historical Perspective: New Dimensions of Race, Class, and Gender. Joe William Trotter, Jr., ed. Bloomington: Indiana University Press, 1991.

Grossman, James R. *Land of Hope: Chicago, Black Southerners, and the Great Migration*. Chicago: University of Chicago Press, 1989.

Guterl, Matthew Pratt. *The Color of Race in America, 1900–1940*. Cambridge: Harvard University Press, 2001.

Hagan, William. *American Indians*. Chicago: University of Chicago Press, 1969.

Henderson, Alexa Benson. *Atlanta Life Insurance Company: Guardian of Black Economic Dignity*. Tuscaloosa: University of Alabama Press, 1990.

Hendricks, Wanda A. *Gender, Race, and Politics in the Midwest: Black Club Women in Illinois*. Bloomington: Indiana University Press, 1998.

Hickey, Georgina. *Hope and Danger in the New South City: Working-Class Women and Urban Development in Atlanta, 1890–1940*. Athens: University of Georgia Press, 2003.

Higginbotham, Evelyn Brooks. *Righteous Discontent: The Women's Movement in the Black Baptist Church, 1880–1920*. Cambridge: Harvard University Press, 1993.

Higham, John. *Strangers in the Land: Patterns of American Nativism, 1860–1925*. New Brunswick: Rutgers University Press, 1988.

Hine, Darlene Clark. *Black Women in White: Racial Conflict and Cooperation in the Nursing Profession, 1890–1950*. Bloomington: Indiana University Press, 1989.

Historical Roots of the Urban Crisis: African Americans in the Industrial City, 1900–1950. Henry Louis Taylor, Jr. and Walter Hill, eds. New York: Garland, 2000.

Hofstadter, Richard. *The Age of Reform: From Bryan to F. D. R.* New York: Alfred A. Knopf, 1972.

Huggins, Nathan I. *Harlem Renaissance*. New York: Oxford University Press, 1973.

Hunter, Jane E. *A Nickel and a Prayer*. Cleveland: Elli Kani Publishing Company, 1940.

Jackson, Kenneth T. *The Ku Klux Klan in the City*. New York: Oxford University Press, 1970.

Jenkins, William D. *Steel Valley Klan: The Ku Klux Klan in Ohio's Mahoning Valley*. Kent: Kent State University Press, 1990.

Jones, Adrienne Lash. *Jane Edna Hunter: A Case Study of Black Leadership, 1910–1950*. Brooklyn, NY: Carlson, 1990.

Jones, Maldwyn Allen. *American Immigration*. Chicago: University of Chicago Press, 1974.

Jordan, William G. *Black Newspapers and America's War for Democracy, 1914–1920*. Chapel Hill: University of North Carolina Press, 2001.

Keller, Frances R. *An American Crusade: The Life of Charles Waddell Chesnutt*. Provo: Brigham Young University, 1978.

Katzman, David M. *Before the Ghetto: Black Detroit in the Nineteenth Century*. Urbana: University of Illinois Press, 1973.

Kellogg, Charles F. *NAACP, A History of the National Association for the Advancement of Colored People*. Baltimore: Johns Hopkins University Press, 1967.

Kenzer, Robert C. *Enterprising Southerners: Black Economic Success in North Carolina, 1865–1915*. Charlottesville: University Press of Virginia, 1997.

Knupfer, Ann Meis. *Toward a Tenderer Humanity and a Nobler Womanhood: African American Women's Clubs in Turn of the Century Chicago*. New York: New York University Press, 1996.

Kornweibel Theodore, Jr. *"Investigating Everything": Federal Efforts to Compel Black Loyalty during World War I*. Bloomington: Indiana University Press, 2002.

Kusmer, Kenneh L. *A Ghetto Takes Shape: Black Cleveland, 1870–1930*. Urbana: University of Illinois Press, 1976.

Lewis, Earl. *In Their Own Interests: Race, Class, and Power in Twentieth Century Norfolk*. Berkeley: University of California, 1991.

Lutholtz, M. William. *Grand Dragon: D. C. Stephenson and the Ku Klux Klan in Indiana*. West Lafayette: Purdue University Press, 1991.

McBride, David. *Integrating the City of Medicine: Blacks in Philadelphia Health Care, 1910–1965*. Philadelphia: Temple University Press, 1989.

McWilliams, Wm. A. *Columbus Illustrated Record, 1919–1920*. Columbus, OH: W. A. McWilliams, Publisher, 1920.

Mark, Mary Louise. *Negroes in Columbus*. Columbus: The Ohio State University Press, 1928.

Meier, August and Elliott Rudwick, *From Plantation to Ghetto*. New York: Hill and Wang, 1970.

Meyer, Stephen Grant. *As Long as They Don't Move Next Door: Segregation and Racial Conflict in American Neighborhoods*. Lanham: Rowan & Littlefield, 2000.

Miller, Zane L. *Boss Cox's Cincinnati: Urban Politics in the Progressive Era*. New York: Oxford University Press, 1968.

———. *Visions of Place: The City, Neighborhoods, Suburbs, and Cincinnati's Clifton, 1850–2000*. Columbus: The Ohio State University Press, 2001.

Miller, Zane L. and Bruce Tucker. *Changing Plans for America's Inner Cities: Cincinnati's Over-the-Rhine and Twentieth-Century Urbanism*. Columbus: The Ohio State University Press, 1998.

Moon, Henry Lee. *Balance of Power: The Negro Vote*. Garden City, NY: Doubleday, 1948.

Moore, Jacqueline M. *Leading the Race: The Transformation of the Black Elite in the Nation's Capital, 1880–1920*. Charlottesville: University Press of Virginia, 1999.

Moore, Leonard J. *Citizen Klansmen: The Ku Klux Klan in Indiana, 1921–1928*. Chapel Hill: University of North Carolina Press, 1991.

Moore, Shirley Anne Wilson. *To Place Our Deeds: The African American Community in Richmond, California, 1910–1963*. Berkeley: University of California Press, 2000.

Morais, Herbert M. *The History of the Negro in Medicine*. New York: Publishers Company, 1969.

Mumford, Kevin J. *Interzones: Black/White Sex Districts in Chicago and New York in the Early Twentieth Century*. New York: Columbia University Press, 1997.

Olson, James S. and Raymond Wilson, *Native Americans in the Twentieth Century*. Provo: Brigham Young University Press, 1984.

Osofsky, Gilbert. *Harlem, The Making of a Ghetto: Negro New York, 1890–1930*. New York: Harper & Row, 1966.

Patterson, James T. *American in the Twentieth Century: A History*. New York: Harcourt Brace, Jovanovich, 1976.

Peretti, Burton W. *The Creation of Jazz: Music, Race, and Culture in Urban America*. Urbana: University of Illinois Press, 1992.

Phillips, Kimberly L. *Alabama North: African-American Migrants, Community, and Working-Class Activism in Cleveland 1915–1945*. Urbana: University of Illinois Press, 1999.

Reed, Christopher Robert. *The Chicago NAACP and the Rise of Black Professional Leadership, 1910–1966*. Bloomington: Indiana University Press, 1997.

Rice, Mitchell F. and Woodrow Jones, Jr. *Public Policy and the Black Hospital: From Slavery to Segregation to Integration*. Westport: Greenwood, 1994.

Roseboom, Eugene H. and Francis P. Weisenburger. *A History of Ohio*. Columbus: The Ohio State Archaeological and Historical Society, 1961.

Roseboom, Eugene H. *A History of Presidential Elections*. New York: The Macmillan Company, 1959.

Rudwick, Elliott M. *Race Riot at East St. Louis, July 2, 1917*. Carbondale: Southern Illinois University Press, 1964.

Russell, Francis. *The Shadow of Blooming Grove: Warren G. Harding in His Times*. New York: McGraw-Hill, 1968.

Schneider, Mark R. *Boston Confronts Jim Crow, 1890–1920*. Boston: Northeastern University Press, 1997.

Scott, Emmett J. *Negro Migration during the War*. Carnegie Endowment for International Peace, Division of Economics and History, *Preliminary Economic Studies of the War*, ed. David Kinley. No. 16. New York: Oxford University Press, 1920.

————. *The Negro American in the World War*. Chicago: Homewood Press, 1919.

Senechal, Roberta. *The Sociogenesis of a Race Riot: Springfield, Illinois, in 1908*. Urbana: University of Illinois Press, 1990.

Sernett, Milton C. *Bound for the Promised Land: African American Religion and the Great Migration*. Durham: Duke University Press, 1997.

Sherman, Richard B. *The Republican Party and Black America: From McKinley to Hoover, 1896–1933*. Charlottesville: University of Virginia Press, 1973.

Sitkoff, Harvard. *A New Deal for Blacks, The Emergence of Civil Rights as a National Issue: The Depression Decade*. New York: Oxford University Press, 1981.

Spear, Allan H. *Black Chicago: The Making of a Negro Ghetto*. Chicago: University of Chicago Press, 1967.

Springfield and Clark County, Ohio. Compiled by Workers of the Writers' Program of the Works Progress Administration in the State of Ohio. Springfield, OH: Springfield Tribune Printing Company, 1941.

The State of Afro-American History: Present Past, and Future. Darlene Clark Hine, ed. Baton Rouge: Louisiana State University Press, 1986.

Suggs, Henry L. *The Black Press in the Middle West, 1865–1985*. Westport: Greenwood Press, 1996.

Taiz, Lillian. *Hallelujah Lads & Lasses: Remaking the Salvation Army in America, 1880–1930*. Chapel Hill: University of North Carolina Press, 2001.

Terborg-Penn, Rosalyn. *African American Women in the Struggle for the Vote, 1850–1920*. Bloomington: Indiana University Press, 1998.

Thornbrough, Emma Lou. *Indiana Blacks in the Twentieth Century*. Lana Ruegamer, ed. Bloomington: Indiana University Press, 2000.

Tracy, Steven C., *Going to Cincinnati: A History of the Blues in the Queen City*. Urbana: University of Illinois Press, 1993.

Trotter, Joe William, Jr. *Black Milwaukee: The Making of an Industrial Proletariat, 1915–1945*. Urbana: University of Illinois Press, 1985.

————. *Coal, Class, and Color: Blacks in Southern West Virginia, 1915–1932*. Urbana: University of Illinois Press, 1990.

———. *River Jordan: African American Urban Life in the Ohio Valley*. Lexington: The University Press of Kentucky, 1998.

Tuck, Stephen G. N. *Beyond Atlanta: The Struggle for Racial Equality in Georgia, 1940–1980*. Athens: University of Georgia Press, 2001.

Tucker, Richard K. *The Dragon and the Cross: The Rise and Fall of the Ku Klux Klan in Middle America*. Hamden: Archon, 1991.

Tuennerman-Kaplan, Laura. *Helping Others, Helping Ourselves: Power, Giving, and Community Identity in Cleveland, Ohio, 1880–1930*. Kent: Kent State University Press, 2001.

Tuttle, William M., Jr. *Race Riot: Chicago in the Red Summer of 1919*. Urbana: University of Illinois Press, 1996.

Urbana and Champaign County. Compiled by Workers of the Writers' Program of the Works Progress Administration in the State of Ohio. Sponsored by the Urbana Lions Club. Urbana, OH: Gaumer Publishing Company (c. 1942).

Ward, David. *Poverty, Ethnicity, and the American City, 1840–1925: Changing Conceptions of the Slum and the Ghetto*. New York: Cambridge University Press, 1989.

Waskow, Arthur I. *From Race Riot to Sit-in: 1919 and the 1960s: A Study in the Connections between Conflict and Violence*. Garden City, NY: Anchor Books, 1967.

Weems, Robert E., Jr. *Black Business in the Black Metropolis: The Chicago Metropolitan Assurance Company, 1925–1985*. Bloomington: Indiana University Press, 1996.

Weiss, Nancy J. *Farewell to the Party of Lincoln: Black Politics in the Age of FDR*. Princeton: Princeton University Press, 1983.

———. *The National Urban League, 1910–1940*. New York: Oxford University Press, 1974.

Weisenfeld, Judith. *African American Women and Christian Activism: New York's Black YWCA, 1905–1945*. Cambridge: Harvard University Press, 1997.

Wesley, Charles H. *The History of the Prince Hall Grand Lodge of Free and Accepted Masons of the State of Ohio, 1849–1960*. Wilberforce, OH: Central State College Press, 1961.

Williams, Charles H. *Sidelights on Negro Soldiers*. Boston: B. J. Brimmer Company, 1923.

Wolcott, Victoria W. *Remaking Respectability: African American Women in Interwar Detroit*. Chapel Hill: University of North Carolina Press, 2001.

Woodson, Carter G. *The Negro in Our History*. Washington, D.C.: The Associated Publishers, Inc., 1947.

Wright, George C. *A History of Blacks in Kentucky: Vol. 2: In Pursuit of Equality, 1890–1980*. Frankfort: Kentucky Historical Society, 1992.

Articles, Chapters, and Miscellaneous Materials

"Address of President William S. Scarborough upon the opening of the academic year 1918–1919 at Wilberforce University, September 17, 1918." *The Wilberforcian* 1 no. 6 (March 1919), Carnegie Library, Wilberforce University, Ohio.

Allen, Anne Beiser. "Sowing Seeds of Kindness—and Change: A History of the Iowa Association of Women's Clubs." *Iowa Heritage Illustrated* 83 (Spring 2002): 2–13.

Allen, Nimrod B. "East Long Street." *The Crisis* 25 (November 1922): 12–16.

Barnhart, J. D. "The Southern Influence in the Formation of Ohio." *Journal of Southern History* 3 (Feb. 1937): 28–42.

Berquist, Goodwin and James Greenwood. "Protest Against Racism: 'The Birth of a Nation' in Ohio." In *Rhetoric of the People*, ed. Harold Barrett. Amsterdam: Rodopi, N. V., 1974.

Boynton, Virginia R. "Contested Terrain: The Struggle over Gender Norms for Black Working-Class Women in Cleveland's Phillis Wheatley Association, 1920–1950." *Ohio History* 103 (Winter–Spring 1994): 5–22.

Carby, Hazel. "Policing the Black Woman's Body in an Urban Context," *Critical Inquiry* 18 (Summer 1992): 738–55.

Carter, Patricia A. "Housing the Women Who Toiled: Planned Residences for Single Women, Cincinnati 1860–1960." *Ohio History* 103 (Winter–Spring 1996): 46–71.

Chesnutt, Charles W. "The Negro in Cleveland." *The Clevelander* 5 (Nov. 1930): 3–4, 24–26.

"Cleveland's *Call and Post*." *The Crisis* 45 (Dec. 1938): 391, 404.

Cleveland, Committee Investigating the Admittance of Colored Internes [sic] and Nurses to the Staff of City Hospital. "Report, Dec. 12, 1927." Western Reserve Historical Society Library, Cleveland, Ohio.

Collins, Ernest M. "Cincinnati Negroes and Presidential Politics." *Journal of Negro History* 41 (April 1956): 131–37.

Columbus Urban League. *Twenty Years of Service in the Field of Social Work for Negroes and Inter-race Relations 1917–1937*. Columbus: Columbus Urban League, 1937 (Printed pamphlet). PA, Box 534 44. Ohio Historical Society Archives/Library, Columbus, Ohio.

Columbus Urban League: "An Inventory of Its Papers in the Ohio Historical Society (Manuscript Division), Ohio Historical Society, Columbus, Ohio, 1969." Ohio Historical Society Archives/Library, Columbus, Ohio.

Fairbanks, Robert B. "Cincinnati Blacks and the Irony of Low-Income Housing Reform, 1900–1950." In *Race and the City: Work, Community, and Protest in Cincinnati, 1820–1970*, ed. Henry Louis Taylor, Jr. Urbana: University of Illinois Press, 1993.

Garvin, Charles H. "The Negro Physicians and the Hospitals of Cleveland." *Journal of the National Medical Association* 22 (July–September 1930): 124–27.

Giffin, William W. "Black Insurgency in the Republican Party of Ohio, 1920–1932." *Ohio History* 82 (Winter–Spring 1973): 25–45.

———. "The Mercy Hospital Controversy among Cleveland's Afro-American Civic Leaders, 1927." *The Journal of Negro History* 61 (Oct. 1976): 327–50.

———. "Mobilization of Black Militiamen in World War I: Ohio's Ninth Battalion." *The Historian* 40 (August 1978): 696–703.

———. "The Political Realignment of Black Voters in Indianapolis, 1924," *Indiana Magazine of History* 79 (June 1983): 133–66.

Gordon, Rita W. "The Change in the Political Realignment of Chicago's Negroes during the New Deal," *Journal of American History* 56 (December 1969): 584–603.

Green, H. M. "A Brief Study of the Hospital Situation among Negroes." *Journal of the National Medical Association* 22 (July–Sept. 1930): 112–14.

Hannah, Eleanor L. "A Place in the Parade: Citizenship, Manhood, and African American Men in the Illinois National Guard, 1870–1917." *Journal of Illinois History* 5 (Summer 2002): 82–108.

Haynes, George E. "The Opportunity of Negro Labor." *The Crisis* 18 (Sept. 1919): 236–38.

———. "Negroes Move North." *Survey* 42 (January 4, 1919): 459.

Hendricks, Wanda A. "Child Welfare and Black Female Agency in Springfield: Eva Monroe and the Lincoln Colored Home." *Journal of Illinois History* 3 (Summer 2000): 86–104.

Himes, J. S., Jr. "Forty Years of Negro Life in Columbus, Ohio." *The Journal of Negro History* 27 (April 1942): 133–54.

Hoffman, Steven J. "Progressive Public Health Administration in the Jim Crow South: A Case Study of Richmond, Virginia, 1907–1920." *Journal of Social History* 35 (Fall 2001): 175–194.

"How Shall We Vote?" *The Crisis* 29 (Nov. 1924): 12–15.

Hoy, Suellen. "Illinois Technical School for Colored Girls: A Catholic Institution on Chicago's South Side, 1911–1953." *Journal of Illinois History* 4 (Summer 2001): 103–22.

Jackson, Mary E. "The Colored Woman in Industry." *The Crisis* 17 (Nov. 1918): 12–13.

Johnson, Wray R. "Black American Radicalism and the First World War: The Secret Files of the Military Intelligence Division." *Armed Forces and Society* 26 (Fall 1999): 27–53.

Kenny, John A. "The Negro Hospital Renaissance." *Journal of the National Medical Association* 22 (July–Sept. 1930): 109–12.

Kilson, Martin. "Political Change in the Negro Ghetto, 1900–1940's." In *Key Issues in the Afro-American Experience*, eds. Nathan I. Huggins, Martin Kilson, and Daniel M. Fox. New York: Harcourt Brace Jovanovich, Inc., 1971.

Kornbluh, Andrea Tuttle. "James Hathaway Robinson and the Origins of Professional Social Work in the Black Community." In *Race and the City: Work, Community, and Protest in Cincinnati, 1820–1970*, ed. Henry Louis Taylor, Jr. Urbana: University of Illinois Press, 1993.

Krawcheck, Julian. "The Negro in Cleveland, A History, 1809–1963." Reprint from *Cleveland Press*, May 27–31 and June 1, 1963. PA, Box 297, 1. Ohio Historical Society Archives/Library, Columbus, Ohio.

Lindenmeyer, Kristie. "Saving Mothers and Babies: The Sheppard-Towner Act in Ohio, 1921–1929." *Ohio History* 99 (Summer–Autumn 1990): 105–34.

McDermott, Stacy Pratt. "'An Outrageous Proceeding': A Northern Lynching and the Enforcement of Anti-Lynching Legislation in Illinois, 1905–1910." *Journal of Negro History* 84 (Winter 1999): 61–78.

McKenzie, Roderick Duncan. "The Neighborhood: A Study of Local Life in the City of Columbus, Ohio." *American Journal of Sociology* 27 (Sept. 1921), 145–68, (Jan. 1922), 486–509, (May 1922): 780–99.

Mennell, James. "African Americans and the Selective Service Act of 1917." *Journal of Negro History* 84 (Summer 1999): 275–87.

Mercy Hospital Association. *Does Cleveland Need a Negro Manned Hospital? Facts Are the Answer* (Printed pamphlet). Western Reserve Historical Society Archives/Library, Cleveland, Ohio.

Meier, August and Elliott Rudwick. "Early Boycotts of Segregated Schools: The Case of Springfield, Ohio, 1922–23." *American Quarterly* 20, no. 4 (Winter 1968): 744–58.

Morton, Marian J. "'Go and Sin No More': Maternity Homes in Cleveland, 1869–1936." *Ohio History* 93 (Summer–Autumn 1984): 117–46.

Murage, Njeru. "Making Migrants an Asset: The Detroit Urban League-Employers Alliance in Wartime Detroit, 1916–1919." *Michigan Historical Review* 26 (Spring 2000): 67–93.

"Negro Health and Race Relations." *Cincinnati Sanitary Bulletin* 8, no. 4 (Oct. 14, 1925), 1–3, Cincinnati Historical Society Library.

Ohio Federation for Uplift Among Colored People. *Are You With Us?* Cleveland, 1918 (Printed pamphlet). PA Box 226, 32. Ohio Historical Society Archives/Library, Columbus, Ohio.

Phillis Wheatley Association, Cleveland. *Annual Report for the Year, 1923.* Ohio Historical Society Archives/Library, Columbus, Ohio.

Pierce, David H. "White Children and Their Colored Schoolmates." *The Crisis* 26 (June 1923): 63–64.

Robinson, James H. "The Negro Migration." *Social Service News: "A Magazine of Human Helpfulness"* 1: 7 (July 1917): 100–101.

Savitt, Todd L. "Four African-American Proprietary Medical Colleges: 1888–1923." *Journal of the History of Medicine and Allied Sciences.* 55 (July 2000): 203–55.

Scarborough, William S. "Race Riots and Their Remedy." *The Independent* 99 (1919): 223–24.

Schmidlapp, Jacob G. *Low Priced Housing for Wage Earners.* No. 34, New York City: National Housing Association Publications, 1919 (Printed pamphlet). Box 62, Folder 18, Cincinnati Model Homes Company, 1912–1977, Cincinnati Historical Society Library.

Shilling, David Carl. "Relations of Southern Ohio to the South during the Decade Preceding the Civil War." *Historical and Philosophical Society of Ohio Quarterly* 8, no. 1 (1913): 3–62.

Taylor, Henry Louis, Jr. "City Building, Public Policy, the Rise of the Industrial City, and Black Ghetto-Slum Formation in Cincinnati, 1850–1940." In *Race and the City: Work, Community, and Protest in Cincinnati, 1820–1970,* ed. Henry Louis Taylor, Jr. Urbana: University of Illinois Press, 1993.

Van Duesen, John G. "The Negro in Politics." *Journal of Negro History* 21 (July 1936): 256–74.

Weisenburger, Francis P. "William Sanders Scarborough, Early Life and Years at Wilberforce." *Ohio History* 71 (Oct. 1962): 203–26.

———. "William Sanders Scarborough, Scholarship, the Negro, Religion, and Politics." *Ohio History* 72 (Jan. 1963): 25–50, 85–88.

White, Walter. "The Test in Ohio." *The Crisis* 36 (Nov. 1930): 373–74.

Williams, Lee. "Newcomers to the City: A Study of Black Population Growth in Toledo, Ohio, 1910–1930." *Ohio History* 89 (Winter 1980): 5–24.

Index

Addams, Jane, 66
Adelphi Loan and Savings Company (Columbus), 102
Advocate (Cleveland), 25, 26, 84, 98
African Methodist Episcopal Church, 28, 39, 43, 66, 137
Afro American Republican Club (Cleveland), 228
Ailer, Charles C., 105
Akron, 65, 81, 210; black business, 25, 98, 102, 103; black churches, 107; black population growth, 14–15, 217, 220; black residential patterns, 124; blacks and employment, 11; blacks in politics, 212–13; discrimination in public accommodations, 140–41; equal rights struggle, 167–68, 169, 170; public schools and blacks, 135; welfare associations and blacks, 144, 146; white hostility, 115; YMCA, 155, 168. *See also* NAACP, Akron branch
Akron Negro Business League, 103
Akron University, 134
Alabama, 10, 11, 14, 83, 105, 132
Alabama North: African-American Migrants, Community, and Working Class Activism in Cleveland, 1915–1945 (Phillips), 3, 221
Alexander, Harry, 96
Allen County, 46
Allen, Nimrod B., 59, 186; and biog-

raphy, 65; on black businesses in Columbus, 97, 102–3; and Columbus Urban League, 144, 229; and middle class values, 154; on public accommodations in Columbus, 138–39; on public schools in Columbus, 130, 182; on real estate color line in Columbus, 125; on residential locations of blacks in Columbus, 123–24
Allen Theater (Cleveland), 140, 170
Alpha Hospital Association (Columbus), 186
Alpha Hospital (Columbus), 185–86
Alpha Phi Alpha fraternity (Dayton), 178
Al Smith League of Colored Voters of Ohio, 202
American Medical Association, 30
American Red Cross (Cincinnati), 144
American Rolling Mill Company, 42
Anchor Life Insurance Company (Cleveland), 102
Anglo-Saxon Protestants, 33, 34, 110, 141
anti-crime activities, black, 152, 153–54
Antioch Baptist Church (Cincinnati), 106, 155
Antioch Baptist Church (Cleveland), 66, 156, 190

Antioch College, 44
Anti-Tuberculosis League
    (Cincinnati), 149
Arkansas, 1, 11, 102, 132
Ashtabula, 10
Associated Charities (Cincinnati), 144
Associated Press All American foot-
    ball team, 135
Athens, 182
Atlanta, GA, 102, 222

Baber, Vivian, 46
Bad Lands (Columbus), 23
Bagnall, Robert W., 162, 163, 177,
    178, 181, 182
Bailey, Edward A., 126, 128
Bailey, Horace C., 66, 187, 190, 191,
    192
Baker, Elbert H., 172
Baker, Newton D., 71, 72, 83, 126–27
Baltimore, MD, 135
Baltimore, OH, 40
Baptist Ministerial Association
    (Columbus), 39
Baptist Ministers' Alliance
    (Cincinnati), 77, 137
Baptist Ministers' Alliance
    (Cleveland), 39, 71, 79, 137
Baptists, 10, 28, 29, 227
Barberton, 11
Barcus, Robert, 198
Barnhardt, John D., 48
Beaty, A. Lee, 77, 78, 198, 208, 209
Bee (Cincinnati), 25
Beito, David T., 29
Bell, William, 135
Bellamy, Paul, 172
Belmont County, 203
Benson, Ozie, 128
Better Housing League of Cincinnati,
    58, 62, 92, 93, 144, 147, 148
Biblus Kluklus: in Columbus, 30
Biddle College, 64
Big Four Roundhouse (Columbus),
    84
Birmingham, AL, 27
"The Birth of a Nation," 34, 71,
    73–79

"black metropolises," 89, 90, 108,
    216–17
Black Ohio and the Color Line,
    1860–1915 (Gerber), 3
Black and White Chronicle (Akron),
    25, 98
Blade (Toledo): on black migrants in
    Toledo, 10, 12
Blaine Club (Cincinnati), 197
Blossom, Dudley S., 188, 189
Blue, Welcome T., 26
blues music, 215, 216
Bolshevism, 34, 81
Booker T. Washington School
    (Middletown), 42
Boston University, 106, 163
Boult, Peter, 203, 209
Bowman School (Mansfield), 132,
    174–76, 228
Boyd, Albert D. (Starlight), 197, 205
Branch, Lizzie, 229
Brascher, Nahum D., 25, 26
Bricker, John W., 43
Bridgeport, 203
Broadway Theater (Columbus), 139
Brookside Park (Cleveland), 170
Brotherhood (Cincinnati), 25
Brown, Hallie Q., 225
Brown, Russell S., 190, 191, 192, 207
Brown, Samuel A., 161
Brown, Stanley, 189
Brown, Walter L., 203
Buffalo, NY, 10
Bulkley, Robert J., 212
Bundy, Leroy, 192–93, 208
business, black: barbering and food
    catering, 99–100; black patrons of,
    26, 27, 99; business associations,
    103; and business districts, 24, 97;
    funeral homes, 100–101; growth of,
    24, 97, 98 101; life insurance, 102;
    limitations of, 103–4; migrants in
    business, 26–27, 102–3; and news-
    papers, 24–26, 98; other small
    enterprises, 27; real estate compa-
    nies, 101; retail stores, 26, 101; sav-
    ings banks, 101–2. See also hospitals
    and blacks; women, black

business and professional classes, black, 31, 107, 222–23
Business and Professional Men's Club (Columbus), 103
Butler County, 115

California, 221
Calloway, Cab, 216
Calvary Methodist Episcopal Church (Cincinnati), 136
Canton, 14, 107, 124, 144, 146, 154, 212
Carby, Hazel, 60
Carroll, James, 74
Carter, Patricia A., 147
Case School of Applied Sciences, 44, 134
Caterer's Association (Cleveland), 30, 45, 68
Catholic Charities (Cincinnati), 144
Catholic Columbian, 74
Cayton, Andrew, 215
Cayton, Horace R., 89
Cedar Avenue YMCA, (Cleveland), 154
Centenary Methodist Episcopal Church (Columbus), 125
Center Street YMCA building (Springfield), 118
Central Avenue (Cleveland), 21, 24, 26, 35, 38, 47, 57, 97, 105, 120, 125, 152
Central Body (Cleveland), 205
Central High School (Cleveland), 129, 132
central Ohio: and black population in cities, 14, 90; and black social service institutions, 143; and color line intensity, 218; and the equal rights struggle,159, 169, 218–19; and NAACP branches, 66, 161, 162; and public accommodations, 44, 139; and protest heritage, 51, 52; and public schools, 39, 40, 129, 130, 131, 132, 133, 173, 179, 182; and race relations heritage, 48, 49
Chaddock, Robert E., 48

Champion Avenue School (Columbus), 41, 130, 146, 182
Champion Chemical Company (Springfield), 65, 181
Charlotte, NC, 64
Charter Party (Cincinnati), 211
Chauncey, Herbert S., 101, 102, 103, 186
Chesnutt, Charles W.: on black barbers in Cleveland, 100; on black businesses in Cleveland, 103–4; and literary fame, 215; and politics and protest, 166; on settlement house plan in Cleveland, 57–58
Chicago, 35, 45, 52, 79, 102, 140, 188
Childers, O. W., 45, 47
Chillicothe, 27, 40, 65
China, 33
Chinese Americans, 33
Chinese Exclusion Act, 33
Chisum, Melvin J., 11–12
Chittenden Hotel (Columbus), 139
churches, black, 104–5; and buildings, 105–7; and denominations, 28, 105; growth of, 28–29, 95; and the Social Gospel, 155–56. *See also* ministers, black
Church of the Living God, 28
Cincinnati, 4, 9, 28, 29, 38, 43, 55, 56, 63, 64, 72, 75, 78, 81, 109, 111, 115, 116, 122, 139, 141, 158, 167, 169, 176, 177, 215, 216, 217, 218, 223, 228, 229; black business, 24, 25, 26, 27, 97–104 *passim*; black churches, 39, 105, 106, 107, 136, 137, 149, 155, 156; black fraternal orders, 107–8; black migrants' conditions, 17, 20, 92–93; black migrants' numbers, 9–10; black-police issues, 22, 94, 95, 153; black population growth, 14, 31, 89, 90, 217, 220; black residential patterns, 31, 35, 37, 119, 120, 121, 123, 124, 221; blacks and employment, 24, 96–97; blacks and hospitals, 183–85; blacks in politics, 197,198, 202, 204–5, 208, 209, 210, 211; blacks

and public schools, 40, 41–42, 129, 130–31, 133, 134, 136, 156, 157, 224; blacks and public welfare institutions, 51, 53–54, 58–59, 62, 143, 146–47, 149–50; blacks and welfare associations, 61, 62, 64–65, 142, 143–44, 145, 148, 149; discrimination in public accommodations, 44, 138; equal rights struggle, 50, 77, 166, 168, 171, 182, 183, 185, 230; vice in black districts, 22, 94, 152; YMCA, 53–54, 61, 154–55; YWCA, 54, 59, 61, 147. *See also* NAACP, Cincinnati branch

Cincinnati Business Men's League, 103

Cincinnati City Council, 204

Cincinnati Clericus, 137

Cincinnati College of Embalming, 100

Cincinnati Council for Social Agencies, 54, 62, 229

Cincinnati Department of Health, 148

Cincinnati Enquirer, 81, 171

Cincinnati Federation of Women's Clubs, 108

Cincinnati General Hospital, 183, 185

Cincinnati, Hamilton and Dayton Railroad, 16

Cincinnati Health Board, 20

Cincinnati Medical Association, 184

Cincinnati Normal School, 136

Cincinnati Police Department, 95, 204

Cincinnati Protective and Industrial Association for Colored Women and Children, 54

Cincinnati Sanitary Bulletin, 93

Cincinnati Settlement School of Music, 156

Citizen (Dayton), 25

City Free Labor Exchange of Cleveland, 16

Civil Rights Protective League (Springfield), 180, 181

Clark, Peter, 198

Clark, R. Eugene, 184

class structure, black, 32, 221–23

clerkships, retail, blacks barred from, 97

Cleveland, 11, 12, 30, 48, 49, 50, 70, 78, 80, 81, 82, 84, 89, 108, 109, 118, 141, 165, 166, 168, 169, 175, 176, 180, 212, 215, 221, 226, 227, 228, 229; black business, 24, 25, 26, 27, 97–104 *passim*; black churches, 28, 29, 32, 39, 105, 107, 136–37, 155, 156; black fraternal orders, 107; black migrants' conditions, 17–21 *passim*, 92–94 *passim*; black migrants' numbers, 9–10, 91; black-police issues, 21–22, 94–95, 152–53; black population growth, 14, 31, 90–91, 216–17, 220; black residential patterns, 35, 37, 38, 119, 120–21, 124, 125–27; black-white relations, 51, 68; blacks and employment, 16, 23–24, 96–97; blacks and hospitals, 183, 186–93; blacks in politics, 197–98, 200, 201, 205–8, 209, 210–11, 225; blacks and public schools, 40, 43, 129–30, 132–33, 134, 224; blacks and public welfare institutions, 51–52, 56–61 *passim*, 143, 145, 146, 147, 149–50, 154, 218; blacks and welfare associations, 61, 63–64, 142, 144, 145–46, 151; discrimination in public accommodations, 44–45, 138, 139–40; equal rights struggle, 51, 68, 71–72, 73–74, 76–77, 79, 167, 170, 171–72, 173–74, 183, 230; vice in black districts, 21, 94, 152; white hostility, 45, 47, 128; YMCA, 143, 154. *See also* NAACP, Cleveland branch

Cleveland Anti-Tuberculosis League, 151

Cleveland Area Church Federation, 188

Cleveland Association of Colored Men, 30, 65, 68, 79

Cleveland Board of Education, 173, 207
Cleveland Business Men's Association, 103
Cleveland Call, 98, 192
Cleveland Call and Post, 98
Cleveland Chamber of Commerce, 18, 63, 93, 140
Cleveland City Council, 21, 77, 164, 188, 190, 191–92, 205, 206, 207, 208, 228
Cleveland City Hospital, 187–93, 208, 228, 230
Cleveland Civil Service Commission, 206–7
Cleveland Clinic, 189
Cleveland Community Chest, 187
Cleveland Federation of Colored Women's Clubs, 77, 150
Cleveland Finance Company, 102
Cleveland Heights, 125
Cleveland Herald, 98
Cleveland Home for Aged Colored People, 56, 57
Cleveland Hospital Association, 186
Cleveland Hotel, 140
Cleveland Juvenile Court, 225
Cleveland Medical Reading Club, 229
Cleveland News, 17, 18, 45
Cleveland Plain Dealer, 18, 171–72, 190, 207
Cleveland Real Estate Board, 18, 19
Cleveland Realty, Housing, and Investment Company, 26
Cleveland School of Education, 132
Cleveland Welfare Federation, 63, 150
Cleveland Women's Civic Association, 151
Cleves, 117
Cohen, Isadore B., 170
Cole, Charles, 46
College Hill, 120, 221
colleges, universities, and blacks, 43–44, 134–36
Colley, E. Duval, 204
Colored Big Brothers (Columbus), 144, 153

Colored Big Sisters (Columbus), 144, 153
Colored Citizen (Cincinnati), 25
Colored Democratic Clubs (Ohio), 202
Colored Industrial School of Cincinnati, 42, 131, 146
Colored Lutheran Emanuel Church (Cincinnati), 137
Colored Women's Association (Lorain), 73
Colored Women's Independent Political League (Columbus), 30, 225
Colored Women's Republican Club (Columbus), 209, 225
Columbia Chemical Company, 11
Columbia University, 64
Columbiana County, 78
Columbian Fraternal Association, 102
Columbus, 13, 20, 70, 78, 82, 84, 109, 111, 115, 136, 141, 166, 167, 171, 179, 225; black business, 26, 27, 97, 98, 100–103 *passim;* black churches, 28, 39, 105, 106, 107, 226; black fraternal orders, 30, 108; black migrants' conditions, 17, 92; black-police issues, 95, 152–53; black population growth, 14, 31, 89, 90, 220; black residential patterns, 35, 36, 37, 119, 120, 121, 123, 124, 125; blacks and employment, 11, 24, 91, 96; blacks and hospitals, 183, 185–86; blacks in politics, 199, 202, 203, 208, 212–13; blacks and public schools, 40, 41, 129, 130, 133; blacks and public welfare institutions, 53, 56, 59, 61, 146; blacks and welfare associations, 61, 62–63, 65, 142, 143, 144, 146, 152, 153, 154, 168; discrimination in public accommodations, 44, 68, 138–39; equal rights struggle, 74, 168, 169, 182–83, 186, 229, 230; vice in black districts, 22–23, 94; white hostility, 47, 79; YMCA, 56, 61,

62; YWCA, 56, 61. *See also* NAACP, Columbus branch

Columbus Citizen, 119

Columbus Citizen's Law and Order League, 79

Columbus Commercial High School, 41

Columbus Dispatch, 84, 119

Columbus East High School, 41

Columbus Home for Colored Girls, 56, 61, 146

Columbus Hotel, 139

Columbus Industrial Mortgage and Security Company, 102

Columbus North High School, 41

Columbus Police Department, 152

Columbus Urban League, 65, 97, 102, 111, 112, 113, 123, 125,138, 144, 146, 152, 153, 154, 162, 168, 183, 186, 229; origins, 62–63

Columbus Voice, 98

Columbus Weekly News, 98

Committee on Public Information, 84

Community Chest: in Cincinnati, 62, 145, 149

Congregational churches, 28, 39

Connecticut Western Reserve, 44, 49, 51, 159

Conners, William R., 10, 64

Conrad, George W. B, 204

Coolidge, Calvin, 201, 211, 225

Cooper, Myers Y., 201–2

Cottrill, Charles, 166, 198

Court of Calanthe: in Columbus, 30

Covington, KY, 101

Cox, George B., 197

Cox, James M., 18, 20, 76, 78, 79, 83–84

Crawford Old Men's Home (Cincinnati), 53, 62

Credential Mortgage Company (Columbus), 102

Crescent Club (Cincinnati), 108

Crisis, 177, 181; on a cemetery color line, 169; on college and university degrees awarded to blacks, 135–36; on numbers of black

migrants in Ohio, 9, 10; and politics, 211, 212

Crittenden, Florence, 150

Crittenden Home (Cleveland), 150

Crosby, Bing, 216

culture of the South, 225–27

Cumminsville, 120

Curry, E. W., 198

Cuyahoga County, 76, 197, 203, 205, 206, 207, 208–9, 218

Dabney, Wendell P.: on black churches in Cincinnati, 156; on black businesses in Cincinnati, 97–98, 100, 104; and black men's clubs and lodges, 108; on black professionals in Cincinnati, 104; on black residential segregation in Cincinnati area, 120, 123; on Cincinnati UNIA, 210; on daily newspaper's reporting, 171; and home for unwed mothers, 54; on hospitals in Cincinnati, 185; and Klan legislation, 168; and middle class values, 154; on NAACP branch, 66, 162; in the newspaper business, 25, 98; and politics and protest, 166, 197, 204; on public accommodations in Cincinnati, 44, 138; on schools in Cincinnati, 133; on vice activities and crime in Cincinnati, 22, 94; and women's shelter in Cincinnati, 58

Daily Journal (Toledo), 18

Daniels, Charles, 46

Daniels, George W., 181

Daughters of Hope, 29

Davey, Martin L., 202

Davis, Charles R., 160

Davis, Estelle Rickman, 108

Davis, Harry E., 164; as civil service commissioner, 206–7; as state representative, 168, 209; on public accommodations in Cleveland, 45; and public schools, 174; on recruiting of black migrants, 12

Davis, Harry L., 76–77, 118, 167, 201

Davis, John W., 201

Dayton, 65, 78, 82; black business, 98; black churches, 115; black population growth, 14–15, 90, 217; black residential patterns, 119, 121, 124, 127; blacks in politics, 202; blacks and public schools, 40, 129, 130, 131, 132; equal rights struggle, 76, 166–67, 173, 177–79, 183, 219, 230; white hostility, 115, 119. *See also* NAACP, Dayton branch

Dayton Board of Education, 127, 177, 178, 179

Dayton City Commission, 76

Dayton Federation of Churches, 76

Dayton News, 78

Decatur, William J., 131

Democratic Party and Democrats, 3, 76, 77–78, 110, 195, 196, 198, 199, 200, 201, 202, 203, 206, 207, 208, 209, 211, 212, 214

Denison University, 44

dentists, black, 104

Deshler Hotel (Columbus), 139

Detroit, MI, 220

Dewey, John, 66

Dickinson, C. E., 212

District of Columbia, 45, 79, 102, 184, 188, 189

Dixon, Thomas, 73

doctors, black, 28, 103, 104, 232

domestic and personal service, blacks in, 24, 96

Donahey, A.Victor (Vic), 117, 201

Dorsey, George R., 43

Drake, St. Clair, 89

Du Bois, W. E. B., 66, 112, 114, 161, 181, 212

Dunbar, Paul Lawrence, 215

Dyer anti-lynching bill, 161–62, 195

East End Investment and Loan Company (Cincinnati), 102

East High School (Akron), 135

East Long Street Branch YWCA (Columbus), 56

East Long Street (Columbus), 23, 24, 35, 41, 97, 103, 120, 125, 154, 186

East St. Louis, IL, 45, 79, 208

East Side (Cleveland), 125, 154, 205, 221

East Side (Columbus), 153

Eichelberger, James W., 140

Eley, Sherman, 46

Elks, 107

Elyria, 203, 227

Emancipation Day, 201

Emerson, H. I., 79

Emery, Mary, 54, 59

Empire Building and Loan Association (Cleveland), 102

Empire Steel Company (Mansfield), 175

employment, black, 96; impact of the national economy on, 91–92; in industry, 16; of women, 16, 96, 97; and World War I, 10–13. *See also* business, black; domestic and personal service; individual occupations; industrial workers; professions

Episcopal church and Episcopalians, 105, 137

Epoch Producing Company, 75, 77

equal rights struggle in Ohio against discrimination: black professionals role in, 160; in cemeteries, 169; in employment, 71, 97; in entertainment (film), 71–79; in government and politics, 195–96, 199, 213–14; and Ku Klux Klan activities, 167–69; in law enforcement, 21; new protest leadership of, 85, 86, 193–94; in news reporting, 171–72; old protest leadership of, 67, 85–86, 165–67, 193; in professions, 187–88, 189, 190, 192–93; in public accommodations (retail stores, restaurants, theaters, hotels, streetcars, etc.), 67–68, 169–71; in public hospitals, 185, 186–93; in public schools, 69–71, 173–82; as racial violence, 71, 79–80; in residential housing, 126, 127, 128; in universities, 182–83. *See also* Dyer anti-lynching bill; individual

cities; the New Negro; NAACP;
   NAACP branches; regional variations, Ohio's
Evangeline Home (Cincinnati), 54,
   59, 150, 156

Fairbanks, Robert B., 147, 148
Faulkner, James W., 81
Fayette County, 203
Federated Churches of Cleveland,
   126, 137
Ferguson, Daniel, 43
Fifth Street (Cincinnati), 97
First Congregational Church
   (Columbus), 65
Fisher, B. Harrison, 174
Fisher, Ruth Anna, 73
Fisk University, 64, 163
Fitzgerald, William S., 167, 169
Fleming, Lethia, 200, 225
Fleming, Thomas W., 26, 167, 205,
   206, 207, 208
Florida, 1, 11
"Flytown," (Columbus), 153
Forte, Ormonde O., 25, 98
Fortnightly Club (Columbus), 30
Fort Wayne, IN, 220
Forum (Dayton), 26, 76, 98
Fourth Liberty Loan, 84
Fox Film Corporation, 71
Franklin County, 77, 79, 115, 203,
   208
fraternal orders, black, 29–30, 107–8
Frederick Douglass Elementary
   School (Cincinnati), 41, 42, 64,
   130, 131, 149, 156–57, 182, 202
Frederick Douglass Recreational
   Center (Toledo), 157
Freedman's Hospital (Washington,
   D.C.), 184, 189
Freeman (Indianapolis), 76
Friendly Service Bureau (Columbus),
   144, 153
Friendship Home for Colored Girls
   (Cincinnati), 54, 61, 146, 147
Fulton, John C., 83
Fulton School (Springfield), 131,
   179–82, 228

Gallagher, Rachel S., 16
Gallia Academy (Gallipolis), 70
Gallipolis, 40, 69–71, 85
Gallipolis High School, 70
Gamble, G. W., 27
Gamble, James N., 59
Garfield Heights, 128
Garfield Park (Cleveland), 47
Garfield School (Dayton), 130, 131,
   177–79
Garvey, Marcus, 210, 228
Garvin Charles, 82, 125–26, 128,
   186, 189, 229
Gary, IN, 220
Gazette (Cleveland), 68, 81, 84, 140,
   166, 177, 219, 227, 228, 230; as
   business enterprise, 25, 98; on
   Cleveland City Hospital issues,
   189, 192; on daily newspapers,
   171; on Klan legislation, 168; on
   motion pictures, 78–79; on num-
   bers of black migrants in
   Cleveland and other cities, 9–10;
   on politics, 78, 201; on rising
   rents, 19, 92; on Springfield riot
   (1921), 118; on vice activities and
   crime, 21, 94, 152
Gentlemen's Agreement, 33
George, Clayborne, 126, 161, 163,
   164, 175–76, 189, 190, 191,
   192–93, 206, 207, 208
George Steele Woman's Relief Corps
   (Columbus), 30
George Street (Cincinnati), 22, 223
Georgia, 1, 10, 11, 101
Gerard, AL, 65
Gerber, David A, 1, 3, 51, 216, 219
Germans, 19, 123
ghetto school, 2, 217, 219
A Ghetto Takes Shape: Black
   Cleveland, 1870–1930 (Kusmer), 3
Gillespie, Chester K., 170, 208
Gilliam, Edward L., 66, 160
Gladden, Washington, 74
Gongwer, W. B., 206, 207
Good Citizenship League
   (Mansfield), 174, 176
Goode, William, 203

Good Samaritans, 29; in Columbus, 30

Goodyear Tire and Rubber Company, 11

Gottlieb, Peter, 13, 91

Graduate Nurses' Association (Cincinnati), 149

Grannum, Stanley E., 106

Grant, Stephen, 37

Gray, E. B., 184

Greater Cincinnati Bicentennial Series (Miller and Louis, eds.), 4

Greater Dayton Association, 76

Great Migration, 3, 9, 14, 33, 220

Greece, foreign born from, 19–20

Greene County, 66

Green, William R., 83, 169, 206

Greenwood Cemetery (Zanesville), 141, 169

Gregg, E. J., 151, 164, 188–89, 190, 191, 201, 206, 207, 208

Griffin, Eva L., 151

Griffith, D. W., 73

Hall, Frank A. B., 204–5

Hamilton, 121, 124

Hamilton County, 77, 131, 132, 176, 204, 208, 209

Hamilton County Juvenile Court, 153

Hand of Ethiopia (Dayton), 178

Hanna, Marcus, 99–100, 165, 197–98

Harding, Warren G., 200

Harriett Beecher Stowe School (Cincinnati), 41, 84, 130–31, 134, 136, 146, 149, 157, 182; and Jackson Colony, 131

Harris, Willie, 27

Harrod, Charles L., 115, 167

Harshman, Ralph G., 124–25, 133, 138, 139

Hartman Hotel (Columbus), 139

Hartman Theater (Columbus), 139

Harvard Law School, 162

Harvard University, 137

Haskell, Carl W., 199

Hayes, George W., 58

Haynes, George E., 12, 13

health standards, black, 20–21, 93

Hector, Flora, 27

Heintzman, Joseph W., 75

Helter, Henry H., 174

Hickey, Georgina, 222

Hicks, George Ryan, 26–27

Hicks, Mary L., 183

Higginbotham, Evelyn Brooks, 224–25

Hill, Arthur, 128

Hillsboro, 40

Hill, T. Arnold, 146

Hill, William H., 27

Himes, Chester, 215

Himes, J. S., Jr.: on black churches in Columbus, 105, 106; on southern newcomers in Columbus' black society, 226; vice enterprises in Columbus, 22–23

Hine, Darlene Clark, 226

Hi-Y Club (Columbus), 30

Hobbs, Alexander (Smoky), 197

Holiness Assembly Church (Cincinnati), 105

Hollenden Hotel (Cleveland), 99–100, 165, 197, 230

Holy Trinity Catholic Church (Cincinnati), 137

Hollywood, 34

Home for Aged Colored Women (Cincinnati), 53, 62, 108

Home for Colored Girls (Cincinnati), 53, 58, 228

Honolulu, HI, 198

Hoover, Herbert, 202, 212

Hope, Anna, 59

Hopkins, William R., 188, 189, 190, 208, 230

hospitals and blacks, 183–93

Hotel Statler (Cleveland), 140

housing conditions, black migrants, 1–18, 19, 92, 93

housing shortage, 17, 18–19, 92

Houston, TX, 90

Houston, Walter S., 101

Howard University, 137, 162, 184, 189, 198

Hughes, Ann, 65

Hughes High School (Cincinnati), 136

Hunt, Charles E. A., 160

Hunter, Clay E., 136

Hunter, Jane Edna, 140, 191, 228; and origins of a women's shelter in Cleveland, 57. *See also* Phillis Wheatley Association; Phillis Wheatley Home

Hunton, Addie, 181

Huron Road Hospital (Cleveland), 189

Illinois, 221

immigration and immigrants, European, 122, 175, 220; and fraternal orders, 29; and historiography, 217; and labor supply, 11, 14, 91, 221–22; and mid-19th century urban life, 19; as objects of intolerance, 33, 34, 37, 110, 111, 115, 116, 141; and Ohio settlement, 49; and prewar urban life, 19–20; and racial tensions, 47, 128; and "tenderloin" districts, 21; and urban slum conditions, 31; white ethnic areas and black residential patterns, 38, 123, 128; and welfare institutions, 52. *See also* individual immigrant and ethnic groups.

The Independent, 80

Independent Colored Voters League of Cuyahoga County, 201

Indiana, 1, 110, 115, 201, 220

Indianapolis, 76, 201

Industrial Savings and Loan Company (Cincinnati), 102

industrial workers, black, 23–24, 96; in skilled labor, 24, 96; in unskilled labor, 24, 96

Informer (Akron), 98

Informer (Dayton), 25–26

Informer (Springfield), 98

institutions, black: *See* churches, black; color line; fraternal orders, black; leadership, black; women, black. *See also* individual churches, black; individual cities; public

welfare institutions, black; and YMCA and YWCA, black facilities

intermarriage, anti-racial intermarriage bill, 168

International Workers of the World, 81

Iowa, 168

Irish, 19, 123

Italy, foreign born from, 19–20

Jackson, Andrew, 196

Jackson, Kenneth T., 115

Jackson, Perry B., 209

Japan, 33

Japanese Americans, 33, 111

Jaymes, Sully, 181–82

jazz music, 215, 216

Jefferson Hotel (Columbus), 139

Jefferson, Thomas, 99

Jeffrey Manufacturing Company (Columbus), 96

Jelliffe, Rowena, 58

Jelliffe, Russell, 58

Jenkins, William D., 115

Jews, 37, 110, 135, 167

Jim Crow, 2, 141, 185, 189, 214, 216

Johnson, Charles S., 65, 181

Johnson, James Weldon, 211

Johnson, Joseph L., 198, 202

Johnson Reed Act, 110

Johnson, Tom L., 94

Johnson, William B., 98

Johnston, Arthur, 203

Jones, George D., 78

Jones, Joseph L., 11–12

Jones, Robert G., 173

Journal (Cleveland), 25

Juvenile Protective Association (Cincinnati), 153, 156

Kansas City General Hospital (MO), 184

Kansas City, MO, 27, 184

Karb, George J., 74

Keith's Theater (Columbus), 139

Kelly, Samuel T., 168

Kelly, S. T., 66, 160

Kentucky, 1, 48, 49, 101, 106, 123
Kilson, Martin, 214
Kingsley, H. C., 168
Knights of Pythias, 29, 107; in
    Cincinnati, 108; in Columbus, 30
Knox, George L., 76
Kornbluh, Andrea Tuttle, 144
Kornfield, Rabbi, 74
Ku Klux Klan, 34, 75, 110, 111,
    114–17, 128, 179, 180; and anti-
    Klan activity, 162, 164, 167–69,
    209, 211; and politics, 195, 196,
    200–202, 213
Kusmer, Kenneth L., 218, 219, 226

labor, black-white competition and
    strikes, 47
LaFollette, Robert M., 201
Lakeside Hospital (Cleveland), 128,
    186, 189, 229
Lane, Aubrey, 198
lawyers, black, 28, 103, 104, 232
leadership, blacks: contrasting styles of
    new and old leadership, 67, 85–86,
    165–67, 193; differing emphases on
    "racial uplift" activities and equal
    rights protest work, 227–30 passim;
    migrants as leaders in business,
    NAACP branches, and welfare
    associations, 26–27, 64, 65, 102–3,
    161; new leadership in equal rights
    struggles, 66–79 passim, 159–94 pas-
    sim; new leadership in social welfare
    work, 53–65 passim, 142–58 passim;
    views regarding all-black institu-
    tions and organizations, 51–52,
    227–29. See also equal rights strug-
    gle; National Urban League; politics
    and politicians, black; welfare asso-
    ciations and blacks; welfare services
    and blacks; regional variations,
    Ohio's; women, black
Lewis, Courtland, 160
Lewis, Fountain, Jr., 58, 99, 101
Lewis, Fountain, Sr., 99
Liberia, 198
Liberty Garment Company
    (Cleveland), 96

Lima, 45, 46
Lincoln Elementary School
    (Gallipolis), 70
literature and writers, black, 215
Livingston College, 64
Local People (Dittmer), 2
Lockland, 120, 131, 221
Loews' Ohio Theatre (Cleveland),
    170
Lorain, 66, 78
Lorain County, 203
Louisiana, 1
Louisville, KY, 113
lower class, black, 31, 221–23
Loyal Legion of Lincoln
    (Youngstown), 116
Lucas County, 38
Luna Park (Cleveland), 45, 68, 140
Lyceum Theater (Columbus), 139
lynching, 5, 66, 110, 117, 161–62,
    165, 195, 199

McCall, Sallie Peters, 42
McClain, R. P., 184
McClean, John R., 171
McCord, George E., 180
McCulloch, Roscoe C., 212–13
McElroy, Silas D., 67
McKinley, William, 165, 197–98
McMorries, John H., 189
Mack, Clark L., 93
Madisonville, 120
Mahoning County, 168
Mahoning Valley cities, 116
Majestic Theatre (Springfield), 73
Male, A. D., 199
Manning, A. E., 76
Mansfield, 132, 173, 174–76
Mansfield Board of Education, 174
Manual Products Company
    (Cleveland), 96
Marietta, 48
Marion, 45, 47
Martin, Alexander H., 126, 132
Martin, Mary E., 132, 207
Mary B. Talbert Home (Cleveland),
    145, 146, 150
Maschke, Maurice, 197, 205, 207

Masons, 29, 30, 39, 107
Mason, William, 43
Maurer, Irving, 65
Meharry Medical College, 184
Mercy Hospital Association
    (Cleveland), 186–87
Mercy Hospital (Cincinnati), 184–85
Mercy Hospital proposal (Cleveland),
    187–88, 189, 190–91
Methodist Episcopal church, 43, 227
Methodists, 28, 105
Method, W. A., 186
Metropolitan Baptist Church
    (Cincinnati), 204
Metropolitan Church (Cleveland),
    79
Michigan, 67, 168
middle class values, 60, 153–54
Middletown, 42, 66
migration, black: authorities' reac-
    tions to, 12–13; impetus behind,
    10–12, 90–92; and migrants' con-
    ditions and adjustment to urban
    life, 15–23, 92–95; and migrants'
    initiatives, 13–14; and number of
    migrants, 9–10, 91; in the twen-
    ties, 90–91; in wartime, 9–14. *See
    also* business, black; churches,
    black; employment, black; equal
    rights struggle in Ohio; leadership,
    black; Ohio color line; NAACP;
    regional variations, Ohio's; south-
    ern culture; southern newcomers
    versus old residents; welfare asso-
    ciations and blacks; welfare insti-
    tutions and blacks
Miles Heights, 203
Miles Theatre (Cleveland), 68
Miller, Edith Fossett, 99
Miller, Herbert A., 168
Miller, Kelly, 226
Mills Brothers (Harry, Herbert,
    Donald, John, Jr.), 216
ministers, black, 28, 103, 104, 232
Minister's Union (Cleveland), 76
Mississippi, 1, 11, 29, 46
Missouri, 26, 184
Mitchell, L. Pearl, 225

Model Drug Company, 184
Model Drug Store, 27
Model Homes Company
    (Cincinnati), 55, 92, 148, 157
Monroe, J. P., Mrs., 58
Montgomery County Court of
    Appeals, 179
Monticello, 99
Moore, Leonard J., 115
Morgan, Daniel E., 208
Morgan, Garrett A., 98
Morrison, Toni, 215
Moton, Robert R., 140
Mount Carmel Presbyterian Church
    (Cincinnati), 161
Mount Sinai Hospital (Cleveland),
    189
Mount Zion Congregational church
    (Cleveland), 29, 32, 39, 207
Mount Zion Methodist Episcopal
    Church (Cincinnati), 106
"The Moving Picture World," 72
Murrell, Howard, 126
Myers, George A.: and black barber-
    shops, 99–100; on black businesses
    in Cleveland, 103–4; on black
    professionals in Cleveland, 104;
    on black welfare associations in
    Cleveland, 145; on employment of
    blacks in Cleveland, 97, 98; on
    motion pictures, 76; on numbers
    of black migrants in Cleveland, 9,
    91; and politics and protest,
    165–66, 170, 172, 187, 188, 192,
    193, 196–97, 229–30
"The Mystery of Morrow's Rest," 73

NAACP, Akron branch, 66, 162,
    167, 168, 170–71
NAACP, Cincinnati branch, 66, 77,
    161, 162, 167, 168, 177, 228, 229
NAACP, Cleveland branch, 45,
    66–67, 77, 79, 133, 134, 139, 161,
    162–63, 164, 168, 169, 170, 173,
    174, 187, 188, 189, 190–91, 192,
    206–7, 212, 225, 228, 229, 230
NAACP, Columbus branch, 62, 66,
    74, 78, 162, 212

NAACP, Dayton branch, 66, 119, 177, 178
NAACP (Flint), 2
NAACP, Mansfield branch, 174, 176
NAACP, Springfield branch, 66, 73, 179, 180, 181
NAACP, Toledo Branch, 66, 161–62, 170, 172
Nashville, TN, 64, 184
National Association for the Advancement of Colored People (NAACP), 9, 37, 67, 85, 134, 160, 161, 162, 163, 164, 165, 167, 174, 177, 178, 181–82, 196, 211–13; and branches in Greene County, Lorain, Middletown, Oberlin, Urbana, Wellsville, Youngstown, 66; and motion pictures, 73; and Ohio branches, 193, 209, 210, 212, 214, 224, 228; and origins, 66
National Baptist Convention, 39, 137, 225
National Carbon Company, 12
National Colored Soldiers Comfort Committee, 84
National Conference on Social Work (1926), 93
National Federation of Negro Women's Clubs, 225
National Medical Association, 30
National Negro Business League, 149
National Negro Health Week, 149, 152
National Urban League, 61, 85, 142, 143, 146, 153, 226; in Cleveland, 63, 64; in Akron, Canton, Cincinnati, and Warren, 144, 146; and leadership in Ohio affiliates, 224; and origins, 52. See also individual cities; Columbus Urban League; Negro Civic Welfare Association (Cincinnati); Negro Welfare Association (Cleveland)
Native Americans, 33
Negro Civic Welfare Association (Cincinnati), 64–65, 144, 145, 148, 149, 153, 154, 156, 228, 229; origins, 62

Negro Welfare Association (Cleveland), 10, 28, 38, 91, 96, 144, 145, 151, 154, 229; origins, 63–64
Negro Welfare League (Columbus), 62, 65
Neil Hotel (Columbus), 139
Newark, 107
Newburgh Heights, 118–19
New Deal, 3, 214
New Hope Baptist Church (Cincinnati), 105
"New Negro," 84, 161, 166
New Orphan Asylum for Colored Children (Cincinnati), 53, 62, 108
New York Central Railroad, 11, 17
New York City, 19, 35, 66, 67, 76, 106, 161, 178, 188, 216
New York Times, 116
Niagara Movement, 66
"The Nigger" (motion picture), 71–73
Ninth Street Branch YMCA (Cincinnati), 54, 59, 61, 154–55, 184
North Carolina, 100, 212
northern Ohio: and anti-Klan sentiment, 167; and black population in cities, 14, 90; and black social service institutions, 143; and the color line, 2, 218; and daily newspapers, 171, 172; and the equal rights struggle, 159, 169, 193, 219; and NAACP branches, 66, 161, 162, 219; and public accommodations, 44 139, 141; and protest heritage, 51, 52, 218–19; and public schools, 40, 129, 132, 173, 224; and race relations heritage, 48–49
Northwest Community Center (Columbus), 154
Norwegians, 19
Norwich Hotel (Columbus), 139
nurses and nursing, 82

Oatmeal, John T., 203
Oberlin, 66
Oberlin College, 44, 134, 135

Odd Fellows, 29, 30, 39, 107, 108, 179

Ohio Avenue Day Nursery (Columbus), 56, 65

Ohio Board of Motion Picture Censors, 72, 74, 75, 76

Ohio Civil Rights Law, 170

Ohio color line: in business, 99, 103; in churches, 38–39, 136–37; in colleges and universities, 43–44, 134–36; in employment, 97; in entertainment (film, sports, and music), 71–79, 134–35, 215–16; in fraternal orders, 39, 137–38; in funerals and cemeteries, 100–101, 169; in government and politics, 195–96, 213; in health standards, 20–21, 93; in law enforcement, 21, 22, 94–95, 119, 152–53; in news reporting, 119; in public accommodations (retail stores, restaurants, theaters, hotels, streetcars, etc.), 44–45, 138–41; in public hospitals, 183–84, 185, 188, 189, 190; in public schools, 39–43, 129–34; in professions, 30, 39, 137; in residential housing, 18, 35–38, 92, 119–21, 123–24, 125–29; in voluntary organizations, 30 39, 103, 137–38. *See also* Ohio's regional variations; public welfare institutions

Ohio Council of National Defense, 84

Ohio Department of Health, 20

Ohio Federation for Uplift Among Colored People, 65

Ohio Federation of Women's Clubs (African American), 30, 108, 224

Ohio House of Representatives, 77–78, 116, 168, 197, 206–7, 208–9

Ohio National Guard, Ninth Separate Battalion and World War I, 82; and regiment issue, 82–83

Ohio National Guardsmen, 118

Ohio Negro Workers' Advisory Committee, 12–13

Ohio Northern University, 134

Ohio Recorder (Columbus), 98

Ohio Senate, 116

Ohio State College of Pharmacy, 27

Ohio State Journal (Columbus), 84, 119

Ohio State Lantern, 134

Ohio State Monitor (Columbus), 26

The Ohio State University, 43, 44, 134, 135, 136, 168, 198, 229; and Inter-Racial Council, 134; and Phi Beta Kappa, Pi Lambda Theta, Scarlet Mask, and other extracurricular student organizations, 135

Ohio Supreme Court, 75–76, 177, 179

Ohio Torch (Columbus), 98

Ohio University, 44, 134, 182–83, 201

Ohio Wesleyan University, 44, 134

Old Folks Home (Columbus), 56, 59

Oliver, Cora, 59

Omaha, 79

Omaha Monitor, 12

Optimist (Cincinnati), 98

Osborne, Clyde W., 116

Ottawa, 46

Ott, C. J., Mrs., 168

Otterbein College, 134

Our Lady of the Sacrament Catholic Church (Cleveland), 136

Outhwaite School (Cleveland), 129, 132, 134, 173

Owen, James A., 207–8

Oxley, Edmund H., 59, 137, 156

Parents' Protective Association (Dayton's Willard School), 177

Parker, John J., 212

Passing of the Great Race (Grant), 34

Payne, Lawrence O., 164, 192–93, 208

Pennsylvania, 1, 13, 48, 49, 67, 221

Pennsylvania Railroad, 11, 47

People's System Finance Company (Akron), 102

Perkins Street YMCA (Akron), 155, 168

Peters, W. H., 93, 183, 184
Petrach, Louis, 151
Philadelphia, 35
Phillips, Kimberly L., 14, 215, 217–18
Phillips, William, 177
Phillis Wheatley Association
    (Cleveland), 57, 59, 61, 140, 145,
    147, 187, 191, 228
Phillis Wheatley Club of St. Paul's
    A.M.E. Church (Columbus), 30
Phillis Wheatley Home (Cleveland),
    59, 60, 61, 146
Pickaway County, 115
Pierce, David, 133
Pilot (Cincinnati), 25
Piqua, 65, 216
Pittsburgh, 13
Pittsburgh Valve Company, 11
Playhouse Settlement (Cleveland),
    57, 218
Pleasant Company Club (Cleveland),
    30
Poland, foreign born from, 19–20
police, 21, 95, 128, 152–53
politics and politicians, black: as can-
    didates for state legislature, 208–9;
    and color lines, 213; and equal
    rights, 195, 213; and the Klan,
    195, 201–2; in municipal elec-
    tions, 203–8; and NAACP,
    211–13; and new leadership,
    209–10, 214; and patronage poli-
    tics, 196–99, 214; in presidential
    campaigns, 200–201, 202–3; and
    protest, 195–96, 199, 213–14; as
    Republican independents,
    195–214 passim; as state represen-
    tatives, 209; in statewide cam-
    paigns, 201–2; and Universal
    Negro Improvement Association,
    210–11. See also Democratic Party
    and Democrats; individual cities;
    Republican Party and Republicans;
    women, black
population, 232; and migrants, 9–10;
    during 1910–1920, 14–15; during
    1920–1930, 90
Porter, Ethlinda, 136

Porter, Jennie D., 42, 59, 131, 136
Porter, William, 136
Post (Cleveland), 98, 101, 192
Presbyterian church, 28, 105
Presbyterian Church in the United
    States of America, 38
Prince Hall Grand Lodge of Free and
    Accepted Masons of the State of
    Ohio, 107
Procter and Gamble Company, 59
professions and professionals, black:
    associations of, 30, 39, 137; black
    clients of, 27, 104; expansion and
    prosperity of, 24, 28, 103, 104,
    232; limitations of, 28, 104. See
    also individual occupations
Progressive Government Committee
    (Cleveland), 208
Progressive Party, 201
Protestant Episcopal church, 28
Public Health Federation
    (Cincinnati), 149
Pulley, Robert W., 203

Race and the City: Work, Community,
    and Protest in Cincinnati,
    1820–1970 (Taylor, ed.), 4
The Races of Europe, (Ripley), 34
racial uplift versus equal rights
    protest, 227–30
radicalism: blacks accused of, 80–81
Record ((Dayton), 25–26
Red Scare, 34, 80–81
Reese, Carrie, 179
Reese, Earl, 178
regional variations, Ohio's. See cen-
    tral Ohio; northern Ohio; south-
    ern Ohio
Rendville, 202
Renfro, Inez, 100
Renfro, St. Julian, 100
Republican Party and Republicans, 3,
    25, 67, 77–78, 110, 165, 193,
    195–214 passim, 225, 230
residential patterns. See black business
    and professional classes; Ohio's
    color line; individual cities; lower
    class, black; and urbanization

restrictive covenants, 37
Rives, John, 26, 98
"Roaring Third" or Third Police
    Precinct (Cleveland), 21, 22,
    94–95, 151, 152
Roberts, George H., 168
Robinson, James H.: biography, 64;
    and welfare association, 144; on
    numbers of black migrants in
    Cincinnati, 9, and protest, 229.
    See also Negro Civic Welfare
    Association (Cincinnati)
Rockwood, Harvey L., 93
Roman Catholic church, 28, 39, 105,
    136, 202
Roosevelt, Franklin D., 214
Roosevelt High School (Dayton),
    127
Rosenwald, Julius, 52, 54, 56
Rostrum (Cincinnati), 25
Rumanians 123
Russell, Francis M., 131, 156
Russell, Paul, 116
Russia, foreign born from, 19–20
Rutherford B. Hayes School
    (Cleveland), 129, 132, 134, 173

St. Andrews Episcopal Church
    (Cincinnati), 59, 137, 146, 149,
    155, 156
St. Andrews Episcopal Church
    (Cleveland), 29, 32
St. Ann's (Catholic) Church
    (Cincinnati), 39
St. Ann's (Catholic) School and
    Social Center for Colored
    (Cincinnati), 157
St. Clairsville, 84
St. James Methodist Episcopal
    Church (Cleveland), 45, 47
St. Louis, MO, 27, 188
St. Luke's Hospital (Cleveland), 189
St. Mark's Presbyterian Church
    (Cleveland), 29, 32
St. Paul's Church (Cincinnati), 136
St. Vincent's (Charity) Hospital
    (Cleveland), 189
Salisbury, NC, 64

Salvation Army, 59; in Cincinnati,
    54, 149–50; in Cleveland, 149–50;
    origins, 53
Salvation Army Rescue Home
    (Cleveland), 150
Sandusky, 11, 65
Scarborough, William S., 80, 83–84,
    166, 198
Schmidlapp, Jacob G., 54–55, 56, 59
Schofield, Mrs. Levi T., 57, 59
schools, public, and blacks, 39–43,
    134–36. See also individual cities;
    equal rights struggle in Ohio;
    Ohio color line; regional varia-
    tions, Ohio's
Scott, Emmett J., 13, 20, 63
Second Presbyterian Church
    (Cleveland), 57
Sellsville area (Columbus), 154
Selma University, 106
Seventh Day Adventist denomina-
    tion, 28, 105
Shaker Heights, 125, 126, 128, 173
Shaker Heights Protective
    Association, 126–27
Sharpsburg, KY, 64
Sheppard-Towner Act, 149
Sherman, Richard B., 2
Shilling, David C., 48
Shiloh Cumberland Presbyterian
    Church (Cincinnati), 39
Shoemaker Health and Welfare
    Center (Cincinnati), 145
Simmons University, 106
Skillman's barbershop (Cincinnati),
    99
Smith, Al, 202, 203, 211
Smith, Beulah, 169
Smith, Harry C.: on Cleveland City
    Hospital issues, 189, 192; on daily
    newspapers, 171, 172; on housing
    conditions, 17; and Klan legisla-
    tion, 168; and middle class values,
    154; on motion pictures, 71, 72;
    and NAACP, 164, 230; in news-
    paper business, 25, 98; on old ver-
    sus new black Cleveland residents,
    226; and politics and protest, 78,

166, 187, 199, 200, 201–2, 205, 227–28, 229–30; on public accommodations, 68; and public schools, 173, 180; and Red Scare, 81; on rioting, 79–80, 219; on vice enterprises, 21, 152; and UNIA, 211; and World War I, 84. See also *Gazette*

Smith, Kate, 216

Social Gospel Movement, 155

South Bend, IN, 220

South Carolina, 27

Southern Baptist Church (Cincinnati), 29

Southern Christian Recorder, 65

southern culture, 225–26

Southern Hotel (Columbus), 139

southern newcomers versus old residents, 225–27

southern Ohio: and black population in cities, 14, 90; and black social service institutions, 143; and color line, 2, 218; and the equal rights struggle, 159, 169, 218–19; and NAACP branches, 66, 161, 162; and public accommodations, 44, 139; and public schools, 39, 40, 129, 130, 131, 132, 133, 173, 182, 224; and protest heritage, 51, 52, 219; and race relations heritage, 48, 49

Spiritualist Church of God (Cincinnati), 105

Springfield, 65, 82; black business, 98; black churches, 155; black population growth, 14–15, 90, 220; black residential patterns, 124; blacks in politics, 198, 201, 202, 203, 211; blacks and public schools, 40, 129, 131, 182; discrimination in public accommodations, 44; fraternal orders, black 179; equal rights struggle, 173, 179–82, 219, 225, 230; white hostility, 115, 117–18; YMCA, 118. See also NAACP, Springfield branch

Springfield Board of Education, 180, 181

Spring Street Branch YMCA (Columbus), 56, 59, 61, 65, 103, 186

Stacel, Jacob, 167

Standard Theatre (Cleveland), 71

Star Building and Loan Association (Toledo), 102

Stephenson, D. C., 169

Sterling Hotel (Cincinnati), 108

Steubenville, 73

Stevenson, William, 77

Stillman Theater (Cleveland), 140, 170

Sudduth, Horace, 101, 102

Sudduth Real Estate Agency (Cincinnati), 101

Supreme Life and Casualty Company (Columbus), 102

Swedes, 19

Symmes, Elizabeth, 54

Taft, Charles P., II, 144

Taylor, Henry Louis, Jr., 147, 148, 218, 219

teachers, black, 28, 103, 104, 232

"tenderloin" districts and blacks, 31; in Cincinnati, 21, 22, 94; in Cleveland, 21, 94; in Columbus, 23

Tennessee, 27, 136, 163, 184

Texas, 90, 91

Thompson, George W., 168

Thompson, William (Bill), 196–97

Thornbrough, Emma Lou, 220

"Tin Can Alley" and "Tin Town" (Dayton), 127

Toledo, 78, 174, 198; black business, 102; black churches, 137; black migrants' conditions, 17, 18, 19, 20, 92; black migrants' numbers, 10; black-police issues, 153; black population growth, 14–15, 90, 217, 220; black residential patterns, 37–38, 119, 124; blacks and employment, 11; blacks in politics, 202, 212–13; blacks and public schools, 28; blacks and public welfare institutions, 157; discrimina-

tion in public accommodations, 141; equal rights struggle, 169, 230; white hostility, 45–46, 47, 128–29. *See also* NAACP, Toledo branch
Toledo Council of Churches, 137
Tracy, Steven C., 215
Tribbitt, R. M., 186
Trinidad, West Indies, 137
Trotter, Joe William, Jr., 104, 160, 217–18, 220, 222
Trotter, Mamie, 108
Troy, 65
True Reformers, 29
Tuberculosis Institute (Cincinnati), 149
Turner, Edward C., 75
Tyler, Ralph W., 84–85, 165–166, 186, 198

Union Baptist Church Missionary Society (Cincinnati), 108
Union (Cincinnati), 25, 44, 98, 166, 168
Union High School (Gallipolis), 70
Union Station (Columbus), 63
United Brothers of Friendship, 107
United Brothers of Hope, 29
United States Army: 92nd Division, 81–82, 136; 93rd Division, 81–82; 372nd Regiment (93rd Division), 83; Camp Sheridan (AL), 83; Camp Sherman (OH), 82; Camp Stuart (VA), 83; Officer Training School (Des Moines, IA), 81, 82; Student's Army Training Corps, 81, 82; Surgeon General's Office, 82. *See also* World War I, blacks in
United States Department of Agriculture, 198
United States Department of Labor, 12, 16
United States Employment Service, 13, 16
United States Homes Registration Bureau, 61
United States Naval Academy, 135
United States Navy Department, 198

United States Senate, 212–13
United States Supreme Court, 37, 210, 212
United States Thrift Stamps, 65
Universal Negro Improvement Association, 187, 189, 210–11, 228, 229
University of Cincinnati, 44, 134, 135, 137
University of Pennsylvania, 64
University of Toledo, 134
Urbana, 65, 66, 117
urbanization, 121–23. *See also* individual cities; migration, black

violence, racial, 45–46, 119; arson, 128; bombing, 128; and the Klan, 117; physical harassment, 47; race rioting, 45, 46–47, 117–18; threatening rumors, 118; vandalism, 128. *See also* Ohio color line, residential patterns
Virginia, 48, 49, 162, 221
Virginia Hotel (Columbus), 139
Voice of the People (Cincinnati), 25
voluntary associations, black, 30, 103

Wade Park (Cleveland), 125, 126, 128
Wadsworth, 116
Walker, Leroy J., 100–101
Walker, Ruth H., 100–101
Walnut Hills (Cincinnati), 31, 41, 53, 62, 94, 102, 106, 120, 223, 229
Walnut Hills Day Nursery for Colored Children (Cincinnati), 53
Walnut Hills High School (Cincinnati), 42
Walz, F. W., 191–92
War Camp Community Services, 84
Ward, David, 217
Ware, William, 210, 211
Warren, 144
Warrensville workhouse, 22
Warsaw, KY, 27
Washington, Booker T., 52, 112, 114,

140, 230
Washington County, 115
Washington Courthouse, 203
Washington Terrace apartments
    (Cincinnati), 55–56, 148, 157
Washington Terrace Community
    Center (Cincinnati), 157
Washington Terrace Welfare
    Association (Cincinnati), 157
welfare associations and blacks, 65,
    142–43; leadership, 64–65. *See also*
    individual cities; National Urban
    League; welfare institutions and
    blacks; welfare services and blacks;
    women, black; YMCA; YWCA
welfare institutions and blacks,
    53–54, 56–61, 146–47, 149–50,
    154–55. *See also* individual cities;
    individual institutions; welfare
    associations and blacks; welfare
    services and blacks; women, black
welfare services and blacks: and
    churches, 155–56; in health care,
    59, 149–52; in job placement, 62,
    63, 64, 145–46; and new leader-
    ship in, 157–58; recreational and
    social, 61, 154–55; in residential
    sheltering 59–61, 146–48; and
    schools, 156–157; in vocational
    training, 146. *See also* individual
    cities; welfare institutions and
    blacks; women, black; YMCA;
    YWCA
Wellsville, 66
Welsh, 123
Wesleyan University, 106
West End Branch YWCA
    (Cincinnati), 54, 59, 61, 108, 147,
    155, 229
West End (Cincinnati), 35, 38, 62,
    92, 93, 94, 120, 123, 147, 148,
    152, 197, 221, 223
West End Improvement Association
    (Dayton), 127
Western College for Women, 134
Western Reserve University, 44, 134,
    135, 136; and School of Medicine,
    128, 189

West Goodale Street District
    (Columbus), 123
West Virginia, 1, 69, 102, 123, 160,
    221, 222
White, Charles W., 161, 163, 173,
    175–76, 187, 189, 191
white intolerance rising, 33–34,
    110–11. *See also* Ku Klux Klan
White, Walter W., 162, 212
Wilberforce University, 43, 44, 65,
    80, 82, 83, 134, 136, 166, 198, 225
Willard Elementary School (Dayton),
    132, 177, 193
Williams, Charles, 29
Williams, Charles G., 72–73, 74, 75
Williams, W. Henry, 106
William T. Boyd Lodge, Prince Hall
    Masons (Cleveland), 107
Willis, Frank B., 71–72, 74, 76, 78,
    198–99
Wills, J. Walter, 65, 100
Wilson, Woodrow, 34, 83, 84, 127,
    198
Witt, Peter, 94–95
Wittenberg University, 134
WLW radio (Cincinnati), 216
women, black, 32; in business, 99,
    100; in churches, 224–25; in civic
    affairs and leadership, 224–25; and
    clubs in Cincinnati, Cleveland,
    and Columbus, 30, 108, 138; and
    employment, 96–97, 98, 223; and
    job training, 146; and maternity
    homes, 149–50; as migrants, 10;
    and newspaper publishing, 25; and
    politics and suffrage, 200, 209,
    225; and prenatal aid, 149; in pro-
    fessions, 103, 224; and protest
    activities, 225; and shelters for sin-
    gle females, 59–60, 146–47; and
    southern culture, 225–26; and
    wartime employment, 16, 23, 32;
    and wartime nursing, 82. *See also*
    individual cities; individual insti-
    tutions; individual occupations;
    individual persons
Woodland Hills Park (Cleveland),
    140, 170

Woodlawn, 176
Woodlawn School (Hamilton
    County), 132, 173, 176–77
Woodlin, William J., 65
World (Indianapolis), 76
World War I, blacks and, 5, 9, 10–11;
    backing the war on the home
    front, 83–84; and Champaigne
    offensive; 83; and combat service
    in "Red Hand" Division (French
    Army), 83; and journalism, 84, 85;
    and military honors, 83; and Red
    Cross, 82, 84; and Selective
    Service Act, 82; and Verdun sec-
    tor, 83; women in the war effort,
    82. *See also* United States Army
Wyoming, OH, 131

Xenia, 40, 43, 65, 80

Yale University, 64, 65

Yellow Springs, 136
Young, Bernard, Jr., 135
Young Men's Christian Association
    (YMCA), 59, 84, 108, 143; in
    Columbus, 56; origins, 53
Youngstown, 116, 168; black popula-
    tion growth, 14–15, 90, 217; black
    residential patterns, 124; blacks
    and employment, 91; blacks and
    public schools, 40; blacks and wel-
    fare associations, 143; white hos-
    tility, 45–46, 47, 115. *See also*
    NAACP
Young Women's Christian Association
    (YWCA), 59, 108, 143, 224; in
    Cleveland, 57; in Columbus, 56; in
    Dayton, 76; origins, 53

Zanesville, 140, 141, 169, 203
Zion Hill Baptist Church
    (Cleveland), 105

www.ingramcontent.com/pod-product-compliance
Lightning Source LLC
Chambersburg PA
CBHW030640270326
41929CB00007B/152